Online Retrieval
A Dialogue of Theory and Practice

Second Edition

Geraldene Walker
University at Albany
New York

Joseph Janes
Assistant Professor
School of Information & Library Science
University of Washington
Seattle

Edited by Carol Tenopir

1999
Libraries Unlimited, Inc.
Englewood, Colorado

Libraries Unlimited, Inc.
P.O. Box 6633
Englewood, CO 80155-6633
1-800-237-6124
www.lu.com

Library of Congress Cataloging-in-Publication Data

Walker, Geraldene.
    Online retrieval : a dialogue of theory and practice / by
Geraldene Walker, Joseph Janes ; edited by Carol Tenopir. -- 2nd ed.
    xiii, 312 p. 22x28 cm. -- (Database searching series)
    Includes bibliographical references and index.
    ISBN 1-56308-657-3
    1. Online bibliographic searching--United States. 2. DIALOG
(Information retrieval system) 3. Electronic information resource
searching--United States. I. Janes, Joseph. II. Tenopir, Carol.
III. Title. IV. Series: Database searching series (Unnumbered)
Z699.35.O55W35   1999
025.5'24--DC21   99-10206
                                                        CIP

Contents

Online Retrieval

Database Searching Series

Edited by Carol Tenopir

Cases in Online Search Strategy, by Bruce Shuman.

Online Retrieval: A Dialogue of Theory and Practice, second edition, by Geraldene Walker and Joseph Janes.

Preface

"Online searching" isn't what it used to be. In 1993, we published the first edition of this book and intended it to be a guide to students who were learning about searching databases of mainly bibliographic records. In those days, there were lots of databases, with their numbers growing all the time. Online vendors such as DIALOG, LEXIS/NEXIS, Wilsonline, and Dow Jones, and CD-ROM vendors such as UMI and SilverPlatter provided access to a pretty predictable world. And, oh yes, there was this new thing called the Internet, which was just getting important, so we included a final chapter that talked about gophers and FTP and the World Wide Web and how to search them all.

Since things are changing so quickly in the information retrieval area, with Internet use continuing to grow at a phenomenal rate and many of the traditional systems migrating to the Web, we have expanded our scope in this second edition to include discussion of and examples from a number of newer systems, and especially to highlight similarities and differences between systems like DIALOG and the search engines available on the Web.

Searching is now much more a part of the popular consciousness, even to the point of television commercials that talk about the freshness of links in search engines and techniques for searching. The information retrieval "business" includes those search engines, directories, and portals, many of which have capitalization of billions of dollars each.

Our challenge was to revise our first edition to keep up with this new world. What we have chosen to do is to incorporate discussion of Internet searching in the same basic structure of the first edition (in chapters on search technique, free-text searching, etc.). We continue to use the DIALOG system and command language as our examplar, not because it holds the highest share of the professional searching market as it did several years ago, but because it is still the most advanced and sophisticated search language. We continue to believe that if people learn to use a fully featured search system such as DIALOG and, more to the point, understand how it works, how the databases it searches are structured and the concepts of searching that underlie it, then they will be well-prepared for a fast-changing world of new and continually changing companies, systems, databases, and so on. We hope the balance we have tried to strike is a satisfactory and productive one.

The book is laid out in the following way. Chapter 1 gives a broad overview of the search for information in computerized settings. Chapter 2 traces the conceptual and technical history of online systems and summarizes the advantages of their use, and chapter 3 describes the telecommunications connection. Chapter 4 outlines the different types of systems and information that are available for computer searching. Basic information on how databases are constructed and how that structure affects search possibilities are introduced in chapter 5.

The actual practice of searching begins in chapter 6 with a discussion of search protocols, the use of a command language, and the design of a search. Search practice continues in chapter 7 and 8, which deal respectively with controlled vocabulary searching, the use of thesauri, and free-text searching. The searching component ends with an overview of other types of database—citation indexes, full-text files, and reference databases—in chapter 11.

But searching is a practical activity. You cannot become proficient by reading a book. Like learning to drive a car, you need to practice, so after reading each chapter on search technique (chapters 6 to 11), get online and try to replicate the sample search on whatever system you are using. Then try a few examples of your own before going on to the next chapter. This alteration of theory and practice is how we see you using this book to develop your search skills.

We have once again divided the responsibility for chapters based on our backgrounds, areas of interest, and expertise. The boxes we used for commenting on each other's chapters, which we used in the first edition, proved very popular, and so we continue to use them here. When you see a box in the text marked with our initials, you will know we are illuminating points or even disagreeing with each other (and perhaps even with ourselves).

We hope that students, library and information professionals, and others interested in searching in the digital world will find this book to be of interest and help as they make their way through this increasingly complicated and fascinating new information environment.

Acknowledgments

We would like to take the opportunity to acknowledge some people without whose help you would not be holding this book in your hands.

First of all, thanks to the many generations of students in our respective online searching courses. Their comments and questions have provided us with new insights and a continuing search for new and better ways to explain and clarify the more difficult concepts of computer search strategies. We wrote this book (and its predecessor) primarily to help us to make our classes more interesting and our teaching more effective, and we hope that we have succeeded in that aim.

Geraldine would like to give special thanks to her graduate assistant for last year, Mary-Ann Dean, who provided assistance with the preparation and mailing of requests for reprint permissions and with the typing of sections of the manuscript.

Joe would like to thank Bob Summers, who was of great help on several of the early chapters, doing searches and helping with technical matters and moral support. Laura Bost's work on the first edition continues to be invaluable in future generations. He would also like to thank former colleagues at the University of Michigan, Amy Warner and Kanen Drabenstott, for their advice and assistance.

Sample PsycINFO® DIALOG records are reprinted with permission of the American Psychological Association, publisher of the PsycINFO® and PsycLIT® Databases (Copyright 1887-1998 by the American Psychological Association). All rights reserved. For more information contact psycinfo @ apa.org.

Sample DIALOG records are reproduced with the permission of the DIALOG Corporation.

Sample records from Sociological Abstracts are reprinted courtesy of Sociological Abstracts.

Sample records from the Disclosure database are reprinted with permission. Copyright (1998) Disclosure Incorporated.

1 THE SEARCH FOR INFORMATION IN THE ONLINE AGE

This chapter identifies some of the problems facing the information-seeker in a world of information overload. It introduces the concept of online searching and attempts to show the usefulness of such searching by giving examples of the wide variety of information-bearing materials that are available online today. The chapter then explains the basic mechanics of information retrieval, which apply equally to both manual and computerized information systems of all types—library catalogs, CD-ROMs, online database systems, and the Internet.

Information Overload

The problems of organizing information in order to find it when it is required are nothing new. From as early as the seventh century BC, collections of information-bearing artifacts existed in the form of stone tablets, and later parchment scrolls. However, for many centuries, the emphasis was on preservation of the cultural heritage of society in an uncertain world, rather than on its retrieval in response to a request.[1] Documents were relatively rare, and so few people could read that there was little call for access to individual items. Today, the situation has totally changed. The pressures brought about by the explosion in the amount of material being published annually over the last 50 years have highlighted the problems involved in retrieving a single desired item from the proverbial "haystack" of available information. The focus has moved from collection and preservation to retrieval and selection.

It is all too easy to assume that modern technology can solve this retrieval problem, or at least simplify the process. The use of computers and communication technologies has had an enormous influence on the way that information is produced, organized, stored, searched, and transmitted, and has certainly made more information accessible to more people. But these new technologies have failed to solve the intellectual problems of information retrieval. In fact, in some ways they have made retrieval more difficult. On the one hand, technology has speeded the search process, increased the amount of information that can be accessed by a single search, and enabled the searcher to use much more sophisticated search strategies. On the other hand, the amount of information available is daunting, and the variety of different ways to access it means that selection and evaluation are key ingredients to successful searching. Thus, technological developments have resulted in an increased need for user training if the most efficient use is to be made of these powerful new retrieval systems.

What Information Can You Find Online?

The heart of an online retrieval system is the information it contains—the files or databases that are available for searching. Databases come in all shapes and sizes, ranging from vast files such as MEDLINE or CA Search (containing around 9 million and 12 million records respectively), to tiny specialized files such as the Philosopher's Index (just under 200,000 records) or AIDSLINE (144,000 records, but growing fast). Although these are examples of bibliographic files, there is now a wide range in types of information available for searching online, much of it in full text. Different databases not only contain different types of information but also are useful for a variety of purposes, ranging from quick verification of a reference to factual data to in-depth research. Today it is possible to find answers to almost any type of reference query using online resources.

In this book we are going to concentrate on one of these online search services, the DIALOG system (now owned by M.A.I.D. plc). The search language that you will learn will be the DIALOG command language, and the majority of our examples are taken from the DIALOG system, though examples are also given from other systems. The reason for this concentration on DIALOG is our belief that it is very difficult to learn more than one new language at a time, and that it is better to become fluent in one new language before trying another. We also believe that, because most online systems have a very similar range of commands, once one understands the kinds of features available and becomes proficient on one system, it is not difficult to transfer that knowledge to another system with a slightly different command language. Both CD-ROMs and the WWW have attempted to make their systems easier to use by the uninitiated, but better searching on these systems will also result from a general understanding of what the computer is doing in any given situation.

> It is also true that the DIALOG command language is among the most powerful, full-featured (and therefore complex) language. Learning it and what it can do will serve you well in learning, using, and evaluating other systems, including Web-based ones. – JWJ

Some search services provide information in a single subject field. For example, Mead Data Central has specialized in legal information, with two databases covering federal statutes and case law. DIALOG, however, is a multisubject system, so that it provides a particularly useful example to illustrate the diversity of information that can be accessed online.

There are four basic types of databases currently available for online access:

- Bibliographic citations (sometimes including abstracts)
- Full-text documents
- Directory sources
- Numeric data

It is not uncommon for a single search subject to be covered by several databases, which will often provide different types of information. The degree of overlap between files and the occurrence of unique items will vary considerably by both subject field and database. In order to demonstrate the diversity of information available, let us look at how the records in different files provide information suitable for answering a variety of requests.

Bibliographic Information

Although the original use of online systems was normally to produce a bibliography of citations in response to a subject search request, the same type of record is also useful for checking an incomplete or misremembered reference. For example, a request for "that book about tough California writers" can be swiftly identified by using a database such as the Library of Congress MARC file or the online version of R. R. Bowker's *Books in Print*®. The resulting citation in *Books in Print*® (fig. 1.1) contains information not unlike that in a standard catalog record.

Fig. 1.1. Books in Print® record.

```
00598185    1034311XX    STATUS: Out of print (06-92)
   TITLE: California Writers: Jack London, John Steinbeck, the Tough Guys
   AUTHOR: Martin, Stoddard
   PUBLISHER: St Martin   PUBLICATION DATE: 01/1984 (840101)
   NO. OF PAGES: 224p.
   LCCN: 82-020451
   BINDING: Trade - $22.50
   ISBN: 0-312-11420-6
   VOLUME(S): N/A
   ORDER NO.: N/A
   IMPRINT: N/A
   STATUS IN FILE: New (84-02)

   LIBRARY OF CONGRESS SUBJECT HEADINGS: LONDON, JACK, 1876-1916 (00280707)
```

The same record on LC MARC (fig. 1.2) looks rather more complicated.

Fig. 1.2. LC MARC record.

```
1637993  LCCN:  82020451
   California writers  ;  Jack London,  John Steinbeck, the tough guys /
   Stoddard Martin
   Martin, Stoddard, 1948-

   New York : St. Martin's Press,    viii, 224 p. ; 23 cm.
   PUBLICATION DATE(S) : 1983
   PLACE OF PUBLICATION: New York
   ISBN: 0312114206
   LC CALL NO.: PS283.C2 M35 1983  DEWEY CALL NO.: 813/.54/099794
   RECORD STATUS: Increase in encoding level from prepublication record
   BIBLIOGRAPHIC LEVEL: Monograph
   LANGUAGE:  English
   GEOGRAPHIC LOCATION: California
   NOTES:
    Includes bibliographical references and index.
   DESCRIPTORS:
   American fiction -- California -- History and criticism; American fiction
    20th century -- History and criticism; California in literature
```

Here are some other examples of bibliographic records to prove that even a single type of record can vary greatly (see figs. 1.3 and 1.4, p. 4).

Fig. 1.3. Magazine Index record.

```
12535757  DIALOG File 47:  MAGAZINE INDEX  *Use Format 9 for FULL TEXT*
'Hearty' vitamins;  sparing arteries with megadose supplements. (research
   using soybean-oil and vitamin E)
Raloff, Janet
Science News  v142 p76(1) August 1, 1992
SOURCE FILE: MI File 47
CODEN: SCNEB  ISSN: 0036-8423
AVAILABILITY: FULL TEXT Online  LINE COUNT: 00092
ABSTRACT:  Scientists are conducting tests that boost LDL oxidant defensive
   benefits in order to discourage plaque buildup in the human body.  The
   study includes large doses of soybean-oil capsules and vitamin E.
   Researchers say that vitamin therapy will probably be used to ward off
   heart disease.
DESCRIPTORS: Atherosclerosis--Prevention;  Cholesterol,  LDL--Research;
   Oxidation--Research; Vitamin therapy--Research
```

Fig. 1.4. BIOSIS Previews record.

```
9610212     BIOSIS Number: 94115212
   HEPATIC CYTOTOXICITY AND MUTAGENIC POTENTIAL OF SODIUM SELENITE VITAMIN E
ICCF BUCURESTI ON MOUSE BONE MARROW IN-VIVO
   SOCACIU C; PASCA I; LISOVSCHI C
   USACN, STR. MANASTUR NR. 3, CLUJ-NAPOCA 3400, ROMANIA.
   BUL INST AGRON CLUJ-NAPOCA SER ZOOTEH MED VET 46 (0). 1992.  121-127.
CODEN: BIAVD
   Full Journal Title: Buletinul Institutului Agronomic Cluj-Napoca Seria
Zootehnie si Medicina Veterinara
   Language: ROMANIAN
   Subfile: BA (Biological Abstracts)
   The cytotoxic and mutagenic potential of a Natrium Selenite - vitamine E
mixture through "in vivo" treatment was investigated. Swiss-Albino male
mice were orally administered with 0.7, 1.4 or 3.5 mg drug/kg body weight
and sacrificed after 24 hrs. The micronucleus test was applied on bone
marrow cells and the percentage of micronucleated polychromatic
erythrocytes was significantly increased versus control only for 3.5 mg
drug/kg b. w. This effect was comparable with 550 mg/kg cyclophosphamide
(positive control) treatment in the same conditions. The hepatic
cytotoxicity was investigated in the same experimental and control groups
through evaluation of some marker enzymes activities: Ca-ATPase. G-6-Pase,
lactatedehydrogenase (LDH) sorbitolydehydrogenase (SDH), peroxidase (Px)
and also through nucleotide protein ratio (DO260/280). All drug
concentrations revealed a liver metabolic activation, significantly
increased versus control. The experiment revealed a mutagenic and a
cytotoxic potential for Natrium Selenite--Vitamin E mixture especially
around 3.5 mg/kg but for the practical significance of this result we must
consider that the therapeutic dose is always much more inferior to the
toxicity limit.
Descriptors/Keywords: ERYTHROCYTE
Concept Codes:
   *02506  Cytology and Cytochemistry-Animal
   *03506  Genetics and Cytogenetics-Animal
   *10063  Biochemical Studies-Vitamins
   *10066  Biochemical Studies-Lipids
   *13016  Metabolism-Fat-Soluble Vitamins
   *14006  Digestive System-Pathology
   *15008  Blood, Blood-Forming Organs and Body Fluids-Lymphatic Tissue and
            Reticuloendothelial System
   *18004  Bones, Joints, Fasciae, Connective and Adipose Tissue-Physiology
            and Biochemistry
   *22504  Toxicology-Pharmacological Toxicology (1972- )
Biosystematic Codes:
   86375  Muridae
Super Taxa:
   Animals; Chordates; Vertebrates; Nonhuman Vertebrates; Mammals; Nonhuman
   Mammals; Rodents
```

As you can see, the amount of information in the records differs vastly, and they are obviously aimed at very different audiences. Such differences in record content and length affect the ways in which you can search the files, given that any part, or field, of the record is usually searchable.

Full-Text Records

In some databases each record contains the entire text of a document, and online systems are able to search for the occurrence of any single word or phrase in these full-text documents. Many newspapers, legal cases, and reference sources, such as encyclopedias and directories, are now available in full-text format. Full-text is also widely available on the Web, ranging from whole journal articles or even books (e.g., many of the classics that are out of copyright) to personal information and even advertising. Figure 1.5 provides an example from an international newspaper article. Many of these full-text records are very long, so they require special strategies when searching to zero in on the exact information needed and to avoid wasting a lot of time and money.

Fig. 1.5. London *Times* record (extract).

```
09544138
OJ CHALLENGED TO CONFESS;MURDER
Times of London (TL) - Thursday, February 13, 1997
By: Giles Whittell
Section: Overseas news
Word Count: 193

TEXT:
FRED GOLDMAN, whose son was murdered in 1994 at the same time as Nicole
Brown Simpson, O.J. Simpson's former wife, has issued a challenge to Mr
Simpson, urging him to publish a detailed signed confession to the murders.

    In return, Mr Goldman said he would make no attempt to collect the $21
million (Pounds 12.8 million) in damages awarded to him this week against
Mr Simpson by a civil jury, which held the former football star responsible
for the two deaths.

    It was not clear yesterday whether the Brown family would offer to drop
their claim to $12.5 million in punitive damages, and Mr Simpson has yet to
respond to the challenge. Legal experts pointed out, however, that he was
unlikely to accept, not least because that could expose him to perjury
charges.

    Mr Goldman first issued his challenge on Tuesday on Salem Radio Network
and was asked by Mark Gilman on the Alan Keyes Show if it was that simple.
"Easy to say, easy to do, never going to happen," Mr Goldman said. "This
person hasn't owned responsibility for any of his actions through his
lifetime."

    * Race to replace O.J., page 19.
```

Full-text information on the Web ranges from similar informative records (see fig. 1.6, p. 6), to blatant commercial advertising (see fig. 1.7, p. 7), and it is worth pointing out that the Web is a resource that is unedited and largely unsupervised, so extra careful evaluation of retrieved material is even more essential than with bibliographic records.

Fig. 1.6. Internet full-text journal record (abbreviated).

Eating | Drinking | Playing | Bon Appétit | Gourmet | Forums
Home | Text-Only Index | Go to Epicurious Travel

epicurious
RECIPE FILE

Click here to email a copy of this recipe to a friend

INDONESIAN-STYLE GRILLED EGGPLANT WITH SPICY PEANUT SAUCE WHITE

1 eggplant (about 1 1/4 pounds), cut into 1/2-inch-thick slices
1 garlic clove, minced
1 shallot, minced
a 2-inch-long fresh hot red chili, chopped fine (wear rubber gloves), or 1/4 teaspoon crushed red pepper flakes
2 teaspoons Oriental sesame oil
1/4 cup ground roasted peanuts
2 teaspoons soy sauce
1 teaspoon sugar
2 teaspoons fresh lemon juice, or to taste
vegetable oil for brushing the eggplant

Sprinkle the eggplant lightly with salt, let it drain in a colander for 1 hour, and pat it dry. In a small saucepan cook the garlic, the shallot, and the chili in the sesame oil over moderately low heat, stirring occasionally, until the vegetables are softened, add the peanuts, and cook the mixture, stirring, for 1 minute. Add the soy sauce, the sugar, the lemon juice, and 1 cup water, boil the mixture, stirring occasionally, until it is thickened slightly, and add salt and pepper to taste. Brush the eggplant, patted dry, with the vegetable oil and grill it on an oiled rack set 5 to 6 inches over glowing coals, turning it, for 7 to 8 minutes, or until it is just cooked. Transfer the eggplant to a serving plate and spoon the peanut sauce over it.

Serves 4.

Gourmet
July 1990
Debbie White: Atlanta, Georgia

http://food.epicurious.com

Fig. 1.7. Internet advertisement record.

Energizer Bunny

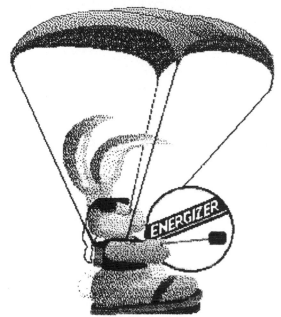

It's the famous **Energizer Bunny**, star of award-winning TV commercials, now appearing on your Mac. Yes! You heard it right. This bunny with an attitude will invade your Mac with cool desktop wallpaper and sizzling hot screen savers. But no! Energizer Bunny doesn't stop there. Just when you least expect it, he proudly parades across your screen beating his drum for everyone to hear. Amaze your friends as the original Energizer Bunny struts his stuff with live-action sound and full animation. Don't wait, don't hesitate! Be the first to have the one and only Energizer Bunny show off on your Mac. He'll dazzle and impress, as he keeps going and going and going...

Requires Mac with 1.44MB floppy, running System 6.0.7 or later, 2MB of RAM, color or gray-scale monitor.

To order a discounted copy of Energizer Bunny (list price: $29.95), consult the chart below for pricing information. There are no hidden charges. I pay taxes where appropriate and ship all orders the same day they are received via First Class Mail service within the United States and Air Mail delivery elsewhere.

Directory Information

Directory files are systematically arranged listings of people, organizations, or institutions, providing addresses, affiliations, qualifications, and so forth. These are used to locate experts or organizations through their addresses, phone numbers, zip codes, specialization, and so on. This kind of information is often among the most popular quick reference types of query in libraries, particularly public libraries. Figures 1.8 (*Marquis Who's Who*) and 1.9 (*American Library Directory*) are examples of this type of directory resource that are available online. (See p. 8.)

Fig. 1.8. *Marquis Who's Who* record.

```
00934100    Record provided by: Marquis
   Perot, H. Ross
   OCCUPATION(S): investments and real estate group executive; data
   BORN:  1930
   SEX: Male
   FAMILY:  married; 4 children.
   EDUCATION:
     Ed., U.S. Naval Acad.
   CAREER:
     founder, Perot Systems Corp., Washington, 1988-
     now with, The Perot Group, Dallas
     chmn., chief exec. officer, also dir., Electronic Data Systems Corp.,
        Dallas, to 1986
     founder, Electronic Data Systems Corp., Dallas, 1962-84
     data processing salesman, IBM Corp., 1957-62
   MILITARY:
     Served with USN, 1953-57
   AWARDS:
     Recipient Internat. Disting. Entrepreneur award, U. Man., 1988.

   Office: Dallas, TX
```

Fig. 1.9. *American Library Directory* record.

```
00021412   0733532000   LIBRARY RECORD
   OFFICIAL NAME: SYRACUSE UNIVERSITY LIBRARY - E S Bird Library
   LIBRARY TYPE: COLLEGE & UNIVERSITY
   ADDRESS:   222 Waverly Ave
              Syracuse, NY
              13244-2010
   SAN (Standard Address Number): 354-2645
   TELEPHONE  NUMBER(S):  315-443-2573;  Interlibrary Loan Service Tel. No.:
      443-3725

   LIBRARY HOLDINGS:
   BK VOLS: 2,650,995    PER SUB: 9015   MICRO: Total 3,238,652
```

SPECIAL COLLECTIONS: Stephen Crane First Editions & Manuscripts; Spire Collection on Loyalists in the American; Revolution; Novotny Library of Economic History; William Hobart-Royce Balzac Coll; Library; Sol Feinstone Library; Leopold Von Ranke Library; Shaker Coll; Oneida Community Coll; Margaret Bourke-White Coll; Marcel Breuer Coll; Peggy Bacon Papers; Anna Hyatt Huntington Papers; Earl R Browder Papers; Rudyard Kipling First Editions; Cartoonist Coll; Science Fiction Books & Manuscripts; Modern American Private Press Books; Gerrit & Peter Smith Coll; C P Huntington Papers; Averill Harriman Gubernatorial Papers; Dorothy Thompson Papers; Street & Smith Archive; Arna Bontemps Papers; Grove Press Archive; Continuing Education Coll; Benjamin Spock Papers; Mary Walker Papers; Albert Schweitzer Papers; William Safire Coll
  US DOC DEP   STATE DOC DEP

Numeric Data

Databases containing numeric information of various types are also available for online searching. A file such as Donnelly Demographics can provide selected information from the most recent U.S. census, enhanced with estimates of the current situation and even offering five-year projections for certain categories of data. Figure 1.10 (pp. 9-11) presents a very abbreviated section of a single record, but it gives some idea of the wealth of data that can be found in numeric files. It is particularly useful to be able to retrieve this type of information in machine-readable form because the data can then be uploaded to a statistical or database program for analysis and manipulation.

Fig. 1.10. Donnelly Demographics record (extract).

```
00007912
ST JOHNSVILLE (Zip Code 13452)

Level:          ZIP
State:          NY (New York)
County:         MONTGOMERY
SMSA:           ALBANY-SCHENECTADY-TROY NY (0160)
PMSA/MSA:       ALBANY-SCHENECTADY-TROY, NY MSA (0160)
ADI:            ALBANY-SCHENECTADY-TROY
DMA:            ALBANY-SCHENECTADY-TRO
SAMI:           ALBANY
Zip Code:       13452 (ST JOHNSVILLE, NY)
City or Place:  ST JOHNSVILLE
```

Totals & Medians

	1980 Census	1991 Estimate	% Change 80 to 91	1996 Projection
Total Population	4,766	4,494	-5.7	4,358
Total Households	1,647	1,570	-4.7	1,529
Household Population	4,763	4,487	-5.8	4,351
Average Household Size	2.9	2.9	-1.2	2.8
Average Household Inc.	$14,254	$28,152	97.5	$34,720
Median Household Income	$13,019	$23,833	83.1	$29,070

Population by Age and Sex

	1980 Census Number	Pct.	1991 Estimate Number	Pct.	1996 Projection Number	Pct.
Population by Age						
Total	4,766	100.0%	4,494	100.0%	4,358	100.0%
0 - 4	362	7.6%	374	8.3%	356	8.2%
5 - 9	414	8.7%	352	7.8%	351	8.1%
10 - 14	421	8.8%	321	7.1%	331	7.6%
15 - 19	454	9.5%	347	7.7%	302	6.9%
20 - 24	326	6.8%	367	8.2%	324	7.4%
25 - 29	334	7.0%	390	8.7%	344	7.9%
30 - 34	299	6.3%	297	6.6%	363	8.3%
35 - 39	285	6.0%	287	6.4%	278	6.4%
40 - 44	216	4.5%	266	5.9%	267	6.1%

Fig. 1.10. Donnelly Demographics record (continued).

45 - 49	206	4.3%	237	5.3%	246	5.6%
50 - 54	259	5.4%	189	4.2%	219	5.0%
55 - 59	300	6.3%	169	3.8%	168	3.9%
60 - 64	270	5.7%	196	4.4%	150	3.4%
65 - 69	225	4.7%	221	4.9%	168	3.9%
70 - 74	146	3.1%	191	4.3%	178	4.1%
75 - 79	102	2.1%	142	3.2%	144	3.3%
80 - 84	73	1.5%	79	1.8%	97	2.2%
85 +	73	1.5%	69	1.5%	74	1.7%
< 15	1,197	25.1%	1,047	23.3%	1,038	23.8%
65 +	619	13.0%	702	15.6%	661	15.2%
75 +	248	5.2%	290	6.5%	315	7.2%
Median Age	31.2		31.6		32.4	
Median Age Adult Pop.	45.1		42.6		42.6	

Female Population by Age

Total	2,464	100.0%	2,322	100.0%	2,253	100.0%
0 - 4	171	6.9%	182	7.8%	174	7.7%
5 - 9	223	9.1%	172	7.4%	171	7.6%
10 - 14	200	8.1%	152	6.5%	162	7.2%
15 - 19	239	9.7%	183	7.9%	143	6.3%
20 - 24	170	6.9%	178	7.7%	172	7.6%
25 - 29	161	6.5%	202	8.7%	167	7.4%
30 - 34	166	6.7%	156	6.7%	189	8.4%
35 - 39	136	5.5%	142	6.1%	146	6.5%
40 - 44	108	4.4%	142	6.1%	132	5.9%
45 - 49	110	4.5%	119	5.1%	132	5.9%
50 - 54	128	5.2%	95	4.1%	110	4.9%
55 - 59	165	6.7%	91	3.9%	85	3.8%
60 - 64	137	5.6%	101	4.3%	82	3.6%
65 - 69	116	4.7%	124	5.3%	89	4.0%
70 - 74	74	3.0%	105	4.5%	104	4.6%
75 - 79	66	2.7%	83	3.6%	84	3.7%
80 - 84	48	1.9%	46	2.0%	61	2.7%
85 +	46	1.9%	49	2.1%	50	2.2%
< 15	594	24.1%	506	21.8%	507	22.5%
65 +	350	14.2%	407	17.5%	388	17.2%
75 +	160	6.5%	178	7.7%	195	8.7%
Median Age	32.0		32.9		33.6	
Median Age Adult Pop.	46.2		43.6		43.7	

Male Population by Age

Total	2,301	100.0%	2,172	100.0%	2,107	100.0%
0 - 4	191	8.3%	192	8.8%	182	8.6%
5 - 9	191	8.3%	180	8.3%	180	8.5%
10 - 14	221	9.6%	169	7.8%	169	8.0%
15 - 19	215	9.3%	164	7.6%	159	7.5%
20 - 24	156	6.8%	189	8.7%	152	7.2%
25 - 29	173	7.5%	188	8.7%	177	8.4%
30 - 34	133	5.8%	141	6.5%	174	8.3%
35 - 39	149	6.5%	145	6.7%	132	6.3%

Fig. 1.10. Donnelly Demographics record (continued).

40 - 44	108	4.7%	124	5.7%	135	6.4%
45 - 49	96	4.2%	118	5.4%	114	5.4%
50 - 54	131	5.7%	94	4.3%	109	5.2%
55 - 59	135	5.9%	78	3.6%	83	3.9%
60 - 64	133	5.8%	95	4.4%	68	3.2%
65 - 69	109	4.7%	97	4.5%	79	3.7%
70 - 74	72	3.1%	86	4.0%	74	3.5%
75 - 79	36	1.6%	59	2.7%	60	2.8%
80 - 84	25	1.1%	33	1.5%	36	1.7%
85 +	27	1.2%	20	0.9%	24	1.1%
< 15	603	26.2%	541	24.9%	531	25.2%
65 +	269	11.7%	295	13.6%	273	13.0%
75 +	88	3.8%	112	5.2%	120	5.7%

Median Age	30.1		30.1		31.0	
Median Age Adult Pop.	44.0		41.5		41.5	

Population by Race

Total	4,766	100.0%	4,494	100.0%	4,358	100.0%
White	4,739	99.4%	4,449	99.0%	4,304	98.8%
Black	2	0.0%	7	0.2%	8	0.2%
Other	24	0.5%	38	0.8%	46	1.1%
Hispanic	20	0.4%	21	0.5%	22	0.5%

	1980 Census		1991 Estimate		1996 Projection	
	Number	Pct.	Number	Pct.	Number	Pct.
Household Income						
$ 0- 7,499	399	24.2%	181	11.5%	145	9.5%
$ 7,500-14,999	569	34.5%	270	17.2%	197	12.9%
$15,000-24,999	507	30.8%	377	24.0%	306	20.0%
$25,000-34,999	120	7.3%	319	20.3%	285	18.6%
$35,000-49,999	38	2.3%	256	16.3%	292	19.1%
$50,000-74,999	13	0.8%	123	7.8%	200	13.1%
$75,000 +	1	0.1%	44	2.8%	104	6.8%

	1991 Estimate
Neighborhood Mobility	
Household Moved In:	
Most Recent Year	179
Last 5 Years	539
6 - 9 Years Ago	221
10 - 14 Years Ago	226
15+ Years Ago	528
SocioEconomic Status:	
Socioeconomic Status Score	27
Private Sector Employment	1,295

Other numeric databases are of particular interest in the business environment, such as the various U.S. and international financial and company files. For example, information regarding U.S. import and export figures is available from a file such as Piers Exports (see fig. 1.11). It is also easy to collect data on the financial status of a particular U.S. or international public corporation using one of the Moody files. Figure 1.12 provides the record for the IBM Corporation from Moody's Corporate Profiles.

Fig. 1.11. Piers Exports record.

```
08532492
Product Exported: VOLKSWAGEN 85 JETTA
Product Code: 6921000 (AUTOMOBILES,MOTOR VEHICLES,TRAILERS)
    Weight of Cargo:              1900 POUNDS
    Number of Units of Cargo:        1 UNITS

Date of Shipment (YY/MM/DD): 920831

U.S.-Based Exporter: A & M INTL SERVICE
    Company Location: MIAMI, FL

U.S. Port of Loading: PT EVERGLADES (5203)

Destination Point: CALLAO (33303), PERU (333)
```

Fig. 1.12. Moody's Corporate Profiles record (abbreviated).

```
0004427
INTERNATIONAL BUSINESS MACHINES CORP.

MOODY'S NUMBER: 00004427
DUNS NUMBER: 00-136-8083
```

	STATISTICAL RECORD			
12/31/91	12/31/90	12/31/89	12/31/88	12/31/87
Operating profit margin%				
1.5	16.0	11.0	14.7	14.3
Book value				
56.96	67.79	61.28	62.23	60.09
Return on equity%				
NIL	14.1	9.8	13.9	13.7
Return on assets%				
NIL	6.9	4.8	7.5	8.3
Average yield%				
4.3	4.4	4.2	3.8	3.2
P/E ratio-high				
NIL	11.7	20.2	14.0	20.2
P/E ratio-low				
NIL	9.0	14.4	11.2	11.7
Price range-high				
139 3/4	123 1/8	130 7/8	129 1/2	175 7/8
Price range-low				
83 1/2	94 1/2	93 3/8	104 1/4	102

```
7-YEAR PRICE SCORE: 54.40  12-MONTH PRICE SCORE: 64.61

    NYSE COMPOSITE INDEX=100
```

CAPITALIZATION (12/31/91):		
	($000)	(%)
Long Term Debt	13,231,000	25.4
Deferred Income Tax	1,927,000	3.7
Common & Surplus	37,006,000	70.9
Total	52,164,000	100.0

```
INSTITUTIONAL SHARES: 262,516,211
INSTITUTIONAL HOLDERS: 1,197
NUMBER OF COMMON STOCKHOLDERS: 772,047
```

Examples such as these could be almost endless. They are included here to give a feeling for the depth and breadth of information available from online databases. They should help convince you that computer resources and the retrieval skills they require are a vital resource, both for personal information gathering and for the provision of an effective search service to others.

How Does Information Retrieval Work?

Any formal search for information involves some interaction with an information retrieval (IR) system. The word *system* is used to describe a wide variety of phenomena that we encounter in our daily lives—the educational system, the political system—but may best be seen as some set of components that interact to provide a desired result (see fig. 1.13).

Fig. 1.13. A system.

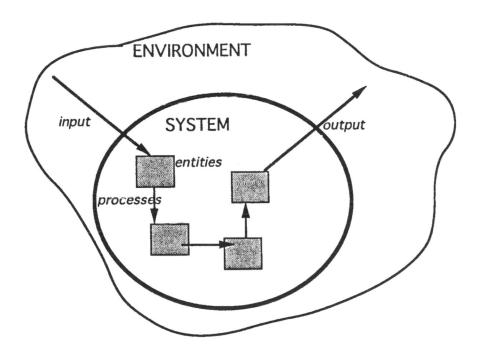

These components consist of a group of interlinked entities (e.g., organizations, people, documents) that participate in a group of interlinked processes (e.g., transmitting, updating, searching). Outside the system, separated from it by a boundary but influencing its operation, lies the system environment. The dynamic nature of the system and the relationships between the elements in it are represented by the information flowing through the system, hence the term IR *cycle.* The transfer of information across the boundary between the system and its environment is known as *input* and *output.* The nature of these inputs, processes, and outputs is governed by the objectives that the system is aiming to fulfill and the external environment within which it operates.

Thus, the typical elements of a document-based IR system consist of inputs and outputs, the matching mechanism, and a series of activities, including:

> the selection of documents;
>
> the conceptual analysis of documents;
>
> the organization of *document representations*;
>
> the storage of documents;
>
> the conceptual analysis of queries;
>
> the matching of documents and queries; and
>
> the delivery of documents.

Let us elaborate on these different elements. The inputs to the system are:

- new documents selected on the basis of user needs;
- ad hoc queries posed by the system users; and
- the indexing language used by both the indexer and the searcher.

The outputs are:

- documents retrieved in response to queries; and
- factual queries answered.

The relationships among the elements of such an IR system are illustrated in simplified form in figure 1.14 (see p. 15).

> *And, of course, the cycle is complete when the users who get the documents use them to assist in creating new works, which make their way into the system, and on and on and on. This "cycle of information" takes place not only in the IR system, but everywhere—and is an important underlying phenomenon in library information work. – JWJ*

The structure in figure 1.14 is generalized in that it makes no assumptions about how any activity will be carried out, and is equally applicable to either manual or computerized systems. In practice a range of other activities are necessary to link the system inputs and outputs. For example, once the documents have been acquired, they need to be organized in some way so they can be identified and located in response to a search request. This involves cataloging (i.e., description), subject indexing, and (sometimes) abstracting. This indexing consists of two separate stages: the determination of subject content (conceptual analysis) and the translation of that concept into the controlled vocabulary of the system (i.e., the assignment of controlled subject terms). Such a system vocabulary may consist of a list of subject headings, a subject thesaurus, or a classification scheme, and is used to represent the subject matter of the documents for purposes of searching. Most computer systems also make use of *keywords*, or uncontrolled natural language terms that occur in the documents themselves; these will also be searchable. In these systems, both terms from the controlled vocabulary and the keywords may thus be considered subject terms that are searched as representing the documents themselves.

Fig. 1.14. The IR cycle (adapted from Lancaster[2]).

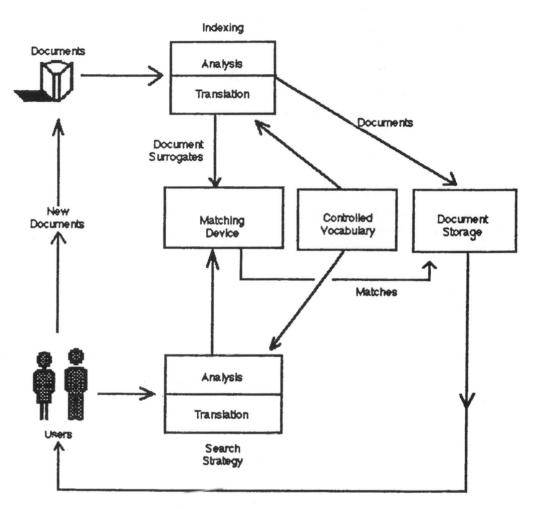

Indexing is a simple term that sometimes causes confusion. The reason for this is probably that it is used in two rather different ways. We use it to talk of assigning index terms from a controlled vocabulary, but we know that one can also search index terms—keywords—from natural language. Further confusion may be added by the fact that classification numbers are also often considered to be a kind of indexing (subject description). Perhaps we can best summarize this by saying that indexing involves any type of subject specification assigned to documents in order to assist with their retrieval. – GW

Other pieces of information about documents (author's name, date of publication, language, etc.) may also be incorporated into the document representation and thus become available for searching. These document representations (or surrogates) are in fact little summaries of the basic characteristics of the documents being input to the system. They are, of course, much easier to search than the documents themselves because of their condensed nature and their ability to be searched in a variety of ways.

Once the indexing process has been completed, the documents are put into storage, and the document representations are entered into the matching mechanism. This file of document surrogates may be as simple as a card file or a printed index, but for the purposes of online retrieval it is a machine-readable file (a *database*) stored on a computer system. The aim is to make the file conveniently searchable on any search keys deemed to be potentially useful as access points to the document. In the case of the library catalog, the available search keys have traditionally been limited to the author, the title, and a single subject heading. Thus, one of the major advantages of computerized IR systems is their ability to permit searching on a much wider range of document keys—by date, by keyword, by language, and so on.

The input from the other end of the system, the user query, is treated in a fashion as similar as possible to that used for inputting the documents. Queries are analyzed for conceptual content, which is then translated into the vocabulary of the system. This translated version of the query (often with natural-language keywords or other desired document attributes added) becomes the *search strategy*, to be used for matching against the document surrogates in the database.

The output from a document-based IR system will consist of a set of records that the computer has found to match the search strategy. Such records are deemed by the system to be relevant to the user's information need. The success of the retrieval process is usually judged by this attribute of *relevance*, which is generally accepted to be qualitative in nature and uncertain in definition. (For more on relevance, see chapter 12.) The search process, which may be iterative, is finally completed when the user is satisfied with the results of the search, or when it becomes clear that there are no more relevant documents to be found.

> A number of researchers have taken a new look at relevance over the past several years. We'll deal with it in more detail in the chapter on evaluation, but for the moment you should know that it appears to be a subtle but measurable phenomenon, dependent on the individual person and situation, and more complicated than one might expect. – JWJ

Information Seeking

It is widely believed that user requests for information usually fall into one of two broad categories:

1. The need to locate and obtain a particular document for which the author or title is known, usually called a *known item search*.

2. The need to locate material dealing with a particular subject or to answer a particular question, known as a *subject search*.

Most information services need to be able to provide answers to both of these types of query. The bibliographic networks (such as OCLC and RLIN) are excellent examples of known item search systems because they are normally used to provide cataloging data for items that are already in hand.

> *Unfortunately we will be coming across acronyms like this all the time. They are a professional pitfall that you will need to negotiate. OCLC and RLIN are large-scale (many millions of records) bibliographic databases used by many libraries to assist in cataloging and inter-library loan functions. They are known as bibliographic utilities. The OCLC database is produced by the Online Computer Library Center in Ohio, and RLIN is a product of the Research Libraries Group.* —GW

The use of these bibliographic utilities is fairly straightforward because they can be searched on accurate and relatively stable elements, such as the ISBN (International Standard Book Number) or an author's name. Subject searching is far more difficult because one is in effect searching for what is not known and which may not even exist. In such cases users are looking for information that will fill a gap in their personal conceptual frameworks, which are probably unique.

> *A couple of different research approaches have been tried regarding users and gaps in their knowledge states. Belkin, Oddy, and Brooks,[3] in a project now known as ASK, studied the anomalous states of knowledge exhibited by users when approaching information systems. They contend that because users have perceived a gap in their knowledge state, they will be "unable to state precisely what is needed to resolve that anomaly." Instead of being asked what information they wanted, users were asked to give a problem statement describing their current knowledge state and the researchers attempted to derive a structural representation of that state to assist in retrieval.*
>
> *Dervin[4] has developed a similar sense-making model, which states that people are constantly trying to make sense of their situation as they move through time and space. When they find they are unable to continue moving due to a gap in their sense of the world, they express that gap as an information need, which must be filled for the gap to be resolved and the person to continue on. Both of these theories have been very useful in thinking about and designing information systems.* – JWJ

The problems involved in trying to answer this type of subject search arise not only from the difficulty in defining the question but also from the intangible nature of information itself. Information is difficult to define accurately; it is perceived differently by different individuals, and their perceptions are likely to change over time. Although information can reasonably be regarded as anything that helps to answer an information need and may be presented in any way—oral, written, graphic—or in any format—print, microform, computer data, etc.—the mere provision of information-bearing documents does not necessarily mean that information has been effectively transferred.

The growth of funded research and the escalation of publication rates in recent years have posed enormous problems for those whose task it is to acquire and organize the files of published information that have resulted. The organization and processing of this information is far from simple, and the increased amounts of it have merely served to exacerbate a long-standing conceptual problem. As early as 1960 Maron and Kuhns[5] highlighted the difficulties involved in identifying the subject content of either documents or queries, because such decisions are not only restricted by the nature of the controlled vocabulary in use but are also bound to contain an element of subjectivity. This was confirmed by Lancaster's early research on the MEDLARS search system,[6] which suggested that search vocabulary and human errors were the major causes of retrieval failure. The move to computerized systems has undoubtedly speeded up the mechanical parts of IR but has done little to help with the conceptual problems involving subject description.

In fact, the term *information retrieval* itself is something of a misnomer, because what is retrieved by most IR systems is usually either a set of documents or citations to documents that are believed to contain the required information. For example, a library catalog can be searched by subject terms to retrieve records related to the subject required. But the documents identified must then be tracked to the shelves and further searched for particular items of information. The catalog entries are used for the purpose of identifying potentially useful items because they are easier to search than the shelves themselves, but they do not necessarily provide the requested information.

Notice that in this situation we are matching the terms that represent our required subject with the terms that represent the content of the documents. Thus the IR system (in this case the library catalog) is a *matching device* for comparing individual words or phrases between documents and queries. Crucial to the success of this type of retrieval is the vocabulary used to index the documents and to search the document surrogates. It is clear that the same vocabulary has to be used by both the indexer and the searcher, or no matches will be found. This standardization is the role of a *controlled vocabulary*. For example, if we are searching a file for the term "motor cars" when the indexer has entered documents on this subject under the heading "automobiles," we will retrieve nothing, although relevant material is available in the collection. Notice also that although an IR system does not usually retrieve information, information retrieval (IR) is the term commonly used to describe many types of literature searching. Many of the newer systems, however, do provide direct access to the information itself.

As we shall see in chapter 2, the growing problems faced by the traditional search systems (the card catalogs and printed indexes) as they attempted to cope with escalating publication rates led to the early experiments with automated and semiautomated IR systems during the 1950s.

Notes

1. Peter Briscoe, et al. (March 1986), "Ashurbanipal's Enduring Archetype: Thoughts on the Library's Role in the Future," *College & Research Libraries* 47(2): 121–26.

2. F. Wilfred Lancaster (1979), *Information Retrieval Systems: Characteristics, Testing and Evaluation*, 2d ed. (New York: Wiley), 8.

3. N. J. Belkin, R. N. Oddy, and H. M. Brooks (1982), "ASK for Information Retrieval: Part I . Background and Theory," *Journal of Documentation* 38(2): 61–71; and N. J. Belkin, R. N. Oddy, and H. M .Brooks (1982), "ASK for Information Retrieval: Part II. Results of a Design Study," *Journal of Documentation* 38(3): 145–64.

4. B. Dervin (1983), "An Overview of Sense-Making Research: Concepts, Methods and Results to Date." Paper presented at the International Communication Association Annual Meeting, Dallas, TX; and B. Dervin and P. Dewdrey (1986), "Neutral Questioning: A New Approach to the Reference Interview," *RQ* 25: 506–13.

5. M. E. Maron and J. L. Kuhns (1960), "On Relevance, Probabilistic Indexing and Information Retrieval," *Journal of Association of Computing Machinery* 7(3): 216–44.

6. F. W. Lancaster (1968), *Evaluation of the MEDLARS Demand Search Service* (Bethesda, MD: National Library of Medicine): 193.

Additional Reading

Lancaster, F. W. (1979), *Information Retrieval Systems: Characteristics, Testing and Evaluation.* 2d ed. (New York: John Wiley): chapters 1, 4, and 5.

2 DEVELOPMENTS IN INFORMATION RETRIEVAL

This chapter looks at the way IR systems have developed over the years. We noted in chapter 1 that the escalation of journal publishing and the detailed level of much of the published research has led to increasing difficulties in retrieving appropriate material in response to information queries. Over the last 50 years, dissatisfaction with the performance of manual systems has led to experiments with alternative methods, and ultimately to the use of computer systems for the storing and searching of information records. All early IR systems were what is now called *pre-coordinate systems*, and many of these traditional systems are still in use for library catalogs and printed indexes today. The best known of these controlled vocabulary systems is probably the Library of Congress Subject Headings list (LCSH). In order to allow documents to be searched and retrieved on the basis of their subject content, the vocabulary of the system must not only permit the subject of the document to be adequately described, but both the indexer and searcher must be aware of the appropriate terminology used by the system.

Problems with Pre-Coordinate Systems

Using this traditional type of indexing system, for example, does one choose MEDIEVAL ARCHITECTURE or ARCHITECTURE, MEDIEVAL, or even ARCHITECTURE—MEDIEVAL as the preferred subject entry for a document on that topic? (Most of these older systems confined their subject access to a single term or phrase.) And supposing the topic to be indexed is "Medieval church architecture." How does one structure a heading to cover all three aspects of this subject? Should it be CHURCH ARCHITECTURE, MEDIEVAL or MEDIEVAL ARCHITECTURE—CHURCHES, or some other of a variety of possibilities? The term *pre-coordinate* is used to indicate that a group of different search terms are to be coordinated (put together) in some prescribed order. This method of indexing is called pre-coordinate because the total coordinated heading is constructed at the input or indexing stage of the IR cycle (i.e., before the document surrogates are entered into the system). The development of such an index "string" is an attempt to specify a multifaceted subject with a single standardized index entry. Terms are linked in a designated order using standardized punctuation, so that documents on the same subject will not be entered into the system under variant combinations of the individual subject terms. One can imagine the problems involved if the order is not standardized, and also the difficulties in trying to specify a compound subject with a single, all-encompassing index entry if there is no set of rules.

The most obvious solution to this problem would appear to be to make multiple entries, one under each of the selected headings. In the previous example this would require three separate entries—one under MEDIEVAL, one under ARCHITECTURE, and one under CHURCHES—so that whichever term the searcher selects as a search term, the relevant document or documents would eventually be retrieved. The operating word here is "eventually" because the searcher would need to scan all the entries under the chosen search term to find any that also use the other search terms. This also raises another problem, in that none of the entries is "specific." That is, none of them completely specifies the content of the document; they are not "coextensive" with the subject of the document.

> *Specificity is a term used in relation to how accurately the document or query is represented in the system. It refers to how completely the terms in the system vocabulary fit with the subject of the document to be indexed. It can also refer to how accurately a search statement represents a particular information need. Specificity is not an inherent, predetermined value for a given term, but varies in relation to a particular document or a particular query. – GW*

In real life this means that one might expend a great deal of time searching a very large section of the file under any one of these individual headings. This is because we have to search much too broadly. We have lost specificity when we search under only one part of the subject involved. The basic aim of any IR system must be to limit the search for a given query to a manageable subset of the collection. In this sense, dividing a compound heading into its individual parts appears to be counterproductive. As we lose topic specificity, we increase search time.

Another possible way to improve retrieval performance is to retain specificity by using the entire pre-coordinated string, but making multiple entries under each of the rotated combinations. We would thus have three entries for the previous example:

```
CHURCHES : ARCHITECTURE : MEDIEVAL
ARCHITECTURE : MEDIEVAL : CHURCHES
MEDIEVAL : CHURCHES : ARCHITECTURE
```

Notice that even this does not cover every reasonable possibility. For example, there is no entry under MEDIEVAL ARCHITECTURE (with or without punctuation), although it is a likely search string. The problem is that the number of entries required to cover all possible combinations of multiple terms grows exponentially with the number of individual terms, and most system managers are not prepared to allow for more than one or two entries per document.

> *This limitation in the number of subject headings normally allocated in traditional systems is a feature of their physical format. Multiple entries bulk out the size of the catalog, already growing unduly as a result of increased acquisitions. But because a book can only be in one place on the shelf, it is an obvious benefit for the catalog to provide multiple pointers to increase access.*
>
> *– GW*

As the content of documents has become more detailed and specialized, the limitations of the pre-coordinate systems have become increasingly evident. We have seen a move away from a total reliance on controlled subject headings such as LCSH even in traditional library catalogs.

Post-Coordinate Retrieval Systems

Not only is there more information needing to be processed nowadays, but that information is becoming ever more specialized and therefore needs more detailed indexing. In response to this problem, a series of experimental systems was developed during the 1950s that were intended to provide greater specificity in indexing and more flexibility in searching. These new systems became known as *post-coordinate systems*, based on the fact that they relied on the combination (or coordination) of multiple subject terms at the search stage rather than the input stage. Index terms were assigned individually, with a single entry made for each term, as suggested earlier, but provision was made for searching them in combination rather than by single terms only.

This totally new approach required new matching mechanisms. It was based on the idea of storing document surrogates in a document-term matrix rather than in a single alphabetic sequence. The original post-coordinate search systems were card-based manual systems that permitted the combination of search terms without the restrictions of linear order. This was accomplished by having the search file used for matching consist of records for subjects rather than records for documents. Document numbers were entered on the subject cards for the index terms selected for a particular document at the input (indexing) stage. The cards were then filed in alphabetical order by each individual subject term. When conducting a search, the subject cards appropriate to a given query were retrieved and compared for document numbers that matched on each subject card (see fig. 2.1.).

These systems were enthusiastically adopted in a number of special libraries, whose users were the ones facing the most severe problems with the retrieval of complicated, multifaceted subjects.

Unfortunately, these new systems also had their limitations. They could handle only a limited number of index terms or records or both, and their matching processes were often complicated and unwieldy. But they did have another big advantage that was not apparent initially. They turned out to be easy to convert to computer operation when the appropriate technology eventually became available, so that they provided ready-made databases as the new computer IR systems become available.

Fig. 2.1. Post-coordinate Uniterm cards (showing document number 15 on the topic of medieval church architecture).

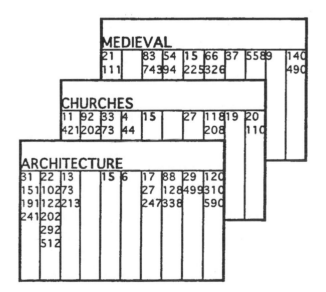

The terms pre-coordinate and post-coordinate tend to confuse some people, so let's recap what we have said about them. Coordination refers to the combining of separate index terms in order to specify a compound subject. Pre- and post- refer to the time at which that combination occurs, with pre- meaning the input (indexing) stage and post- meaning the output (searching) stage.

This means that indexers in pre-coordinate search systems will construct a single compound subject heading for each document that is input, resulting in an index heading such as FRANCE: HISTORY : REVOLUTION, or similar entries with these same terms rotated.

Notice that none of these entries conforms to natural language usage—where the user may well decide to search under FRENCH REVOLUTION—and thus fail to retrieve relevant material unless the controlled vocabulary provides a structure of linkages (references) leading from unused to used terms. In a post-coordinate system the indexer would probably select the same individual terms but make three separate entries—one under FRANCE, one under HISTORY, and one under REVOLUTION—that would be filed separately and not coordinated unless a searcher selected all three as search terms. The problem of combination order is thus eliminated. – GW

Computer Retrieval Systems

The theories behind these manual post-coordinate systems formed the basis for the offline, batch-processed computer retrieval systems that started appearing in the early 1960s. Most of these early systems were developed using U.S. government funding and were initially justified on the basis of being multipurpose. Although many of the early databases were originally developed to speed the production of printed indexes, it was later realized that they could also be used for retrospective searching and current awareness services. These systems used magnetic tape as their storage medium, were usually updated on a periodic basis, and were searched somewhat inefficiently in serial fashion (i.e., scanning each record in linear sequence). Almost all of them were based on human indexing and searching, using controlled vocabularies with terms selected from *thesauri* (lists of preferred subject terms).

These early computer retrieval systems offered a number of advantages over their manual predecessors, including the ability to

- provide multiple access points to a document;
- handle complex search strategies;
- generate printed output;
- collect operating data automatically; and
- produce a variety of services from a single input.

But they also had a number of basic drawbacks, of which the biggest was undoubtedly their lack of interaction. This meant that a search was essentially a one-shot affair with no browsing capability. The process was thus very different from the traditional manual search process. It usually meant that the search was delegated to a specialist searcher, known as the *intermediary*, who often had minimal or even no contact at all with the individual who made the original request for information.

The other big disadvantage was the delayed response time, largely a result of the way in which searches were processed. Because they were collected and saved to be processed in batches, the requester might have to wait several days (or even weeks) for the results, even though the actual search process had been enormously speeded up. This was particularly unsatisfactory in view of the lack of interaction during the search process because it often meant that the complete search cycle had to be repeated if the results proved to be unsatisfactory to the user.

Online Retrieval Systems

Online systems differ in two fundamental ways from the systems that we have been discussing so far. First, when the search is conducted online it progresses in an interactive, conversational fashion, making it more akin to the manual search process, where one selects and discards items based on what else one finds while the search is in progress. Online searches are thus conducted in *real time*—the computer searching and comparing while one is at the terminal. This means that results are available almost immediately because the computer is capable of searching very fast despite the great size of the files involved. This speed of response is attractive to many users. It means that users can take advantage of new information as they find it in order to adapt and refine their search strategies, a process known as *feedback* that has been found to improve the relevance of the material retrieved.

Second, an online system provides *remote access*, which means that the searcher and the file of documents do not have to be geographically adjacent. The user terminal and the search system are linked by a telecommunication network, regardless of their geographical locations. Although most of the search systems commonly used in this country are American, they can be accessed from almost anywhere in the world. All that is needed is a reliable telephone system, a computer terminal, and a password and knowledge of system protocols. This means that not only bibliographic information but also bank, insurance, tax, and even security information is potentially available to users with sufficient expertise. In recent years a number of serious cases of illegal access by *hackers* has heightened recognition of the importance of adequate security measures for computer-held data.

The ability to provide access from remote locations and also the ability of present-day computers to handle multiple tasks in parallel have led to the development of a mass market for online products. The number of online searches performed has been rising steeply each year since online systems first became available (see fig. 2.2, p. 26).

The remote access provided by online systems has had another important by-product. It means that almost all information seeking now takes place on a much wider scale than it ever did in the old days of manual systems. Users are no longer limited in their information gathering to the materials available in their own library or group of local libraries. The question is no longer "What have we got on XYZ?" but "What has been published (anywhere) on XYZ?" This wider access has led to greatly increased use of the journal literature and has escalated interlibrary loan requests in recent years.

Fig. 2.2. Online searches of databases on major U.S. vendors of word-oriented databases.[1]

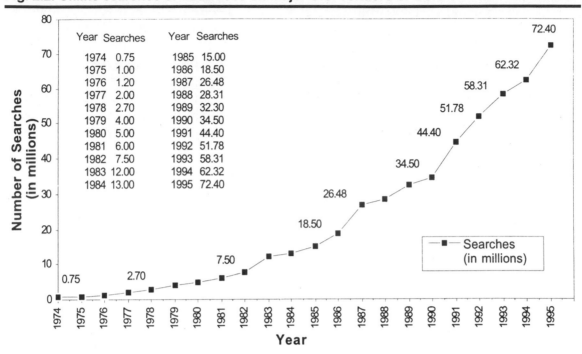

Year	Searches	Year	Searches
1974	0.75	1985	15.00
1975	1.00	1986	18.50
1976	1.20	1987	26.48
1977	2.00	1988	28.31
1978	2.70	1989	32.30
1979	4.00	1990	34.50
1980	5.00	1991	44.40
1981	6.00	1992	51.78
1982	7.50	1993	58.31
1983	12.00	1994	62.32
1984	13.00	1995	72.40

Growth of Online Systems

The widespread use of online computer search systems has thus been a relatively recent phenomenon, dating back only to the early 1970s. During the 1960s, experimental systems were being developed by organizations that faced problems with the storage and retrieval of their own in-house information. In 1964, the U.S. National Library of Medicine offered on-demand batch searching (i.e., offline) of their MEDLARS system to the medical profession at large. By the following year, Lockheed Missiles Corporation (DIALOG), Systems Development Corporation (SDC), and Chemical Abstracts Service were all developing computer search services with funding from the federal government. In 1968, the first online access was accomplished from the State University of New York Biomedical Network in Albany to the MEDLARS database in Bethesda, Maryland, using dedicated lines. By 1969, the first packet-switched data communications network (ARPAnet) had begun test operation, and the necessary components for more general online communication were gradually falling into place.

The first major online dial-up service was MEDLINE, the online version of MEDLARS. It was swiftly followed in 1972 by the offer of commercial online services DIALOG (Lockheed) and ORBIT (SDC). From that date, systems have proliferated; LEXIS from Mead Data Central, the New York Times Information Bank, and the Dow Jones News/Retrieval Service arrived in swift succession. By 1975, more than 300 public access databases were available from a range of different vendors, and online IR was firmly established in both North America and Western Europe. Using these early systems required considerable training, and most of their use was delegated to professional searchers in library settings. But gradually the idea of direct user access developed, and by 1979 two systems were initiated that directly targeted the home user—The Source and CompuServe (see more on this aspect in chapter 4).

Since these beginnings in the early 1970s, the rate of growth of all aspects of online has been truly extraordinary (see fig. 2.3), and the impact of online systems on information-seeking and worldwide information use has been profound.

Fig. 2.3. Growth of online services.[2]

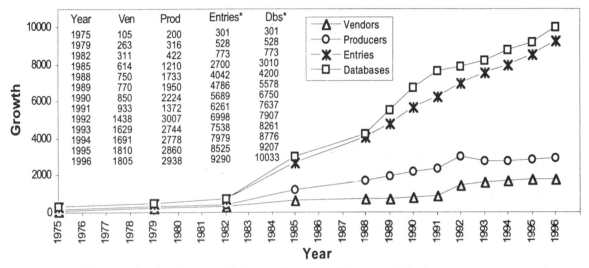

Year	Ven	Prod	Entries*	Dbs*
1975	105	200	301	301
1979	263	316	528	528
1982	311	422	773	773
1985	614	1210	2700	3010
1988	750	1733	4042	4200
1989	770	1950	4786	5578
1990	850	2224	5689	6750
1991	933	1372	6261	7637
1992	1438	3007	6998	7907
1993	1629	2744	7538	8261
1994	1691	2778	7979	8776
1995	1810	2860	8525	9207
1996	1805	2938	9290	10033

*Note: Database and entries that are provided in more than one medium are counted only once.

By 1997, the number of different search services (vendors) available worldwide had grown to 2,115, offering 10,338 databases (including CD-ROM files) with an average size of 9,662 records per file from 3,216 different database producers. These figures indicate the solid establishment of the database industry. But the real measure of acceptance of computer-based resources is indicated by the growth in the number of searches performed. The growth of online use of databases on the major U.S. systems offering word-oriented databases reached a high of 79.9 million searches in 1997. These figures represent a specific subset of vendors. If one were to add in the transactional databases (stocks, electronic ordering, credit checking, airline reservations, etc.) and consumer service systems, the number of searches would be much larger. Unfortunately, such data do not exist, and neither do data for the use of CD-ROM databases.

The expansion and popularity of the Web has been the largest single phenomenon in the information and database industry over the last few years, affecting virtually all players in the information industry. Nobody knows the exact numbers of databases or users on the Web, but figures are in the many millions and growing exponentially. Many publishers are putting up multimedia databases combining audio, image, and video materials and linking to other publications via hyperlinks. The Net is becoming commercialized and is widely used for advertising and online ordering. URLs and E-mail addresses are found not only on catalogs and business cards but also on television, billboards, trains, buses, and even the packaging of a variety of goods. A number of the traditional search services (e.g., DIALOG, Dow Jones) are now making their services available through the Web, where they have the possibilities for an enhanced multimedia interface. In fact, the Internet is fast becoming part of the professional searcher's toolkit (see chapter 4 for more on this). A whole range of factors is being raised by these new developments, including pricing strategies, intellectual property rights, and the security of the information being transmitted.

Although the United States has retained the largest share of the online market, both as a supplier and as a user, Europe has been making considerable strides because national monopolies over their telephone and communications networks (PPTs) are gradually being eroded. Databases are now being produced in 41 languages worldwide.

Like all really good inventions, economical access to online information required input from a range of seemingly unrelated technologies and the coming together of a group of unconnected priorities in order to flourish. These include:

Funding

The first of these priorities was implemented as a result of the growing recognition of the importance of information and information products as a vital national resource. A major impact on the attitudes of the U.S. federal government was the 1959 launching of the Russian satellite. This event, widely regarded in the United States as heralding a major loss of technological superiority, prompted the investment of large amounts of federal funds in the development of computer systems for the storage and processing of information, and for the collection of data in machine-readable files. The most important of these early systems were initiated by the Armed Services Technical Information Agency (later DDC) and the National Aeronautics and Space Administration (NASA), who were swiftly followed by the National Library of Medicine (MEDLINE) and the Educational Resources Information Center (ERIC). Although these early services were initially in-house batch-processed systems and were not generally available to the public, the file structures and search features designed at that time have influenced the way in which most other computer IR systems have developed over the years. Both the Systems Development Corporation (SDC) and Lockheed (DIALOG) information systems also received federal funding to assist with the development of search software and the mounting of additional databases provided by contracts with outside database-producing agencies, such as the National Agricultural Library and the Chemical Abstracts Service. Both SDC and DIALOG quickly developed into major commercial vendors of online information.

Data

The second area to affect the development of online systems was more directly concerned with the provision of information products—the production of printed indexes and abstracts. During the 1960s, it became economically advantageous for the publishers of these secondary services to have their indexes produced by computer-assisted photo-typesetting. One of the prime requirements for this type of current-awareness product is speed of production, and the computer proved to be ideal for duplicating, reformatting, sorting, and printing the multiple entries required by printed indexes.

In addition to saving money and time for the index publishers, computerized typesetting does another important thing: It creates databases. As a by-product of the typesetting operation, the information contained in the printed publication (usually bibliographic citations) became available in machine-readable form at no extra cost to the producer. Database producers realized that there was a potential market for the sale of these databases, which could be mounted for in-house computer searching. A number of information centers started buying the index tapes and using them as sources for *current awareness* and to provide *selective dissemination of information* (SDI) services to their clients. As the numbers of available databases grew, it also became possible to provide access to a whole sequence of years of the same file for comprehensive *retrospective searching*. Eventually this became recognized as a commercially viable operation, and service organizations such as DIALOG and SDC began to buy tapes from a variety of other database producers and, using their own search interfaces, to offer remote searching of them as a product for sale.

Computer Technology

The third area to influence developments and to hasten the move from batch to on-line was developments in the computer field itself. Not only were computers becoming faster and more powerful, but storage costs were going down—an important consideration when dealing with the massive bibliographic files involved in this type of operation. Another vital computer development was the facility for timesharing, which led the way to the commercial possibilities of a mass market. Once multiple searchers were able to use the system at the same time, it became feasible to offer online searching as a viable commercial operation.

Networks

The final piece of the jigsaw that was needed to enable the birth of viable online IR services was the ability to provide remote access in an efficient and economical fashion. This required the development of telecommunications networks designed especially to link two computers (or a computer and a terminal) and to transmit data in digitized form. Early online access to databases was usually through the ordinary telephone network, which was (of course) widely available but not sufficiently reliable for the transmission of digitized data and also too expensive when longer distances were involved. Thus, telecommunication networks, such as TYMNET and TELENET, were developed during the 1970s to cover most of North America; they were linked by satellite to networks like Euronet in other countries to provide worldwide access. Contemporary users enter one of the network nodes via a local telephone call and are routed through the most convenient path to the service of their choice. The United States is particularly well served in this respect, since in most countries local telephone calls are not free and access nodes may be few and far between. Nevertheless, these communications networks have proved to be cheaper and more reliable than telephone lines, and are used today for almost all computer communication that is not hard-wired.

Putting It All Together

The online industry is thus composed of three basic elements:

1. Database producers, who select the documents for input, index them using a controlled vocabulary, and convert the resulting records to machine-readable form. Many of them produce printed indexes as well as machine-readable databases and may also add abstracts to their records. Producers fall into one of three very different groups:
   - Government agencies, such as the National Library of Medicine, producers of the MEDLINE database;
   - professional/academic organizations, such as the American Psychological Association, producers of the PsycINFO database; and

- commercial organizations, such as the Institute for Scientific Information, producers of the SCISEARCH database.

Their differing levels of subject expertise and varying motivations in the production of a database mean that these different agencies operate to their own highly individual standards, and that despite some subject overlap, almost every database has its own vocabulary and specialized record structure.

2. Online vendors (search services), most of whom lease a variety of databases, mount them on their time-sharing computers, and provide an interface and command language with which they can be searched. A few vendors are also database producers, selling only their own products (e.g., H. W. Wilson). The vendor situation has been extremely volatile in recent years, with mergers and takeovers as the norm. The original commercial online systems, SDC and Lockheed, are still in business, though not under the same names, and there is also a plethora of new operators offering a wide range of information services, from popular bulletin boards and access to the Web (e.g., America Online, CompuServe) to highly specialist legal or stock market information (e.g., LEXIS, Dow Jones).

3. Information searchers, who may be the information-seekers themselves but are often professional search specialists in libraries and information agencies. Because the first users of the online search services were technical information centers and specialist scientific libraries, the role of the librarian in these organizations came to include that of professional search intermediary. The specialized contribution of these intermediaries was familiarity with the protocols and search features of a range of online services, and knowledge of the availability and idiosyncrasies of the different databases. Early attempts to encourage users to search for themselves, and the later development of new simplified end-user systems, did not prove very successful, except in specialized subject areas such as medicine. However, the more recent availability of databases for searching on CD-ROM and the Web have been greeted with enthusiasm by users, who now appear keen to do their own searching. Certainly, more people are becoming aware of the advantages of computer online search systems and confident of their ability to use them, though they do seem to expect them to be not only simple to use but also free.

Notes

1. K. L. Nolan, ed. (1998), *Gale Directory of Databases* (Detroit: Gale), xviii.

2. Ibid., xxi.

Additional Reading

Hahn, T. B. (1996), "Pioneers of the Online Age," *Information Processing & Management* 32(1): 33–48.

O'Leary, M. (1997), "Online Comes of Age," *Online* 21(1): 10–20.

Perry, E. M. (1992), "The Historical Development of Computer-assisted Literature Searching and Its Effects on Librarians and Their Clients," *Library Software Review* 11(2): 5.

3 GOING ONLINE

Getting access to an online search system is largely a question of compatibility between one's own machine and the vendor's mainframe. Some attention to the nitty-gritty of telecommunications is essential, so this chapter goes over the various aspects of the topic in considerable detail. Together with a manual for the computer and the vendor's documentation, this chapter should give novice readers a reasonable understanding of what is going on.

> *Several years ago, this chapter was really necessary, but the world has changed dramatically since then. You'll probably just use telnet (to dialog.com or another address) to access systems today, and the computer/software/modem-buying deal is also much simpler. We keep this chapter partly for a sense of history, and partly for those of you who still have to struggle with Neanderthal technology for a while. – JWJ*

The most basic requirement for online searching is to be able to communicate with the host system where the files of information are stored. This involves the use of a terminal, usually a microcomputer, connected via a modem, a telephone line, and a packet-switched telecommunication network to the large timesharing computer on which the databases available for searching are stored.

Getting Connected

One of the most important decisions to be made regarding accessing online information is your choice of ISP (Internet Service Provider). As online use increases, additional networks are being connected, and more people are getting hooked up. As the number of access providers increases and as telecommunications technology and infrastructures change, there will be additional options. At present there are four basic types of ISP:

- online gateway systems (e.g., America Online);
- national services (e.g., TYMNET, Sprintnet);
- regional services (usually Baby Bells); and
- small mom-and-pop modem shops.

The role of the ISP is to manage the connection between users and the Wide Area Network (WAN) that accesses the actual database system. Although the networks take care of the long-distance communications, they rely on the local telephone system to provide the initial link between the searcher and the ISP. The user's choice of ISP depends on the individual's own expertise and how the access is intended to be used. The largest ISPs have more customers, just as large telephone companies do, which means that they have more modems that customers can dial into, which means fewer busy signals. They also offer lots of points of presence (POPs) that allow users to dial into the network from remote phones without incurring long-distance telephone charges, and they may also offer other value-added services. Small ISPs, on the other hand, are generally easier to work with, but they may not have the reliability and 24-hour service of the bigger companies.

The ability to run certain programs depends on the physical connection and available hardware and software. One can use the systems either over phone lines on a terminal or via an Ethernet LAN (Local Area Network). Some kind of computer is obviously required, but a user can connect using quite a range of equipment, from the dumbest of terminals to a UNIX workstation. However, even with the fastest line and most powerful computer, system availability will depend on the appropriate software being loaded on the ISP machine and the connection to the network.

The total picture looks something like the setup displayed in figure 3.1.

Fig. 3.1. The online connection.

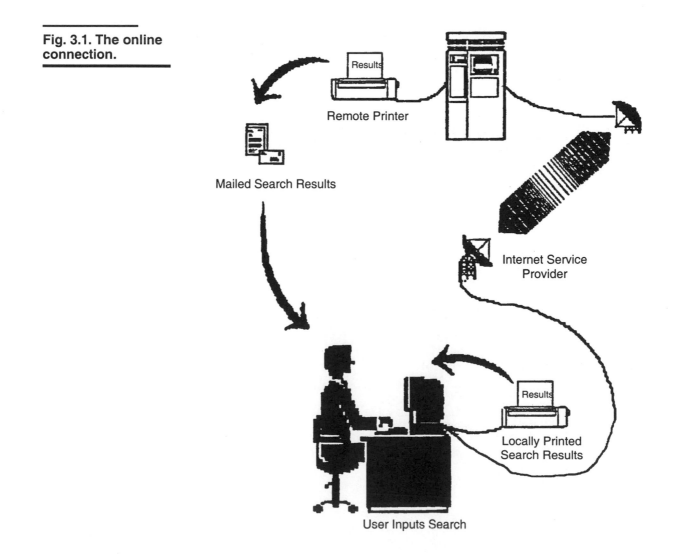

Remote Printer

Mailed Search Results

Internet Service Provider

Locally Printed Search Results

User Inputs Search

To enable your microcomputer to link into this system, four basic items are necessary:

- a plug-in communications card;

- a modem;

- access to a telecommunications network; and

- a communications software package.

Let's look at how these components fit together to get a connection and the role that each of them plays in getting connected.

Communications Card

We all know that computers communicate in terms of *binary digits*, or bits. These bits are grouped together to form *bytes*, just as the letters of the alphabet are grouped to form words. Unfortunately, microcomputers think of these grouped bits as "words," though to humans they are merely single characters, which can lead to some terminological confusion. These computer words usually consist of eight bits, and because they are passed along together, each word requires eight wires. This works fine within one's own machine, but remote access to another machine requires the use of telephone lines that do not have sufficient wires, so that the bits have to travel one at a time instead of in parallel along them. It is thus necessary to change things so that a computer will talk in single bits.

This is the job of the communications card, which is a printed circuit board slotted into one of the serial ports on a computer. (Incidentally, these serial ports can also be used to connect other peripherals, such as a mouse or a printer.) It is responsible for converting the computer's internal parallel communications into a serial output for transmission over telephone lines. For this reason it is sometimes called a serial card. The port at the rear of the card is called an RS 232 interface and is one of the few standardized components in the microcomputer world. It enables the user to connect almost any brand of modem to a computer.

Modems

If computers and telephones spoke the same "language," one would not need a modem. Unfortunately, they do not. Virtually everything in a computer happens electronically, using digital signals to indicate either an on or off condition. This is referred to as binary format, where there are only two options, either a one or a zero, with no in-between. It is rather like Morse code, where everything has to be encoded as either a dot or a dash. If you could hear digital information, it would sound like a series of clicks and clacks, and we might imagine it looking something like figure 3.2.

Fig. 3.2. Digital pattern.

Most telephones, on the other hand, are still analog devices, meaning they use sound waves to function. Sound can rise or fall to cover all levels, rather like an air raid siren in old movies. It might look something like figure 3.3, where we can see a gradual transition from top to bottom. Analog information is not discrete like digital information.

Fig. 3.3. Analog pattern.

As seems evident, digital and analog devices are essentially incompatible. A modem is necessary to translate from one pattern to another—digital signals to analog tones and vice versa—during an online session. The word *modem* is an abbreviation for *modulator/ demodulator*. During any telecommunications session the modem performs two essential operations:

1. When transmitting information, it converts or modulates the digital signals from the PC into sound signals compatible with today's analog telephone systems.

2. When receiving information, it converts or demodulates the analog signals coming over the phone line back into the digital format required by the PC.

There are two types of modems: internal and external. As a rule, installing an internal modem is like adding any other expansion board to a system. It must be inserted directly into an unoccupied expansion slot in the back of a machine. External modems, on the other hand, require an RS 232 cable so they can be connected to the outside of a serial port on the back of a machine. In either case, once the modem is in place, a standard telephone cord connects it to a phone jack or wall plug. In certain locations one may want to add a telephone line surge protector to the modem setup to protect the hardware from damage by voltage spikes on the phone lines.

Most modems today are internal and are directly connected from the computer to a modular telephone jack. The major option with regard to modems is their transmission speed, which is measured in "baud." The number of bits that are transmitted over the communication line each second is the *baud rate*, which is strictly bits per second divided by 10. It currently varies from a slow 9,600 bps up to 56K bps, depending on the choice of modem and communication channel. Speeds have been increasing over the years, and even higher speeds are now becoming available in certain geographic areas using cable modems, which are offered by some ISPs in conjunction with their local television company. A cable modem is the equivalent of T1 access (24 channels of 56K bps), and the main advantage is (of course) speed—up to one million characters per second (10M bps), equal to about 35 times the speed of a 28.8K bps modem, though speeds vary somewhat depending on the equipment used by the cable television company. Compression is one means becoming available for sending 28.8K or 56K bps through 19.2 lines intended for home use.[1] Cable modem connections require an Ethernet card and an external cable modem about twice the size of a standard external telephone modem.

The major problem at present is a limit on the number of households that can access the Internet through a single cable. Because standard cable lines were originally designed for one-way (television) transmission, only a small percentage of U.S. households have access to cable systems capable of handling two-way, high-speed data transmission. The availability of cable modems is of particular interest to libraries and businesses, because they can handle LANs and thus spread the initial costs of expensive T1 lines. Satellite systems are also another way of providing one-way Internet access.

It might appear self-evident that faster access would necessarily be better, but it is difficult to read text that is scrolling up the screen at even 1200 baud, and no one can type fast enough to take advantage of the higher speeds for input. However, if one intends to capture and download large files of data, the faster speeds are more economical. The speed of the host computer is also a consideration because it sets the highest speed at which one can receive data, which is often slower than the speed at which one can send.

Two other concerns regarding terminal compatibility with the system are parity and duplex. *Parity*, used for checking whether data has been corrupted in transit, operates by the computer adding an additional bit (the parity bit) to each character at the time it is being input. (See below for more details on parity.) The system and the terminal need to be operating on the same parity—either even or odd, and the computer will automatically check every character as it is received. *Duplex* refers to the mode of transmission of data down the line. Half duplex is very similar to how people communicate on walkie-talkies or ham radios—one person at a time, and communication switches back and forth. Using full duplex, however, both terminals can send and receive simultaneously, so information transfer is faster and more efficient. Both parity and duplex are settings that one may need to program into the configuration of the communications software (see fig. 3.5 on p. 37).

Telecommunications

The database system that we want to access may be anywhere in the United States or even somewhere in Europe. DIALOG's computers are in California; MEDLINE's are outside Washington, DC; and the European Space Agency's files are at Frascati, outside Rome in Italy. Other databases are scattered all over the world. If we had to pay regular long-distance telephone charges every time we wished to access them, online searching would be very expensive indeed! Fortunately, as we have seen, in most locations one can gain access to online systems through a local telephone call to a node of the network. The technology that makes this possible is provided through *packet-switched networks*, which divide the data traffic into discrete "packets" before routing them. Each packet contains a set number of computer bits, and when the data are too small to fill a complete packet, they are combined with fillers. Each packet is stamped with an electronic address telling the system its destination and is then sent along the most efficient route currently available on the network. Luckily, this complex process is transparent to the user, who needs to know only the telephone number of the ISP that provides the gateway into the network. Once the connection to the host system has been made, the network can, thankfully, be ignored.

The major telecommunication networks have nodes in most large metropolitan centers, so that it is usually possible to link into them via a local (i.e., free) telephone call. Because they are designed especially for the transfer of data, as opposed to voice traffic, they are faster and less prone to interference than the telephone network. The complete connection is represented by figure 3.4, page 36.

Fig. 3.4. The telecommunications link.

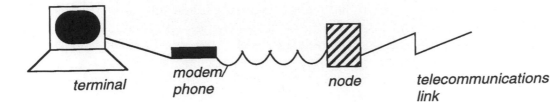

The two largest networks in North America are Sprintnet and TYMNET, though some search services also have their own personal telecommunications networks. Prices vary only slightly among networks, and costs are usually incorporated into system costs, so that one is not billed directly for telecommunications. Europe also has a number of different networks, such as SCANNET and BLAISE, which are linked into Euronet-Diane. Communications between the two continents takes place via satellite links between two of the networks. It is thus possible to use an online search service from almost any place in the world that has a reliable telephone service. This is an important factor for some countries because most database systems are in either the United States or Western Europe.

Each network has slightly different sign-on procedures, or *protocols*, but this is not a major problem because they are explained in the system instruction manuals of subscribers. Subscribers will also probably receive a complete listing of TYMNET and Sprintnet telephone numbers, which will identify the telephone number of a local node that one must call to connect to the system. One will be connected to a computer (hear that funny whine?), and one needs to give it the correct protocols in order to establish a link to the system of choice. Establishing this connection can be vastly simplified by communications software, so let's look next at how that operates.

Communications Software

Perhaps the most important component of the whole setup is the communications software package, the programs that tell a microcomputer how to send and receive information as though it were a dumb terminal with no memory, no storage, and no "intelligence" at all. The DIALOG communications software, DIALINK, is available for downloading from the Internet and is a very easy-to-use program. Once the software is installed on a machine, the configuration program must be used to make the computer and modem compatible with the online system. This initial customizing of the software is a tedious task but will save endless effort in the long run. The configuration program will walk the user through a series of steps that will tell the system about the user's computer equipment and set the correct parameters (e.g., baud rate, parity) to make the machine compatible with the host computer of the online service. WINsock is additional software needed to translate the internal communications of the PC to the TCP/IP language of the network. Figure 3.5 gives an idea of the type of information that needs to be entered, but of course each software package is slightly different, and some of the gateway systems (see chapter 4) will take care of these details and save a lot of hassle.

Fig. 3.5. Customizing software.

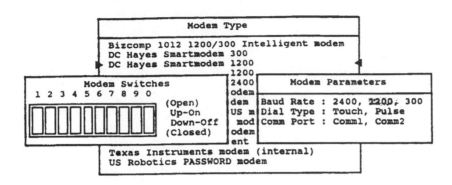

Because noise on the line can cause the receiving computer to misunderstand the message that has been sent, a number of techniques have been developed to help minimize interference with the transmission of data. Probably the most important of these is parity checking. Each character in computer code is made up of eight bits, or binary digits, of which only seven are used to denote the character. The remaining eighth bit is the parity bit. It is used as a kind of check digit, to check that the other seven bits have been correctly transmitted. Parity can be even or odd, and the two systems that want to communicate have to agree on which they are using. It works like this: For each individual character, the "spare" bit is used as a parity bit. At the time when data are sent, the computer totals the value of all the bits and adds a zero or a one to make the total an even or an odd number, depending on the parity in use. At the time of receipt, the receiving computer will check that the total is correct (i.e., odd or even), and if it is not, will issue a message to say that there is noise on the line. In any case, once the parity bit has served its function, the receiving machine discards it. Parity checking is based on the possibility that one of the bits in a character may get transformed, but it is unlikely that two bits in the same character will get changed. Parity checking, a relatively simple checking device, is not foolproof. Notice that if two bits in a character do get changed, the resulting character will have the correct parity and there is no way for the receiving machine to detect the error. That is why one sometimes gets strange characters that one did not type, or the machine does not understand a perfectly correct command.

Normally things like parity and duplex are customized into a communications software package, so that they are performed only once, when the software is installed, and the user does not need to worry about them thereafter. It is usually a case of making sure that everything matches, so that if anything on the system changes (e.g., a faster modem), the configuration program must be revised in order to reconfigure the system.

Choosing a communications software package is particularly important because the user will be living with it for a long time to come. In general, the more expensive the package, the more sophisticated its capabilities. Three important capabilities to look for in a communications package are:

- automatic logon and autodial;

- upload and download capability; and

- ability to access a range of different systems.

The ability to type in complete searches before going online (uploading them) and to download results for post-processing is particularly important, because it saves online time and thus reduces costs. When this feature is available, downloaded data is saved to a buffer (an area of temporary storage space) and can be transferred in offline mode to memory, to a printer, or to disk for export to a word-processing package. Using a word processor in this way makes it possible to customize search results to produce a professional-looking, value-added end product.

The ease of customizing system parameters and protocols depends on the ability of the communications software to allow different settings to be predefined so as to simplify access to a variety of search services. It is then possible to select a system from an initial menu and have the computer automatically adjust to the appropriate configuration without the need for further searcher input.

> *A personal note: Setting up modems and communications software can be a real pain in the neck. These protocols (baud rate, parity, duplex, stop bits) have to exactly match what your network or vendor requires, or it's not going to work. Things have gotten a bit easier over the years as more and more people are connecting, but it still can be a nuisance. (Furthermore, the whole telecommunications business is changing very rapidly with the increasing use of wide area networks). On one level, it really doesn't matter what these settings are, so long as they match. Find out what they are, configure your software and modem accordingly, and hope for the best. The nice part is that in most cases, once you get these set, you'll never have to worry about them again. Also, software is now available that detects many of these settings for you (e.g., plug-and-play in Windows), so the whole process is becoming less and less painful. – JWJ*

Search Databases

The files available for searching are stored at the database system on direct-access storage devices that permit almost instantaneous response. The range of subject information available is one of the great advantages of online searching, as no library can afford to purchase all the texts or printed indexes that are currently being published. For the historical reasons discussed earlier, most of the earliest databases to become available were in the scientific and technical fields. Biological, physical, chemical, and medical sciences were all well represented from the early days, as were engineering and agriculture. Also, a number of multidisciplinary scientific subjects, such as energy and the environment, were added fairly early. Most of these files provide retrospective coverage back to the late 1960s or early 1970s, usually depending on when their producers started computer typesetting because retrospective conversion is not regarded as an economic option. The next group of files to become available online were those covering business and the social sciences—education, law, psychology, and economics—most going back to the early to mid-1970s. Last to be converted were the humanities files, many of which cover a much briefer time span, which is particularly unfortunate in view of the historical nature of many of the humanities disciplines. Large numbers of more popular information resources, such as newspapers and magazines, have more recently become available for online searching, and new full-text files are being mounted almost every month.

In fact, nearly all index and abstract publications are now being produced by computer typesetting, so that many available online databases mirror their hard-copy reference counterparts, and many are also available on compact disc (CD-ROM) or can be leased for in-house mounting. Libraries are increasingly faced with acquisition choices between different versions of the same databases, with decisions being based on their levels of usage of the different files and the types of searches they most commonly perform. Many of the more popular databases are available from more than one vendor, often in slightly different forms and at different prices, so that it pays to do some comparison shopping and to analyze library use patterns over the years, though one also needs to be aware of how rapidly these are changing.

What Will Happen in the Future?

If online has so many advantages, why then are the printed indexing services still in business? Surely searching them must be much slower? It is, but while several writers have forecast the demise of all printed materials,[2] most libraries still regard electronic (online and CD-ROM) resources as useful adjuncts to their traditional print resources. Why? Possibly because libraries are very traditional places, and change comes slowly. Maybe because users and some librarians have been slow to realize the potential and variety of online resources.

It is beginning to look as if the availability of databases on CD-ROM and the Web is bringing about big changes in the perceptions of users with regard to information sources and access choices. Initially, the introduction of databases on CD-ROM led to a big fall in the number of online searches being performed in most libraries, but this may well be a short-term effect. Most recently, the Internet has had a profound effect on IR patterns in almost all libraries. People may start to ask about subjects that are not available on CD-ROM. Will they then want an online search? Will they want to do it themselves? How will they feel about paying for it? People are not used to the idea of paying for information. Should they have to pay for it? (See more on this in chapters 13 and 14.)

What about costs for online searching? Is it cheaper than a manual search? It is difficult to price a manual search in a realistic fashion, but it is clear that online searches save a lot of time because a single search covers the entire retrospective file. Is it cheaper than it was at first? Originally, it was feared that many libraries would cancel subscriptions to printed index publications as a result of having online access, and that search costs would increase to compensate for lost print revenues. In general, that has not happened, and over the years online costs have risen less quickly than prices in general. Some database publishers are offering cheaper online rates to organizations that purchase their printed products. What will happen if CD-ROMs and the Internet cause a serious decline in the income of the traditional online services? At present, many of these services appear to be migrating to the Web. We can only hazard some guesses about the future. Will print, leased databases, online access, and in-house compact discs continue to share the market, or will some entirely new format arrive to take over? Information is a very volatile product, and the products and the players continue to change almost weekly.

Notes

1. Cindy Chick (1997), "Cable Modems: The Future Is Now!—In the Right Neighborhood," *Searcher* 5(9): 22–26.

2. For example, F. W. Lancaster in *Towards Paperless Information Systems* (New York: Academic Press), as far back as 1978.

Additional Reading

Crawford, Walt (1996), "Choosing Your 'Personal Best' Software and Hardware," *Online* 20(3): 78–82.

Mahon, B. (1991), "Telecommunications Networking in Online Retrieval," *Online Review* 15(3/4): 129–46.

Notess, Greg R. (1994), "Understanding Your Access Options," *Online* 18(9): 41–47.

4 ONLINE INFORMATION

We have looked at the problems involved in retrieving information and seen how computers have been used to store information in databases and to speed the search process. We have learned the basics of getting connected to a computer search service via a telecommunications network, and we are now ready to begin some actual searching. This chapter reviews the major resources that are available for searching and discusses the pros and cons of different methods of accessing the information. We will also attempt to evaluate the search features and the information available from the different sources.

The world of published information has expanded rapidly in recent years, and much of that information is now becoming available in digital form. The advent of networked CD-ROMs in 1988, which allowed multiple workstations to access a single disc, made CD-ROM a viable alternative to online searching for many large university and public libraries. The more recent development of the Internet has opened up an additional range of information-providing options. Many vendors have recognized the wisdom of offering their services in a range of information formats. For example, the CD-ROM producer Ovid entered the online world with the purchase of Bibliographic Retrieval Services (BRS) in 1994, and many of the online services, such as DIALOG and MEDLINE, are now also available on the Internet. In fact, most online vendors now appear to believe that their biggest growth will come from Web versions of their systems.

New digital forms are also to be found on the Internet, which have never been and will never be "traditional" in the library sense. These digital forms are aimed at untrained users and are regarded as being "good enough" for the information needs of most people. They use unsophisticated search protocols, which produce widely varying search results based on dynamic collection-building methods with little, if any, human mediation. They provide keyword access to unit records (and advertising) but have none of the advantages of the traditional indexing associated with searching traditional systems.

Effective database searching consists of two very different skills—the conceptual skills in search strategy development, and the technical details particular to a single search system. The conceptual skills in query analysis and search strategy development are basic to searching in any electronic format and are what most of this book is about. The technical details vary from system to system, and many novice searchers are mortified to discover that what they learned on one CD-ROM database does not necessarily apply to others. This chapter attempts to categorize systems into some broad types and uses examples to provide a flavor of the variety of options available to the searcher.

There are two basic approaches to online information: directly using either a command language or a menu-driven search engine, and via a gateway that will always be menu-driven. All the earliest systems were command-driven and intended for use by trained personnel. They required considerable training in order to learn the system commands and search features. Thanks to the spread of microcomputers and the exponential growth of the Internet in recent years, the simplified menu-driven systems tend to be favored, and many of the older command-driven systems are also offering a menu-driven mode for untrained searchers.

> *Professional searchers are heard to suggest that the systems are being "dumbed down" so as to make them more accessible for novice users. As you might imagine, this simplification can have undesirable side effects because the computer takes command of the search and the searcher has less control. It also often means that the full range of system features may not be available. – GW*

Digital Libraries

Probably most people first become acquainted with online information through an online public access catalog (OPAC) at their local public or college library. Quite a variety of OPACs exist, and differences relate mainly to the interface presented to the user. Most of the older DOS-based catalogs are somewhat unattractive (see fig. 4.1).

Fig. 4.1. Main menu of a DOS-based catalog (GEAC).

WELCOME to the University at Albany Online Catalog

(What's New?)

Use arrow keys or spacebar to select an item, then press ENTER

Title	Title keyword(s)
Author	Author keyword(s)
Subject heading	Subject keyword(s)
Series	Series keyword(s)
All of the above	Notes keyword(s)
	Keywords in all fields

Number searching
Search Reserve Materials
Library Services (Interlib. Loan, Patron, Classes)
Research Databases
Tutorials
START OVER
--->
    Press ENTER to see news, up/down arrow to choose search type.
    Enter OP to change OPAC search parameters. Enter E to exit.

The spread of Windows software and access to the WWW has provided an opportunity to present standard cataloging information in a much more attractive format with point-and-click available for scanning (see fig. 4.2).

Most large libraries are now offering not merely their own catalog online but a whole range of other library catalogs, area union catalogs, and access to the OCLC database of holdings (WorldCat). Many libraries are also mounting other databases in-house to be accessed through their catalog interface. These developments have provided access to vast collections of bibliographic references from the monograph holdings of practically all major libraries and have escalated interlibrary loan requests to previously unknown heights. Many libraries are now moving towards Web-based versions of their catalogs, and the trend is towards providing an increasingly attractive and easy-to-use interface.

Fig. 4.2. Main menu of a Windows-based catalog (innovative interfaces).

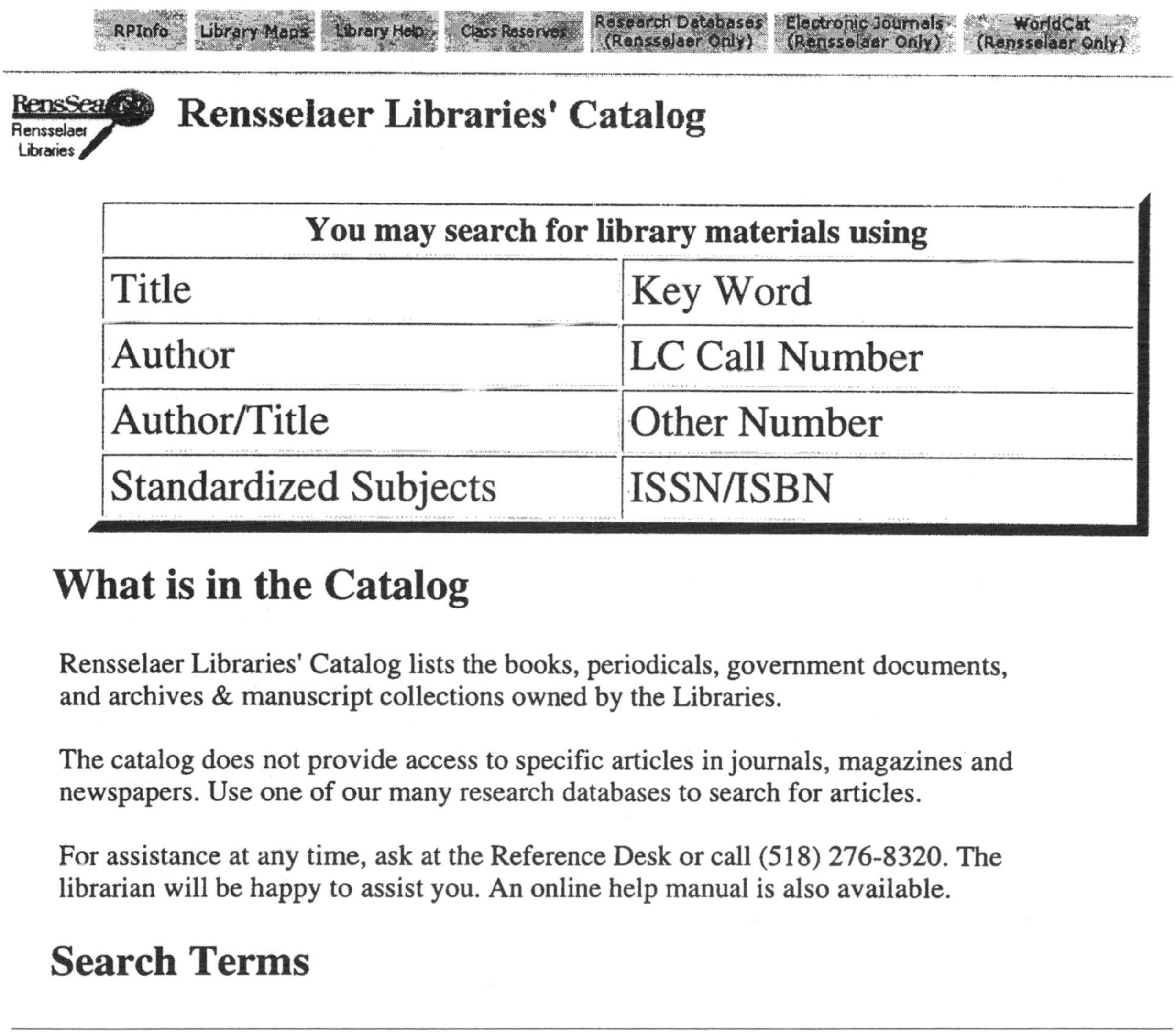

| RPInfo | Library Maps | Library Help | Class Reserves | Research Databases (Rensselaer Only) | Electronic Journals (Rensselaer Only) | WorldCat (Rensselaer Only) |

Rensselaer Libraries' Catalog

You may search for library materials using	
Title	Key Word
Author	LC Call Number
Author/Title	Other Number
Standardized Subjects	ISSN/ISBN

What is in the Catalog

Rensselaer Libraries' Catalog lists the books, periodicals, government documents, and archives & manuscript collections owned by the Libraries.

The catalog does not provide access to specific articles in journals, magazines and newspapers. Use one of our many research databases to search for articles.

For assistance at any time, ask at the Reference Desk or call (518) 276-8320. The librarian will be happy to assist you. An online help manual is also available.

Search Terms

In the same way that library catalogs provide access to books, the availability of databases on CD-ROM has provided access to vast collections of journal literature, some of it in the form of bibliographic references and some of it in full-text. These products are available from a range of producers, and once again, it is the interface that varies. Sometimes the same database will be available from several vendors (and even from the Web) with a vendor's proprietary search software. The data will be the same, but the interface and search engine will differ. Despite these variations, the techniques and strategies we will learn for searching on DIALOG will stand us in good stead with these other products too. But let us look first at different ways of accessing these vast information resources.

Gateways for the General User

Gateways are aimed at the general market of novice online users. They offer their own customized menu-driven interface to provide access to a range of online services from a wide variety of producers. They are a kind of middleman between the searcher and the system itself, buying wholesale access for themselves and then selling it with their own software with the intention of simplifying access, database selection, and search strategy construction. Gateways are rather like asking help from a reference librarian in a library, rather than conducting one's own search for information, except that a computer is acting as the reference assistant instead of a trained professional. The machine may make decisions regarding the best resource to use for the search, how to structure the search request, and which are the most relevant results. This is more than most professionals would be willing to delegate.

Online systems are a particularly volatile sector of the information marketplace, with consolidation, buyouts and takeovers the norm, so that many companies may come and go. Probably the best-known and most entrenched gateway is America Online (AOL), with more than 12 million subscribers as of summer 1998. As the earliest stand-alone service, AOL has had to painstakingly develop an arcade of features over the years and now offers the full gamut of online options: discussion groups, newswires, bulletin boards, live chat rooms, online shopping, full access to the Internet via browsers such as the Netscape Explorer Web browser, and bibliographic databases of magazines and newspaper articles. AOL distributes its access software through direct mail, shrink-wrapped with magazine issues, and prepackaged with other software programs. They offer many hours of free time to be used within 30 days after one signs up as an incentive to try the service. The bulk of AOL revenues still comes from monthly subscriber fees ($21.95 for unlimited access), but the company's goal is to steadily increase the percentage of money it earns from advertising and transaction fees (which is what the Web browsers rely on).

AOL can be accessed via AOLnet (in selected cities), Sprintnet, TYMNET, the Internet using TCP/IP, or even a toll-free telephone line (800-716-0023). The logon sequence is done through AOL's proprietary software, so that it is not necessary to know anything about modem or terminal settings, network addresses, or even sign-on commands. The software requires an IBM-compatible or Mac 386 processor or better, 4 MB of RAM, and Windows 3.1 or higher. Modem speeds vary according to the network used but need to be at least 2400 bps.

When one first logs on to AOL one reaches the main menu, which offers icons for 19 topic groupings, though the same file may appear under more than one heading (see Fig. 4.3).

Fig. 4.3. AOL main menu.

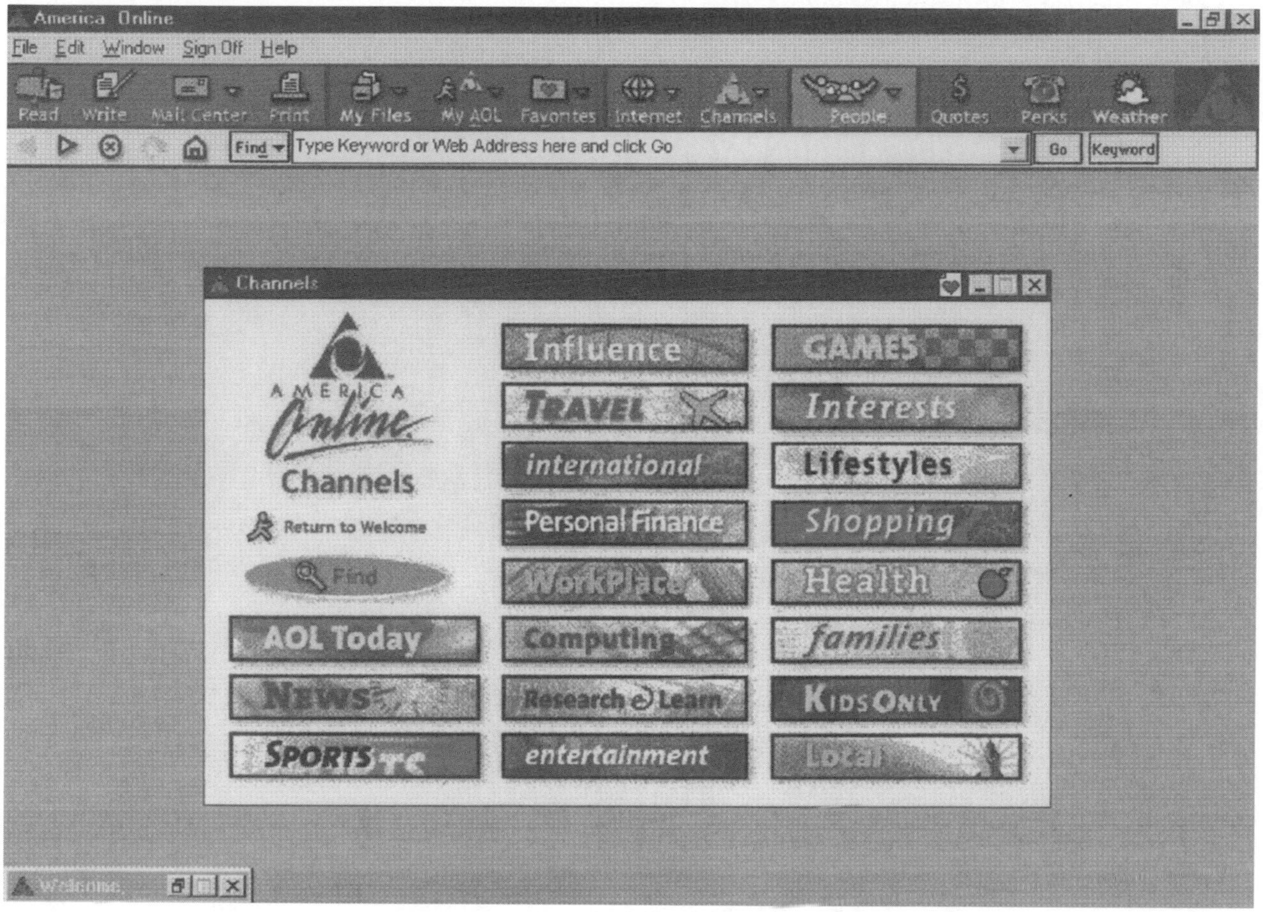

Most of these groupings are relatively self-explanatory. For example, Today's News offers continuously updated major newswires; Reference Desk provides links to bibliographic databases of journal articles; Personal Finance gives current stock quotes and access to discount brokerages; Travel offers airline reservations and travel guides; Marketplace is online shopping; and People Connection connects to online chat rooms. Figure 4.4, page 46, offers an example of the main menu from one of these groups.

Unfortunately, each group must be searched separately, so it pays to invest some time in finding the most useful resources and bookmarking them to the Personal Choices icon as a method for speeding future reference. (It is also possible to bookmark Internet URLs through AOL using the Favorite Places icon.)

As an alternative to finding information resources through these groups, the Directory of Services offers additional access points that are separate from the keyword access provided via Go To on the pull-down menu. The Directory offers access through descriptive words across all AOL's main groups, though the indexing is not very reliable. AOL documentation is limited to basic technical information. It offers no help on the selection of databases, the design of a search strategy, or how search results are sorted. As with most general online services, AOL offers inadequate documentation and no training courses, though technical support is available 24 hours daily via telephone, E-mail, fax, and a live chat area. Context-sensitive online help is also available for almost every screen, and the User Services icon provides extensive help files with collections of the most frequently asked questions and their answers.

Fig. 4.4. Reference Desk main menu.

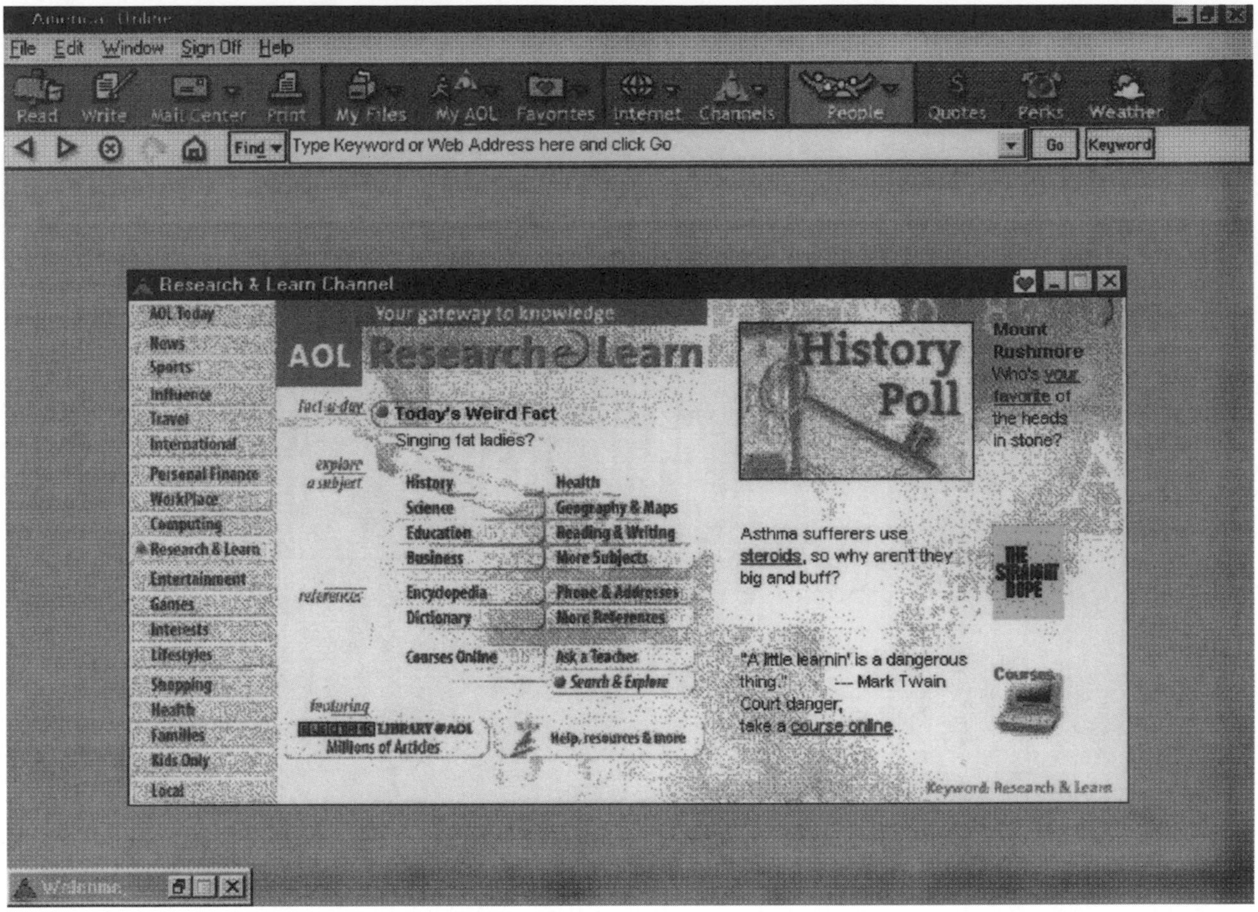

It is probably fair to say that AOL is not a primary resource for bibliographic research. On the other hand, it is a useful source for stock quotes, newswire stories, and a wide range of resources for the casual searcher, particularly for up-to-date information. Unfortunately, the speed of update is frequently offset by busy lines and slow access, especially for graphical materials.

Similar gateway services include CompuServe, Prodigy and the newer Microsoft Network (MSN). They all offer similar types of information, though MSN offers better tools (linked to the operating system) and more advanced technology. MSN is especially attractive for commercial organizations, offering the ability to structure a customized business plan. Microsoft is focusing its information content on "beachhead" areas where it sees potential for high growth. However, these and other established gateways are likely to face competition from some of the other giants of the computer world, such as IBM and AT&T, who are staking out positions in this area.

The value of general online services such as these is a function of both the information content available (remember, all of them offer similar information groupings) and the depth of helpful experts participating in the service's discussion forums and chat areas. As the "old man" of gateways, AOL has an obvious edge.

Information on the Internet

The Internet has been described variously as a network of networks, the Information Superhighway, a sea to be navigated, or just plain information chaos. It has also been suggested that it is the electronic equivalent of the Library of Congress with all the books thrown on the floor. In many ways it is similar to the gateway services discussed previously, in that it is an intermediary, providing access to a wide variety of services: electronic mail, file transfer, numerous information sources, interest group membership, interactive conversation (chat), multimedia displays, and more. The difference lies in the fact that anyone (with an account) can put information (true or false, high quality or inane, pleasant or objectionable) onto the Internet. It is a self-publishing medium. Thus it is not like a library in which all the available items are identified and can be retrieved by a single catalog. In fact, nobody knows how many individual files reside on the Internet, though the number runs in the millions and is growing daily. Each Internet site is created and organized in a different way. Some sites demonstrate an expert's knowledge, while others are amateur efforts.

The Internet consists of a variety of protocols, including E-mail, FTP (File Transfer Protocol), Gopher, HTTP (Hypertext Transfer Protocol), Telnet, Usenet News, and WAIS (Wide Area Information Systems). Many of these protocols feature programs that allow users to search for and retrieve materials made available by the protocol. One of the most efficient (and popular) ways of conducting research on the Internet is to use the World Wide Web because it provides a single interface for accessing all of these protocols and can work with multimedia.

The WWW was developed in 1989 by Tim Berners-Lee of the European Particle Physics Lab (CERN) in Switzerland. The initial purpose was to use networked hypertext to facilitate communication among its members, who were located in several countries. The WWW soon spread beyond CERN and was further developed so as to incorporate graphics, video, and sound. It is now the fastest-growing component of the Internet, and the two are often regarded as synonymous.

The operation of the Web relies primarily on *hypertext* as its means of information retrieval. Hypertext is a document containing words or pictures that connect to other documents via *links* that can be selected by the user. Links may or may not follow a logical path because each connection is programmed by the creator of the source document. Thus, the WWW consists of a virtual web of connections among a vast number of texts, images, video, and sounds. Each file (known as a *page*) is identified by a unique address known as its URL (Uniform Resource Locator).

The URL has a standard format, consisting of:

```
protocol://host/path/filename
```

For example:

```
http://www.albany.edu/library/index.html
```

Web software programs use the URL to retrieve the file from the host computer and display it on the user's computer monitor. It may be accessed directly, if the user knows the URL, or via a link from another page. (In fact, the links are how most people use the Web.)

In order to access the Web, one must use a software program called a Web browser. For graphical access, a browser such as Netscape Navigator or Internet Explorer needs to be installed on one's own machine. The example URL is a good starting point. Just type it in and then try some of the links it offers. The links are usually colored differently from the body text. Just click on one with the mouse, and the linked page will appear on your screen. On Netscape there are also preinstalled links accessible via the narrow buttons across the top of the screen (What's New, What's Cool, etc.). These are programmed to go to documents written by the employees of Netscape. Interesting pages can be marked for future use by using the Bookmark option on the top menu bar.

There are two basic approaches to searching on the Internet—*subject directories* and *search engines.*

Subject Directories

A subject directory is a database of Internet sites submitted by site creators or evaluators and organized into subject categories, though the directory does not always discriminate in its choice of sites to be included. In fact, some directories do not discriminate at all. An increasing number of companies, organizations, libraries, and even volunteers are creating subject-based directories to catalog portions of the Internet. These directories are organized by subject and consist of links to Internet resources relating to each subject. The major subject directories available on the Internet tend to include overlapping but different databases. Most directories provide a search capability that allows keyword searching of a group of files. Yahoo!, for example, indexes thousands of links to a wide variety of sources and is ideal for browsing with its broad subject coverage. It runs a search against a variety of search engines, but the search itself has to be very basic. Magellan, on the other hand, is a more selective database that accepts only reviewed sites. It allows complex Boolean searching and is ideal for in-depth coverage. The Argus Clearing House is one of the highest quality subject directories on the Internet, consisting of collections of recommended sites organized into subject-specific guides. The authors of these recommended sites are often subject specialists, so these collections are particularly good for academic research. The WWW Virtual Library at CERN is another recommended subject directory, with many of its collections maintained at universities throughout the world.

Search Engines

An Internet search engine usually allows for more complicated searching using keywords and Boolean operators. The user enters a search request into a box and asks for the search to proceed. Most Web search engines build their databases with programs called crawlers, robots, spiders, or worms. These programs roam the Internet and gather resources for their databases based on keyword matching. Indexing is created indiscriminately from the collected site (e.g., title, first heading, first "x" number of words, size, URL). Because crawlers have no discrimination, much of what they collect may be outdated, inaccurate, or incomplete. It is not uncommon for links to have vanished, so it is particularly important to evaluate search results carefully.

Each search engine has its own conventions regarding logical combinations, phrases, and truncation. Sometimes the logic or truncation is implicit, so one needs to do some homework on relevant conventions before starting a search. Probably the best-known search engine is AltaVista, a large database that allows complex Boolean searching with nested parentheses, use of phrases, and selected truncation. Lycos selects sites based on their frequency of linking from other sites (i.e., that are frequently selected by other searchers). It reduces search terms to the word root level (stemming), which can result in false drops, and only allows a single Boolean operator in its Advanced Search option.

It is unnerving (to say the least) to have a search return thousands of postings. This is because the system selects records containing each individual search term and pair of terms, as well as the complete request. (It is not a good idea to enter a single search term on Internet because the files are so large.) However, the search results are returned in ranked order (i.e., most relevant first). These relevance rankings are based on unknown algorithms, believed to be based on factors such as frequency of occurrence of the term(s) in the document, their frequency in the database as a whole, and their position in the document. Given that many of these databases are collected haphazardly and that the results are ranked somewhat arbitrarily, it is no surprise that the final output may be bizarre. Be aware that the system's idea of "most relevant" may not be the same as yours. Scan the results for several pages in order to determine whether anything useful was retrieved.

Since the Internet is now widely available in many public and most academic libraries, untrained users are now doing independent searching on the Web. They are happy doing what we would consider to be really bad searches, probably in the wrong places, and believing the results that they get. (The computer must be right!) It is clear that libraries will need to institute extensive training programs, though it seems likely that many users will believe they can manage alone. Despite the potential for poor retrieval and waste of time with the Internet, it can also be extremely useful for the professional librarian. For some topics the WWW can be more valuable than "traditional" resources—for up-to-date news and financial information, for personal memoirs, for access to other library catalogs, for many quick-reference queries, and for nontraditional information that may not be available from the standard library reference collection. This is a new tool that librarians need to master, not only as a reference source but also in order to instruct users in how to use it effectively and efficiently.

Professional Online Services

The professional online services are the "traditional" online services. They have been available since the early 1970s and have been the territory of the trained professional searchers. They are command-driven systems that have the full range of "bells and whistles," and thus searchers require a considerable investment of time and effort to become proficient with them. They were generally only available through library search services manned by trained searchers, known as *intermediaries*. Originally searching was delegated to these librarians, and in general users showed little inclination to perform their own searches. As we shall see, the advent of CD-ROM and Internet has changed that situation.

Menu-Driven Systems

For many years the only market for these online search systems was the library market, but the spread of microcomputers in the early 1980s led vendors to believe there were opportunities for expansion. Many of the original vendors produced "end-user" systems targeted at the general population of microcomputer owners. The systems clearly needed to be simpler in order to attract novice searchers, so most new products offered the same data accessed via a menu-driven interface. In effect they were the same systems with a new face. Both DIALOG and BRS produced end-user versions of their systems and started to market them. Unfortunately, their reception was less enthusiastic than expected, except in limited subject areas. Eventually the end-user search services focused entirely on the medical, legal, and business subsections of the information market, which are seen as having the need for current information and the means to pay for it. Many of these menu-driven services have now migrated to the Web. Examples of such services are DIALOG Select, a WWW version of Knowledge Index (see fig. 4.5), and the Academic Universe from LEXIS-NEXIS (see fig. 4.6).

Fig. 4.5. DIALOG Select home page.

DIALOG SELECT OVERVIEW

Features & Benefits Web Windows®
Frequently Asked Questions Web
Alerts Web only
Price & Database List Web
Sources Database List
Journal List
Applications Web
Technical Requirements Web Windows®

Welcome to Dialog Select, the information service for people who need easy access to authoritative business, legal, scientific, and technical information. The point-and-click interface guides you to the most objective, respected publications and documents available online.

Virtually any topic is covered in the Dialog Select library of more than 50,000 authoritative publications, including full-text journals, magazines, newsletters, newswires, and newspapers. You'll be assured of accessing a comprehensive collection of documents and publications written by professional journalists, analysts, auditors, and industry experts.

That means you get all the facts, figures, and statements you need for a complete picture, quickly and easily. Dialog Select is ideal for keeping up-to-date on exactly what's happening in your industry...or any industry. It can also help you accelerate your product development cycles and reduce your time to market.

Dialog Select is available on the Web or through a Windows® interface.

CORPORATE HOME   LIBRARY   PRODUCT SELECTION GUIDE   PRODUCTS HOME

©1998. The Dialog Corporation
last updated: 6/9/98

Fig. 4.6. LEXIS-NEXIS home page.

LEXIS®-NEXIS® Academic Universe provides access to a wide range of news, business, legal, and reference information.

Your use of this service is governed by Terms & Conditions. *Please review them.*

- Top News
- General News Topics
- Company News
- Industry & Market News
- Government & Political News
- Legal News
- Company Financial Information
- Country Profiles
- State Profiles

- Biographical Information
- Reference & Directories
- General Medical & Health Topics
- Medical Abstracts
- Accounting, Auditing, & Tax
- Law Reviews
- Federal Case Law
- U.S. Code, Constitution, & Court Rules
- State Legal Research

Command-Driven Systems

But what about the original command-driven systems, the major tools for the serious researcher? These services range from the original major vendors of multiple databases, such as the DIALOG Connection from M.A.I.D plc and LEXIS-NEXIS from Reed Elsevier, to small systems that may have only a single specialized database.

Despite their online charges, these professional services are frequently the lowest-cost option for timely and accurate information, especially for the trained searcher. The service's primary customers are professional information users who understand and appreciate the value of information. The vast quantity of information available, combined with the complex search languages, has meant a steep learning curve for efficient use. These professional information services are characterized by the following:

- Excellent access

- Accurate, high-quality data

- Comprehensive data

- Powerful command language search tools

- User-friendly communications software
- Complete customer support, including
    extensive documentation
    training classes
    telephone support

Command search interfaces are frequently complex in order to provide the most sophisticated search tools. Boolean logic (combining search terms with operators such as AND, OR, and NOT) is the basis of the search language in all the various systems. Each database has its own record format (as seen in chapter 1) and selection of fields and search options. Common important features of the search tools include the following:

- The use of truncation or wild cards. For example, if "*" is the wild card, "cat*" searches for all words whose first three letters are "cat." "Wom*n" finds "women" or "woman."

- The ability to limit searches to a particular field, such as title or lead paragraph.

- An online or print thesaurus that lets one check controlled vocabulary terms used in indexing, and also to find related terms. These thesauri vary greatly from database to database but are very helpful in the construction of accurate and cost-effective searches.

- Proximity operators, which allow the selection of search terms in specified relationships to one another, such as adjacent or in a particular order. These are useful for natural language searching and essential for databases that have no thesaurus.

- The ability to select output formats to customize for a bibliography or for mailing labels.

- Search feedback, so that the searcher can check retrievals for each search term input and modify sets to improve search results.

- Help in choosing an appropriate database and the ability to search multiple files for a single search strategy.

- Inexpensive or free browse formats, such as Title or KWIC (Keyword in Context), to enable the searcher to judge relevance before printing a complete set of documents.

The professional search services have the best access, the highest quality and most comprehensive data, and the best customer support. In the hands of a trained searcher, they are the most cost-effective data sources for the retrieval of serious research information. We believe that it is best to pick one professional service and invest the time and effort necessary to become a skillful searcher. The rest of this book concentrates on one such service (DIALOG Connection) and teaches how to use it effectively.

Additional Reading

Bates, Mary Ellen (1996), *The Online Deskbook: ONLINE Magazine's Essential Desk Reference for Online and Internet Searchers*. Wilton, CT: Pemberton Press.

Berkman, Robert I. (1993), *Find It Online!* New York: Windcrest/McGraw-Hill.

Diaz, Karen R. (1997), *Reference Sources on the Internet: Off the Shelf and onto the Web*. Binghamton, NY: Haworth Press.

Lescher, John F. (1995), *Online Market Research: Cost-Effective Searching of the Internet and Online Databases*. Reading, MA: Addison-Wesley.

Notess, Greg R. (1994), *Internet Access Providers: An International Resources Directory*. Westport, CT: Meckler.

5 DATABASE CONSTRUCTION AND STRUCTURE

When building a database, there are a number of important decisions to be made, and these decisions have profound effects not only on what the database looks like but also on how it can be searched and used. In this chapter we'll discuss two of these decisions: the construction of the inverted file and the use of structure.

First of all, it's not really necessary to use either of these in searching at all. The documents or document surrogates to be included in the search system are usually stored in their full, native form in something called a *linear file*. Suppose one wanted to build an information system to search old E-mail messages. One might choose to simply save them in one big word processing file and not go to the trouble of building an inverted file or adding any structural elements at all. Almost all word processors have simple search facilities, and would allow the user, say, to look for all the occurrences of the word "project" to find E-mail messages from the boss about the current project.

> *Which might not be what you wind up with. Searching on the word "project" will get you documents that include that word, but there are other uses of "project" besides "the thing I'm working on now." It can also be used as a verb "I project this book will sell really well" or "Project the slides on that wall over there." Most word processor search engines also automatically truncate, so you'd get words like "projectile" and "projection" as well. Just some of the difficulties we encounter in searching. – JWJ*

For collections of documents that are small or rarely searched, such a setup is probably not all that impractical. But, if the database has several million documents, searching through each word of each document each time a search is performed makes both the inverted files and structure begin to look very attractive indeed.

Inverted Files

The inverted file is used to make searching easier by providing access to the content-bearing words in all documents without needing to search through the entire texts of the documents themselves. The best way to discuss this is to show it, so let's walk through an example of the construction of an inverted file, using a small "toy" collection of documents.

Step 0. Make some initial decisions.

Before starting the process of creating the inverted file, there are some important decisions to be made up front. For example:

Collection & Coverage. What is the database about? Which documents will be included and which ones won't? Where will the collection come from?

Technological Infrastructure. What kinds of hardware and software (including search engine) will be used in building and searching the database?

Technical Details. What, if any, words will be on the stop list? What about punctuation? Will capitalization be preserved, or not? What fields will be used for records? Will phrases be indexed, or just individual words?

The first two categories are beyond the scope of this chapter, but we'll discuss these technical matters as we go and see the effect the decisions will have. As an example, we'll construct a file in the way that DIALOG does. Although other systems will do things in somewhat different ways, especially Internet-based systems, the same basic steps apply.

Step 1. Make a list including all the words in each field of the record.

Our toy database has three fields: title, abstract (really short abstracts, to be sure), and descriptor. We'll talk more about records and structure later in this chapter, but for now it needs to be said that a *field* is an individual piece of information about a document, and a *record* is a collection of fields about the same document.
Here are our documents, with their document numbers:

```
101
The Origins of Don Giovanni
Discusses the history and sources Mozart used in his opera Don Giovanni.
DE: Mozart, Opera, Historical Analysis

102
Handel: Two Great Operas
Plot summaries, textual analysis of libretti, and musical explication
of two of Handel's operas: Giulio Cesare (1724) and his first Italian
opera, Rodrigo (1707).
DE: Handel, Opera, Musical Analysis

103
English Orchestral Music of the Early 18th Century
A discussion of the major features in English music of the mid-1700s,
focusing on Handel and his "Music for the Royal Fireworks" and his
capacity for realizing the common mood.
DE: Handel, Orchestral Music, English Music, Musical Analysis

104
The Art of the Oratorio
One of the greatest writers of the English oratorio, Handel, is
featured, with extensive focus on Messiah, Alexander's Feast, and
his final work, Jephtha.
DE: Handel, Oratorio, English Music, Musical Analysis
```

In this stage, we also deal with a couple of other technical details. We remove all punctuation, including commas, periods, hyphens, apostrophes, quotation marks, and the like, and replace them with spaces. We also choose to ignore capitalization, so we convert all words to capital letters. This means, for example, that the words

"Alexander's Feast"

in document 104 will become

ALEXANDER S FEAST

with no quotation marks. There are other ways this could be handled; for example, one could decide to preserve capitalization to make it easier to search for capitalized words, or not to insert spaces in place of punctuation marks, to keep words like "Alexander's" together. There is nothing magical or even ideal about these decisions; as we said, they are DIALOG's way of doing things, but later we will see the kinds of effects they have on searching.

Doing all these things gets us a list that looks like this:

```
101              PLOT
THE              SUMMARIES
ORIGINS          TEXTUAL
OF               ANALYSIS
DON              OF
GIOVANNI         LIBRETTI
                 AND
DISCUSSES        MUSICAL
THE              EXPLICATION
HISTORY          OF
AND              TWO
SOURCES          OF
MOZART           HANDEL
USED             S
IN               OPERAS
HIS              GIULIO
OPERA            CESARE
DON              1724
GIOVANNI         AND
                 HIS
MOZART           FIRST
OPERA            ITALIAN
HISTORICAL       OPERA
ANALYSIS         RODRIGO
                 1707
102
HANDEL           HANDEL
TWO              OPERA
GREAT            MUSICAL
OPERAS           ANALYSIS
```

103
ENGLISH
ORCHESTRAL
MUSIC
OF
THE
EARLY
18TH
CENTURY

A
DISCUSSION
OF
THE
MAJOR
FEATURES
IN
ENGLISH
MUSIC
OF
THE
MID
1700S
FOCUSING
ON
HANDEL
AND
HIS
MUSIC
FOR
THE
ROYAL
FIREWORKS
AND
HIS
CAPACITY
FOR
REALIZING
THE
COMMON
MOOD

HANDEL
ORCHESTRAL
MUSIC
ENGLISH
MUSIC
MUSICAL
ANALYSIS

104
THE
ART
OF
THE
ORATORIO

ONE
OF
THE
GREATEST
WRITERS
OF
THE
ENGLISH
ORATORIO
HANDEL
IS
FEATURED
WITH
EXTENSIVE
FOCUS
ON
MESSIAH
ALEXANDER
S
FEAST
AND
HIS
FINAL
WORK
JEPHTHA

HANDEL
ORATORIO
ENGLISH
MUSIC
MUSICAL
ANALYSIS

Step 2. Number all the words, including phrases and excluding stop words.

We now assign a number to each of these words. These numbers will serve as pointers to the documents from which they come; when we search the file for a given word, it will tell us its exact location in the file. So, for example, DISCUSSES will get this code:

101 AB 1

to indicate that it comes from document 101, is in the abstract field, and is the first word in that abstract.

An inverted file is intended to aid in searching, but this aid does not come without some cost. One can already get a sense from looking at the preliminary list above that not only does a great deal of thought go into the creation of an inverted file, but also a considerable amount of computing time and storage. There are ways to make the storage issue a bit easier without sacrificing too much access; one of them is the use of a list of words that are either so common or devoid of search potential that they are excluded at this stage and thus not able to be used in searching. Some systems have quite extensive lists of these *stop words* (sometimes called *noise words*); some have none at all. DIALOG, our exemplar system, uses these nine:

AN AND BY FOR FROM OF THE TO WITH

These words will be excluded from the inverted file, but only *after* the words have been numbered. This will permit more precise searching of multiple-word combinations of words.

The other detail to be dealt with here concerns the phrases in the descriptor field. DIALOG and other systems use a technique here called *phrase indexing*, the inclusion of complete phrases from the descriptor field (and sometimes other fields as well) in the inverted file as well as the individual words themselves. So the descriptor

MUSICAL ANALYSIS

would receive three entries: one for MUSICAL, one for ANALYSIS, and the third for MUSICAL ANALYSIS.

> *We call this multiple indexing double posting. It is particularly useful to be able to search phrases in this fashion, as they are more specific search terms than single words. – GW*

This is possible in fields such as the descriptor because it is clear what the phrases are. In other fields (titles and abstracts) humans are good at telling where phrases begin and end, but it has been very difficult to get computers to figure this out. A number of researchers in natural-language processing and automatic indexing have been working on this problem for many years with some success, but such techniques are nowhere near being ready for commercial systems yet. In the meantime, we do the best we can with only *word indexing* of those fields, and make up for it by being more clever in searching. More about this when we discuss free-text searching technique in Chapter 8.

When these three steps have been completed, our list now looks like this:

ORIGINS	101	TI	2	IN	103	AB	7
DON	101	TI	4	ENGLISH	103	AB	8
GIOVANNI	101	TI	5	MUSIC	103	AB	9
DISCUSSES	101	AB	1	MID	103	AB	12
HISTORY	101	AB	3	1700S	103	AB	13
SOURCES	101	AB	5	FOCUSING	103	AB	14
MOZART	101	AB	6	ON	103	AB	15
USED	101	AB	7	HANDEL	103	AB	16
IN	101	AB	8	HIS	103	AB	18
HIS	101	AB	9	MUSIC	103	AB	19
OPERA	101	AB	10	ROYAL	103	AB	22
DON	101	AB	11	FIREWORKS	103	AB	23
GIOVANNI	101	AB	12	HIS	103	AB	25
MOZART	101	DE	1	CAPACITY	103	AB	26
OPERA	101	DE	2	REALIZING	103	AB	28
HISTORICAL	101	DE	3	COMMON	103	AB	30
ANALYSIS	101	DE	4	MOOD	103	AB	31
HISTORICAL ANALYSIS	101	DE	3,4	HANDEL	103	DE	1
HANDEL	102	TI	1	ORCHESTRAL	103	DE	2
TWO	102	TI	2	MUSIC	103	DE	3
GREAT	102	TI	3	ENGLISH	103	DE	4
OPERAS	102	TI	4	MUSIC	103	DE	5
PLOT	102	AB	1	MUSICAL	103	DE	6
SUMMARIES	102	AB	2	ANALYSIS	103	DE	7
TEXTUAL	102	AB	3	ORCHESTRAL MUSIC	103	DE	2,3
ANALYSIS	102	AB	4	ENGLISH MUSIC	103	DE	4,5
LIBRETTI	102	AB	6	MUSICAL ANALYSIS	103	DE	6,7
MUSICAL	102	AB	8	ART	104	TI	2
EXPLICATION	102	AB	9	ORATORIO	104	TI	5
TWO	102	AB	11	ONE	104	AB	1
HANDEL	102	AB	13	GREATEST	104	AB	4
S	102	AB	14	WRITERS	104	AB	5
OPERAS	102	AB	15	ENGLISH	104	AB	8
GIULIO	102	AB	16	ORATORIO	104	AB	9
CESARE	102	AB	17	HANDEL	104	AB	10
1724	102	AB	18	IS	104	AB	11
HIS	102	AB	20	FEATURED	104	AB	12
FIRST	102	AB	21	EXTENSIVE	104	AB	14
ITALIAN	102	AB	22	FOCUS	104	AB	15
OPERA	102	AB	23	ON	104	AB	16
RODRIGO	102	AB	24	MESSIAH	104	AB	17
1707	102	AB	25	ALEXANDER	104	AB	18
HANDEL	102	DE	1	S	104	AB	19
OPERA	102	DE	2	FEAST	104	AB	20
MUSICAL	102	DE	3	HIS	104	AB	22
ANALYSIS	102	DE	4	FINAL	104	AB	23
MUSICAL ANALYSIS	102	DE	3,4	WORK	104	AB	24
ENGLISH	103	TI	1	JEPHTHA	104	AB	25
ORCHESTRAL	103	TI	2	HANDEL	104	DE	1
MUSIC	103	TI	3	ORATORIO	104	DE	2
EARLY	103	TI	6	ENGLISH	104	DE	3
18TH	103	TI	7	MUSIC	104	DE	4
CENTURY	103	TI	8	MUSICAL	104	DE	5
A	103	AB	1	ANALYSIS	104	DE	6
DISCUSSION	103	AB	2	ENGLISH MUSIC	104	DE	3,4
MAJOR	103	AB	5	MUSICAL ANALYSIS	104	DE	5,6
FEATURES	103	AB	6				

Step 3. Alphabetize the list.

This is really the easiest part, but alphabetization is what makes an inverted file so darn useful. Put these entries in alphabetical order (actually, usually in the order of the ASCII character set used by computers—numbers first, followed by letters), and what results is an inverted file.

1707	102	AB	25	HIS	102	AB	20
1724	102	AB	18	HIS	103	AB	18
1700S	103	AB	13	HIS	103	AB	25
18TH	103	TI	7	HIS	104	AB	22
A	103	AB	1	HISTORICAL	101	DE	3
ALEXANDER	104	AB	18	HISTORICAL ANALYSIS	101	DE	3,4
ANALYSIS	101	DE	4	HISTORY	101	AB	3
ANALYSIS	102	AB	4	IN	101	AB	8
ANALYSIS	102	DE	4	IN	103	AB	7
ANALYSIS	103	DE	7	IS	104	AB	11
ANALYSIS	104	DE	6	ITALIAN	102	AB	22
ART	104	TI	2	JEPHTHA	104	AB	25
CAPACITY	103	AB	26	LIBRETTI	102	AB	6
CENTURY	103	TI	8	MAJOR	103	AB	5
CESARE	102	AB	17	MESSIAH	104	AB	17
COMMON	103	AB	30	MID	103	AB	12
DISCUSSES	101	AB	1	MOOD	103	AB	31
DISCUSSION	103	AB	2	MOZART	101	AB	6
DON	101	TI	4	MOZART	101	DE	1
DON	101	AB	11	MUSIC	103	TI	3
EARLY	103	TI	6	MUSIC	103	AB	9
ENGLISH	103	TI	1	MUSIC	103	AB	19
ENGLISH	103	AB	8	MUSIC	103	DE	3
ENGLISH	103	DE	4	MUSIC	103	DE	5
ENGLISH	104	AB	8	MUSIC	104	DE	4
ENGLISH	104	DE	3	MUSICAL	102	AB	8
ENGLISH MUSIC	103	DE	4,5	MUSICAL	102	DE	3
ENGLISH MUSIC	104	DE	3,4	MUSICAL	103	DE	6
EXPLICATION	102	AB	9	MUSICAL	104	DE	5
EXTENSIVE	104	AB	14	MUSICAL ANALYSIS	102	DE	3,4
FEAST	104	AB	20	MUSICAL ANALYSIS	103	DE	6,7
FEATURED	104	AB	12	MUSICAL ANALYSIS	104	DE	5,6
FEATURES	103	AB	6	ON	103	AB	15
FINAL	104	AB	23	ON	104	AB	16
FIREWORKS	103	AB	23	ONE	104	AB	1
FIRST	102	AB	21	OPERA	101	AB	10
FOCUS	104	AB	15	OPERA	101	DE	2
FOCUSING	103	AB	14	OPERA	102	AB	23
GIOVANNI	101	TI	5	OPERA	102	DE	2
GIOVANNI	101	AB	12	OPERAS	102	TI	4
GIULIO	102	AB	16	OPERAS	102	AB	15
GREAT	102	TI	3	ORATORIO	104	TI	5
GREATEST	104	AB	4	ORATORIO	104	AB	9
HANDEL	102	TI	1	ORATORIO	104	DE	2
HANDEL	102	AB	13	ORCHESTRAL	103	TI	2
HANDEL	102	DE	1	ORCHESTRAL	103	DE	2
HANDEL	103	AB	16	ORCHESTRAL MUSIC	103	DE	2,3
HANDEL	103	DE	1	ORIGINS	101	TI	2
HANDEL	104	AB	10	PLOT	102	AB	1
HANDEL	104	DE	1	REALIZING	103	AB	28
HIS	101	AB	9	RODRIGO	102	AB	24

ROYAL	103	AB	22	TWO	102	TI	2
S	102	AB	14	TWO	102	AB	11
S	104	AB	19	USED	101	AB	7
SOURCES	101	AB	5	WORK	104	AB	24
SUMMARIES	102	AB	2	WRITERS	104	AB	5
TEXTUAL	102	AB	3				

And that's how an inverted file is created. Almost all information retrieval systems and search engines you use will have something like this (if not precisely this structure or format) underlying it. New documents are processed in the same way and added to the file; if documents are removed from the database, their pointers are excised from the file, and life goes on.

> What we have described here is the subject inverted file (called the Basic Index in DIALOG), but each database has a whole range of other inverted files too. In fact, it is necessary for the system to construct an inverted file for every field that is required to be searchable. So we will have an author inverted file, a journal name inverted file, a language inverted file, and so on. They are all built in the same way by the system software, and each consists of a list of search terms and the accession numbers of all the records that have contained those terms (pointers). They are, in fact, a series of indexes (rather like back-of-the-book indexes), which point to selected records in the linear file.
>
> The reason for constructing all these inverted files is that each record will now only need to be stored once (as compared with the duplicated unit records in a card catalog) and searching will be speeded up by searching the inverted file instead of the entire linear file. – GW

Why Inverted Files Aren't Panaceas

A couple of things to think about at this stage: Looking through the final inverted file, notice words like WORK, ROYAL, ENGLISH, MESSIAH, and MOOD. If one knows that the database covers only music, some of these terms have special meanings. However, in a file with, for example, newspaper or magazine articles, these words might have other connotations. We also have here four documents about operas and oratorios, both kinds of vocal compositions. None of them, though, contain the words VOICE or VOCAL.

Imagine also a religion database that nonetheless has a document about the oratorio Messiah. Searching in that database for the word MESSIAH will retrieve that document, but also probably a great deal more, so the search will have to be refined with other words and techniques.

The computer can say yes, these documents have those words in them and no, those don't, but not much more than that. The system alone is not able to take advantage of the context of words in a document, which people can do very easily. It is simply unable to identify relationships among terms.

This is one of the most important things to know about information systems in general. The only things that go into inverted files are *words*—either directly from the texts of documents or from some indexing added later (called "controlled vocabulary"). These words are, at best, clues to the actual content and subject matter of these documents, but because of the nature of language, they are often not perfect (or, for that matter, even very good) indicators of that content.

If a document has the word "oratorio" in the text, it is probably about oratorios—that is a fairly specific word. If "oratorio" is in the title, the odds go up. But what about the word "pitcher"?

Here is the bottom line, and what a great deal of the whole profession of library and information science is about: *We want to look for concepts, but we are forced to search for words.* The better that information professionals understand that, and the better they are able to cope with it, the better they will be at searching.

There. Now that we have revealed the secret of the universe, all the rest should be pretty easy.

Structure

Several times in the preceding discussion, we talked about the structure of the records to be included in the database. This is one of the senses of "structure" that we will use here. In this section, we will review what both senses are; give some examples of each; talk about how and why they arose; how they can be used in searching, now and in the future; and elaborate further on overhead issues in database building.

Two Kinds of Structure

In the inverted file construction example above, we used a crude kind of document in a toy database. That document had only a very few pieces of information. In most bibliographic retrieval systems, the records have much more information in them and contain more kinds of information. We might say these records have more elaborate (or at least bigger) *record structures.*

Here, for example, is a record from the *ERIC* database:

Fig. 5.1. ERIC database record.

```
AN   EJ355024 TM511910

TI   An Experimental, Exploratory Study of Causes of Bias
     in Test Items

AU   Scheuneman, Janice Dowd

JO   Journal of Educational Measurement, v24 n2 p97-118 Sum 1987

AV   Available from: UMI

LA   Language: English

DT   Document Type: JOURNAL ARTICLE (080); RESEARCH REPORT (143)

JA   Journal Announcement: CIJSEP87

AB   This study evaluated 16 hypotheses concerning possible sources of
     bias in test items on the Graduate Record Examination General Test.
     Ten of the hypotheses showed interactions between group membership
     and the item performance of Black and White examinees. (Author/LMO)

DE   Descriptors: *Blacks; *College Entrance Examinations; Higher Educa-
     tion; Hypothesis Testing; *Racial Differences; Sex Differences;
     Statistical Bias; *Test Bias; *Test Items; *Whites

ID   Identifiers: *Graduate Record Examinations; Log Linear Analysis
```

The two-letter codes point to the different fields of the record. Remember we said that a field is an individual piece of information about a document, and the collection of these fields about the same document is called a *record*. The fields shown above are described here:

AN—accession number: a number assigned by the database producer as a document is entered into the database. This number uniquely identifies each record in the file. Documents in the ERIC database have two accession numbers: one assigned by the individual ERIC clearinghouse where the document was produced (here TM 511 910), and one by the overall ERIC system (here EJ 355 024).

TI—title: the title of the original document.

AU—author: the author of the original document. There may be more than one author; if so, all may or may not be listed. An agency or organization may also be credited with authorship. This is referred to as a *corporate author.*

JO—journal name and citation: the name of the journal where the original document appeared (if it is indeed a journal article; if not, identifying information about the original source is given). In addition, the journal's volume, number, pages, and year of publication are given.

AV—availability: where the document may be obtained, in addition to the source journal. In this case, the document is available from University Microfilms International (UMI).

LA—language: the language in which the original document is written.

DT—document type: ERIC assigns a code to each document to describe its "type": journal article, guidebook, manual, dissertation, report, and so on. Other databases have similar information, although the specific types involved will differ.

JA—journal announcement: all documents in the ERIC database are also listed in the two ERIC manual indexes: CIJE (*Current Index to Journals in Education*) for journal articles and RIE (*Resources in Education*) for all other documents. This field shows that this document appeared in CIJE in September 1987.

AB—abstract: a brief summary of the document (typically a paragraph), which may either have been written by the original author or by the indexers. This abstract was written by the author, then later edited—the initials are of the indexer.

DE—descriptors: index terms assigned, generally from a predetermined list, by a professional indexer to represent this document and assist searchers in looking for it. This list is known as a controlled vocabulary, which we will discuss later. The descriptors in this record are taken from the *Thesaurus of ERIC Descriptors.* The starred descriptors are referred to as major descriptors, which have been identified by the indexer as the terms that best describe what the document is about and are the only descriptors that appear in the print version of the file.

ID—identifiers: terms assigned by the indexer—similar in form to descriptors, but these are freely assigned and are not from a predetermined list. Often, identifiers are terms so new in an area that they are not yet widely used or known and have not yet been added to the accepted vocabularies. In ERIC this field is also used for proper names (i.e., names of places, people, projects, and programs).

Different databases have different record structures, as we have seen: different fields, different codes for the same fields, and different orderings of the fields. But this ERIC record is a good example of the type of bibliographic record stored in an online database. This record will act as a surrogate for the real document, an article that appeared in the *Journal of Educational Measurement* in 1987.

As an aside, another kind of record in an information system might be familiar: here's the MARC (MAchine-Readable Cataloging) record for the first edition of this book.

Fig. 5.2. MARC record.

```
001  28257554
003  OCoLC
005  19950309081456.0
008  930520s1993 coua b 001 0 eng pam a
010  93004955
020  1563080710 (cloth) :
020  1563081571 (paper) :
040  DLC|cDLC
043  n-us--
050  00 Z699.35.O55|bW35 1993
082  00 025.5/24|220
100  1 Walker, Geraldene
245  10 Online retrieval :|ba dialogue of theory and practice /
     |cGeraldene Walker, Joseph Janes
260  Englewood, Colo. :|bLibraries Unlimited,|c1993
300  xi, 221 p. :|bill. ;|c28 cm
440  0 Database searching series
504  Includes bibliographical references (p. 2-8) and index
650  0 Online bibliographic searching|zUnited States
650  0 DIALOG (Information retrieval system)
700  10 Janes, Joseph
```

The catalog of a library that owns this book will include a MARC record very like this and will create an inverted file much as we have seen to allow people to search for it and find it based on words in the title, one or both of our names, or one of the two subject headings. You will notice that although there are many similarities between the two records and the systems that search them, there are some important differences. The MARC record, representing a 200-plus-page book, has only those two subject headings and no abstract to represent the subject matter of the original document. For a 20-page journal article, the ERIC record has a paragraph-length abstract and a dozen subject indicators. Something to bear in mind—searchers will typically have fewer access points to retrieve book records than journal article records *because of the nature of the records used to represent them.*

The other use of the word "structure" has a somewhat different meaning. Over the last several years, there has been greater attention and awareness of *structured text*, largely fueled by its use in the publishing industry and the Internet. Using structured text is a way of representing the *internal* structure of documents (e.g., acts of a play, chapters of a book, stanzas of a poem, captions of photographs) as well as *meta-information* such as version, edition, authorship, or date. This can be an enormous aid in textual analysis and scholarship, printing, description, and, of course, searching.

There are two common schemes used in creating structured text: *HTML (HyperText Markup Language)* and *SGML (Standard Generalized Markup Language)*. Note that they are both called "markup languages"; we often refer to the creation or conversion of structured documents as "marking them up." Here are examples of each of these languages.

This is an HTML document. HTML is the language used to create documents that can be served and viewed over the World Wide Web on the Internet. It is the "About the Library" page from the Internet Public Library:

Fig. 5.3. Internet Public Library HTML page.

```
<!DOCTYPE HTML PUBLIC "-//W3C//DTD HTML 3.2//EN">
<html>
<head>
<title>IPL About the Library</title>
</head>
<body bgcolor="#FFFFFF">
<h3><a href=="/"><img src="/images/ipl.logo.small.gif" alt="To the
lobby of"></a>the Internet Public Library</h3>


<h1>About the Internet Public Library</h1>


<p><a href="iplfaq.html">Frequently Asked Questions about the IPL</a>
(updated 7 June 96)</p>
<p><strong>NEW!</strong> A more user-friendly <a href="stats.html">
summary of our statistics</a></p>


<ul>
<li><a href="message.html">A welcome message from the Director</a>
<li><a href="bios.html">Meet the IPL Staff</a>
<li><a href="statement.html">Our Statement of Principles</a>
<li><a href="newmission.html">Our Mission Statement and Goals</a>
```

Figure 5.3. Internet Public Library HTML page (continued).

```html
<li><a href="update.html">Our listserv</a>
<li><a href="releases.html">Press Releases</a>
<li><a href="awards.html">Awards Received by the IPL</a>
<li><a href="ifpol.html">Policy regarding requests to reconsider
resources</a>
<li><a href="circpol.html">Policy regarding release of access log
information</a>
<li><a href="repropol.html">Policy regarding reproduction of our
pages and images</a>
<li><a href="telecom.html">Position on S.652 HR.1555</a>, the
Telecommunications Reform Bill.
<li>Thoughts on <a href="bannedbooks.html">Banned Books</a> Week 1996.
</ul>


<p>


<p>The Library is hosted by the <A href="/cgi-bin/redirect?http://
www.si.umich.edu/">School of Information</A> at the <A href="/cgi-
bin/redirect?http://www.umich.edu/">University of Michigan</A>.


<p><STRONG>You may also want to <A HREF="mailto:ipl@ipl.org">Send Us
Feedback</A> | View the IPL <A HREF="/cgi-bin/stats.pages.pl">Access
Statistics</A>.</STRONG></p>


<p><strong>Return to <a href="/">the IPL Main Lobby</a>.</strong>
<hr>


<address>the Internet Public Library - = - http://www.ipl.org/ - = -
ipl@ipl.org</address>
Last Updated Oct 16, 1996


</body>
</html>
```

Here's what this page would look like when viewed over the Web:

Fig. 5.4. Internet Public Library page (as viewed).

---

the Internet Public Library

About the Internet Public Library

<u>Frequently Asked Questions about the IPL</u> (updated 7 June 96)

NEW! A more user-friendly <u>summary of our statistics</u>

- <u>A welcome message from the Director</u>
- <u>Meet the IPL Staff</u>
- <u>Our Statement of Principles</u>
- <u>Our Mission Statement and Goals</u>
- <u>Our listserv</u>
- <u>Press Releases</u>
- <u>Awards Received by the IPL</u>
- <u>Policy regarding requests to reconsider resources</u>
- <u>Policy regarding release of access log information</u>
- <u>Policy regarding reproduction of our pages and images</u>
- <u>Position on S.652 HR.1555</u>, the Telecommunications Reform Bill.
- Thoughts on <u>Banned Books</u> Week 1996.

The Library is hosted by the <u>School of Information</u> at the <u>University of Michigan</u>.

You may also want to <u>Send Us Feedback</u> | View the IPL <u>Access Statistics</u>.

Return to <u>the IPL Main Lobby</u>.

---

the Internet Public Library - = - http://www.ipl.org/ - = - ipl@ipl.org
Last Updated Oct 16, 1996

If the two are compared, one can see that the text of the document is intermingled with lots of things in angle brackets, like <title> and <h1> and <li>. These are HTML tags, and they define the structure of the document and how it will be displayed by a Web browser. The <h1> tag is a first-level header, and its text is displayed as large type. The <ul> tag defines the beginning of an unordered list, and each <li> is a list item, which is preceded by a bullet in the page.

One can imagine ways in which the HTML tags would be quite useful for searching. The <title> tag is an obvious one, but being able to search in important headers or addresses could also come in handy. We will talk more about Web searching in the next chapter.

The next example is an SGML document. SGML has a more complete set of tags and is used by many publishing companies to assist in formatting and printing. We are indebted to the Humanities Text Initiative of the University of Michigan for this document, which is the descriptive information about and opening lines of a book of Longfellow poetry.

Fig. 5.5. SGML document.

```
<TEI.2 ID="BAD8947">
<TEIHEADER>
<FILEDESC>
<TITLESTMT>

    <TITLE TYPE="245">Courtship of Miles Standish : and other
    poems / Henry Wadsworth Longfellow [electronic text]</TITLE>
    <AUTHOR>Longfellow, Henry Wadsworth, 1807-1882</AUTHOR>
    <RESPSTMT>
    <NAME>Nigel Kerr, Mark Holman, Anne Noakes, William
    M. Wines, University of Michigan Humanities Text
    Initiative</NAME><RESP>creation of machine-readable
    edition</RESP>
    </RESPSTMT>
    </RESPSTMT>
    <NAME>Jason J. Chu, University of Michigan Humanities Text
    Initiative</NAME><RESP>correction of machine-readable
    edition</RESP>
    </RESPSTMT>
    <RESPSTMT>
    <NAME>Kevin Butterfield, University of Michigan</NAME>
    <RESP>creation of AACR2-conformant header</RESP>
    </RESPSTMT>

</TITLESTMT>
<EXTENT>ca. 172 kb.</EXTENT>
<PUBLICATIONSTMT>

    <PUBLISHER>University of Michigan Humanities Text
    Initiative</PUBLISHER> <PUBPLACE>Ann Arbor, Mich.</PUBPLACE>
    <IDNO>LongfCourt</IDNO>
    <AVAILABILITY>
    <P>This work is the property of the University of Michigan.
    It may be copied freely by individuals for personal use,
    research, and teaching (including distribution to classes)
    as long as this statement of availability is included in
    the text. It may be linked to freely in Internet editions
    of all kinds, including for-profit works.<P>
```

(Fig. 5.5 continues on page 70.)

Fig. 5.5. SGML document (continued).

```
        <P>Publishers, libraries, and other information
        providers interested in providing this text in a
        commercial or non-profit product or from an information
        server must contact the University of Michigan Press for
        licensing and cost information.</P> <P>Scholars interested
        in changing or adding to these texts by, for example,
        creating a new edition of the text (electronically or in
        print) with substantive editorial changes, may do so with
        the permission of the University of Michigan Press. This
        is the case whether the new publication will be made
        available at a cost or free of charge.</P> <P>Accessible
        at http://www.hti.umich.edu/english/amverse/</P>
        </AVAILABILITY>
        <DATE>1996</DATE>

</PUBLICATIONSTMT>
<SOURCEDESC>

        <BIBLFULL>
        <TITLESTMT>
        <TITLE>The Courtship of Miles Standish, and other poems</TITLE>
        <AUTHOR>Henry Wadsworth Longfellow</AUTHOR>
        </TITLESTMT>
        <PUBLICATIONSTMT>
        <PUBLISHER>Ticknor and Fields</PUBLISHER>
        <PUBPLACE>Boston</PUBPLACE>
        <DATE>1859</DATE>
        </PUBLICATIONSTMT>
        <NOTESSTMT>
        <NOTE><P>Call number: 828 L853c</P></NOTE>
        </NOTESSTMT>
        </BIBLFULL>

</SOURCEDESC>
</FILEDESC>
<ENCODINGDESC>
<EDITORIALDECL>

        <P>All poems, line groups, and lines are represented.
        Indentation has not been preserved.<P>
```

Fig. 5.5. SGML document (continued).

```
</EDITORIALDECL>
</ENCODINGDESC>
</TEIHEADER>
<TEXT>
<FRONT>
<TITLEPAGE>

    <DOCTITLE>
    <TITLEPART TYPE="main">THE COURTSHIP OF MILES STANDISH,
    <LB>AND <LB>OTHER POEMS.</TITLEPART>
    </DOCTITLE>
    <BYLINE>BY<DOCAUTHOR>HENRY WADSWORTH LONGFELLOW.</DOCAUTHOR>
    </BYLINE>
    <DOCIMPRINT>
    <PUBPLACE>BOSTON:</PUBPLACE> <PUBLISHER> TICKNOR AND
    FIELDS.</PUBLISHER> <DOCDATE>M DCCC LIX.</DOCDATE> <PB
    ID="P1" N="[verso]">Entered according to Act of Congress, in
    the year 1858, by <LB>HENRY WADSWORTH LONGFELLOW, <LB>in the
    Clerk's Office of the District Court of the District of
    Massachusetts. <LB>CAMBRIDGE: <LB>ELECTROTYPED AND PRINTED
    BY <NAME>METCALF AND COMPANY.</NAME>
    </DOCIMPRINT>

</TITLEPAGE>
<PB ID="P2" N="[iii]"
</FRONT>
<BODY>
<PB ID="P4" N="[5]">
<DIV0 ID="DIV0.2" N="1" TYPE="poem">

    <HEAD>THE COURTSHIP OF MILES STANDISHHEAD</HEAD>
    <PB ID="P5" N="[6]">
    <PB ID="P6" N="[7]">
    <DIUI ID="DTV1.3" TYPE="section">
    <HEAD>I. <LB>MILES STANDISH.</HEAD>
    <LG ID="LG1" TYPE="stanza">
    <L ID="L1"IN the Old Colony days, in Plymouth the land of
    the Pilgrims,</L>
```

(Fig. 5.5 continues on page 72.)

Fig. 5.5. SGML document (continued).

```
<L ID="L2">To and fro in a room of his simple and
primitive dwelling,</L>
<L ID="L3">Clad in doublet and hose and boots of Cordovan
leather,</L>
<L ID="L4">Strode, with a martial air, Miles Standish the
Puritan Captain.</L>
<L ID="L5">Buried in thought he seemed, with his hands
behind him, and pausing</L>
<L ID="L6">Ever and anon to behold his glittering weapons
of warfare,</L>
<PB ID="P7" N="8">
<L ID="L7">Hanging in shining array along the walls of the
chamber, &mdash;</L>
<L ID="L8">Cutlass and corslet of steel, and his trusty
sword of Damascus,</L>
<L ID="L9">Curved at the point and inscribed with its
mystical Arabic sentence,</L>
<L ID="L10">While underneath, in a corner, were
fowling-piece, musket, and matchlock.</L>
<L ID="L11">Short of stature he was, but strongly built
and athletic,</L>
<L ID="L12">Broad in the shoulders, deep-chested, with
muscles and sinews of iron;</L>
<L ID="L13">Brown as a nut was his face, but his russet
beard was already</L>
<L ID="L14">Flaked with patches of snow, as hedges
sometimes in November.</L>
<L ID="L15">Near him was seated John Alden, his friend,
and household companion,</L>
<L ID="L16">Writing with diligent speed at a table of pine
by the window;</L>
<PB ID="P8" N="9">
<L ID="L17">Fair-haired, azure-eyed, with delicate Saxon
complexion,</L>
<L ID="L18">Having the dew of his youth, and the beauty
thereof, as the captives</L>
<L ID="L19">Whom Saint Gregory saw, and exclaimed, "Not
Angles but Angels."</L>
<L ID="L20">Youngest of all was he of the men who came in
the May Flower.</L>
</LG>
```

There are even more indications of the structure of the document in the SGML document than in the HTML one, giving the lines of the poem, where the pages begin and end, and so on. But you also see a large amount of information about the work itself (publisher, date, author, title, imprint) and this electronic version (who created the SGML version, the size of the file, its availability, etc.). This is often called *meta-information*, and, because it is part of the same file as the work itself, it can also be used in searching in rather sophisticated ways.

Searching and Structure

The use of the structure of bibliographic records in searching is pretty basic. It permits searches to be restricted to a particular field, so one doesn't have to search for all occurrences of the word "Bush" if one only wants documents *written* by someone named Bush, for example. This kind of searching is often used as an auxiliary method to searching by content. We well see more of this in a later chapter, but consider a search for documents about the *Challenger* disaster—if only things written right after it happened were wanted, a search could be conducted for documents with the word "Challenger" with the results restricted to those written in 1986.

Some of the benefits of structured text in searching should be clear. It permits searching by field, but in a much more detailed way than in the bibliographic example—not just words in fields like author, title, and abstract, but also where they occur, in which chapter or heading or subheading or table or caption, and so on. It also allows searching in the meta-information for such data as version or edition.

It is true that in this situation the full text is available to be searched, which is not true with just a bibliographic record. That may seem like an inherent advantage, but this is not necessarily the case. It may well be that the addition of structure helps the full-text searching problem, but this is as yet an emerging area of investigation. As yet, searching using structured documents is pretty crude and largely limited to the HTML/Internet domain, where some search engines allow one to restrict searching to words in the <title> or <h1> tags, for example. And, of course, this kind of searching depends on the right tags being assigned to the appropriate parts of the document at the input stage and the search engine being able to take advantage of them.

Overhead Issues

In both cases, a lot of work is involved in implementation. Indexing or marking up documents takes a great deal of time and intellectual effort, and the more one wants to be able to use this structure as an aid to searching these documents, the more work it will be. To search within chapters or captions, HTML or SGML tags have to be added. For short texts such as poems, this is not an enormous burden, but imagine the work involved in novels; technical documents incorporating formulas, graphs, diagrams, and pictures; or the works of Shakespeare. Because it is difficult to predict exactly what kinds of searching people are going to want to do, a great deal of structure will have to be included to allow for a variety of possibilities. This can be incredibly tedious and very costly. More documents are being created with SGML in "native" form, but there are a lot of pre-SGML documents out there, and their conversion is a daunting prospect indeed.

In a bibliographic database, if one just wants to be able to search for words anywhere, the inverted file does not have to be all that complicated—just list the words and what documents they are in:

ENGLISH 104

If, though, one wants to be able to restrict searching by field (e.g., only look for ENGLISH in the abstract field), the field indicator must be included in the pointer:

ENGLISH 104 AB

And to be able to search for multiple-word phrases, those words have to be found near each other, so position must be included within the field in the inverted field entry. To be able to find the phrase ENGLISH ORATORIO, the searcher has to know if they ever occur next to each other, which they do:

ENGLISH 104 AB 8

ORATORIO 104 AB 9

All of this falls into the general category of overhead—the more one wants to be able to do in searching a database, the more preparation and processing will be needed. We will see this several times in the discussions to come, and this issue should be kept in mind for all kinds of features of information systems.

Additional Reading

Morton, Douglas (1993), "Refresher Course: Boolean AND," *Online* 17(1): 57–59.

Tenopir, Carol (May 1, 1997), "Common End User Errors," *Library Journal*: 31–32.

6 SEARCH TECHNIQUE

This chapter introduces many of the major concepts and basic mechanics of searching. Again, we will use the DIALOG system's commands as illustrations but also include a discussion of current Internet-based search technique at the end. As a framework for presenting the particular commands and ideas, we outline an eight-step procedure, really a codification of common sense, which we hope will help formulate effective search strategies and conduct successful searches. We will also use a particular search as an example to walk the reader through these steps.

1   Read the query.

1a   Listen to the query.

1b   Understand the query.

This is only somewhat flippant. Whatever triggers a search—a phone call or electronic mail message from a patron, a written search request form, a panicky visit to the reference desk—this is the first, best resource. No matter how much the person requesting the search knows about the actual topic, he or she is the one requesting the search, and so is the only one who knows how many documents they want, what kinds of documents, what focus to put on the search, and so on. We will talk more about the search interview process later on, but for now, know that any information that can be obtained from the user could be very helpful. Examples include potential search terms, known authors or titles of good documents (but be careful—these could do more harm than good, especially if the names are wrong), the results of any previous search attempts they made, and so on. Many search services use forms to elicit this sort of information; here are a couple of samples following on pages 76–78.

An important note: it is entirely possible that a query presented for an "online search" really does not belong there. It might be more of a traditional ready-reference question, or one for which a manual or Internet search would be quicker or more appropriate or more successful. Do not get seduced into believing that online searching will answer all questions, because it will not. There are situations in which a search via a commercial online service would be faster and cheaper, but this is not always the case.

On page 79 is the sample query we will use as a demonstration. It is a real query from a psychology doctoral student working on the literature review for her dissertation.

Fig. 6.1. Sample search request form.

Online Search Request Form

Please give a brief narrative description of your topic (use back if necessary):

Do you know of any index terms, vocabulary terms, or search terms that would be useful in searching for documents on this topic? Please list them here, or underline them in the above description.

Do you know of any authors or documents relevant to this topic? Please specify them here.

Types of materials of interest to you (circle):

Journal Articles	Y	N	Conference Papers	Y	N
Reports	Y	N	Dissertations	Y	N

Other (specify): _____

Years to be covered: _____

Languages of interest (list): _____

Please give any other information you think might be helpful in formulating a search strategy on the back.

Fig. 6.2. Internet Public Library reference question form.

---

the Internet Public Library

IPL Ask A Question Form

IPL Reference Question

Reminder:

We are not able to perform lengthy research. However we can provide brief answers to factual questions or suggestions for locations and sources which might help to answer your question.

PLEASE READ! About the IPL Ask-A-Question Service

Before you ask a reference question, please check to see if your question is in the Frequently Asked Reference Questions list. You could save yourself, and us, a lot of time.

---

1 **What is your name?**

What is your email address?

If you don't give us your correct, complete Internet email address (example: fluggly@aol.com), we can't send you an answer to your question.

Where do you live? (City/State/Country)

We can usually help you better if we know where you live, and how far away you are from the resources we may recommend to you.

2 **I won't need this information after:** [   ] (date)

Click here if you are in a hurry.

3 **The Subject Area of the Question:** (click to see list -- choose one)

(None Selected) ▼

4 **Please tell us your question.**
A human being will read your question -- please use complete sentences!
The more you tell us, the better our answer will be. What do you already know about your subject or question?

(Fig. 6.2 continues on page 78.)

Fig. 6.2. Internet Public Library reference question form (continued).

5 **How will you use this information?** Why are you asking your question?

It really helps librarians to know this part! Sometimes we can use our subject knowledge and imaginations to think of other places to look for answers and information, if we know how you will use it.

Will you use this information for a school assignment? ◯ Yes ◯ No

Are you: ▢ A librarian? ▢ A teacher? ▢ A businessperson?

6 **Type of answer preferred:** (choose one of the following)

◯ A brief factual answer to your question
◯ Some ideas for sources to consult for exploration:

▢ Internet sources ▢ Print sources ▢ I don't care which kind

Sometimes the information you want isn't available on the Internet, but might be available through a library near you. We can almost always get you started, at least.

7 **Sources Consulted:**
Please list any places on the Net or off that you've already checked regarding your question. We don't want to duplicate your attempts. Don't forget to try using our Ready Reference Collection and your local library to answer your question.

Reminder: Please take a moment to re-check the e-mail address you are submitting to us, since it is **impossible** for us to communicate with you unless it is correct. Thanks!

8 **SEND IT!**

[Submit Question to IPL Librarians] [Reset Form To Default Values]

If you have problems using this form, you can also submit a question by e-mail. For instructions, consult the E-Mail Guidelines.

Return to Ask a Question | IPL Reference Center | IPL Lobby

the Internet Public Library - = - http://www.ipl.org/ - = - ipl@ipl.org
Last updated Jul 24, 1997.

Fig. 6.3. Completed search request form.

Online Search Request Form

Please give a brief narrative description of your topic (use back if necessary):

> I am interested in information about the psychosocial and behavioral effects of traumatic brain injury in children, and about effective methods of psychological intravention with brain injured children.

Do you know of any index terms, vocabulary terms, or search terms that would be useful in searching for documents on this topic? Please list them here, or underline them in the above description.

traumatic brain injury	psychosocial
closed head injury	behavioral
children	neuropsychology
adolescents	intravention
pediatric	

Do you know of any authors or documents relevant to this topic? Please specify them here.

> The following have been recommended but I haven't yet read them:
>
> —Rutter, Chadwich and Shaffer (1985). Head injury. In M. Rutter (Ed.). *Developmental Neuropsychiatric*.
>
> —Klonoth, Lon and Clark (1977). Head injuries in children. *Journal of Neurology, Neurosurgery and Psychiatric* 40, 1211–1219.

Types of materials of interest to you (circle):

Journal Articles	(Y) N		Conference Papers	(Y) N
Reports	(Y) N		Dissertations	(Y) N

Other (specify): _book chapters_

Years to be covered: _1975-present_

Languages of interest (list): _English only_

Please give any other information you think might be helpful in formulating a search strategy on the back.

A quick read of the request form gives us the sense that the user has thought about this topic quite a bit. In fact, she has given us two known documents with authors and several potentially good search terms. These may well be helpful in the search. We will talk more about the search interview process in a later chapter; for now we shall assume that the conversation reinforces what we see on the form, and that the student is looking for as much as we can possibly give her. This makes sense for a doctoral student in the bibliography-building stage, so we should be looking for larger rather than smaller sets—a *high-recall search*. She is not sure how much is out there but thinks it might be as many as 100 or 150 documents, perhaps more.

2 Identify the major concepts in the query.

Most requests for information that can be searched most effectively online involve more than one concept. One-concept searches can certainly be searched online, but often there is a second concept lurking in the user's mind. For example, a patron seeking information on bilingual education may actually be interested in bilingual education in elementary schools, or materials used in bilingual education, or the controversy sometimes raised about such education.

It is not always easy or straightforward to identify these concepts, sometimes called *facets*. Different people will find different concepts and act on them differently, and there is often no one "right" analysis.

Concept Analysis

We decide that an online search would help answer this query—it does indeed have multiple concepts, and the user is looking for articles, conference papers, and other materials that are included in online databases—so we begin to analyze the concepts it contains.

> *Concept means the abstract idea of a thing, regardless of what it may be called in a given instance. This is because often a single concept (e.g., teacher) will have more than one recognizable name (e.g., instructor, tutor, professor, lecturer, master, coach).*
>
> *The controlled vocabulary in an information retrieval system is an attempt to standardize these words to one preferred term that will always be used to represent a single concept, so that we will not find the same subject entered under different headings. A golden rule for most retrieval systems is to try to gather together under one heading all the material on one subject. – GW*

For this search, we identify three concepts: *traumatic brain injuries*, *their effects*, and *children*. Again, there is nothing magical about this process; it is something you get better at with practice and experience, and you probably thought of the same words when you first looked at the query. If not, don't worry, but look at your analysis and ours and see how they differ. Are they roughly similar? Did you see two concepts, or even four? How might the way you conceptualized the search affect how you do the search? This set of concepts makes sense to us, but it is not the only one, and different ones might well produce equally good results.

Building Blocks

Most searchers use a technique called *building blocks* in constructing their search strategies. It might help to think of a search strategy as a structure, built up from individual pieces, each of which corresponds to a concept derived from the analysis of the query. A good analogy is Lego. Each term is an individual Lego block; put a number of them together, and they form a bigger block. Then put those bigger blocks together and make something even more complicated. If a particular piece looks wrong, or if it is in the wrong place, it can be moved or even taken out. Searching is like that—finding terms that might work, putting them together in concept blocks, combining the concept blocks to see what they produce, and revising the search as necessary. The steps below will follow that process through our sample search.

3   **Identify potential terms to correspond to those concepts.**

Term Selection

We have identified three concepts, so all we need to do is go into the database, look them up, put them together, and go home, right? Unfortunately, the process is not so simple. Remember what we said in the last chapter: We want to look for concepts, but we are forced to search for words. There is often no obvious way to go into a database and pull out only the documents about a particular concept. In some cases one can, when the concept is very specific and there is really only one way to refer to it. But most of the time that is not the case, so we have to try to find multiple terms that might be used to represent each concept. Several might be identified but only one is chosen for strategic reasons, but we will get to that later.

In this case, the user appears to be a good source of terms: TRAUMATIC BRAIN INJURY, CLOSED HEAD INJURY, PSYCHOSOCIAL, PEDIATRIC, and so on. But the terms are really all over the place. It would help to have a way to organize the process and make it easier to keep track of all of this. Have a look at the search grid (see fig. 6.4, p. 82).

It is a bit overwhelming at first, but if you look at it for a time, it will start to make some sense. Look first at the boxes marked "Concept 1," "Concept 2," and "Concept 3." In these boxes we have written in the concepts we previously identified. Right below each of these is a series of lines marked "S#" and "Terms." These are spaces for recording potentially good terms, and we have taken the user's terms and phrases and entered them under the corresponding concepts. (Although we have not quite gotten there yet, the "S#" spaces can be used to record set numbers to help in keeping track of what's what.)

A couple of things to point out. First of all, in a couple of cases, we have terms that are exactly the same as our concept names. Nothing special about this; sometimes it happens and sometimes it does not, as with the second concept.

Second, a few terms are recorded here in a slightly different way. Look at BEHAVIOR(AL) and CHILD(REN), and ADOLESCENT(S). This is Joe's shorthand and is a note to remember that there may be varying forms of these terms. Documents might use the word "behavior" or "behavioral," "child" or "children," "adolescent" or "adolescents." This can be a way to remind oneself about plurals or other variant forms. We just suggest finding a comfortable way of working that helps one get quality results.

Fig. 6.4. Search grid.

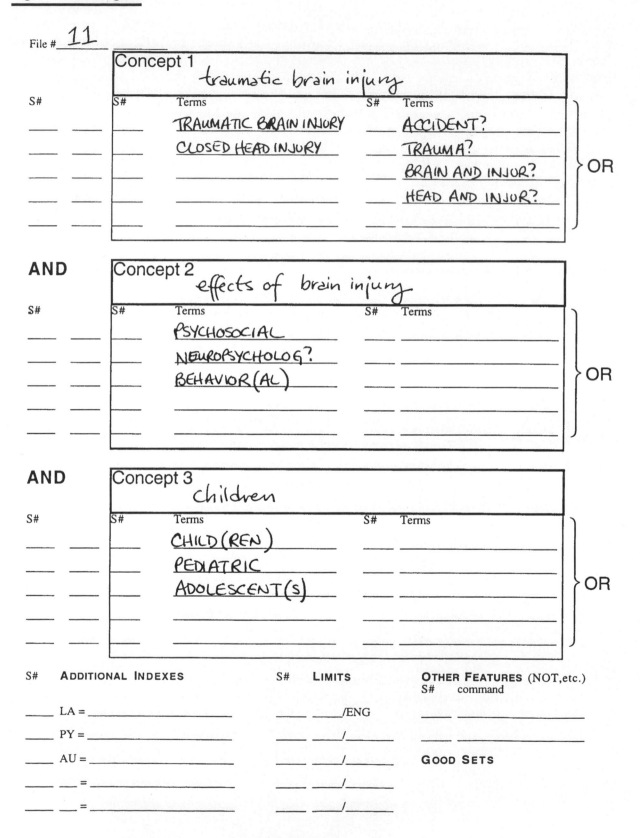

File # _11_

Concept 1	traumatic brain injury

S# | S# | Terms | S# | Terms
TRAUMATIC BRAIN INJURY | ACCIDENT?
CLOSED HEAD INJURY | TRAUMA?
 | BRAIN AND INJUR?
 | HEAD AND INJUR?

} OR

AND

Concept 2	effects of brain injury

S# | S# | Terms | S# | Terms
PSYCHOSOCIAL
NEUROPSYCHOLOG?
BEHAVIOR(AL)

} OR

AND

Concept 3	children

S# | S# | Terms | S# | Terms
CHILD(REN)
PEDIATRIC
ADOLESCENT(S)

} OR

S# | **ADDITIONAL INDEXES** | S# | **LIMITS** | **OTHER FEATURES** (NOT, etc.)
S# command

____ LA = _____ | ____ ____/ENG | ____ _____
____ PY = _____ | ____ ____/____ | ____ _____
____ AU = _____ | ____ ____/____ | **GOOD SETS**
____ __ = _____ | ____ ____/____
____ __ = _____ | ____ ____/____

There is also no one right way to pick terms. In a group of five searchers working on the same query, they might identify five different sets of terms. There would be some overlap, to be sure, but there is rarely only one way to go about doing a search.

> *I often tell my classes that there's no right way to do a search, but there are bad ways. Some conceptualizations and terms will just work better than others in producing sets of documents that the user actually wants and will find useful. It's a very difficult process shot through with ambiguity at more than one level. Don't be intimidated—just keep at it and keep improving. – JWJ*

4   Select alternative (narrower, broader, or related) terms to use if the original strategy needs help.

When doing term selection, terms may come up that are possibly or marginally useful but do not immediately seem ideal. They may in fact be good, but if the initial instinct is ambivalent, hold them out as reserves or alternatives and perhaps put them in the right-hand column of the grid. One's initial, beautifully honed crafted search strategy might not be perfect. More terms, narrower terms, broader terms, different terms, or even fewer terms may be needed. Thus, it is usually a good idea to have a few additional terms up one's sleeve—just in case.

In this search, we have a couple of really interesting (and specific) terms from the user in the first concept, but they might not work, or they may be too specific. We may try a few other ideas, combining some of the same words but in different ways.

5   Determine logical (Boolean) relationships between terms.

We have a good list of terms to use in finding documents for our patron, but we cannot just enter them all and have the answers come out. We have to group them by concepts and then combine those concepts in the appropriate ways. There is a specific way to do this, based on the logic that underlies the construction of many information retrieval systems. This logical understructure comes to us from set theory and is usually called *Boolean logic*.

Boolean Logic and Boolean Searching

Boolean logic is part of a set of techniques used in mathematics for manipulating sets in a rigorous, logical fashion. It is named for the English mathematician George Boole, who developed the framework on which it is based. Boolean logic provides three ways in which sets can be combined, and online systems use all three.

When a search term is entered, a set of documents that contain that term is created. Boolean search techniques allow the searcher to manipulate and combine these sets to provide the user with a set that corresponds to the logic of the initial query. We will discuss each of these three Boolean operators in turn. Before we begin, though, know that the use of Boolean logic and searching is neither universal nor identical across information retrieval systems. Most commercial systems like DIALOG use them in very similar ways, but most Internet-based systems at present have only fragmentary and simple Boolean search capabilities. We will talk about Internet-based systems more at the end of this chapter, but be aware that although full Boolean capability has many advantage, it is not the only game in town.

OR

We could, if we wanted to, go through the database and find all the documents with, say, the word "trauma" in them, another set with the word "psychosocial," and a third with "children," and then compare them to see which terms they all have in common. If we were doing the search manually, using print indexes, we would do precisely that, but it would be tedious and time consuming and we would make lots of mistakes. Using Boolean search tactics with the inverted file for the database will make it much easier and quicker.

We have several terms for the "effects of brain injury," and we want to use them all. Look again at the grid where we have recorded these terms; specifically, look on the right-hand side of that box. See the brace and the big OR there? This tells us that we should use the Boolean operator OR to combine those terms and create a concept block, and that is precisely what we will do.

OR is used to *build up concepts* and can be helpful in several circumstances:

- For *synonyms* or *equivalent terms*

      GARBANZOS **OR** CHICK PEAS

      STUDENTS **OR** PUPILS

      OCCUPATIONS **OR** JOBS **OR** CAREERS

- For *spelling variations*

      HONOR **OR** HONOUR

      ORGANIZATION **OR** ORGANISATION

      JUDGMENT **OR** JUDGEMENT

- For *related terms*

      CLOSED HEAD INJURY **OR** TRAUMATIC BRAIN INJURY

      PSYCHOSOCIAL **OR** NEUROPSYCHOLOGICAL **OR** BEHAVIORAL

      CHILDREN **OR** ADOLESCENTS **OR** PEDIATRIC

This is necessary for a variety of reasons. Authors may use different forms of these words or variant spellings. Words in titles or abstracts may also be slightly different from those used as subject headings. Finally, there simply may be more than one term or word used to represent a single concept or idea. We want the *concept* to be present in the documents we retrieve—the concept of "dogness" or "children" or "Europe"—but human languages are ambiguous and permit multiple ways of saying the same thing. So, once again, we often have to use alternative words to get at a single concept.

For example, suppose a patron is looking for documents about the trade policies within Europe. To represent the concept of "Europe," we might look for "Europe" but also "EC" (an abbreviation for the European Community), "EEC" (the European Economic Community), "EU" (the European Union, the more recent name for the economic community) or even the names of individual countries. In the *ABI/Inform* database, which covers periodicals in business, we find the following postings figures:

EUROPE	80371
EC	16007
EEC	2663
EU	6757
EUROPE OR EC OR EEC OR EU	86934

Notice that the final number is less than the sum of the individual sets due to overlap between them.

A tool known as a *Venn diagram*, named after John Venn, is often used to represent sets and Boolean operations. The figure below is a Venn diagram that represents our first ORed concept:

Fig. 6.5. Venn diagram for OR.

CLOSED HEAD INJURY

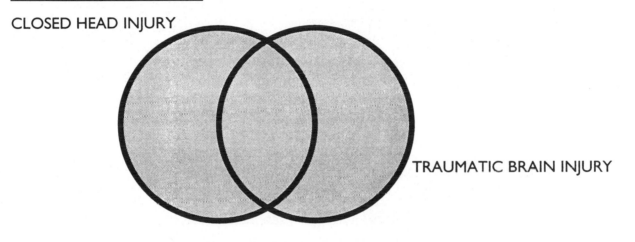

TRAUMATIC BRAIN INJURY

OR will create a set that will retrieve any documents that contain any individual term or any combination of the terms. Because it can only add documents, it will retrieve more documents than any term individually would, and it makes sets bigger.

Be careful, though, of individual terms that *dominate* a concept set. In the Europe example above, most of those documents are probably about Europe in general and not the EU specifically, because the "Europe" set is so much larger than the others. This is not necessarily a problem, but can be. If results seem to be too general, not specifically about a particular concept, a concept set may need to be restructured, dropping a dominant term and using only the more specific, focused terms.

AND

Once we have constructed sets for the individual concepts, we need some way of connecting them so we can find documents that (we hope) are "about" all of them. The way we do this is by use of the Boolean operator AND. Look again at the grid and notice the big ANDs between the concept boxes. This is a reminder that we use AND to pull these concepts together and see what they have in common.

Combining two or more sets with AND will produce a set that contains documents in all of those sets only. That set must be smaller than the individual concept sets, and will therefore produce fewer documents. We call this set the *result set*.

Here is a Venn diagram illustrating how AND works, with two or three concept sets.

Fig. 6.6. Venn diagram for AND.

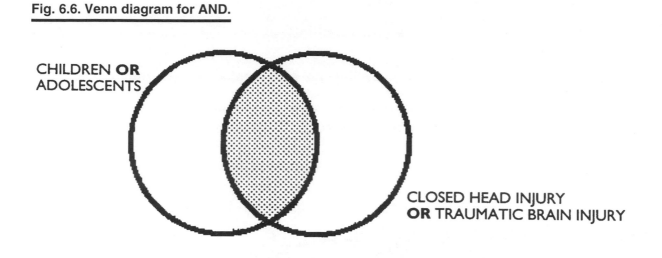

CHILDREN **OR** ADOLESCENTS

CLOSED HEAD INJURY **OR** TRAUMATIC BRAIN INJURY

Another word of caution: Before performing an AND operation, look at the sizes of the individual original concept sets. Because AND can only reduce size, if one or more of the concepts sets are small (e.g., fewer than 50 documents, or about the size that the user said they wanted), the AND may not need to be done. For example, the user says she wants about 60 documents, and one of your concept sets has 47. Before ANDing it in with one or two other sets, it might be prudent to first have a look at it. Maybe *that's* the result set desired, or maybe more terms or broader terms are needed in there. If the set is ANDed in with other concept blocks, the result is likely to be a very small result set. It might even come up with no documents at all. So just take a second and look at those numbers before continuing.

NOT

The third Boolean operator is also the least often used, at least in the same way as AND and OR, for a couple of reasons. It is not even on the search grid, or at least is only tucked down in the corner under "other features." Many beginning searchers do not fully appreciate NOT and its uses, though it is a very powerful tool. Too powerful, in many situations. NOT is used to *exclude* items from a set, but it is a blunt instrument and can have unintended and quite nasty consequences, especially if used in haste or panic.

It is difficult to come up with a good example of its fruitful use in working with concepts, because it does have such power. (We will see it used in another way shortly.) In the next chapter, we will do a search about distance education in library schools in the United States. It turns out that there is no good search term for "United States" in the ERIC database because so many of the documents in there cover it. But there is a term, *foreign countries*. So, to eliminate documents from abroad, we could NOT out the ones with *foreign countries*. Even here, we could lose good documents that are about both U.S. and foreign programs because any document that has that term will be eliminated, but in this case it is appropriate and we will not lose too many documents.

So, NOT should not be a first thought. If you find yourself wanting to use NOT to eliminate a concept, think first whether there might be another way. If a term is making trouble, maybe the concept set should be reconstructed without it. For example, go from

OCCUPATIONS OR JOBS OR CAREERS

to

OCCUPATIONS OR CAREERS

if "jobs" is producing junk, like documents about Steven Jobs.

Or perhaps something new needs to be ANDed in, a new concept or focusing mechanism like date or language. There are places to use NOT, but it should almost always be a second choice.

Here's a Venn diagram for NOT:

Fig. 6.7. Venn diagram for NOT.

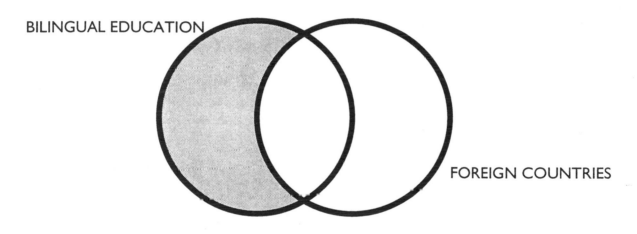

BILINGUAL EDUCATION

FOREIGN COUNTRIES

Order of Operation

Also take care in the order in which search terms are entered. Terms from more than one concept can be entered in a single search statement. We do not recommend this tactic, especially for beginning searchers, because it can be confusing, but one should know how to do it correctly. Most (but not all) retrieval systems will perform NOTs first, followed by ANDs, and finally ORs, and will allow the use of parentheses to override this order.

Thus, a statement such as

(ORATORIO OR OPERA) AND HANDEL

would be different from

ORATORIO OR OPERA AND HANDEL

The first (correct) statement would be interpreted this way: Things in parentheses are done first, so the system would find all documents with either the word ORATORIO or OPERA or both. Then, those would be ANDed with the documents that have HANDEL. This produces a set that, we hope, contains documents about vocal works of Handel. Here's the Venn diagram for that (see fig. 8, p. 88):

Fig. 6.8. Handel's vocal work.

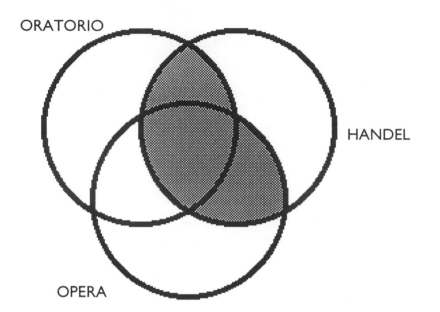

The second statement, though, would be interpreted quite differently. Because there are no parentheses, the AND goes first, so the system would find all documents that satisfy OPERA AND HANDEL. Then those would be ORed with all the documents with ORATORIO. The resulting set would consist of all documents about Handel's operas mixed in with everything about oratorios—not what we had in mind. See how different this Venn diagram is:

Fig. 6.9. Oratorios, with Handel's operas.

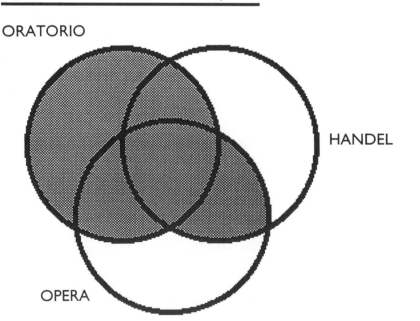

There is nothing really wrong with doing something like the first statement, and most experienced searchers would be quite comfortable doing it, especially for something with only three terms and a simple relationship between them. Just be sure the word order is right!

6   Begin the search.

Here is where to find out if a well-planned strategy will work or not. Even the most experienced and skillful searchers have times when it just does not work, when they just cannot find anything of use, or when the search comes up dry. Sometimes there is nothing to be found—there are no documents in that database in the area the user wants. And sometimes, the right search terms or combinations to pull up the good stuff are elusive.

> *Actually, there are times when the user probably doesn't want anything to come up. There are circumstances, for example in patent searching, when finding something is a bad sign. Someone else has patented your device, or written a book on your dissertation topic, so your work has gone for naught. Another reason why it's good to know what the user wants, and why. – JWJ*

It will probably be most effective to enter all the terms (ORed together) for each concept block together, see how many hits each concept block retrieves, and then AND the remaining sets together to produce a result set. In some cases, that result set will be a good one and will contain useful documents for the patron. Often, though, it could be improved (more about that in step 8). These early stages should provide a good idea of possible steps for refining the search if necessary.

Most Specific First

It might seem that it does not really matter which concept block is entered first because they will all be ANDed together shortly anyway. Although that is true, there is more to it than that. An important and widely used convention is *most specific first*, which can be very helpful. Imagine doing a search on the reliability of children as witnesses in child abuse trials in the *Criminal Justice Information System* (CJIS) database. Here are three concept blocks: children, witnesses, and child abuse. (They could also be two: child-witnesses and child abuse, and if there is a subject heading for child-witnesses, that might well work.)

In a database that covers criminal justice, there are likely to be many more documents on child abuse and witnesses than on children per se. If we search for "child abuse" first, we will get a large set and not learn very much. However, if we search for "children" first, it will be a smaller set and will give us some indication of how many documents we are likely to end up with. If the database supported controlled vocabulary searching, a term like "child witnesses" would be an ideal first choice.

If that first and most specific set is really small (say, 10 documents or less), we might decide to stop right there and either try new terms, reevaluate the search overall, or just inspect that first set—it might be easier than continuing the search. If, though, we get several hundred documents, we proceed, but with the knowledge that our overall result set is likely to be smallish. Experienced searchers can use this kind of information to help guide how they will search from that point on.

Note, though, that if we were doing this same search in, say, *Child Abuse & Neglect & Family Violence*, we would probably enter the "witnesses" concept first because it is probably the most specific. Computer searching is by no means an exact science, and if the broadest concept set is searched for first, it probably will not hurt, but "most specific first" can be very helpful in many circumstances, especially in small databases or with narrow topics.

Logging-On Protocols and Choosing a File (BEGIN)

The major online search services, such as DIALOG, LEXIS/NEXIS, and Dow Jones, are accessed via telecommunications networks or the Internet, as described in chapter 3. When one connects to the service, one must log on in order to start the search. To do this, one must have established an account with the system; they will provide an account number and password used to authenticate your access to the system. This prevents unauthorized use of the service (i.e., freeloading).

We begin our sample search with this login procedure. In search transcripts, we will show what the user types in *italics*, and the system's responses in Roman type.

```
DIALOG INFORMATION SERVICES
PLEASE LOGON:
  ********
ENTER PASSWORD:
  ********
Welcome to DIALOG

Dialog level 98.04.30D

Last logoff:    26may98 12:23:59
Logon file001   26may98 12:28:41


File  1:ERIC  1966-1998/Mar
       (c) format only 1998 The Dialog Corporation

  Set   Items  Description
  ---   -----  -----------
?
```

Notice that in the above, only the system's responses are shown. The searcher has typed in her password, but the system does not display it for security reasons.

The greeting tells us that the last use of the system from this user number was on May 26, 1998, and that we are in the ERIC database, which is file 1 in DIALOG. This is the *default database* selected by the user, meaning that when she logs in, this is the file she will be in, usually selected as being the file she searches most often.

Typically, at this stage, system news will come up: new databases that are available, files not working at present, revisions or reloads of older files, and so on. After this system news (here omitted) comes the *file header*. This tells us what we are currently searching in (ERIC), with the dates of coverage of that file (1966 to March 1998). Then come the headings Set, Items, and Description. The results that appear after these will tell us the numbers of the sets we create, how many documents are in them, and what they represent. Finally, we get a question mark, which is DIALOG's system prompt. This tells us that the system is ready and waiting for us to give it a command.

The first command should always tell the system in which file you want to search. It is quite possible that ERIC, which covers education, will have documents of interest to our user (and indeed, it does), but our intention was to search in PsycINFO, as it is likely that documents in psychology will be more helpful. To move to PsycINFO, file 11 in DIALOG, we use the BEGIN command to change files. The form of the command is

$$\texttt{begin} \le \texttt{file-number} \ge$$

where "≤file-number≥" is the number of the file to be entered. If in the middle of a search, the BEGIN command is given, it will clear out all the previously created sets and move to the file requested. BEGIN is also good to use if you make some horrible mistakes and wants to start over; give the BEGIN command for the same file to achieve a blank slate and recommence the search with Set 1.

Many of the most common DIALOG commands can be abbreviated, so we could also just say

$$\texttt{b} \le \texttt{file-number} \ge$$

which is what we do here:

```
?b 11

26may98 12:29:51 User007659 Session D172.1
          $0.50     0.033 Hrs File1
    $0.50   Estimated cost File1
    $0.10   INTERNET
    $0.60   Estimated cost this search
    $0.60   Estimated total session cost  0.033 Hrs.

File 11:PsycINFO(R)   1967-1998/May
     (c) 1998 Amer. Psychological Assn.

   Set  Items  Description
   ---  -----  -----------
?
```

Now that we are in PsycINFO, we can proceed with our search by starting to create sets based on the terms we selected.

Choosing Search Terms (SELECT)

The command use to search for a given term is SELECT. Its form is

$$\texttt{select} \le \texttt{what-to-search-for} \ge$$

and is often abbreviated as

$$\texttt{s} \le \texttt{what-to-search-for} \ge$$

When the SELECT command is issued, the system searches through the inverted file (DIALOG calls this the *Basic Index*) for all the documents that contain that term. SELECT can be used to search for individual words

```
?s children
```

or phrases

    ?s traumatic brain injury

but those phrases will only work in phrase-indexed fields. Recall our discussion about word- and phrase-indexing in the section on inverted files. The descriptor "traumatic brain injury" could be found this way, but if the phrase appears in a title or abstract, we will not get it by entering the phrase. We can get it, but we have not learned how to do that quite yet.

Another form of the SELECT command is useful if one is searching for several terms at once. It is known as SELECT STEPS and abbreviated SS. The format is

select steps ≤what-to-search-for≥

and its abbreviated form is

ss ≤what-to-search-for≥

When SELECT STEPS is used, it performs the same operations as SELECT. The terms requested are searched for in the inverted file, and a set is produced. The difference between this and SELECT is that when SELECT STEPS is used, sets are created for the individual terms in the statement as well as for the overall statement. These intermediate sets can be useful if, as the search continues, the searcher decides to use these terms in other combinations. The sets have already been created, so typing and time (and money!) can be saved by using the set numbers rather than reentering the terms.

SS can be used anywhere S can be used, but it is not necessary when searching for single terms or phrases. Notice that a lot more sets are created this way, and many beginning searchers find that a bit difficult to contend with, especially when it comes to deciding which sets to use later in a search. Some people like it, others do not, and some wind up using it after they gain some experience. Try it a few times, to learn it and get comfortable with it.

AND, OR, and NOT can be used inside SELECT statements in several ways. As we have seen, two or more terms can be joined by a Boolean operator, as in

    ?s children or pediatric or adolescents

Set numbers can be used in place of terms, as in

    ?s s3 or altruism
    ?s s9 and s12

Also, more than two components may be searched for, as in

    ?s s3 and s8 and s17

A few cautionary words about SELECT: Always be sure to put a space after the word SELECT or S or SS. The system expects it, and if the space is omitted, there may be unexpected results, such as

    ?ssystem

DIALOG sees the SS, searches for the remainder of the statement (YSTEM), and gets zero hits.

Also be careful about spelling and typing errors. Computers are very literal beasts, and a mistake such as this will, more than likely, achieve no hits:

    ?s infomation

Beginning searchers often either fail to notice such an error or find it difficult to recover from it. If this sort of mistake is made (and we all do it), just enter the correct word and proceed as planned, but check the set numbers carefully.

> One of the golden rules of online searching is stated thus: Always be suspicious when you get a set with zero postings. Have you spelled the term or terms correctly? Have you entered the command correctly? Notice the computer responds by repeating your requested term or terms, so see that it received what you intended. When using set numbers, check that the postings look consistent with what you have previously seen. – GW

Another common error among new searchers occurs during searches involving previously created sets. Sometimes, instead of the statement:

        ?s s5 and france

the searcher enters

        ?s 5 and france

or even (more commonly)

        ?s5 and france

In both these cases, it is not set S5 that is ANDed with FRANCE; it is the numeral 5, and only documents containing that number somewhere in the indexed fields will be retrieved. Again, if this should happen, simply reenter the statement. These errors are especially pernicious and difficult to catch because they create sets that may look right. However, if an error like this is carried through an entire search, it will probably result in an almost useless set of citations. One might be able to spot the error later if the result set seems to be fine but is missing one concept altogether; it is usually far easier, though, to catch this mistake as it happens and correct it then.

Truncation (?)

One last piece of DIALOG mechanics before we get into the actual search. Imagine we are doing a search on the effects of technology on libraries, librarians, and the profession of librarianship. We could, of course, search for this second concept by entering

        ?s libraries or librarians or librarianship

or something similar. But look at those three words. They're very similar and, in fact, differ only in the ways they end. It would be nice if there were a shortcut way to search for each of those terms (and perhaps other variants) without having to think of them all and ORing them together. Conveniently enough, there is such a shortcut, using the truncation operator, which in DIALOG is the question mark:

        ?s librar?

This statement will retrieve any document that contains any word that begins with the letters LIBRAR; the words listed above, plus LIBRARY, and so on. There will be only one set, and the system will not explain what the precise words searched on were. Take care, then, not to truncate too far to the left or inadvertently include a word with an enormous number of postings. Go as far to the left as necessary, but the farther one goes, the more records are retrieved, and the greater the potential for irrelevant terms.

> *I vividly recall a search I was doing in a large full-text database of newspaper articles, looking for things about fast-food companies trying to reduce the fat content of their foods. Everything was fine until I was trying to do the FAT part, and I blithely searched on*
>
> *?s fat?*
>
> *and as soon as I'd done it, I knew I had blown it. I got FATE and FATHER and who knows what all else. Took forever, and cost a fortune. Learn from my terrible example. – JWJ*

The "fat" error could probably have been avoided by using a variation of the truncation operator. The general one, as illustrated above, will get all words that begin with the specified characters, regardless of how much comes after. You can control that by using, for example

    ?s statistic? ?

which will retrieve STATISTIC itself and any word that begins with STATISTIC and has *one* additional character. Thus, it will retrieve STATISTIC and STATISTICS, but not STATISTICAL, STATISTICALLY or STATISTICIAN.

If more than one extra character is desired but still a limited number, use as many question marks as characters. Thus,

    ?s retriev??

will get RETRIEVE, RETRIEVAL, RETRIEVED, and RETRIEVER, each of which has two or fewer characters after the stem, but not RETRIEVING, which has three.

The question mark may also be useful inside a word to retrieve variant spellings. Perhaps the most common example of this use of truncation is

    ?s wom?n

which will retrieve WOMAN and WOMEN as well as the less-frequent WOMYN. Such a use of truncation would not work for most British or Canadian spelling variations, seen in such words as COLOUR and HONOUR; they must be searched using OR, since embedded truncation only allows for a single letter:

    ?s behavior or behaviour

So now let us begin our search and see what we get. Our most specific concept is probably the head injury terms, and we had two good ones (or at least they looked good) from the user, so we shall see what they produce:

```
?s closed head injury or traumatic brain injury

          0   CLOSED HEAD INJURY
        370   TRAUMATIC BRAIN INJURY (1997)
    S1  370   CLOSED HEAD INJURY OR TRAUMATIC BRAIN INJURY
```

Maybe the search terms were not all that good. It would appear, because everything is spelled right, that CLOSED HEAD INJURY is not a subject heading in this database, and that TRAUMATIC BRAIN INJURY is a new term in this database and thus has not had many documents indexed with it. In either event, this 370-document set is probably too narrow, so we will have to fall back on alternative terms right away. Now we try this:

```
?s (brain or head) and (trauma? or injur?)

        67917   BRAIN (1967)
        11676   HEAD
        15436   TRAUMA?
        15539   INJUR?
   S2    8103   (BRAIN OR HEAD) AND (TRAUMA? OR INJUR?)
```

These results are better, but the documents we get will be far less specific on "head injuries" than we'd hoped. What we'll get is any document with the word BRAIN or HEAD that also has some form of TRAUMA or INJURY, but these words do not necessarily have to be together or even connected in the document. Still, the set of results is bigger than S1. Our other terms work somewhat better:

```
?s psychosocial or behavioral

        28364   PSYCHOSOCIAL
        81543   BEHAVIORAL
   S3  107312   PSYCHOSOCIAL OR BEHAVIORAL
```

```
?s children or pediatric or adolescents

       207327   CHILDREN (1967)
         3395   PEDIATRIC
        57731   ADOLESCENTS (1967)
   S4  243078   CHILDREN OR PEDIATRIC OR ADOLESCENTS
```

Note that in S4, the number of documents with the word CHILDREN is dramatically larger than the others. Does CHILDREN dominate that set? Perhaps, but the terms are otherwise good, and the user is interested in both. It probably means that the result set will have more in it about children than adolescents, but that may just be the way it is.

So now let us connect them with an AND and see how big our result set will be:

```
?s s2 and s3 and s4

         8103   S2
       107312   S3
       243078   S4
   S5     268   S2 AND S3 AND S4
```

7   Have a look at a few documents.

We know that this original strategy (somewhat modified) produced 268 documents—documents that have one or more of the terms from each concept set. But now we really need to find out whether those documents are any good or not, and we can do that by having a look at a few.

Viewing Results (TYPE)

The DIALOG command used to display records from a set is TYPE, which can be abbreviated as T. The format of the TYPE command is

`TYPE ≤set-number/format/records-to-see≥`

`T ≤set-number/format/records-to-see≥`

So this command

    ?t 5/8/1-9

will show us the first through the ninth documents of set 5, in format 8. In DIALOG, documents usually come out in reverse chronological order (actually, the reverse of the order in which they went into the database), so asking for the first few will result in the most recent, newest ones. Here is an example of format 8:

```
5/8/1
DIALOG(R)File 11:(c) 1998 Amer. Psychological Assn. All rts. reserv.

01532776        1998-07266-014
Parent training.
SERIES TITLE: The LEA series in personality and clinical psychology.

DESCRIPTORS: *Behavior Modification; *Daily Activities; *Disorders; *Parent
   Child Relations; *Parent Training; Adults; Children; Developmental
   Disabilities; Head Injuries; Schizophrenia
IDENTIFIERS: planned activities parent training behavioral technique,
children & adults with normal intelligence or developmental disabilities
or head injuries or schizophrenia or other disorders
SUBJECT CODES & HEADINGS: 3200 (Psychological & Physical Disorders); 3312
   (Behavior Therapy & Behavior Modification)
```

This is sometimes called the "searcher's format" because it gives quite a bit of information that can be useful as the search progresses. It includes not only the title but also the subject headings (here descriptors and identifiers). These will help you to know whether or not the documents are likely to be of value to the user and also can be sources of good potential terms to use if the search needs to be expanded.

There are many other potential formats to use in TYPEing out documents, and they can all be found in the DIALOG Bluesheets, either in print or on the Internet at www.dialog.com. A few, though, are worth mentioning here. Format 6 is often useful for getting a quick sense of what is in a set because it gives only titles of documents. Format 2 is usually bibliographic citation, which may be what the user most wants (although it is always good to ask). Formats 5 and 9 are called "full format"; they will display all the information in the record. Take care with these formats because the records could be quite long and using these formats usually carries an additional charge. More databases are including full-text records, so being able to get the full record in this way is a great time-saver, but be sure that is what is wanted!

At this stage you're looking both to evaluate the quality of the set and think of ways to modify the search to improve it. Look at the rest of this set and do both: see what you think **and** try to find some new good terms to try in the search.

5/8/2

01532586   1998-07195-000
Neuropsychology.
SERIES TITLE: Human brain function: Assessment and rehabilitation.

DESCRIPTORS: *Human Development; *Nervous System Disorders;
 *Neuropsychological Assessment
IDENTIFIERS: developmental considerations & aspects of specialized
assessment in & how disorders in brain function relate to
neuropsychological assessment
SUBJECT CODES & HEADINGS: 3297 (Neurological Disorders & Brain Damage);
 2225 (Neuropsychological Assessment)

TABLE OF CONTENTS:
(Abbreviated)
  Introduction to neuropsychological assessment / Gerald Goldstein
Part I: Developmental considerations
SEE - Neuropsychology of infants and young children / Ida Sue Baron and
  Gerard A. Gioia
SEE - Neuropsychological assessment of older children / Keith Owen Yeates
  and H. Gerry Taylor
SEE - Neuropsychological assessment of adults / Gerald Goldstein
SEE - Neuropsychological assessment of the elderly / Paul David Nussbaum
Part II: Clinical considerations
SEE - Evaluation of high-functioning autism / Don J. Siegel
SEE - Evaluation of head trauma / Randy J. Smith, Jeffrey T. Barth, Robert
  Diamond and Anthony J. Giuliano
SEE - Evaluation of cerebrovascular disease / C. Della Mora and Robert
  A.Bornstein
SEE - Evaluation of demyelinating and degenerative disorders / Daniel N.
  Allen, David G. Sprenkel, Rock A. Heyman, Carol J. Schramke and Nicole
  Englund Heffron
SEE - Assessment following neurotoxic exposure / Lisa A. Morrow
SEE - Assessing medically ill patients: Diabetes mellitus as a model
  disease / Christopher M. Ryan
SEE - Evaluation of neoplastic processes / Richard A. Berg
SEE - Evaluation of patients with epilepsy / Michelle C. Dolske, Gordon J.
  Chelune and Richard I. Naugle
SEE - Evaluation of neuropsychiatric disorders / Doug Johnson-Greene and
  Kenneth M. Adams
Part III: Specialized assessment
SEE - Neuropsychological assessment of abstract reasoning / Gerald
  Goldstein
SEE - Neuropsychological assessment of memory / Joel H. Kramer and Dean C.
  Delis
SEE - Neuropsychological assessment of aphasia / Nils R. Varney
SEE - Assessment of spatial abilities / Bruce M. Caplan and Sarah Romans
SEE - Neuropsychological assessment of motor skills / Kathleen Y. Haaland
  and Deborah L. Harrington
SEE - Assessment methods in behavioral neurology and neuropsychiatry /
  Robert M. Stowe
Index

5/8/3
DIALOG(R)File 11:(c) 1998 Amer. Psychological Assn. All rts. reserv.

01532208   1998-07011-014
Oncologic disorders.

DESCRIPTORS: *Distress; *Illness Behavior; *Neoplasms; *Pain; *Treatment;
  Adjustment; Children; Coping Behavior; Family Relations; Physical
  Treatment Methods
IDENTIFIERS: medical treatment & individual & familial psychological
adjustment & coping & distress due to & treatments for coping with acute
painful medical procedures, children with oncological disorders
SUBJECT CODES & HEADINGS: 3360 (Health Psychology & Medicine); 3293
  (Cancer)

5/8/4
DIALOG(R)File 11:(c) 1998 Amer. Psychological Assn. All rts. reserv.

01532201   1998-07011-007
Traumatic brain injury.

DESCRIPTORS: *Diagnosis; *Measurement; *Traumatic Brain Injury; *Treatment;
  Children; Epidemiology
IDENTIFIERS: description & psychological & psychiatric assessment issues &
epidemiology & medical & psychological & behavioral & pharmacological
treatments, children with traumatic brain injury
SUBJECT CODES & HEADINGS: 3297 (Neurological Disorders & Brain Damage);
  3360 (Health Psychology & Medicine)

5/8/5
DIALOG(R)File 11:(c) 1998 Amer. Psychological Assn. All rts. reserv.

01532194   1998-07011-000
Handbook of pediatric psychology and psychiatry, Vol. 2: Disease, injury,
  and illness.

DESCRIPTORS: *Child Psychiatry; *Child Psychology; *Injuries; *Mental
  Disorders; *Physical Disorders; Adolescent Psychiatry; Adolescent
  Psychology; Adolescents; Children
IDENTIFIERS: issues & disease & injury & illness, children & adolescents
with psychological conditions & serious mental illness, handbook
SUBJECT CODES & HEADINGS: 3200 (Psychological & Physical Disorders)

TABLE OF CONTENTS:
Foreword
Preface
About the editors and contributors
Part one: General issues
SEE - Pain management / Kenneth J. Tarnowski, Ronald T. Brown, Arden D.
  Dingle and Elizabeth Dreelin
SEE - Preparation for medical procedures / Barbara G. Melamed
SEE - Child maltreatment / Robert T. Ammerman and Matthew R. Galvin
SEE - Family adaptation to childhood disability and illness / Alexandra L.
  Quittner and Ann M. DiGirolamo
SEE - Treatment adherence and compliance / Sharon L. Manne

Part two: Pediatric disease, injury, and illness
SEE - Feeding and growth disorders / Frances J. Wren and Sally E. Tarbell
SEE - Traumatic brain injury / Jacques Donders and Andrea Kuldanek
SEE - Burns / David S. Chedekel, Lisa P. Rizzone and Alia Y. Antoon
SEE - Gastrointestinal disorders / Ingemar Engstroem and Bo L. Lindquist
SEE - Neurological disorders / Wun Jung Kim and Michael P. Carey
SEE - Endocrine disorders / Alan M. Delamater and Margaret Eidson
SEE - Pulmonary disorders / Marianne Z. Wamboldt and Leslie Gavin
SEE - Hematologic disorders / Robert J. Thompson, Jr., Kathryn E. Gustafson
  and Russell E. Ware
SEE - Oncologic disorders / James W. Varni, Ronald L. Blount and
  Daniel J. L. Quiggins
SEE - Infectious diseases / John P. Glazer, Johanna Goldfarb and Regina
  Smith James
SEE - Organ transplantation / Margaret L. Stuber and Robert D. Canning
Author index
Subject index

 5/8/6
DIALOG(R)File 11:(c) 1998 Amer. Psychological Assn. All rts. reserv.

01529215   1998-00039-003
Social and behavioural effects of traumatic brain injury in children.

DESCRIPTORS: *Adaptive Behavior; *Loneliness; *Self Esteem; *Social
  Behavior; *Traumatic Brain Injury; Adolescence; Aggressive Behavior;
  Antisocial Behavior; Childhood; School Age Children
IDENTIFIERS: traumatic brain injury, self-esteem & loneliness & maladaptive
& adaptive & aggressive/antisocial behavior, 6.5-17.7 yr old patients,
England
SUBJECT CODES & HEADINGS: 3297 (Neurological Disorders & Brain Damage)

 5/8/7
DIALOG(R)File 11:(c) 1998 Amer. Psychological Assn. All rts. reserv.

01529200   1998-00036-003
Homeostasis, stress, trauma, and adaptation: A neurodevelopmental view of
  childhood trauma.

DESCRIPTORS: *Childhood Development; *Emotional Trauma; *Neurobiology;
  Children; Emotional Adjustment; Homeostasis; Psychological Stress
IDENTIFIERS: neurobiological impact of traumatic experiences on
development, children
SUBJECT CODES & HEADINGS: 2800 (Developmental Psychology)

 5/8/8
DIALOG(R)File 11:(c) 1998 Amer. Psychological Assn. All rts. reserv.

01523141   1997-38757-001
Head injury in children.

DESCRIPTORS: *Brain Damage; *Head Injuries; *Literature Review; *Traumatic
  Brain Injury; Children
IDENTIFIERS: head injury in children, literature review
SUBJECT CODES & HEADINGS: 3297 (Neurological Disorders & Brain Damage)

```
5/8/9
DIALOG(R)File 11:(c) 1998 Amer. Psychological Assn. All rts. reserv.

01522928          1997-38595-016
Predictors of family functioning after traumatic brain injury in children
  and adolescents.

DESCRIPTORS: *Family; *Prediction; *Psychosocial Readjustment; *Traumatic
  Brain Injury; Adolescence; Childhood; Followup Studies; School Age
  Children
IDENTIFIERS: predictors of family functioning after traumatic brain injury,
families of patients aged 6-14 yrs at time of injury, 3- & 6- & 12- & 24-mo
followups
SUBJECT CODES & HEADINGS: 3297 (Neurological Disorders & Brain Damage)
```

These results do not in fact look very good. They are close—at least a few of them are in the general area of head injuries to children—but they do not really seem to focus on the areas the user mentioned in the search request. Document 6 looks pretty good, and a couple of others (9, 7) may also be good. Document 8 looks to be a literature review on head injury in children overall, and may be of interest. We also see a couple of potentially good terms: NEUROPSYCHOLOGICAL ASSESSMENT (in document 2) and HEAD INJURIES (in document 8). Other than these, there is not much else here.

8   Revise and refine the search based on those initial results.

Now you get to play around a bit and try to improve your first search strategy.

If your first result set has *very few* documents, fewer than you expected or wanted, you probably want to get more. Think of what you know now that will produce more documents. You might want to try some of your alternative terms and see if they produce useful results. You might truncate a bit further to the left. You might even think about dropping a concept set (going from three concepts to two, for example), eliminating the least specific one first. Also check for errors in spelling or technique. You might use conceptually broader terms (as we did in going from S1 to S2).

If your first result set has *too many* documents, though, you should think about what you know that will produce fewer documents. Use fewer or narrower terms, truncate further to the right, add a concept (but only if you have a good one to add), or NOT something out (but only if you feel reasonably certain you will not lose useful material this way).

If you have the *wrong* results, you may have made a technique error (using a digit instead of a set number), or you may just have picked poor terms. In the real world, there is no sin in doing some initial searching to see what is available, and then logging off to re-evaluate, find some new terms, talk with the user, and get back in and try again.

We seem to be close, but not quite there. We will now try a couple of terms we spotted from the initial set. This is a tactic called *pearl growing*, and it is a very useful and efficient way of getting new search terms, especially controlled vocabulary terms that the user might not know.

```
?s head injuries

    S6    2323  HEAD INJURIES (1973)

?s neuropsycholog?

    S7   14928  NEUROPSYCHOLOG?

?s s7 and s2 and s4

         14928  S7
          8103  S2
        243078  S4
    S8     238  S7 AND S2 AND S4
```

We are now using our new term for "effects" with our old children/adolescent set, and we get 238 documents. We could look at this set right away, but we may well be getting a number of the same documents we have already seen. We can avoid this by using NOT in a "non-conceptual" way—if we NOT out the previous result set, then we will get just new documents that we did not have in the previous set.

```
?s s8 not s5

           238  S8
           268  S5
    S9     156  S8 NOT S5
```

and we see that there are 156 of these. Let's have a look.

```
?t 9/8/1-7
```

```
 9/8/1
DIALOG(R)File 11:(c) 1998 Amer. Psychological Assn. All rts. reserv.

01532592          1998-07195-006
Evaluation of head trauma.
SERIES TITLE: Human brain function: Assessment and rehabilitation.

DESCRIPTORS: *Head Injuries; *Neuropsychological Assessment; Adults
IDENTIFIERS: neuropsychological concepts & methods in evaluation &
management of head trauma, adults
SUBJECT CODES & HEADINGS: 3297 (Neurological Disorders & Brain Damage);
  2225 (Neuropsychological Assessment)

 9/8/2
DIALOG(R)File 11:(c) 1998 Amer. Psychological Assn. All rts. reserv.

01529581          1998-00573-015
The neuropsychiatric rating schedule: Reliability and validity.

DESCRIPTORS: *Neuropsychological Assessment; *Personality Disorders; *Test
  Reliability; *Test Validity; *Traumatic Brain Injury; Adolescence;
  Adulthood; Childhood; Diagnosis; Organic Brain Syndromes; Rating Scales;
  School Age Children
IDENTIFIERS: reliability & validity of Neuropsychiatric Rating Schedule
interview for diagnosis of organic personality syndrome or personality
change, 6-18 yr olds with traumatic brain injury
SUBJECT CODES & HEADINGS: 2224 (Clinical Psychological Testing); 3290
  (Physical & Somatoform & Psychogenic Disorders)
```

9/8/3

01528403   1998-00645-004
Predicting premorbid neuropsychological functioning following pediatric
  traumatic brain injury.

DESCRIPTORS: *Cognitive Ability; *Neuropsychological Assessment;
  *Predictive Validity; *Reading Skills; *Traumatic Brain Injury; Academic
  Achievement; Childhood; Parents; Racial and Ethnic Differences; School
  Age Children; Socioeconomic Status
IDENTIFIERS: maternal ethnicity & SES & retrospectively rated school
performance & word reading skill, prediction of premorbid neuropsychological
functioning, 6-12 yr olds with orthopedic vs traumatic brain injury
SUBJECT CODES & HEADINGS: 3297 (Neurological Disorders & Brain Damage);
  2225 (Neuropsychological Assessment)

9/8/4

01512432   1997-36680-006
Frontal lobe dysfunction following closed head injury in children: Findings
  from neuropsychology and brain imaging.

DESCRIPTORS: *Brain Disorders; *Head Injuries; *Literature Review;
  *Neuropsychological Assessment; *Tomography; Children; Neuropsychology;
  Prefrontal Cortex
IDENTIFIERS: neurobehavioral sequelae of & neuroimaging techniques for &
performance on neuropsychological tests & prefrontal brain dysfunctions
following closed head-injuries, children, literature review
SUBJECT CODES & HEADINGS: 3297 (Neurological Disorders & Brain Damage)

9/8/5

01507523   1997-43861-011
Predictors and indicators of academic outcome in children 2 years following
  traumatic brain injury.

DESCRIPTORS: *Educational Placement; *Neuropsychological Assessment;
  *Traumatic Brain Injury; Adolescence; Childhood; Followup Studies;
  School Age Children
IDENTIFIERS: neuropsychological predictors & indicators of school place-
ment, 9-15 yr olds with traumatic brain injury, Australia, 24 mo followup
SUBJECT CODES & HEADINGS: 3297 (Neurological Disorders & Brain Damage)

9/8/6

01507522   1997-43861-010
Concept formation and problem-solving following closed head injury in children.

DESCRIPTORS: *Head Injuries; *Neuropsychological Assessment; *Severity
  (Disorders); Adolescence; Adulthood; Childhood; Longitudinal Studies;
  Preschool Age Children; School Age Children
IDENTIFIERS: Twenty Questions Test & Tower of London & Wisconsin Card
Sorting Test performance, 5-18 yr olds with mild vs severe closed head
injury, 36 mo study
SUBJECT CODES & HEADINGS: 3297 (Neurological Disorders & Brain Damage)

9/8/7

01507520   1997-43861-008
Longitudinal neuropsychological outcome in infants and preschoolers with
  traumatic brain injury.

DESCRIPTORS: *Cognitive Ability; *Neuropsychological Assessment; *Traumatic
  Brain Injury; Childhood; Infants; Longitudinal Studies; Preschool Age
  Children; School Age Children; Severity (Disorders)
IDENTIFIERS: neuropsychological outcome, 4 mo to 7 yr olds with severe vs
  mild to moderate traumatic brain injury, 24 mo study
SUBJECT CODES & HEADINGS: 3297 (Neurological Disorders & Brain Damage)

These results are better. A few (3, 6, and 7) look pretty good; the rest are more unfocused. We will look at a few more, in format 6 (titles only):

?t 9/6/8-15

9/6/8
01495176   1996-93914-001
Kognitives Funktionstraining in der neurologischen Rehabilitation von
  Schaedel-Hirntraumen.
TRANSLATED TITLE: Functional cognitive training in neurological
rehabilitation of severe head injury.

9/6/9
01493175   1996-93801-001
Planning skills in head-injured adolescents and their peers.

9/6/10
01488860   1997-95021-100
Polysubstance abuse and traumatic brain injury: Quantitative magnetic
  resonance imaging and neuropsychological outcome in older adolescents
  and young adults.

9/6/11
01487809   1997-95017-369
Performance of children with and without traumatic brain injury on the
  process scoring system for the intermediate category test.

9/6/12
01482579   1997-30097-007
Pediatric neuropsychology.

9/6/13
01481491   1997-09033-004
The role of neuropsychology in educating students with ABI.

9/6/14
01481326   1997-08987-021
Rehabilitation of calculation disorders.

9/6/15
01479639   1997-08457-008
Treating traumatic brain injury in the school: Mandates and methods.
SERIES TITLE: Critical issues in neuropsychology.

The titles are not getting much better. We are still really close, and there must be relevant documents available, but we just have not found the right way to get at them yet. This can be pretty frustrating, but we are not done yet. First, we will review and see what we have done so far.

Viewing Searches (DISPLAY SETS)

This is an extremely helpful command. After one starts creating sets, it gets increasingly difficult to remember what exactly you have done, and especially difficult to remember the numbers of particular sets. Just type **DS** (for **DISPLAY SETS**) to get a listing of all the sets created so far.

```
?ds
     Set   Items   Description
     S1      370   CLOSED HEAD INJURY OR TRAUMATIC BRAIN INJURY
     S2     8103   (BRAIN OR HEAD) AND (TRAUMA? OR INJUR?)
     S3   107312   PSYCHOSOCIAL OR BEHAVIORAL
     S4   243078   CHILDREN OR PEDIATRIC OR ADOLESCENTS
     S5      268   S2 AND S3 AND S4
     S6     2323   HEAD INJURIES (1973)
     S7    14928   NEUROPSYCHOLOG?
     S8      238   S7 AND S2 AND S4
     S9      156   S8 NOT S5
```

> *It pays to try to determine what set numbers you expect before you get online, and then check the numbers as they come up on the screen. I find this very helpful. – GW*

So what now? We used all the terms we got from the user, and there do not seem to be any new ones to pearl grow with. If we think a bit about what we have been getting, and what we have not, we might get an idea. The documents seen so far have been fine in many respects; they are mostly about children and mostly about head injuries, but the other concept, the effects of those injuries, does not seem quite right. And if we look back at the search, we find a word, BEHAVIORAL, that does not seem to be helping much. Maybe if we get rid of it, we might get some better-quality documents. It is worth a try, so we will reconstruct the "effects" concept set and try the descriptor HEAD INJURIES:

```
?s psychosocial or neuropsycholog?
         28364   PSYCHOSOCIAL
         14928   NEUROPSYCHOLOG?
   S10   42859   PSYCHOSOCIAL OR NEUROPSYCHOLOG?
```

and create a new result set

```
?s s6 and s4 and s10
          2323   S6
        243078   S4
         42859   S10
   S11      111   S6 AND S4 AND S10
```

and have a look

?t 11/6/1-15

11/6/1
01532592   1998-07195-006
Evaluation of head trauma.
SERIES TITLE: Human brain function: Assessment and rehabilitation.

11/6/2
01523141   1997-38757-001
Head injury in children.

11/6/3
01512432   1997-36680-006
Frontal lobe dysfunction following closed head injury in children:
   Findings from neuropsychology and brain imaging.

11/6/4
01507522   1997-43861-010
Concept formation and problem-solving following closed head injury in
   children.

11/6/5
01495176   1996-93914-001
Kognitives Funktionstraining in der neurologischen Rehabilitation von
   Schaedel-Hirntraumen.
TRANSLATED TITLE: Functional cognitive training in neurological
rehabilitation of severe head injury.

11/6/6
01493175   1996-93801-001
Planning skills in head-injured adolescents and their peers.

11/6/7
01483092   1997-42970-002
A typology of psychosocial functioning in pediatric closed-head injury.

11/6/8
01482579   1997-30097-007
Pediatric neuropsychology.

11/6/9
01471818   1997-05606-001
Mild head injury in children and adolescents: A review of studies
   (1970-1995).

11/6/10
01471169   1997-05423-010
A review of mild head trauma: I. Meta-analytic review of neuropsychological
   studies.

11/6/11
01470273   1997-05105-003
The influence of age and education on neuropsychological performances of
   persons with mild head injuries.

```
11/6/12
01426537          1996-04605-005
Appraising and managing knowledge: Metacognitive skills after childhood
  head injury.

11/6/13
01426534          1996-04605-002
Dimensions of cognition measured by the Tower of London and other cognitive
  tasks in head-injured children and adolescents.

11/6/14
01411695          1997-85262-001
Applicazione della Batteria Neuropsicologica Luria Nebraska nell'analisi
  funzionale di soggetti con pregresso trauma cranico e coma.
TRANSLATED TITLE: Application of the Luria-Nebraska Neuropsychological
Battery in the functional analysis of subjects with head injury and
subsequent coma.

11/6/15
01411183          1997-06130-003
Age at injury as a predictor of outcome following pediatric head injury:
  A longitudinal perspective.
```

Much better indeed. Many of these titles seem to be really close to what the user wanted, and the whole set just seems better overall. We have lost the "behavioral" aspect, but obviously we just did not have the right term or combination of terms for that, so we might try other ideas later. But we do have a good solid set of documents that the user can evaluate to see what she thinks.

Here's a review of the whole search:

?ds

```
Set    Items    Description
S1       370    CLOSED HEAD INJURY OR TRAUMATIC BRAIN INJURY
S2      8103    (BRAIN OR HEAD) AND (TRAUMA? OR INJUR?)
S3    107312    PSYCHOSOCIAL OR BEHAVIORAL
S4    243078    CHILDREN OR PEDIATRIC OR ADOLESCENTS
S5       268    S2 AND S3 AND S4
S6      2323    HEAD INJURIES (1973)
S7     14928    NEUROPSYCHOLOG?
S8       238    S7 AND S2 AND S4
S9       156    S8 NOT S5
S10    42859    PSYCHOSOCIAL OR NEUROPSYCHOLOG?
S11      111    S6 AND S4 AND S10
```

Leaving the System (LOGOFF)

We conclude the search by logging out of the system. (In a real search, of course, we would type out the whole result set for the user, in format 2 or perhaps format 5). The command to get offline is **LOGOFF**, although lots of other words will also work (e.g., BYE, QUIT, EXIT, OFF).

```
?logoff

26may98 12:23:59 User007659 Session D171.4
                  $0.50    0.033 Hrs File11
                     $0.00 23 Type(s) in Format 6
                     $0.00 16 Type(s) in Format 8
                  $0.00 39 Types
            $0.50  Estimated cost File11
            $0.10  INTERNET
            $0.60  Estimated cost this search
            $2.62  Estimated total session cost 0.145 Hrs.
Logoff: level 98.04.30 D 12:23:59
```

When this message appears, the user is off the system and the search is completed. The sets created are gone, and unless the search was saved (which we will talk about later), it would have to be re-run to get the results back. There is a version of this command, though, called **LOGOFF HOLD**, that allows the user to get off and think about the search for a bit. This version will save your sets for about a half hour, so if the user logs back in with the same account number and password during that time, the sets should still be there.

The Internet

So far, we have talked only about how to search using large-scale, well-established, well-organized commercial information retrieval systems such as DIALOG. There are other such systems (e.g., LEXIS, Dow Jones), and while they are all different, they bear substantial similarity to each other. So, if some other system is going to be used, the commands will be somewhat different from those we have discussed here, but the concepts will be very much the same.

The Internet, though, is a different matter. In this section we will talk about searching using the Internet, focusing on the World Wide Web and emphasizing similarities and differences to what we have talked about already in DIALOG. There is much more to the Internet than the Web; it supports E-mail, discussion groups (listservs and Usenet), and other means of moving information around, but in this context, it makes the most sense to concentrate on the Web. To learn more about the Internet in general, there are a great many books and websites available for you to consult.

The *World Wide Web* (sometimes abbreviated as the WWW; we will call it the Web) has been around since 1989. It was thought that it would be helpful to have an easy way for people to make documents and information available in the distributed, networked environment of the Internet. Until that point, it was very difficult to "publish" on the Net. One could create an archive of files that could be accessed using the FTP file transfer protocol, but that was difficult and nonintuitive. One could build a menu-driven, text-only system called a gopher, but that was also limiting. Allowing people to create documents that could include images, text, and links to other documents (we call this *hypertext*) was the real breakthrough, and the Web has grown to global proportions in a few short years.

What was developed is what network people call a *protocol*, really a set of standards that define what is needed to make a document available on the Web so that it can be retrieved and displayed by other, remote machines. This protocol is called *HTTP*, for *Hypertext Transfer Protocol*, and it is this set of standards that forms the backbone that makes the Web work. Recall the HTML document we saw in the previous chapter. If a computer is connected to the Internet, and the user writes an HTML document and decides to put it in a central location to make it available (this is called *serving* the document, and a computer which does that is a *server*), then anybody else in the world who is similarly connected and has the right software can find it and display it (this computer is called a *client*, and the arrangement is called a "*client-server* architecture") .

There are a few other important things to know about this environment. First, it is often referred to as *distributed* or *decentralized*. This means that there is no single "Internet"; the Internet, such as it is, is made up of connections between thousands of individual networks in schools and businesses all over the world. So there is no center, no central authority (other than the protocols we all agree to), and nobody to really "run" it. Thus, one cannot stop anybody from making anything available (including potentially offensive material), and one cannot force anybody to, for example, include indexing or subject headings.

Second, because the Web was developed at a time when lots of people had access to computers, it was taken for granted that any search mechanisms that would work in this environment had to be easy to use and take little if any time to learn. When DIALOG was started in the 1970s, computing was dominated by large, expensive mainframe computers, so that not many people would or could use them. Thus, DIALOG is a large, centralized system, and its command structure, while very sophisticated and permitting powerful searching, is intricate and difficult to learn.

Further, the HTML structure was never really intended to be a help in organizing and searching information, as was the structure of a bibliographic record. So, while we can take advantage of that structure in searching, as we saw in the previous chapter, it will be in different ways than in DIALOG. Typically we will be able to search based on what something *is* (an image, a link, an address) rather than what it *means* (an abstract, a subject heading, an author).

Also, DIALOG contracts with producers of commercial databases to make them available. This information is professionally produced, edited, organized, and indexed, and users can have a great deal of confidence in what they find there. The Internet is not like that. There is quite a bit of interesting and worthwhile material freely available on the Net, and the amount and quality of the "good stuff" is increasingly rising. But there is an enormous amount of what might politely be called trivia and things that are downright wrong, and it all sits there together. There is no "collection development" or "selection" on the Net—it just happens. Users and searchers, therefore, have to be much more vigilant in reading and evaluating the results of searches to decide whether what they get is worth anything.

So the picture that emerges is one of a world where there is a very large collection of "documents" (but certainly not as large as the entirety of DIALOG-accessible databases) available to computers all over the world, searchable in full text but with somewhat cruder search techniques, and using systems that require no training and make few demands on the users.

To further illustrate these points, let us go back through the eight steps we outlined above, commenting on how they might best work in the Web, and discussing a few specific search engines. Keep in mind that the network environment is very volatile; not only can documents and entire resources change without a moment's notice, but search systems can change and add new features and new ones can arise very quickly as well. It is entirely possible that much of the specific discussion of features and technique that follows will be radically different from what is available when you read this.

What is important, though, is the *concepts* we are looking at. If one understands how to think about searching and take advantage of the searching environment, be it DIALOG or the Web or whatever comes next (and something *will* come next), all will be well.

1   Read the query.

1a   Listen to the query.

1b   Understand the query.

2   Identify the major concepts in the query.

There is certainly nothing wrong with these steps. Understanding exactly what is being sought does not get any less important in the Internet environment. What might get *more* important is understanding exactly what might be found there. Although the information available there is getting better, it is probably never going to be of the same quality or comprehensiveness (at least not while things are still free) as in a commercial search system. The best way to know what is out there, as with any retrieval system or collection, is experience, so an investment in time just to browse will certainly pay off.

3   Identify potential terms to correspond to those concepts.

Term selection is still part of the game, but because there is very little of what we would think of as indexing or subject description, and no consistency whatsoever, it will be harder to find "standard" or "preferred" terms. (We will talk more about the uses and benefits of controlled vocabulary in the next chapter.)

It is also worth mentioning that one has to take into account the style of writing involved in the documents being searched. We will say this again when we discuss full-text searching in DIALOG later; newspaper files, for example, will be searched differently from more academic records. The same thing applies here. You will find scholarly papers and children's stories and everything in between all mixed together, along with many things in languages other than English. Again, one will gain a better appreciation for this as one gains experience with the environment, but keep an eye out for writing style and especially word choice.

4   Select alternative (narrower, broader, or related) terms to use
     if the original strategy needs help.

Still a good idea as well, but many of these will not appear in most circumstances. This is because the searching environment is significantly constrained, compared with what we have seen in DIALOG.

5   Determine logical (Boolean) relationships between terms.

Boolean searching is possible in most Web search engines, and it will work in much the same way as we have seen in DIALOG. OR can be used to search for one or more related terms, AND to require all terms to be present, and NOT to exclude terms, and most systems will allow you to use parentheses to affect the order in which these operators are interpreted, as we also saw in DIALOG.

Internet Search Engine Technique

There are a couple of important variations in the use of Boolean operators, however. Some systems require the use of AND NOT rather than simply NOT. Strictly speaking, from a set-theory point of view, this is correct, but commercial systems typically do not make the user do this. Be aware of it, though, because leaving AND out of that expression means searching on the word "not" rather than using NOT as a command.

Some systems also allow the use of the + and - signs in searching. Putting a + in front of a word or phrase requires it to be in documents (like AND); putting a - there excludes it (like NOT). So a search such as this is possible in AltaVista:

```
+noir +film -"pinot noir"
```

which would retrieve documents with both the words "film" and "noir" but not the phrase "pinot noir."

This illustrates another technique: the use of quotes to define a phrase. Although there are almost never subject headings or descriptors in Net documents, the search engines are able to retrieve based on phrases anywhere in those documents. (We'll discuss how to do this in DIALOG later.) Therefore, a search such as

```
"stupid pet tricks"
```

in Infoseek will retrieve documents with those three words exactly in that order.

Capitalization is an issue on the Net. Notice that we never discussed it in DIALOG; that is because all characters are treated as capitals regardless of how they appear in original documents. That is not the case on the Internet. Typically, searches are conducted in lowercase, but if you wish to search on a word or phrase that contains capitals, you may do so. Thus, searching on

```
Turkey
```

in AltaVista will retrieve precisely that—the word "Turkey," capitalized. Many such documents will likely be about the country Turkey, but some will be references to other kinds of turkeys where the word is somewhere capitalized, as in the first word of a sentence. It will not, though, retrieve documents where the word "turkey" appears but is never capitalized. This might be useful in a number of situations, including of course searching on proper nouns.

There is one large difference between searching on the Internet and in commercial systems that dramatically affects the way in which one searches. So far, search engines in the Net world do not allow one to create and manipulate sets.

> Now, of course, since we've said this, the day the book goes to press, some system will announce this as a new feature! – JWJ

Every search in the Net is a one-shot affair. One cannot create separate concept sets and combine them into a result set. This is not as dramatic as it sounds; one can certainly create a sophisticated search in a single statement and then redo it when results have been reviewed, but it is certainly a different way of thinking about constructing and performing searches.

Given the nature of the Net and the information found there, it is often best to do shorter and more specific searches anyway. One is more likely to find searches like

```
fish AND ("America Online" or AOL)
```

on the Web than the extended strategy used for the head injury search on DIALOG.

6 Begin the search.

In discussing searching in commercial services, our first piece of advice was to search on the most specific concept block first to give some idea of how many items one is likely to retrieve. That advice is also useful here. Because it is not possible to create and manipulate sets, and because many other pieces of technique might not be available, it makes sense to search on the most specific aspects of what is being sought. Decide on the narrowest terms, the ones that will retrieve the fewest things that are still of interest.

Subject Directories

There is an exception to this strategy. If a group of documents is being sought on a particular topic, it might be more productive to use a service like Yahoo!, the Argus Clearinghouse, or the Internet Public Library (IPL).

If, say, one is trying to find documents about the TV show *ER*, one might think about using Yahoo!, searching through its general-to-specific menus on Entertainment, Television, Shows and so on, down to the category for *ER* to find all the sites it knows about. Searching on "ER" alone would be difficult if not impossible—some search engines will not search on anything shorter than three or four letters.

Other sites that serve to collect and organize related information resources might be helpful in similar ways. The IPL (http://www.ipl.org) can point visitors to sites about philosophy, for example, in its Ready Reference Collection, selecting ones of high quality and useful content, describing each, giving author and publisher information, and collecting them to make them easier to find and access.

The guides to subject-oriented resources in the Argus Clearinghouse (http://www. clearinghouse.net) are an excellent way to know more about what is available in many topics, and act in many ways as pathfinders do in libraries. Each guide is evaluated on a series of criteria, including the resources involved, the guide's design and organizational scheme, and evaluative techniques it uses.

Both of these resources do some of the things that libraries and librarians usually do (and, in fact, both are staffed by people with library educations and backgrounds): that is, find, evaluate, describe, and organize information resources so they can more easily be found and used.

Ranking of Retrieved Documents

In DIALOG, we said that documents would be retrieved in reverse order of input to the database, so one gets the most recent ones first. That is not the case here. Typically, Internet search engines use some algorithm to rank the documents according to how closely they think they match your query. This sounds like a great method, but it is not without problems, and it does not always work the way the searcher necessarily wants it to or thinks it should.

AltaVista will raise the score of a document (i.e., put it towards the top of the list) if the words searched are in the first few words of the document, if the query words are "close to one another" in the document, and if those words appear more than once. Infoseek uses very similar criteria, but rather than looking at proximity, it will score words higher if they are relatively rare in the database of all documents—in other words, uniqueness helps.

> *The use of these kinds of rating schemes has led to a fascinating phenomenon: trying to influence how search engines rank pages. For a while, people could simply add hundreds of occurrences of words and phrases to their pages to inflate their scores when those words are searched. Sometimes those words were relevant to the actual content, sometimes not. The search engine people got wise and changed their procedures, and then people came up with new ideas. Amazing stuff, really—a cottage industry devoted to trying to "fix" information retrieval. Who knew our field could be so intriguing? – JWJ*

Excite says that it is able to search by concept rather than simply by words, and can look "for ideas closely linked to the words in your query." In their description of how to use their service, they say "Our search engine can figure out that relationships exist between words and concepts—that the term 'elderly people' is related to 'senior citizens.' It learns about related concepts from the documents themselves and learns more from each new document it indexes."

When it presents results, it also presents the opportunity to do a new search for "more like this" for each document to find what it thinks are similar documents.

In no case do you get any further information on what actually goes on. Ranking of documents in relation to queries is an old idea from information retrieval research but has only recently been implemented in commercial systems because it requires yet more overhead, and results have been less than perfect.

> *It is perhaps worth noting that DIALOG-type systems are binary—records either match the search strategy, or they do not. The Web, on the other hand, is a partial match system. The search retrieves anything that matches your search statement or any part of your search statement, so postings are large. And don't expect that the document you consider to be most relevant will necessarily be output first, or even towards the top of your results! – GW*

The increased investment and attention that the Internet has brought to the world of information retrieval means that ideas such as these will probably appear with some regularity. This could well be a major boon to the search for information, and these systems do work reasonably well at present. It will, however, take some time before they can do the kind of reasoning and interpretation we take for granted in people.

Truncation

There are a few more mundane details about searching on the Web to be discussed. The first is truncation. Most systems permit it, but in different ways. AltaVista uses the * as the truncation operator, either at the end of words or in the middle, and in all cases it will match an arbitrary number of characters. So here one can search on

        col*r

to get both "color" and "colour" (but also "collector" and "collider"; perhaps

        colo*r

would be better) and

```
antiq*
```

will get "antique," "antiques," "antiquities," "antiquated," and so on.

Lycos, on the other hand, will automatically interpret words given it as being truncated, unless it is told otherwise. So a search on

```
match
```

here will get "match," "matches," "matching," "matchless," and so on. To get only "match" (to stop truncation) the word must end with a period:

```
match.
```

Searching Using Structure

There is structure in HTML documents, as we saw in the last chapter, and some systems allow you to take advantage of it in searching. Because the kind of structure here is different from that we find in bibliographic records (remember it is used here to describe the internal components of a document, not the fields that describe a document), the searching will also be different. But HTML structure can also be of great help.

AltaVista permits searching on a number of these parts of documents, including the title tag, image tags, links to other documents, and the URL address of a page. Therefore, searches like these are possible:

```
title:"ESPNET" and "Steffi Graf"
```

to get pages with ESPNET in the title and the phrase "Steffi Graf" anywhere

```
image:cow
```

will get things with "cow" in an image tag, not necessarily images of cows!

```
link:albany.edu
```

will get pages with at least one link to any Web site at the University at Albany.

```
echinacea and url:*.org
```

will get documents containing the word "echinacea" that come from not-for-profit organizations.

7 Have a look at a few documents.

One typically has less control over what is displayed when the results of searches on the Web are reviewed. Rather than seeing simple counts of number of hits (although AltaVista permits this), a list of the first 10 or so documents will come up. It is possible to ask for more at a time and to indicate how much information to see about each: the document's title (from the title tag, which many documents do not use), the URL, and perhaps its size, when it was last visited by the search engine, and a line or two from the document.

In many cases, it will be possible to make initial decisions about which of the retrieved documents will be of interest, but these documents almost always will have to be inspected more closely, which is easy to do by simply clicking on the link.

8   Revise and refine the search based on those initial results.

Many search engines provide, along with the list of retrievals, an active window showing the search entered. This makes it easier to make changes to that search or simply clear out the window and try again, without having to go back to the main screen. This is rather different from the process we suggested for DIALOG searching but is a convenience for the searcher.

As we mentioned previously, this is a fluid and rapidly changing area. The best way to know what kinds of searching are possible and the techniques to use is to look at the documentation the service provides: help pages, sample searches, and so on. Knowing what needs to be done and experience in searching in all kinds of environments will greatly assist in understanding what is available and how to use it most effectively.

Additional Reading

Bates, Marcia J. (1989), "The Design of Browsing and Berrypicking Techniques for the Online Search Interface," *Online Review* 13(5): 407–24.

—— (1987), "How to Use Information Search Tactics Online," *Online* 11(3): 47–54.

—— (1984), "The Fallacy of the Perfect Thirty-Item Search," *Reference Quarterly* 24(1): 43–50.

—— (1979), "Information Search Tactics," *Journal of the American Society for Information Science* 30(4): 205–14.

Diaz, Karen R. (Spring 1997), "User Success in a Networked Environment," *RQ* 36(5): 393–407.

Hawkins, D. T. (January/February 1996), "Hunting, Grading, Browsing: A Model for Online Information Retrieval," *Online* 20(1): 71–73.

Quint, Barbara (1991), "Inside a Searcher's Mind: The Seven Stages of an Online Search, Part 1," *Online* 15(3): 13–19.

—— (1991), "Inside a Searcher's Mind: The Seven Stages of an Online Search, Part 2," *Online* 15(4): 28–38.

Schack, E. O., and M. B. Schack (1989), "Online Data Retrieval Using Boolean Logic," In *Online and CD-ROM Databases in School Libraries: Readings* (Englewood, CO: Libraries Unlimited): 99–101.

Tenopir, Carol (April 1, 1997), "Learning from the Experts," *Library Journal*: 37–38.

7 USING CONTROLLED VOCABULARY

The search we conducted in the previous chapter on the after effects of traumatic brain injury in children was somewhat successful. We were able to retrieve a reasonable set of documents, many of which seemed to be relevant to the user's query. However, it also seemed as though there must be good documents we were not able to get, and many of the ones we did retrieve were not really appropriate (including a document on the use of a "rating scale of attentional behaviour"). And yet we tried many good terms from the user, including an alternative or two, and even tried pearl growing terms from good documents.

In fact, those terms seemed to help quite a bit; it is the use of terms like that which we will discuss in this chapter. The use of *controlled vocabulary* terms—subject headings, descriptors, index terms—can often aid in database searching when they are available. We will talk about why they can be so useful and in what kinds of situations, why they sometimes do not work so well, and some techniques for their use in searching on DIALOG. We will conclude, once again, with a look at how controlled vocabulary searching works in the Internet environment.

Why Controlled Vocabulary Searching?

What do you call people whose profession is to help people learn? Are they teachers? Instructors? Faculty? Educators? Tutors? Docents? Professors? Lecturers?

How do you refer to systems that help people find items in a library? Catalogs? Online catalogs? OPACs? Online public access catalogs? Card catalogs?

Who wrote *Huckleberry Finn*? Mark Twain? Samuel Clemens? Samuel Longhorn Clemens? Twain, Mark?

Where would you look in a catalog for the author who wrote *One Hundred Years of Solitude*? Under Marquez, Gabriel Garcia? Or Garcia Marquez, Gabriel?

What do you think of when you read the word "mercury"? A planet? A car? A god? A metal? A thermometer?

These are all illustrations of the need for and advantages of controlled vocabularies, and their cousin, name authority files. Both of these have been developed by librarians over the last hundred years or so as ways of making it easier, more often than not, to find items in a collection.

> *Although we will focus primarily in this chapter on "controlled vocabulary" in the sense of subject headings for concepts like "teacher" and "metal," the use of name authority lists for proper names is closely related, and a number of databases have both. Sometimes they are separate fields, sometimes they are combined, but they work in quite similar ways. – JWJ*

There are two related problems at work here. Remember what we said before—we want to look for concepts but are forced to search for words. Those words, however, sometimes let us down.

First of all, there are often several words or phrases for any given concept. This is the teacher/faculty/instructor issue, and it is called *synonymy*. The inverse problem is *ambiguity* or *polysemy*—more than one concept for the same "word" or series of characters (e.g., Mercury the planet and Mercury the god).

The assembly and appropriate use of controlled vocabularies can assist searchers in both of these situations. When an indexer processes a document, she selects from among a set of possible terms for any given concept. If the preferred term is FACULTY, she assigns that to the document, and subsequent searchers use that term later to retrieve documents about "people who teach." By the same token, a decision is made that subject headings such as MERCURY (MYTHOLOGY) and MERCURY (PLANET) will be used to resolve ambiguity.

There are several advantages to the use of controlled vocabularies in both indexing and searching:

- It facilitates the *gathering of like items*: assembling a set of documents about people in medical school by using and searching on the term MEDICAL STUDENTS.

- It helps with *comprehensiveness*. If the indexing is consistent, there is greater confidence that all or nearly all of the documents about medical students have been retrieved by using that term.

- It also helps with the *precision* of results. Searching on MEDICAL STUDENTS will not get documents about law students, dental students, graduate students, and so on, unless those documents are also about medical students.

- It can help *broaden understanding* of the topic, either by the searcher or the user. Looking for appropriate terms can often help searchers (or users, especially if they are not that familiar with the subject area) to select better search terms, refine strategy, and generate new ideas for terms to use.

It is by no means the case that using controlled vocabulary is a panacea, and we will see in the following chapter where and how other techniques might be chosen, but it is often a good start for most searches.

Thesaurus Structure and Use

So where do we find these terrific terms? Many database producers compile and distribute lists of subject terms that they use for indexing the documents in their files and that we can use for searching. These lists are usually called *thesauri*. Most people are probably familiar with the kind of thesauri we use in writing, like *Roget's*, which are collections of synonyms and antonyms for words in the English language. Thesauri for databases are somewhat similar but much richer. They contain not only synonyms but also information about the relationships between terms. In addition, they aid in selecting the best terms to search for a given concept.

As an example, let's look at one such controlled vocabulary—the *Thesaurus of ERIC Descriptors*, produced by the federally funded Educational Resources Information Center (ERIC). ERIC is the producer of the most comprehensive and most-often-used database in the field of education, also called ERIC, although it covers a number of other areas, including information and library studies. Much of the discussion that follows is specific to this thesaurus. Thesauri can differ greatly. For comparison's sake, we will look at another one briefly before we leave the issue, but if the reader really want to know how a thesaurus (and, thus, a database) is created and used, the best bet is to read the explanatory material included with a thesaurus. Experience doesn't hurt either—use a few thesauri and become skilled at figuring out how unfamiliar ones work!

A look through the *ERIC Thesaurus* gives some examples of how a controlled vocabulary could be useful in searching. If information about drunken driving is being sought, for example, the term used to index this concept in ERIC documents is DRIVING WHILE INTOXICATED. A search for documents about discontinuation of programs would use the term PROGRAM TERMINATION (as opposed to PROGRAM DISCONTINUANCE, PROGRAM ELIMINATION, PROGRAM PHASEOUT, or TERMINATION OF PROGRAMS). If the preferred term to refer to materials that are used in programmed instruction is required, one would find that from 1966 to 1980, the term was PROGRAMED MATERIALS (note the spelling difference), but that it was changed to PROGRAMED INSTRUCTIONAL MATERIALS in March 1980. In each of these instances, searching on the preferred term from the controlled vocabulary will give an increased chance of retrieving documents that are on the topic of interest.

Let's look at a specific example of a search term from ERIC and examine its entry in the thesaurus. The term we choose is INFORMATION SCIENTISTS, and this is what the entry looks like:

```
INFORMATION SCIENTISTS          Jul. 1971
      CIJE: 230   RIE: 182      GC: 710
  SN  Individuals who observe, measure, and describe the behavior
      of information, as well as those who organize information
      and provide services for its use.
  UF  Information Brokers
      Information Professionals
      Information Specialists
  NT  Librarians
  NT  Search Intermediaries
  BT  Professional Personnel
  RT  Information Industry
  RT  Information Science
      Information Science Education
      Library Associations
```

Let's take this document line by line and find out what it means, beginning with

INFORMATION SCIENTISTS   *Jul. 1971*

This first line gives the preferred term (INFORMATION SCIENTISTS) and the date it was added to the thesaurus (July 1971). The *ERIC* file dates back to July 1966, so that is the earliest possible date. Some terms are ambiguous because they could be used in more than one way, and so they have a parenthetical component to resolve the ambiguity. An example is INEQUALITY. The term INEQUALITY could refer to the generic notion of inequality, specific inequalities (e.g., educational, social, economic), or even the mathematical concept of inequality. The descriptor INEQUALITIES was added in 1970 but was used inconsistently and was therefore removed in 1980. Alternatives were proposed, such as EQUAL EDUCATION, DISADVANTAGED, or a series of descriptors referring to social, ethnic, sexual or racial bias and discrimination. But what about mathematical inequality? When INEQUALITIES was removed in 1980, a new descriptor was added for just that concept: INEQUALITY (MATHEMATICS). The parenthetical part of the descriptor is used to remove the ambiguity about the kind of inequality. The point of this seemingly elaborated discussion is this: When one wants to use a term such as this in searching, one must remember that the parenthetical is an essential part of the descriptor. If one searches just on

?s inequality

    S8   972   INEQUALITY

one will get each occurrence of the word "inequality" in all four Basic Index fields. But if one wishes to use the much more specific descriptor, one must search with

?s inequality (mathematics)

    S9   11   INEQUALITY (MATHEMATICS) (MATHEMATICAL EXPRESSION OR
                            PROPOSITION C

which will retrieve only documents indexed with that term. Be sure to include a space before the first parenthesis—the system is very picky. If the space is omitted, the result is

?s inequality(mathematics)

    S10   0   INEQUALITY(MATHEMATICS)

We will go back to the next line on our entry for INFORMATION SCIENTISTS:

    CIJE: 230   RIE: 182   GC: 710

This line lists the number of postings and group code information. *ERIC* is really two databases: a collection of citations to journal articles in the educational area (called the *Current Index to Journals in Education* in the printed version and identified by EJ accession numbers in the database), and a collection of citations to other kinds of documents, such as doctoral dissertations, technical reports, test banks, conference papers, bibliographies, and guides. (The printed version of the second database is called *Resources in Education*, and the records are identified with ED accession numbers in the database). This line in the thesaurus tells how many documents in each of these two collections had been indexed under the given term at the time of publication of this edition of the thesaurus. This can be of help in deciding whether or not to use a term—if it has significantly more or fewer postings, its use may need to be rethought. For INFORMATION SCIENTISTS, we see that as of 1995 (for the 13th edition of the thesaurus), it had been used for 170 journal articles and 162 "other" documents.

The "group code" gives the broadest category to which that term belongs. INFORMATION SCIENTISTS is in Group 710, INFORMATION/COMMUNICATION SYSTEMS. This piece of information is not particularly helpful in searching. Look at the next line.

```
SN   Individuals who observe, measure, and describe the behavior of
     information, as well as those who organize information and
     provide services for its use.
```

SN stands for *scope note* and gives a brief description of the term as it is used in ERIC. Not all terms have scope notes, but such notes can be very useful, especially if the subject field is unfamiliar or when trying to choose between two terms that appear to be very similar. This is perhaps the major fault with the ERIC thesaurus. There is frequently a multitude of terms with overlapping or similar connotations. Without scope notes it is difficult for the beginning searcher (and often the experienced searcher) to choose the most appropriate term to search. Personal experience suggests that ERIC is particularly frustrating in this respect. The scope notes are really aimed at the indexers, but as searchers we can use them, too. They often include notes about the interpretation of terms, warnings against the use of terms in certain ways, and recommendations regarding other potential terms.

```
UF   Information Brokers
     Information Professionals
     Information Specialists
```

UF stands for *Use For*. This indicates that INFORMATION SCIENTISTS is the preferred term for this concept, and that these other three are not to be used. In fact, if one was to look in the thesaurus under any of these, one would see

Information Brokers
use   INFORMATION SCIENTISTS

This is a reciprocal reference, rather like a *see* reference in a library catalog. Having looked up the nonpreferred term, one is referred to the correct form of entry. In some cases these are old terms that have been replaced by newer ones. For example,

College Teachers (1967 1980)
use   COLLEGE FACULTY

This means that from 1967 to 1980, the descriptor was COLLEGE TEACHERS; in 1980 it was changed to COLLEGE FACULTY. However, old documents will not immediately be reindexed, so if one wants to search on a concept with old and new descriptors and get documents going back to the beginning of the database, both terms may need to be ORed together. When databases are reloaded, though, they are usually reindexed, so this is only a temporary problem.

```
NT   Librarians
     Search Intermediaries
```

Here is where we get to the interesting stuff. NT stands for **Narrower Term**. Terms in the ERIC Thesaurus (and many others) are organized in hierarchies of specificity. Just as documents vary in how much detail they give on a particular topic, so do descriptors vary. In this instance, we are told that LIBRARIANS and SEARCH INTERMEDIARIES are narrower terms than INFORMATION SCIENTISTS. If a document is strictly about "librarians," it will be indexed using that term. If it is broader, though, and talks about "information professionals," it will probably be indexed with INFORMATION SCIENTISTS. In searching, be aware of how narrowly the client's search is focused and what kinds of terms best reflect that level of specificity. Also, in perusing the thesaurus, one may find that one has entered a hierarchy at too high or too low a level; the listing of hierarchies will give a better idea of where one should be. It may be that the best search strategy encompasses many different levels of the hierarchy, as in:

```
?s librarians or information scientists
    BT   Professional Personnel
```

BT stands for *Broader Term* and is the opposite of NT. In this particular case, PROFESSIONAL PERSONNEL is unlikely to be much help for a search on information scientists. In some circumstances, though, a broader term might indeed be helpful.

```
    RT   Information Industry
         Information Science
         Information Science Education
         Library Associations
```

The final part of the display is RT, the *Related Terms*. These are terms that are not part of the hierarchy—neither narrower or broader—for this particular descriptor, but that are related (at least in somebody's opinion), and that may also be of use in searching. When constructing a search strategy, one may find that some of the terms in the RT grouping look useful. Notice that BTs, NTs and RTs are all types of the familiar *see also* reference from the library catalog. They are suggestions of other terms that may be useful for a search. If one of them turns out to be a better term than the original choice, turn to the entry for it and start all over.

A caveat: After a while, all terms start to look good. Do not spend more than a few minutes looking through the thesaurus for descriptors, or you will select too many terms, including some real losers, and the search will not be as effective. Find two or three, or maybe only one, that look good, and see if there are maybe a couple of others that look possible and hold them in reserve. But the longer one looks, the more one will find, and that is typically counter-productive. Do not be cavalier about term selection, but too much of a good thing is undesirable here, especially if some of the terms have lots of postings.

Using these print thesauri can be a big help in planning searches. There may be another, additional aid, though. In DIALOG, many databases have online versions of their controlled vocabularies to consult while conducting searches. We will see how to do this shortly.

As we have said, all databases and all thesauri are different. Here is a look at a couple of extracts from the *Thesaurus of Psychological Index Terms*, the controlled vocabulary for *Psychological Abstracts* and its online counterpart, PsycINFO. First, how would we go about searching for information scientists? There is no listing under that term, but there is this:

```
Information Specialists 88
PN 4                              SC 25338
   B  Professional Personnel/ 78
   N  Librarians 88
   R  Information 67
```

This looks familiar. The first line shows the descriptor name and the year in which it was added to the thesaurus (1988). The second line gives postings information (PN for postings notes) showing that four documents had been indexed with this term by June 1994, for the 7th edition. The second line also shows the unique code number (SC for subject code) assigned to this descriptor, which may also be used as a search term. LIBRARIANS is a narrower term, INFORMATION is a related term, and PROFESSIONAL PERSONNEL is a broader term. The slash after this last term indicates that it is an "array term," which represents conceptually broad areas and is used in indexing and searching when a more specific term is not available.

Because this database covers a different, although often related, subject area from ERIC, the terms it uses and the level of detail explored are different. Take, as an example, the term SCHIZOPHRENIA. This is a descriptor in both databases, but the entries are quite different. First, in ERIC:

```
SCHIZOPHRENIA                          Jul. 1966
     CIJE: 460      RIE: 127      GC: 230
  UF  Dementia Praecox
  BT  Psychosis
  RT  Autism
      Echolalia
      Emotional Disturbances
      Paranoid Behavior
```

Compare this with the *PsycINFO* entry:

```
Schizophrenia 67
PN 16934                   SC 45440
   UF Chronic Schizophrenia
      Dementia Praecox
      Process Schizophrenia
      Pseudopsychopathic Schizophrenia
      Reactive Schizophrenia
      Schizophrenia (Residual Type)
      Simple Schizophrenia
   B  Psychosis 67
   N  Acute Schizophrenia 73
      Catatonic Schizophrenia 73
      Childhood Schizophrenia 67
      Hebephrenic Schizophrenia 73
      Paranoid Schizophrenia 67
      Schizophreniform Disorder 94
      Undifferentiated Schizophrenia 73
   R  Anhedonia 85
      Catalepsy 73
      Expressed Emotion 91
      Fragmentation (Schizophrenia) 73
      Schizoaffective Disorder 94
      Schizoid Personality 73
      Schizotypal Personality 91
```

This display shows more postings, many more detailed terms, and possible alternative terms. It could be quite helpful in refining the search, especially through specifying exactly what type or form of schizophrenic disorder is desired. Of course, a search on schizophrenia *per se* would be much more productive in PsycINFO than in ERIC, but a search on the impact of schizophrenia on the learning process might yield equally good results in either database. This gives an idea of the challenges involved in database selection, which we will return to in chapter 10.

At this point, be aware of the following:

1. Not all databases have controlled vocabularies. Some database producers do not have the resources or inclination to produce thesauri, and thus none exist. Other types of databases (e.g., numeric, financial, reference) have no controlled vocabulary because it would make no sense.

2. Not all controlled vocabularies are useful. Some, such as the *Thesaurus of ERIC Descriptors* and the *Thesaurus of Psychological Index Terms*, are quite thorough and helpful in searching. Others are barely more than word lists (e.g., the thesaurus for *The Philosopher's Index*). Quite a number of databases use the *Library of Congress List of Subject Headings (LCSH)* in place of a thesaurus (e.g., *Magazine Index* or *Books in Print ®*). This suggests that both indexing languages and indexing standards vary greatly among different databases.

3. Not all indexing is done perfectly. In one's experience in searching, one will undoubtedly find index terms that will confuse, amuse, or infuriate.

Mechanics of Controlled Vocabulary Searching

The DIALOG commands we saw in the previous chapter for creating and manipulating sets and truncating and displaying records are basic techniques, but there are more commands and ways of searching, some of which are particularly applicable for controlled vocabulary searching. We will present several ways of searching using controlled vocabulary: searching bound descriptors, searching for an individual word in the descriptor field, and searching for a single-word descriptor, searching for major descriptors, and the *explode* feature of DIALOG.

Searching Bound Descriptors

If, after rummaging through the thesaurus, one or more terms to search have been found, simply enter them as a search statement. For example:

```
?s choral music or rock music or vocal music
            117    CHORAL MUSIC (MUSIC INTENDED FOR GROUP SINGING)
             73    ROCK MUSIC
            276    VOCAL MUSIC (MUSICAL COMPOSITIONS WRITTEN FOR VOICES,
                   EIT...
      S11   430    CHORAL MUSIC OR ROCK MUSIC OR VOCAL MUSIC
```

Thus, for *bound descriptors* (as these intact multiple-word descriptors are often called), we merely search on the phrase as given in the thesaurus. Recall that this will only work in the descriptor field, or in some other field that is phrase-indexed. These phrases were entered into the inverted file as phrases as well as individual words, so a search on the word ROCK would retrieve the 73 documents above, but also any other use of the word ROCK in any field of the database.

In the search in the previous chapter, we had difficulty finding documents about the behavioral aspects of head injury in children. Finding things about neuropsychological and psychosocial aspects was easier, but we never quite got our hands on their behavioral aspects. And yet, you would think that a database focusing on psychology would have a great many documents about behavior.

In fact, it does, and that was part of the problem we had with that aspect of the search, though it was not obvious at the time. We searched on the word BEHAVIORAL correctly, but quite broadly—in titles and abstracts as well as in the descriptor field. We got more than 60,000 hits on that term, and the result sets of which it was a part were all broad and unfocused. (And that was using BEHAVIORAL; had we searched broadly on the word BEHAVIOR, we would get about 212,000 hits, and truncating on BEHAVIOR? gets more than 250,000!) We need some way of making that search a bit more specific so it will get more useful results.

There are a great many descriptors about "behavior" in the PsycINFO database, and we could pick our way through them all, finding a handful that appear to be most helpful. Or, we could take an easier path. Wouldn't it be nice to be able to find all the places that the word BEHAVIOR appears in the descriptor field? That means that the indexers of those documents thought that there was some "behavioral" component present in each, which is at least more specificity than we have with the really broad BEHAVIORAL search.

There is a way to do precisely that, using a DIALOG technique called *qualifiers*.

Using Qualifiers (Suffix Searching)

The search statement

```
?s alcohol

    S1      3228      ALCOHOL
```

searches for ALCOHOL in all the Basic Index fields. However, we may wish to search for the word only in the title field. We could use the statement

```
?s alcohol/ti

    S2      1139      ALCOHOL/TI
```

to increase specificity. We *qualify* a search statement with a suffix, using the slash and the field codes of the field or fields we wish to search in, such as:

```
                    S TERM/field code(s)
```

The most often used codes for bibliographic databases are AB (abstract), DE (descriptor), ID (identifier), and TI (title), but there are many others, especially in nonbibliographic files. Other databases may have other fields and codes in their Basic Indexes, so check the bluesheets carefully. One could also use the statement

```
?s computer?/ab

    S3      32375     COMPUTER?/AB
```

This statement searches for the word stem COMPUTER in the abstract field only and will retrieve COMPUTER, COMPUTERS, COMPUTERIZATION, and so on in that field only.

We can specify more than one field to search in, as in this example:

```
?s frog/ti,de

     S4       72      FROG/TI,DE
```

This statement searches for the word FROG in either the title or the descriptor field. It is the logical equivalent of

```
?s frog/ti or frog/de

              25      FROG/TI
              54      FROG/DE
     S5       72      FROG/TI OR FROG/DE
```

This technique will only work on Basic Index fields. To search in other fields, such as author, journal name, or publication year, we use prefix searching, which will be described in chapter 8.

Qualifiers may be used also with sets that have already been created, as in the following example:

```
?s newspaper

     S6     3940      NEWSPAPER

?s s6/ti

     S7      940      S6/TI
```

The first statement produces S6, which contains all documents with the word NEWSPAPER in any Basic Index field and has 3,940 documents. Using *post-qualification* (as it is called in this instance of qualifying a previously existing set), we limit the search to the title field only and so create a new set S7, with only 940 documents.

This illustrates one of the primary uses of qualifying—to improve the quality of terms or sets by focusing them. Often a document is more likely to be about a subject if that term is in the title or descriptor fields rather than in the abstract, a longer and often less specific indicator of content. Probably the most frequently used qualifier will be DESCRIPTOR (or sometimes TITLE), as in:

```
?s cats/ti,de
```

because these two fields will provide the most relevant retrievals. Using qualifiers is a good way to narrow searches, because one can check retrieval at each step. Back to our music terms.

```
?s music/de

     S14    5537      MUSIC/DE
```

will retrieve any document with the word MUSIC anywhere in the descriptor field. That would include all the documents from the search statements above (ROCK MUSIC, CHORAL MUSIC, etc.) and also any indexed with MUSIC ACTIVITIES, APPLIED MUSIC, MUSIC EDUCATION, or even just MUSIC.

Why would anyone want to do this? Sometimes, as with "behavior," one may wish to search on a broad concept that has many descriptors associated with it, all of which have a certain word in common. If there was interest in documents that discussed the use of music in foreign-language education, a search on the music concept might need to be very broad. There are many good descriptors—perhaps too many. MUSIC itself is only used for documents generically about music but not for a document about, say, Japanese music, which would be indexed with ORIENTAL MUSIC. (Of course, this document would be entered in the Basic Index under both ORIENTAL and MUSIC. This is called *double posting*.) One may decide, then, to provisionally accept any document with any descriptor that includes the word MUSIC. This is a good initial strategy but will produce some *false drops*.

Searching One-Word Descriptors

But what if the descriptor was just MUSIC? Not all descriptors are phrases. Many are single words. As we just said, the descriptor MUSIC is used when the document is generically about "music" but not any particular kind of music or for any particular purpose. Another example is a term such as SLEEP in PsycINFO. This is a descriptor unto itself, but there are also descriptors, such as SLEEP DISORDERS, SLEEP APNEA, REM SLEEP, and SLEEP WAKE CYCLE, that incorporate the word SLEEP. Furthermore, SLEEP is relatively frequently used in abstracts, but that is not as good an indicator of document content.

For example, searching on

```
?s sleep

    S1      9706      SLEEP
```

will retrieve all documents with the word SLEEP in any of the Basic Index fields. Searching

```
?s sleep/de

    S2      6729      SLEEP/DE
```

will retrieve all documents with the word SLEEP in the descriptor field. But that is not the same thing as retrieving documents that have the one-word descriptor SLEEP. To get those, one must search

```
?s sleep/df

    S3      3945      SLEEP/DF
```

where the suffix /df ("descriptor full") qualifies the search to *one-word descriptors only*. This is an important and subtle distinction and is not always easily grasped initially. A tip: To search a one-word descriptor as a one-word descriptor, use /DF.

There are a couple of other techniques we can use to make controlled vocabulary searching more efficient or more precise: restricting to major descriptors and exploding.

Major Descriptors

You'll recall in chapter 6, when we discussed record structures, we saw that some descriptors were starred. (There are many instances of this in the search examples.) We called these *major descriptors* and said that the indexer had decided that these terms best described the document and were the only index terms used in the printed index. We can use these decisions to try to improve the quality and precision of our search results.

If we wish to restrict our searching to major descriptors, we can give the command

```
?s music education/maj
```

to retrieve only those documents that were assigned MUSIC EDUCATION as a major descriptor. If, as often happens, we had already gotten a set for MUSIC EDUCATION, say S6, and now wish to improve the specificity of that set, we can type

```
?s s6/maj
```

and the set will be so restricted.

A couple of comments here. First, this command looks a lot like the suffixes we called *qualifiers* earlier. It is very similar, but note that with qualifiers we were restricting to a particular field (title or abstract), and now with descriptors we are reducing within a field—a slight difference. Technically, /MAJ is not a qualifier, but a limit, which we will discuss in chapter 9, but it makes sense to introduce it here. Second, there is a companion limit, /MIN, which, as you might have guessed, limits to minor descriptors (the unstarred ones). It escapes these writers why anyone would want to do that, but it can be done if desired.

> MAJOR descriptors are those that are also used in the printed indexes (RIE and CIJE) of ERIC. They are obviously regarded as the most important index terms and are identified on your printout by having an asterisk beside them. They provide a useful and simple way of making your search more specific. But check your bluesheets for suffix codes, because they are not available on many files. – GW

Explode

Exploding is a nice technique that can save a lot of typing and improve the breadth and recall of a search. If one explodes on a controlled vocabulary term, one will search on it and all its narrower terms, all ORed together. In some files (e.g., ERIC), only the terms that are directly narrower (one level down) in the hierarchy are returned. In other files (e.g., PsycINFO), narrower terms of narrower terms, all the way down, are returned. Check documentation and thesauri to see what a particular file does. This feature is available only in files that have online thesauri.

The technique is very simple:

```
?s music!
```

is the equivalent of

```
?s music/df or applied music or jazz/df or oriental music or rock
   music or vocal music
```

Very handy. Note that using exploding, one will get a term like JAZZ, which is a narrower term to MUSIC in the thesaurus but does not have the word "music" in it, so it would not appear by searching on MUSIC/DE.

However, there are some terms in the MUSIC hierarchy that will not come up by doing this. CHORAL MUSIC, for example, is a narrower term under VOCAL MUSIC, but because ERIC's explode only goes down one level, it will not be included. Again, this can save a lot of typing and possibly retrieve documents that might otherwise be overlooked. Beware of overuse, though—sometimes there are undesirable narrower terms, so it pays to examine the print or online thesaurus before trying to use explode.

We have mentioned this "online thesaurus" several times—we will now see how it works and how it might be used. To access it, we use a DIALOG command that has several other uses: EXPAND.

Viewing the Basic Index and Online Thesaurus: EXPAND

The EXPAND command's primary function is to allow one to view an alphabetical display of a portion of the Basic Index. (We will use it with prefix searching in chapter 9 and citation searching in chapter 11.) It can be very useful when one is not sure of the spelling of a word, or when there may be variant spellings or misspellings in the database. The format of the command is

    expand ≤**term**≥

which may be abbreviated as

    e ≤**term**≥

The result is a display like the following:

```
?e bias

        Ref    Items    RT    Index-term
        E1       1            BIARD
        E2       1            BIARTS
        E3     9929     8     *BIAS (AN INCLINATION, OR A LACK OF BALANCE (NOTE: ...))
        E4       2            BIAS (LEONARD)
        E5       1            BIAS ELIMINATION PROCEDURES
        E6       1            BIAS IN ATTITUDE SURVEY
        E7       2            BIAS IN ATTITUDES SURVEY
        E8       1            BIASE
        E9     986            BIASED
        E10      2            BIASEDNESS
        E11    821            BIASES
        E12     99            BIASING

             Enter P or E for more
```

The display has four columns. The first gives reference numbers that we can use later to select terms from the display. The second gives the number of postings, which is the number of documents that contain each term. The third, RT, shows the number of related terms in the thesaurus; an entry in this column indicates that this term is a descriptor. Finally, we see the alphabetical list of terms themselves. Notice that E3 is BIAS, the term we began with, and it has an asterisk in front of it as an indication that this is in fact the term expanded. Also notice that there is a parenthetical expression after BIAS in E3. This is not part of the descriptor; it is the very beginning of the scope note from the thesaurus. It should be reasonably clear when using an EXPAND display which of these parentheticals are scope notes and which are parts of descriptors. Another point of interest is E4, BIAS (LEONARD). This is an identifier (proper nouns cannot be descriptors in ERIC, but this is not true of other files) and refers to Leonard Bias, the college basketball star who died of a drug overdose in 1986. E5, E6, and E7 are also identifiers; we know this because they are multiple-word phrases but have no related terms. E8, BIASE, is probably a spelling or typing error in one of the documents.

To see the next "page" of the display (the next 12 entries), just type

    p (for PAGE)

or

    e (for more EXPAND)

```
?p

       Ref     Items       Index-term
       E13        1        BIASING EFFECTS
       E14        1        BIASNESS
       E15        3        BIATHLON
       E16        1        BIAZHUN
       E17       20        BIB
       E18       10        BIBB
       E19        1        BIBB COUNTY INSTRUCTIONAL MATERIALS CENTER GA
       E20        1        BIBBIDIBOBBIDIBOO
       E21        1        BIBBINS
       E22        1        BIBBITS
       E23        1        BIBCON
       E24        2        BIBDATA
```

Here we see more of the same. Because none of these are descriptors, there is no RT column (E19 is an identifier).

The reference numbers of these terms are now available for use in searching. We have as yet created no sets by using the EXPAND command, but we can do this by selecting terms from the display using the E numbers:

> ?s e3, e8-e14

This command will create a set containing documents with the terms specified. As can be seen, more than one term at a time can be selected, separating them with commas or using a hyphen. The selected terms are then ORed together. The command above is equivalent to

> ?s e3 or e8 or e9 or e10 or e11 or e12 or e13 or e14

The EXPAND display goes up to e50. If further EXPAND statements are used, they are, in effect, overwriting in the same computer space. This means that one can only SELECT from that most recent display. The others have been lost and must be recreated to be seen or used.

There are two ways to enter the online thesaurus. If there is a descriptor in an alphabetical EXPAND display (such as BIAS above), one can look at its online thesaurus entry to display the related terms by expanding on its E number, as in the following example:

```
?e e3

Ref     Items     Type    RT    Index-term
R1       9929               8    *BIAS (AN INCLINATION, OR A LACK OF BALANCE (NOTE: ...)
R2       1069      U        1    PREJUDICE
R3       1449      N       20    SOCIAL BIAS
R4        376      N       10    STATISTICAL BIAS
R5       1557      N       19    TEST BIAS
R6        653      N        8    TEXTBOOK BIAS
R7      82045      R       52    ATTITUDES
R8        316      R       14    EGOCENTRISM
R9         60      R        3    MENTAL RIGIDITY
```

Now there is a new display, similar to the other but slightly different. Instead of the reference numbers beginning with E, they begin with R. This means that one is in an online thesaurus display rather than an alphabetical one. The Items column is the same, but now we see an additional column, Type, which indicates whether the listed term is a Use For (U), Narrower (N), Broader (B), or Related (R) Term in the thesaurus. The final two columns are the same as before. The full entry is not visible as it would be in the print version of the thesaurus, including scope notes, but the relationships and hierarchies are preserved and available for online consultation.

This process can continue indefinitely, as now any terms in the display can be expanded by EXPANDing on R numbers, as in this example:

```
?e r5

Ref    Items   Type   RT   Index-term
R1     1557           19   *TEST BIAS (UNFAIRNESS IN THE CONSTRUCTION, CONTENT,
                           ADM...)
R2     9929    B       8   BIAS
R3      420    R      10   CULTURE FAIR TESTS
R4     1379    R       9   ERROR PATTERNS
R5      581    R      15   OBJECTIVE TESTS
R6     1449    R      20   SOCIAL BIAS
R7     1277    R      23   SOCIAL DISCRIMINATION
R8      376    R      10   STATISTICAL BIAS
R9      302    R      11   TEST COACHING
R10    6052    R      29   TEST CONSTRUCTION
R11    2786    R      24   TEST INTERPRETATION
R12    2100    R      23   TEST ITEMS

            Enter P or E for more
```

The other way to enter the online thesaurus does not depend on having a previous e-display in hand. If it is already known that a certain term is a descriptor, one may just EXPAND directly on it by using parentheses, as shown in this example:

```
?e (graduate students)

Ref    Items    Type   RT   Index-term
R1     3052            12   *GRADUATE STUDENTS
R2      140     N       5   DENTAL STUDENTS
R3      169     N       5   LAW STUDENTS
R4     1680     N       8   MEDICAL STUDENTS
R5    22586     B      26   COLLEGE STUDENTS
R6     1936     R      13   COLLEGE GRADUATES
R7     1154     R      12   DOCTORAL PROGRAMS
R8     5313     R      22   GRADUATE STUDY
R9     9385     R       7   GRADUATES
R10  126309     R      29   HIGHER EDUCATION
R11     442     R       9   MASTERS PROGRAMS
R12      30     R      14   RESEARCH ASSISTANTS

            Enter P or E for more
```

These R numbers can now be SELECTed in groups in exactly the same way as before. (Remember, we do not create sets using EXPAND; we have to SELECT from the R-display.) For example:

```
?s r1-r4

          3052    GRADUATE STUDENTS
           140    DENTAL STUDENTS
           169    LAW STUDENTS
          1680    MEDICAL STUDENTS
    S2    4985    R1-R4
```

There are advantages and disadvantages to using the online version of the thesaurus. Its major disadvantage is that one is paying online time to work with the thesaurus. It is useful when there is no printed thesaurus available, but it is not a substitute for thorough preparation.

However, if the online controlled vocabulary is used cleverly, it can save time, money, and effort. One can SELECT from the R-display directly, which will allow one to avoid typing long descriptors and possibly making typing or spelling errors. Because the online thesaurus is sometimes updated more frequently that the print version, there may be new descriptors or relationships online to help, and certainly the postings information will be more up-to-date, so the potential size of the retrieved sets can be better gauged.

Search Example

For the sample DIALOG search, we will rerun the search from the last chapter on the various effects of closed head injuries in children. Using controlled vocabulary techniques, we are likely to get higher-quality results more quickly and easily.

First of all, a trip through the *Thesaurus of Psychological Index Terms* yields some interesting potential terms: HEAD INJURIES, BRAIN DAMAGE, and TRAUMATIC BRAIN INJURY for that concept block (probably the most specific); several that contain the words PSYCHOSOCIAL, NEUROPSYCHOLOGICAL (in various forms); and many with BEHAVIOR, not surprisingly. We will try searching on them in various ways, as will be seen below. Finally, the preferred terms for CHILDREN and ADOLESCENTS are children and adolescents. We begin the search with these terms.

```
File 11:PsycINFO(R) 1967-1998/May
 (c) 1998 Amer. Psychological association

     Set    Items     Description
     ---    -----     -----------
?ss head injuries or brain damage or traumatic brain injury

     S1     2323     HEAD INJURIES (1973)
     S2     4677     BRAIN DAMAGE (1967)
     S3      370     TRAUMATIC BRAIN INJURY (1997)
     S4     7023     HEAD INJURIES OR BRAIN DAMAGE OR TRAUMATIC BRAIN INJURY
?ss psychosocial or neuropsych? or behavior/de

     S5    28364     PSYCHOSOCIAL
     S6    18301     NEUROPSYCH?
     S7   139787     BEHAVIOR/DE (1967)
     S8   181319     PSYCHOSOCIAL OR NEUROPSYCH? OR BEHAVIOR/DE
?ss children/df or adolescents/df

     S9    30379     CHILDREN/DF (1967)
     S10   32256     ADOLESCENTS/DF (1967)
     S11   58049     CHILDREN/DF OR ADOLESCENTS/DF
```

The "head injury" concept is by far the narrowest, as we suspected. There are obviously a lot of documents with BEHAVIOR in the descriptor field, but we can have more confidence in those documents than searching just for BEHAVIOR anywhere, precisely because the word is in the descriptor field. It is a large component of that set, but not necessarily dangerously so. If all we get in the results are behavior-oriented documents, to the exclusion of psychosocial/neuropsychological ones, we may try those terms separately to see how they are contributing. The age set seems fine; we will put them all together.

?s s4 and s8 and s11

```
        7023    S4
      181319    S8
       58049    S11
S12      135    S4 AND S8 AND S11
```

This set seems reasonable; let's have a look:

?t 12/8/1-8

```
 12/8/1
DIALOG(R)File 11:(c) 1998 Amer. Psychological Assn. All rts. reserv.

01532776          1998-07266-014
Parent training.
SERIES TITLE: The LEA series in personality and clinical psychology.

DESCRIPTORS: *Behavior Modification; *Daily Activities; ^Disorders; *Parent
  Child Relations; *Parent Training; Adults; Children; Developmental
  Disabilities; Head Injuries; Schizophrenia
IDENTIFIERS: planned activities parent training behavioral technique,
children & adults with normal intelligence or developmental disabilities or
head injuries or schizophrenia or other disorders
SUBJECT CODES & HEADINGS: 3200 (Psychological & Physical Disorders); 3312
  (Behavior Therapy & Behavior Modification)

 12/8/2
DIALOG(R)File 11:(c) 1998 Amer. Psychological Assn. All rts. reserv.

01532201          1998-07011-007
Traumatic brain injury.

DESCRIPTORS: *Diagnosis; *Measurement; *Traumatic Brain Injury; *Treatment;
  Children; Epidemiology
IDENTIFIERS: description & psychological & psychiatric assessment issues &
epidemiology & medical & psychological & behavioral & pharmacological
treatments, children with traumatic brain injury
SUBJECT CODES & HEADINGS: 3297 (Neurological Disorders & Brain Damage);
  3360 (Health Psychology & Medicine)

 12/8/3
DIALOG(R)File 11:(c) 1998 Amer. Psychological Assn. All rts. reserv.

01523141          1997-38757-001
Head injury in children.

DESCRIPTORS: *Brain Damage; *Head Injuries; *Literature Review; *Traumatic
  Brain Injury; Children
IDENTIFIERS: head injury in children, literature review
SUBJECT CODES & HEADINGS: 3297 (Neurological Disorders & Brain Damage)
```

12/8/4
DIALOG(R)File 11:(c) 1998 Amer. Psychological Assn. All rts. reserv.

01522010   1997-36671-015
Central nervous system dysfunction: Brain injury, postconcussive syndrome,
   and seizure disorder.
SERIES TITLE: Issues in clinical child psychology.

DESCRIPTORS: *Behavior Therapy; *Central Nervous System Disorders; *Drug
   Therapy; *Medical Treatment (General); *Rehabilitation; Brain Concussion;
   Children; Convulsions; Students; Traumatic Brain Injury
IDENTIFIERS: medical management & rehabilitation & pharmacological issues &
behavioral interventions, students with pediatric traumatic brain injury or
postconcussion syndrome or seizure disorders
SUBJECT CODES & HEADINGS: 3570 (Special & Remedial Education); 3300 (Health
   & Mental Health Treatment & Prevention)

12/8/5
DIALOG(R)File 11:(c) 1998 Amer. Psychological Assn. All rts. reserv.

01512432   1997-36680-006
Frontal lobe dysfunction following closed head injury in children: Findings
   from neuropsychology and brain imaging.

DESCRIPTORS: *Brain Disorders; *Head Injuries; *Literature Review;
   *Neuropsychological Assessment; *Tomography; Children; Neuropsychology;
   Prefrontal Cortex
IDENTIFIERS: neurobehavioral sequelae of & neuroimaging techniques for &
performance on neuropsychological tests & prefrontal brain dysfunctions
following closed head-injuries, children, literature review
SUBJECT CODES & HEADINGS: 3297 (Neurological Disorders & Brain Damage)

12/8/6
DIALOG(R)File 11:(c) 1998 Amer. Psychological Assn. All rts. reserv.

01494841   1996-93815-012
Behavior modification with brain-injured children: A brief note on
   directions for research.

DESCRIPTORS: *Behavior Modification; *Experimentation; *Traumatic Brain
   Injury; Children
IDENTIFIERS: directions for research on behavior modification with
brain-injured children
SUBJECT CODES & HEADINGS: 3297 (Neurological Disorders & Brain Damage)

12/8/7
DIALOG(R)File 11:(c) 1998 Amer. Psychological Assn. All rts. reserv.

01482579   1997-30097-007
Pediatric neuropsychology.

DESCRIPTORS: *Brain Disorders; *Developmental Stages; *Neuropsychological
   Assessment; *Neural Development; Adolescents; Preschool Age Children;
   School Age Children; Oral Communication; Motor Skills; Head Injuries;
   Cognitive Processes
IDENTIFIERS: development of nervous system & motor & speech & higher
cognitive functions & application to development of neuropsychological
assessment approach, 2-5 & 6-14 yr olds with neuropsychological deficits
SUBJECT CODES & HEADINGS: 3297 (Neurological Disorders & Brain Damage)

```
12/8/8
```

```
01482317          1997-09204-008
```
Children with brain injury.

DESCRIPTORS: *Biopsychosocial Approach; *Brain Damage; *Neuropsychological
  Assessment; *Systems Theory; Children
IDENTIFIERS: nature of various brain disorders & methodological &
biobehavioral systems approaches to neuropsychological assessment,
children with brain injury
SUBJECT CODES & HEADINGS: 2225 (Neuropsychological Assessment); 3297
  (Neurological Disorders & Brain Damage)

Pretty good—a reasonably sized set, with many potentially interesting documents. We might try to improve it a bit by focusing the BEHAVIOR term down to documents in which it is part of a major descriptor. We first reconstruct that set, with the narrower version of BEHAVIOR, then recombine the concept sets to form a new result set:

?s s5 or s6 or behavior/maj

```
        28364    S5
        18301    S6
         4565    BEHAVIOR/MAJ (1967)
  S13   50523    S5 OR S6 OR BEHAVIOR/MAJ
```

?s s4 and s13 and s11

```
         7023    S4
        50523    S13
        58049    S11
  S14     116    S4     AND S13 AND S11
```

and it appears to make very little difference. We only lose 19 documents by doing this. This would probably not be done in a real search, but we will take a moment and see what those look like. We can use the Boolean operator NOT to do this:

?s s12 not s14

```
         135    S12
         116    S14
  S15      19    S12 NOT S14
```
?t 15/8/1-6

```
15/8/1
```

```
01532776          1998-07266-014
```
Parent training.
SERIES TITLE: The LEA series in personality and clinical psychology.

DESCRIPTORS: *Behavior Modification; *Daily Activities; *Disorders;
  *Parent Child Relations; *Parent Training; Adults; Children;
  Developmental Disabilities; Head Injuries; Schizophrenia
IDENTIFIERS: planned activities parent training behavioral technique,
children & adults with normal intelligence or developmental disabilities
or head injuries or schizophrenia or other disorders
SUBJECT CODES & HEADINGS: 3200 (Psychological & Physical Disorders); 3312
  (Behavior Therapy & Behavior Modification)

15/8/2
DIALOG(R)File 11:(c) 1998 Amer. Psychological Assn. All rts. reserv.

01522010   1997-36671-015
Central nervous system dysfunction: Brain injury, postconcussive syndrome,
  and seizure disorder.
SERIES TITLE: Issues in clinical child psychology.

DESCRIPTORS: *Behavior Therapy; *Central Nervous System Disorders; *Drug
  Therapy; *Medical Treatment (General); *Rehabilitation; Brain Concussion;
  Children; Convulsions; Students; Traumatic Brain Injury
IDENTIFIERS: medical management & rehabilitation & pharmacological issues &
behavioral interventions, students with pediatric traumatic brain injury or
postconcussion syndrome or seizure disorders
SUBJECT CODES & HEADINGS: 3570 (Special & Remedial Education); 3300 (Health
  & Mental Health Treatment & Prevention)

15/8/3
DIALOG(R)File 11:(c) 1998 Amer. Psychological Assn. All rts. reserv.

01494841   1996-93815-012
Behavior modification with brain-injured children: A brief note on
  directions for research.

DESCRIPTORS: *Behavior Modification; *Experimentation; *Traumatic Brain
  Injury; Children
IDENTIFIERS: directions for research on behavior modification with
brain-injured children
SUBJECT CODES & HEADINGS: 3297 (Neurological Disorders & Brain Damage)

15/8/4
DIALOG(R)File 11:(c) 1998 Amer. Psychological Assn. All rts. reserv.

01481495   1997-09033-008
A positive, communication-based approach to challenging behavior after ABI.

DESCRIPTORS: *Behavior Problems; *Classroom Behavior Modification; *Special
  Education; *Communication Skills Training; *Traumatic Brain Injury;
  Adolescents; Cognitive Rehabilitation; School Age Children
IDENTIFIERS: critical intervention themes in & communication-based approach
to preventing evolution of problem behaviors, child & adolescent students
with acquired brain injury
SUBJECT CODES & HEADINGS: 3570 (Special & Remedial Education)

15/8/5
DIALOG(R)File 11:(c) 1998 Amer. Psychological Assn. All rts. reserv.

01481494   1997-09033-007
Understanding and overcoming the challenging behaviors of students
  with ABI.

DESCRIPTORS: *Behavior Problems; *Classroom Behavior Modification; *Special
  Education Students; *Traumatic Brain Injury; Adolescents; School Age
  Children
IDENTIFIERS: problem behaviors & behavior change strategies, students
with acquired brain injury
SUBJECT CODES & HEADINGS: 3570 (Special & Remedial Education)

```
   15/8/6
DIALOG(R)File 11:(c) 1998 Amer. Psychological Assn. All rts. reserv.

01480852           1997-08859-009
Pediatric traumatic brain injury: Challenges and interventions for
   families.

DESCRIPTORS: *Coping Behavior; *Family Therapy; *Traumatic Brain Injury;
   *Needs; Advocacy; Behavior Therapy; Parents; Roles; School Psychologists;
   Professional Consultation; Parent School Relationship; Family Members;
   Children; Client Education
IDENTIFIERS: coping experiences & needs for & psychologist's role in
education & support & advocacy & behavioral therapy & home-school
consultation, children with traumatic brain injury & their families
SUBJECT CODES & HEADINGS: 3313 (Group & Family Therapy)
```

Not so good, but again, it is a small change. This search is much improved over the previous version, but there is still room for improvement. The techniques we pick up in the next chapter, for searching free text, will help even more. In the meantime, here are the first 20 titles of that good set 14, to give a better idea of what this set looks like:

```
   14/6/1
01532201           1998-07011-007
Traumatic brain injury.

   14/6/2
01523141           1997-38757-001
Head injury in children.

   14/6/3
01512432           1997-36680-006
Frontal lobe dysfunction following closed head injury in children: Findings
   from neuropsychology and brain imaging.

   14/6/4
01482579           1997-30097-007
Pediatric neuropsychology.

   14/6/5
01482317           1997-09204-008
Children with brain injury.

   14/6/6
01481491           1997-09033-004
The role of neuropsychology in educating students with ABI.

   14/6/7
01481334           1997-08987-030
Traumatic brain injury in children: Neuropsychological, behavioral, and
   educational issues.

   14/6/8
01481171 1997-08958-008
Recent advances in neuropsychological assessment of children.
SERIES TITLE: Critical issues in neuropsychology.
```

14/6/9
01480853   1997-08859-010
Children and adolescents with traumatic brain injury: Reintegration
   challenges in educational settings.

14/6/10
01480848   1997-08859-005
Neuropsychological consequences of traumatic brain injury in children
   and adolescents.

14/6/11
01480845   1997-08859-002
Assessing children with traumatic brain injury during rehabilitation:
   Promoting school and community reentry.

14/6/12
01480843   1997-08859-000
Childhood traumatic brain injury: Diagnosis, assessment, and intervention.

14/6/13
01479633   1997-08457-002
Pediatric brain injury: Mechanisms and amelioration.
SERIES TITLE: Critical issues in neuropsychology.

14/6/14
01471818   1997-05606-001
Mild head injury in children and adolescents: A review of studies
   (1970-1995).

14/6/14
01461782   1997-97163-001
Specificity of brain-behavioural relationships revisited: From epileptic
   personality to behavioural phenotypes.

14/6/16
01457377   1997-03731-002
A taxonomy of neurobehavioral functions applied to neuropsychological
   assessment after head injury.

14/6/17
01456899   1997-03303-005
Factors contributing to successful return to school for students with
   acquired brain injury: Parent perspectives.

14/6/18
01451651   1996-98606-010
Cognitive rehabilitation for children with traumatic brain injury.

14/6/19
01437777   1996-06915-007
Assessing children with traumatic brain injury during rehabilitation:
   Promoting school and community reentry.

14/6/20
01427791   1996-04856-003
Behavioural adjustment and parental stress associated with closed head
   injury in children.

Controlled Vocabulary Searching on the Internet

This will not take long, because there really is nothing that could sensibly be called "controlled vocabulary searching" in the Internet environment. The search engines say they "index" Web documents, but they do not mean that in the sense that the ERIC clearinghouses or Psychological Abstracts do. They do not create abstracts, add descriptors, or even have any real contact with documents. When they say "indexing," they really mean "inverted file creation of words in the full document," perhaps with a stoplist.

So why is this section here, and why is it not over yet? First, to promote awareness of this situation, and second, to provide a few ideas for ways to search for networked resources using techniques that could only loosely be referred to as resembling the use of controlled vocabularies. In general, though, searching on the Net is full text and free text all the way, and we will deal with those types of searching in more detail in the next chapter.

If the point of a controlled vocabulary is to lead the searcher to a collection of resources all on a single topic (what cataloging theorists would call the "gathering" function), then the category structure of Yahoo! probably comes the closest on the Net. Yahoo! is the de facto "catalog" of the Net, but one should in no way believe it shares important characteristics with library catalogs or indexed DIALOG files. For example, they make no claim of comprehensiveness or selectivity (beyond the "cool" ratings on some sites).

However, it is a good place to start looking for a list of potentially interesting sites, especially if the words for the concept of interest are not very specific. (For example, if I were looking for sites about the US Open Tennis championships, *Babylon 5*, or Jimmy Carter, I would probably start with Yahoo!). Yahoo!'s category labels serve as a very broad categorization, and in fact, when searching in Yahoo, I try to search for words I think will be in category labels rather than site names or their very brief (sometimes nonexistent) descriptions. Search engines are also starting to add category features, but they so far cover dramatically fewer sites than Yahoo!

If Yahoo! does not help, one might also work with search engines but try to identify the right, really specific word or phrase that everybody uses to describe a particular concept. (Assuming there is one, of course, which there may well not be.) Book/movie/TV/album titles and personal and geographical names are easy, but there are no name authority files out there, either, so variants may have to be searched. More generic concepts can be harder—one might actually try using database thesauri to identify "official" terms such as "attention deficit disorder" or "hebephrenic schizophrenia," but as always on the Net, one is at the mercy of the people who write the documents. "Official" terms will help to find documents written by people who use "official" language, but miss altogether alternative or nontraditional points of view that might use different language. Welcome to the Net.

A final idea is to directly search for websites by guessing at domain names. There are some obvious ones (e.g., ford.com for the Ford Motor Company, nbc.com for the NBC network), and some that are slightly less obvious but can be worked out (e.g., ala.org for the American Library Association, umich.edu for the University of Michigan). There is interesting information about the impact of eating eggs on cholesterol levels from the American Egg Board. If we worked there, we would suggest they be at eggs.org, but they went for aeb.org, as we discovered from one of their commercials. A little guesswork, possibly supplemented by searching using Yahoo or a search engine, can pay off.

But it still remains the case that the Net is almost entirely a controlled-vocabulary-free zone and probably will be for the foreseeable future. This makes the techniques of free-text searching very important there, and we will explore those in the next chapter.

Additional Reading

Bates, Marcia J. (1988), "How to Use Controlled Vocabularies More Effectively in Online Searches," *Online* 12(6): 45–56.

Fidel, Raya (Winter 1992), "Who Needs Controlled Vocabulary?" *Special Libraries* 83: 1–9.

Morton, Douglas (1994), "Refresher Course: Expanding Your Outlook," *Online* 18(3): 77.

Tenopir, Carol (November 15, 1987),"Searching by Controlled Vocabulary or Full Text?" *Library Journal* 112: 58–59.

SEARCHING USING FREE TEXT

In chapter 7, we saw that searching using controlled vocabulary techniques can be effective and efficient. In many cases, it is preferable to search using controlled vocabulary terms because we often get higher-quality, more specific results. Sometimes, though, controlled vocabulary searching is either not good enough or not even possible. In these situations, we must rely on another set of techniques described in this chapter: searching free text.

Free-text searching is sometimes called keyword searching and is used in many online library catalogs and other computerized information retrieval systems. Essentially, searching with free-text techniques involves using terms from everyday or specialized language rather than controlled vocabulary terms. Take a peek at the search example at the end of this chapter now, just to get a feel for what we are describing and see how different it is from what we have done so far. It will look familiar because it is another version of the brain injury search, but now taking advantage of all the new techniques we will learn here.

In this chapter, we will explore online searching techniques used with free text, the situations in which this searching works best, where free-text terms come from, some problems with free-text searching, and how to refine searches to broaden or narrow results. A search example and a discussion of Internet free-text searching conclude the chapter.

Proximity Operators

Recall once again how the inverted file is constructed. Each word (excluding stop-words) that occurs in a document is marked with its position, and then an alphabetical list of all such words is created. Index terms that are intact phrases, such as descriptors and identifiers, are often included both as individual words and as full phrases (we said these fields are both word-indexed and phrase-indexed). We do not know yet how to search for phrases in other word-indexed fields, such as titles or abstracts.

We can, at this point, search for such phrases, but in a very crude way, using single words joined by the AND operator. If we were looking for documents about the Graduate Record Examinations, for example, we could simply search GRADUATE AND RECORD AND EXAM? and see what comes up. But there would be no guarantee that documents we retrieved would have anything to do with the Graduate Record Examinations. We could get documents that talk about examinations of record-buying habits of graduate students. Or we might retrieve a paper about record keeping of graduate schools for foreign-language examinations. AND does not allow us to specify relationships between concepts; we can only say that terms occur in the same record.

There are techniques, however, that allow us to be more specific. These are called proximity operators, and they are used to specify how close two or more words should be in the documents retrieved. There are several proximity operators, but they all work in essentially the same way.

The simplest of these allows one to retrieve documents that have two or more words in direct proximity, that is, right next to each other. In this way one can search for a phrase in word-indexed fields. For example, to search for the phrase "information industry" in titles (a rather specific tactic, by the way), use the (W) proximity operator, as in the following example from ERIC:

```
        Set     Items    Description
        ---     -----    -----------
?s information(w)industry/ti

                13082    INFORMATION/TI
                 2152    INDUSTRY/TI (PRODUCTIVE ENTERPRISES, ESPECIALLY MANUFACTU...)
        S1          12    INFORMATION(W)INDUSTRY/TI
```

This command tells DIALOG to retrieve all documents that have the word "information" directly followed by the word "industry" in the title field.

More than two words can be chained together, as in the following example:

```
?s management(w)information(w)systems

                41955    MANAGEMENT
               125433    INFORMATION
                53499    SYSTEMS
        S2       2173    MANAGEMENT(W)INFORMATION(W)SYSTEMS
```

This expression will retrieve documents with these three words in this order, in any Basic Index field.

The general form of the command is

s ≤term≥(W)≤term≥
s ≤term≥(W)≤term≥(W)≤term≥
... etc.

Compare the following three expressions, again in *ERIC*:

```
?s day care

        S3       4735    DAY CARE (CARE OF CHILDREN BY PERSONS OTHER THAN
THEIR...)
```

```
?s day(w)care/de

                 7651    DAY/DE
                11423    CARE/DE
        S4       6841    DAY(W)CARE/DE
```

```
?s day()care

                22753    DAY
                27177    CARE
        S5       7907    DAY()CARE
```

The first of these searches uses the bound descriptor DAY CARE. The second searches for the word DAY followed by the word CARE in the descriptor field, and retrieves more than 2,000 more documents. Why? Because several descriptors incorporate those two words in that order, including ADULT DAY CARE, DAY CARE CENTERS, FAMILY DAY CARE, SCHOOL AGE DAY CARE, and so on. S4 includes all of these. Finally, S5 includes all documents that have these two words in this order in any field and retrieves more than 1,000 more records than S4. This example illustrates the power and some of the potential problems of free-text searching.

Also note that there is no W between the parentheses in the search expression for S5. That is not a mistake—in this situation *only*, the W can be left out. (W) and () work in exactly the same way, and the W can be either upper or lower case.

Suppose one wanted to search for documents about the University of Michigan. Using this same technique, one could search on

```
?s university(w)of(w)michigan
```

but would get no hits. Not because none exist, but because OF is a stopword in the DIALOG system, as we discussed in the chapter on database construction. Recall the process: When a document containing the phrase "University of Michigan" is processed to go into a DIALOG database, each of those three words is numbered with its position in the field. Then the stopwords are eliminated, but their positions are preserved. So we have to reconstruct those phrases by allowing for the presence of stopwords (or any other words, for that matter). We do this by extending the (w) operator, and allowing for space between the words we search on. The command is

s ≤term≥(nW)≤term≥

where n is any number one or greater.[1] To search for documents containing the phrase "University of Michigan" in the Basic Index, we would search the following:

```
?s university(1w)michigan
        66777     UNIVERSITY
         6678     MICHIGAN
    S6    890     UNIVERSITY(1W)MICHIGAN
```

which retrieves all documents with the word UNIVERSITY followed by the word MICHIGAN, with at most one word in between.

This tactic can also be used when two words close together but not necessarily next to each other are wanted, as in the following example:

```
?s (online or information)(2w)retrieval
        5646      ONLINE
      125433      INFORMATION
        7013      RETRIEVAL
    S7  5555      (ONLINE OR INFORMATION)(2W)RETRIEVAL
```

This set contains all documents with either ONLINE or INFORMATION followed by the word RETRIEVAL with zero, one, or two words in between. Documents that have the phrases "information retrieval," "online retrieval," "online bibliographic retrieval," "online systems for retrieval of information," and so on might be of interest, so the search is broadened a bit.

> *In practice, a number higher than (3W) or (4W) tends to be counter-productive, as the farther apart terms get, the more we revert to the simple Boolean AND. – GW*

Notice that we have a Boolean expression on the left side of the (2W). There can also be set numbers here, truncations, or anything legal, as in the following:

```
?s s7(w)system?

          5555    S7
        110345    SYSTEM?
   S8      662    S7(W)SYSTEM?
?t 8/5/1

   8/5/1
EJ546260                 IR535161
  Shape Measures for Content Based Image Retrieval: A Comparison.
  Mehtre, Babu M.; And Others
  Information Processing & Management; v33 n3 p319-37 May 1997
  ISSN: 0306-4573
  Language: English
  Document Type: JOURNAL ARTICLE (080); PROJECT DESCRIPTION (141)
  Journal Announcement: CIJNOV97
  Explores the evaluation of image and multimedia information-retrieval
systems, particularly the effectiveness of several shape measures for
content-based retrieval of similar images. Shape feature measures, or
vectors, are computed automatically and can either be used for retrieval or
stored in the database for future queries. (57 references) (Author/LRW)
  Descriptors: Comparative Analysis; Content Analysis; Databases;
*Evaluation Methods; Futures (of Society); *Information Retrieval;
*Information Systems; Mathematical Formulas; *Measurement Techniques;
*Multimedia Materials
  Identifiers: *Digital Imagery; Query Processing; *Shapes; Similarity
(Concept); Vector Methods
```

Can you see why this document was retrieved? English grammar being what it is, the words wanted may not always be in the same order. An author writing a document about relativity theory might use that phrase, but she might also use "theory of relativity," "theory of general relativity," "relativity theories," or "theory of special relativity." If one was looking for these documents, one might be tempted to use a command like the following:

```
?s relativity(w)theory

           384    RELATIVITY
         38845    THEORY
   S9       13    RELATIVITY(W)THEORY
?t 9/5/1
   9/5/1
EJ456369                 RC509090
  Relativity, Relatedness and Reality.
  Deloria, Vine, Jr.
  Winds of Change; v7 n4 p34-40 Fall 1992
  ISSN: 0888-8612
  Language: English
  Document Type: JOURNAL ARTICLE (080); POSITION PAPER (120)
  Journal Announcement: CIJMAY93
```

Anticipated the modern physics relativity theory, American Indians gained
information about the natural world through careful observation based on
the principle that all things are related. American Indian students could
radically transform scientific knowledge by grounding themselves in
traditional knowledge about the world and working this understanding into
the Western scientific format. (SV)
   Descriptors: *American Indian Culture; American Indian Education;
American Indians; Epistemology; Higher Education; *Holistic Approach;
Science Education; Scientific Attitudes; *Scientific Methodology
   Identifiers: *Knowledge Acquisition; World Views

One might also want documents that contain the other phrases, so perhaps one could try the following:

```
?s relativity(2n)theor?

          384     RELATIVITY
        63161     THEOR?
  S10      49     RELATIVITY(2N)THEOR?
```

Notice the postings have gone from 13 to 49.

```
?t 10/5/1
 10/5/1
EJ531451            SE556552
  The Utilization of Fiction When Teaching the Theory of Relativity.
  Hellstrand, Ake; Ott, Aadu
  Physics Education; v30 n5 p284-86 Sep 1995
  ISSN: 0031-9120
  Language: English
  Document Type: TEACHING GUIDE (052); JOURNAL ARTICLE (080)
  Journal Announcement: CIJFEB97
  Describes a way of teaching the theory of relativity with the help of a
novel. Aims to contribute to the formation of didactic theories by means of
an evaluation of alternative methods. (AIM)
  Descriptors: *Fiction; Physics; *Relativity; Science Instruction;
Secondary Education; Teaching Methods
  Identifiers: Theory of Relativity
```

This command uses the (N) proximity operator, which retrieves documents that have the two terms near each other (hence the "N") with the possibility of intervening words, in this case as many as two. The general form

$$s \leq term \geq (nN) \leq term \geq$$

is similar to that of (W), and the same guidelines apply about using set numbers, Boolean expressions, truncation, and so on. In many cases, (nN) is more useful than (nW) because of this tendency in English to invert phrases and insert words.

A couple of further examples illustrate the use of (nN): If a patron requests documents on hypothesis testing (a technique from statistics), the concept might be referred to in documents as "hypothesis testing," but "testing the hypothesis" or "a test of two null hypotheses" might also appear. So instead of HYPOTHESIS(W)TESTING, HYPOTHES?S(3N)TEST??? might be preferred to get many variant forms of the phrase.

Also, (nN) can be used to save typing. If seeking documents about public universities in Michigan, one could try a strategy such as UNIVERSIT?(1N)MICHIGAN, which would retrieve documents with "University of Michigan" and also "Eastern Michigan University," "Michigan Technological University," and even "Michigan State University." Of course, some things would be missed (notably Wayne State University), but these could be ORed in, and quite a bit of typing would still be saved.

> *The use of proximity operators is available on most of the major online systems, though their exact formats vary. On some systems, for example, the (W) operator is replaced by ADJ (adjacent to). So we may have a command in search mode, such as DAY ADJ CARE, that will be equivalent to DAY()CARE in DIALOG. Similar features are also available on the Internet, though formats vary in different search engines. – GW*

There are other, broader proximity operators in DIALOG. The (F) operator will seek documents that have two words in the same field (e.g., both in the title, both in the abstract). The field to be searched in can be specified or left unqualified. See the following examples:

S ≤term≥(F)≤term≥
S ≤term≥(F)≤term≥/≤field code≥

A search for documents about the use of CD-ROMs in school libraries might go something like the following:

```
?s cdrom? or cd()rom?
            14      CDROM?
          2029      CD
          4426      ROM?
          1431      CD(W)ROM?
    S11   1436      CDROM? OR CD()ROM?
?s school(w)(librar? or media)
        291966      SCHOOL
         41884      LIBRAR?
         34797      MEDIA
    S12   4874      SCHOOL(W)(LIBRAR? OR MEDIA)
?s s11(F)s12
          1436      S11
          4874      S12
    S13     77      S11(F)S12
?t 13/5/1-3

 13/5/1
DIALOG(R)File      1:ERIC
(c) format only 1998 The Dialog Corporation. All rts. reserv.

EJ544898           PS526458
  Using a CD-ROM Encyclopedia: Interaction of Teachers, Middle School
Students, Library Media Specialists, and the Technology.
  Albaugh, Patti R.; And Others
  Research in Middle Level Education Quarterly; v20 n3 p43-55 Spr 1997
  ISSN: 1082-5541
  Language: English
```

Document Type: RESEARCH REPORT (143); JOURNAL ARTICLE (080)
Journal Announcement: CIJOCT97
Observed sixth-grade students and their ways of gathering information for
a science report from Encarta 94, a CD-ROM encyclopedia. Developed
recommendations for collaboration between the classroom teacher and the
school library media specialist during the implementation of CD-ROM
technology for information gathering, as well as ways to manage a
CD-ROM-based project. (AA)
   Descriptors: Access to Information; Case Studies; Classroom Techniques;
*Computer Attitudes; Computer Uses in Education; Educational Media;
Educational Strategies; Educational Technology; Elementary School Students;
*Encyclopedias; Grade 6; Information Seeking; Intermediate Grades;
Librarian Teacher Cooperation; *Multimedia Materials; Naturalistic
Observation; *Optical Data Disks; *Student Attitudes; Teacher Attitudes

13/5/2
DIALOG(R)File   1:ERIC
(c) format only 1998 The Dialog Corporation. All rts. reserv.

EJ544781   IR535023
   Technology Use in North Carolina Public Schools: The School Library Media
Specialist Plays a Major Role.
   Truett, Carol
   North Carolina Libraries; v55 n1 p32-37 Spr 1997
   For related earlier study, see EJ 488 280. Journal availability: State
Library of North Carolina, 109 East Jones Street, Raleigh, NC 27601-1023.
   ISSN: 0029-2540
   Language: English
   Document Type: RESEARCH REPORT (143); JOURNAL ARTICLE (080)
   Journal Announcement: CIJOCT97
This report on teachers and technology in North Carolina schools
continues an earlier report based on a survey of North Carolina schools
that focused on media specialists. Highlights include how teachers
incorporate CD-ROM and videodisk technologies, school library media
specialists as technology instructors, and teacher expectations of media
specialists. (LRW)
   Descriptors: *Computer Uses in Education; Curriculum Development;
*Educational Technology; Elementary Secondary Education; Learning Resources
Centers; Librarian Teacher Cooperation; Library Instruction; *Library Role;
*Media Specialists; Optical Data Disks; Public Schools; *School Libraries;
School Surveys; Staff Development; Teacher Attitudes; *Teacher Role; Use
Studies; Videodisks
   Identifiers: North Carolina; *Technology Utilization

13/5/3
DIALOG(R)File   1:ERIC
(c) format only 1998 The Dialog Corporation. All rts. reserv.

EJ515154   IR532273
   Government Publications: A Forgotten Treasure.
   Ekhaml, Leticia
   School Library Media Activities Monthly; v12 n4 p28-31 Dec 1995
   ISSN: 0889-9371
   Language: English
   Document Type: PROJECT DESCRIPTION (141); JOURNAL ARTICLE (080)
   Journal Announcement: CIJAPR96
Presents information on government publications for school library media
specialists, notes problems, and identifies selection aids. Topics include:
the "Monthly Catalog" on CD-ROM, the Superintendent of Documents

```
Classification System, GPO bookstores and depository libraries, how to
purchase and promote the use of government publications, and a list of
current documents useful to teachers and students. (AEF)
   Descriptors: Classification; Depository Libraries; *Government
Publications; *Information Sources; *Library Collection Development;
*Library Material Selection; Media Specialists; Optical Data Disks; *School
Libraries
   Identifiers: Bookstores; Government Printing Office; Monthly Catalog of
US Government Publications; Superintendent of Documents Classification
```

The first two documents in S13 look promising, but the third is off the track because the strategy is so broad. However, we notice the good descriptor SCHOOL LIBRARIES, so we use the following instead:

```
?s school libraries
    S14     3479     SCHOOL LIBRARIES
?s s11 and s14
            1436     S11
            3479     S14
    S5       103     S11 AND S14
?t 15/6/1-4

 15/6/1
EJ544781           IR535023
  Technology Use in North Carolina Public Schools: The School Library Media
Specialist Plays a Major Role.

 15/6/2
EJ539702           IR534431
  Mediagraphy: Print and Nonprint Resources.

 15/6/3
EJ529708           IR533359
  Full-Text Magazine Indexes & More on CD-ROMs.

 15/6/4
EJ523175           IR532797
  What CD-ROMs Are Other Schools Using?
```

With this strategy, we get improved results. There are other proximity operators; we will see how to use some in later chapters.

Why Use Free-Text Searching?

As we have seen, controlled vocabulary searching is often an excellent way to go. But that is not always the case. The following examples illustrate several situations in which searching using terms selected from a thesaurus or controlled vocabulary is not the best method.

- *There is no thesaurus.* Obviously, if there is no controlled vocabulary, it cannot provide search items. Some databases have no thesaurus at all. Others use one, but it is unavailable because it is not published or one may not have access to it. If there is no indexing at all (often the case with newspaper databases, for example), all that are left are free-text techniques. If documents in the database have been indexed in some way, but in an unknown fashion, one can begin with free-text searching and then use pearl-growing techniques to weave in controlled vocabulary terms. This is an often-used and successful approach.

- *There are no good controlled vocabulary terms.* In some cases, the vocabulary may simply not cover the subject area of the query very well. There may be several related, marginal terms, but no single good term.

- *The term is new.* It may also be the case that the subject area or terminology of the query is new, so no term or terms have yet been accepted into the thesaurus. In general, it will take some time, probably years rather than months, for a new term to become widely used and incorporated into the printed controlled vocabulary. Some disciplines and databases move faster than others, but in swiftly developing areas or for very new terms, controlled vocabulary may not work. Further, when the term is included in the thesaurus, older documents may not be reindexed, so they will be accessible only using free-text searching.

- *There is only one good term, and it is not an index term.* This is particularly the case when a good term is outside of a subject area. For example, if one was searching for documents about how to develop good search strategies in Web-based search engines, one might decide to search in ERIC, but ERIC, as of this writing, has no good descriptor or term for the concept "search engine." There are other possibilities—INFORMATION RETRIEVAL, ONLINE SEARCH, and ACCESS TO INFORMATION—but in this case, it might be better to search for this phrase as a free-text expression like the following:

```
?s search()engine? ?
          13234    SEARCH
           1023    ENGINE? ?
   S10        77    SEARCH()ENGINE? ?
?s s10 and search strategies
             77    S10
           2350    SEARCH STRATEGIES (COMPREHENSIVE PLANS FOR FINDING
                   INFORMATION ...)
   S11        20    S10 AND SEARCH STRATEGIES
?t 11/5/1
 11/5/1
EJ546200              IR535073
  "Just the Answers, Please": Choosing a Web Search Service.
  Feldman, Susan
  Searcher; v5 n5 p44-50,52-57 May 1997
  Language: English
  Document Type: NON-CLASSROOM MATERIAL (055); JOURNAL ARTICLE (080);
PROJECT DESCRIPTION (141)
  Journal Announcement: CIJNOV97
  Presents guidelines for selecting World Wide Web search
  engines. Real-life questions were used to test six search engines.
  Queries sought company information, product reviews, medical
  information, foreign information, technical reports, and current
  events. Compares performance and features of AltaVista, Excite,
  HotBot, Infoseek, Lycos, and Open Text. (AEF)
  Descriptors: *Comparative Analysis; *Computer Software
  Evaluation; Computer Software Selection; Guidelines;
  *Information Retrieval; Information Services; *Online Searching;
  Search Strategies; *World Wide Web
  Identifiers: *Query Processing; *Search Engines; Web Sites
```

- *There are not many hits, either in the database or for controlled vocabulary.* Free-text strategies are inherently broader than controlled vocabulary and thus will generally retrieve more documents. If an initial controlled vocabulary search pulls up very few or no good hits, or if it is known that there will be little good material in the database, a free-text strategy might be used to widen the net and pull in more records. There is no guarantee that these will be relevant, but at least they will be a starting point. Always keep in mind that the file may not contain the right material, no matter how good the strategy.

- *A known item is being sought.* Known-item searches are a special case. If the document's title, or a portion of it, is known (to provide a bibliographic verification, for example), there is no need to do an elaborate controlled vocabulary search. Just do a reasonable free-text attempt. Be careful, though, not to over-specify—the user's memory may not be perfect. In looking for Marcia Bates's well-known article on "the perfect thirty-item search," one might search in Library & Information Science Abstracts for the following:

```
?s perfect()thirty()item()search/ti
            90      PERFECT
            62      THIRTY
           463      ITEM
          4890      SEARCH/TI
    S1       0      PERFECT()THIRTY()ITEM()SEARCH/TI
```

Nothing is retrieved, but then try a broader strategy like the following:

```
?s thirty()item
            62      THIRTY
           463      ITEM
    S2       1      THIRTY()ITEM
```

This approach retrieves one item, which is correct:[2]

```
?t 2/6/1

  2/6/1
168472      85-2684
  TITLE: The fallacy of the perfect thirty-item online search
?t 2/3/1

  2/3/1
168472      85-2684    Library and Information Science Abstracts (LISA)
  TITLE: The fallacy of the perfect thirty-item online search
  AUTHOR(S): Bates, Marcia J.
  JOURNAL: RQ
  SOURCE: 24 (1) Fall 84, 43-50. 11 refs
```

- *You do not want to deal with a new controlled vocabulary.* As we have seen, thesauri and vocabulary differ, sometimes widely, from database to database. If confronted with a search in an unfamiliar database, one might decide that it is not really worth learning an entirely new vocabulary for one search. If time is pressing, an initial free-text strategy might be employed to see what happens, perhaps pearl growing from good documents as they come up. This can work, but clearly it is not a preferred method. Some people, though, are good at this sort of thing; if their style works in this setting, more power to them.

It should be pointed out early and often that neither technique—controlled vocabulary nor free-text searching—is superior to the other. In some cases, one will be preferable, but often they work in tandem: One begins with a free-text search and pearl grows using index terms from good documents; or one begins with a good index term or two, discovers a useful free-text expression, and uses it. The blending of these two techniques to produce high-quality searches is part of the real art of searching.

Choosing Free-Text Terms

Once the decision is made to use free-text techniques, how are terms generated? There may be no controlled vocabulary from which to draw. Or, a controlled vocabulary term or two may be employed, but in free-text fashion. This is not done frequently, though, so where do these terms come from?

The first and potentially best source of free-text terms is the user. He or she may have quite a good idea about the vocabulary of the subject area to be searched and will be able to provide helpful clues for further searching. This is particularly true with university faculty, researchers, and other specialists looking for new or new-to-them documents in their fields. In this situation, use the information they provide on search request forms and through interviews.

However, many users do not have that much background or experience in the areas of their topics and may not be reliable sources of terms. They are still certainly worth discussing, and if they know of any good documents, titles, or authors, these are often sources of good terms.

Further, one can also try pearl growing with free-text terms from good documents, in addition to index terms, if any. Look for additional good terms in abstracts and especially in titles. If a word or phrase is used in the title, it is often an indication that the document is really about that concept.

A balance must be struck between generality and specificity. If a very general, single-word free-text term is used, one may retrieve thousands of documents, only a few of which are of interest to the user. On the other hand, if the expression is too specific, one may retrieve very little, miss good things, or perhaps get nothing at all. This balancing act can be very tricky, but it gets easier with experience.

Problems with Free-Text Searching: False Drops

Free-text searching is certainly not a panacea, although it can be a helpful complement to controlled vocabulary techniques. However, there are situations in which free-text searching can be problematic. The major difficulty we encounter in searching free-text is *false drops*: retrieved documents that are not germane to the topic. Because there is no control over the vocabulary in title and abstract fields when words are searched for in those fields, the author or abstracter may or may not be using them in the same way as the searcher.

The following are a few examples of common sources of false drops and a few pieces of advice to help avoid them:[3]

Problem: Reverse concepts. If one were doing a search on school libraries and used the expression LIBRAR? AND SCHOOL?, one would get not only "school library" material but also "library school" material, which is not what is wanted.

Solution: Use proximity operators to more closely tie concepts together. A search on SCHOOL(W)LIBRAR? would not retrieve "library schools," but neither would it retrieve "libraries in schools" nor "libraries in elementary schools." One might be tempted to try SCHOOL?(2N)LIBRAR?, but that would bring the search back right where it started. In many cases, one can avoid reverse concepts by using (W), but in some instances one might have to go to controlled vocabulary.

Problem: Homographs/conflation. These are two terms for the same problem: two or more concepts that use the same word or words. Examples include words like CRACK (cocaine or seismic fault?), FIELD (part of a bibliographic record or a meadow?), and SDI (Strategic Defense Initiative or selective dissemination of information?). We say that these terms are conflated.

Solution: Qualify or focus the expression. If crack cocaine is the preferred topic, try something like CRACK AND (DRUG? OR COCAINE). This will focus the results and eliminate seismic or other extraneous material. Alternatively, try CRACK/TI, qualifying the term down to the title field. Some nonrelevant records will still come up, but marginal or off-hand mentions of the word in the abstract field will be eliminated.

Problem: Excessive truncation. Truncation is a wonderful thing, but too much of any good thing is too much. It would not be a good idea, for example, to search on BOOK? in ABI/Inform (which will also get BOOKKEEPING), or to search on INTERN? in ERIC, which would get INTERN and INTERNS but also INTERNAL and INTERNATIONAL.

Solution: Do not truncate too far to the left. Try to imagine all the variant forms that the word can take (e.g., COMPUTER, COMPUTING, COMPUTERS, COMPUTE, etc.) and either truncate further to the right (COMPUT? - still pretty bad) or restrict the length of your truncation (COMPUT??? will only get up to three more characters; COMPUTER? ? will only get up to one more) or do not truncate at all (COMPUTER OR COMPUTING OR COMPUTERS OR COMPUTE), depending on the database and the vocabulary.

Problem: Acronyms. Many acronyms (CBS, USA, NASA) are not a problem because they have essentially entered the language as words in their own right. Some, however, will conflate with other common words. Acronyms such as ADD (attention deficit disorder, from psychology), SAD (seasonal affective disorder), AIDS (acquired immune deficiency syndrome), and so on will retrieve many more documents than intended because they will also retrieve based on the words "add," "sad," and "aids."

Solution: There are several things to try. Focus or qualify the set (ADD AND ATTENTION). Use the full expression (SEASONAL()AFFECTIVE()DISORDER?). Search in the descriptor field and see if the expression or acronym is an index term (ACQUIRED()IMMUN?/DE).

Problem: Negation. Suppose one is searching for documents about programs to teach older people how to use computers. A strategy like COMPUTER? ? AND (OLDER OR ELDERLY) might seem like a good start, but it retrieves documents that contain sentences like, "We had hoped to include elderly people in our program, but our funding wouldn't allow us to." Although many databases instruct their indexers and abstracters not to incorporate negative phrases, it is not a universal instruction, and the instructions are not necessarily followed.

Solution: Shy of completely reworking abstracts and the way they are written, there is not a lot that can be done about this. It is not a major problem, but it is particularly frustrating when it happens.

Good Places to Use Free-Text Searching

There are several situations in which free-text techniques are especially useful—situations in which controlled vocabulary simply will not work or cannot be used. The following are a few examples:[4]

- *Geography.* Some databases have geographical descriptors (ABI/Inform, PAIS) or identifiers (ERIC), but many do not. If searching for documents that make mention of a particular geographic name, free-text techniques may be the only option: ANN()ARBOR, NEW()YORK. Keep in mind, though, that several geographic names may refer to the same area. For a search on New England, the following might be wise to do:

```
(NEW()ENGLAND OR MAINE OR VERMONT OR NEW()HAMPSHIRE OR CONNECTICUT
OR RHODE()ISLAND) OR MASSACHUSETTS)
```

and even then you might miss records which refer to Boston or Providence or the White Mountains or the Berkshires.

- Other proper names. Again, some databases have personal name fields or include names as descriptors or identifiers, but if these are not available or if one is looking for other proper names, use free-text: GROUCHO(W)MARX, HOUSE(1W) REPRESENTATIVES, MICROSOFT()WORD.

> *When searching for personal names it is worth remembering that they may be entered in some databases in inverted form (both as Groucho Marx and Marx, Groucho), so GROUCHO(N)MARX might be a more useful strategy. – GW*

- *Concepts marginal to the database.* Say one is looking for documents about virtual reality systems and their potential impact on teaching. Searching in ERIC uncovers a number of descriptors on "teaching" but none on virtual reality, so one might use VIRTUAL()REALITY as a free-text expression.

The Ladder of Specificity:
Broadening and Narrowing Searches

As we have discussed searching techniques using controlled vocabulary and free text, the idea of broadening and narrowing search statements has come up more than once. It is possible to think of these methods of searching as falling on a continuum, or ladder, of specificity.

We have already seen that controlled vocabulary searching is a very specific technique. The fact that an indexer, after evaluating a document, has assigned it a particular term, gives us a reasonably good idea that the document is about that concept. With free-text techniques, because one is dealing with parts of the document that are in natural language (titles and abstracts), one does not have that kind of confidence about the topic covered based on the simple presence of a word or phrase.

Consider the diagram in figure 8.1:

Fig. 8.1. The ladder of specificity.

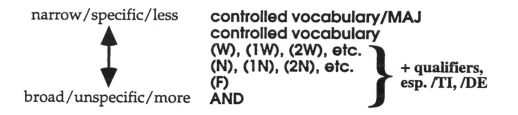

As one moves from the bottom of this ladder toward the top, the strategies become more specific and narrower and will retrieve fewer documents. Conversely, as one moves down, the strategies become less specific and broader and retrieve more documents. The /MAJ limit moves up the ladder, as do field qualifiers, especially /TI to qualify to titles and /DE to limit to the descriptor field.

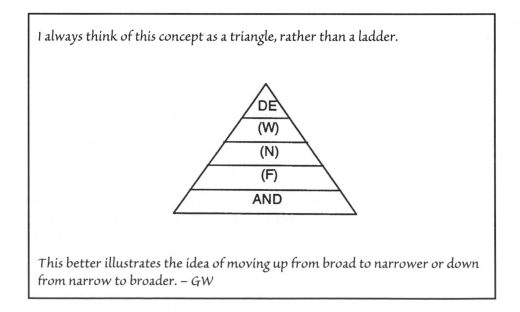

This may be intellectually interesting, but it is also of considerable use in searching. Depending on the nature of the topic, the user, and the database, one can choose to begin a search with a strategy or set of strategies at a selected level on the ladder. After reviewing initial results, the results may be too broad, or there are too many or too few documents. One of the ways to cope with this is to move up or down on the ladder.

Similarly, if there are fewer documents than expected or even none, or if they may be a bit too narrow, move down the ladder. One can move from controlled vocabulary to free text, drop /MAJ or field qualifiers, or move to a broader free-text strategy: (W) to (1W) or (2W) or (N), (N) to (1N) or (2N) or (F), and so on.

These are not the only ways to broaden or narrow searches, though. A search can be broadened by using more terms (ORing them together), using broader controlled vocabulary terms as they are indicated in the thesaurus, or dropping a marginal concept altogether. A search can be narrowed by using fewer terms, using narrower controlled vocabulary terms, adding another concept, or NOTing out a concept.

> I am not a big fan of NOT—it is a seductively easy way of reducing the size of sets, but I think that it is often a bad idea. It is really easy to lose good documents that way. If you NOT a term out, especially using free text, any good documents that happen to have that term will also go away. If you are positive that any document that contains that term is not useful, under any circumstances, you might think about trying NOT, but I would be very careful about it. – JWJ

The following is a brief example showing this "ladder" at work in *ERIC* on the two-word phrase "test bias." We begin with the broadest strategy, by searching for the two words in the same document, using AND:

```
    Set    Items    Description
    ---    -----    -----------
?s test and bias

           71282    TEST
           14735    BIAS (AN INCLINATION, OR A LACK OF BALANCE (NOTE: ...)
    S1      3127    TEST AND BIAS
```

More than 3,000 documents in ERIC contain both the word TEST and the word BIAS. Now we move to a slightly narrower strategy, (F), and look for those words in the same field:

```
?s test(f)bias

           71282    TEST
           14735    BIAS (AN INCLINATION, OR A LACK OF BALANCE (NOTE: ...)
    S2      2767    TEST(F)BIAS
```

We get fewer documents. Let us NOT to see what we lost when we went to a narrower strategy:

```
?s s1 not s2

          3127      S1
          2767      S2
    S3     360      S1 NOT S2
?t 3/5/1


  3/5/1
DIALOG(R)File       1:ERIC
(c) format only 1998 The Dialog Corporation. All rts. reserv.

EJ531824           UD519585
  Teacher Disapproval, Delinquent Peers, and Self-Reported Delinquency: A
Longitudinal Test of Labeling Theory.
  Adams, Mike S.; Evans, T. David
  Urban Review; v28 n3 p199-211 Sep 1996
  ISSN: 0042-0972
  Available from: UMI
  Language: English
  Document Type: REVIEW LITERATURE (070); RESEARCH REPORT (143); JOURNAL
ARTICLE (080)
  Journal Announcement: CIJFEB97
  Uses data from the National Youth Survey to assess the effects of
individual students" perceptions of teacher disapproval on self-reported
delinquency. Results indicate that the perceptions of teacher disapproval
are associated with subsequent delinquency. This relationship was
significant when controlling for prior delinquency, thus weakening the
argument that labeling is merely a result, not a cause of delinquency. (GR)
  Descriptors: *Delinquency; High School Students; Junior High School
Students; *Labeling (of Persons); *Peer Influence; *Secondary Education;
*Social Bias; Social Science Research; Socioeconomic Status; Stereotypes;
*Teacher Attitudes
  Identifiers: National Youth Survey
```

The above is one of those documents excluded by limiting to the same field (F). The words TEST and BIAS appear, but they are in different fields and are unrelated. The document has nothing to do with "test bias," and the extremely broad strategy using AND did not serve us well. We will continue to use narrower strategies like the following and view documents we exclude to demonstrate how moving up the ladder focuses searching more closely at each step.

```
?s test(10w)bias

          71282     TEST
          14735     BIAS (AN INCLINATION, OR A LACK OF BALANCE (NOTE: ...)
    S4     2103      TEST(10W)BIAS
?s s2 not s4

          2767      S2
          2103      S4
    S5     664      S2 NOT S4
?t 5/5/1-3


  5/5/1
DIALOG(R)File       1:ERIC
(c) format only 1998 The DialogCorporation. All rts. reserv.

EJ546738           TM520217
  Estimating the Importance of Differential Item Functioning.
```

Rudas, Tamas; Zwick, Rebecca
Journal of Educational and Behavioral Statistics; v22 n1 p31-45 Spr 1997
ISSN: 1076-9986
Language: English
Document Type: JOURNAL ARTICLE (080); EVALUATIVE REPORT (142)
Journal Announcement: CIJNOV97
The mixture index of fit (T. Rudas et al, 1994) is used to estimate the fraction of a population for which differential item functioning (DIF) occurs, and this approach is compared to the Mantel Haenszel test of DIF. The proposed noniterative procedure provides information about data portions contributing to DIF. (SLD)
  Descriptors: Comparative Analysis; *Estimation (Mathematics); *Item Bias; *Maximum Likelihood Statistics; *Test Items
  Identifiers: Item Bias Detection; *Mantel Haenszel Procedure

5/5/2
DIALOG(R)File   1:ERIC
(c) format only 1998 The Dialog Corporation. All rts. reserv.

EJ546729   TM520205
  A Multidimensionality-Based DIF Analysis Paradigm.
  Roussos, Louis; Stout, William
  Applied Psychological Measurement; v20 n4 p355-71 Dec 1996
  ISSN: 0146-6216
  Language: English
  Document Type: JOURNAL ARTICLE (080); EVALUATIVE REPORT (142)
  Journal Announcement: CIJNOV97
A multidimensionality-based differential item functioning (DIF) analysis paradigm is presented that unifies substantive and statistical DIF analysis approaches by linking both to a theoretically sound and mathematically rigorous multidimensional DIF conceptualization. This approach results in the potential for DIF analysis more closely integrated with the whole test development process. (Author/SLD)
  Descriptors: Cluster Analysis; *Estimation (Mathematics); Hypothesis Testing; Identification; *Item Bias; *Models; Test Construction; *Test Items
  Identifiers: Item Bias Detection; *Multidimensionality (Tests)

5/5/3
DIALOG(R)File   1:ERIC
(c) format only 1998 The Dialog Corporation. All rts. reserv.

EJ545074   PS526650
  Restricting a Familiar Name in Response to Learning a New One: Evidence for the Mutual Exclusivity Bias in Young Two-Year-Olds.
  Merriman, William E.; Stevenson, Colleen M.
  Child Development; v68 n2 p211-28 Apr 1997
  ISSN: 0009-3920
  Language: English
  Document Type: RESEARCH REPORT (143); JOURNAL ARTICLE (080)
  Journal Announcement: CIJOCT97
Used new test to determine whether 24-month olds interpret novel words in accordance with Mutual Exclusivity Bias. Found that when asked to select exemplars of a familiar noun, they avoided objects from previously read story in which novel nouns were used as atypical exemplars of familiar noun. When pronouns and proper names replaced novel nouns, toddlers did not avoid story objects. (KB)

```
  Descriptors: *Familiarity; Measures (Individuals); Novelty (Stimulus
Dimension); *Toddlers; *Vocabulary Development
  Identifiers: *Mutual Exclusivity Bias; Naming Response; *Word Learning
```

The above are documents that have TEST and BIAS in the same field but not within 10 words of each other in that order. A couple of these are close, referring to item bias in tests, but they are still not quite on the mark. Another attempt yields the following:

```
?s test(3n)bias

         71282    TEST
         14735    BIAS (AN INCLINATION, OR A LACK OF BALANCE (NOTE: ...)
    S6    2068    TEST(3N)BIAS
?s s4 not s6

          2103    S4
          2068    S6
    S7      69    S4 NOT S6
?t 7/5/1-3


 7/5/1
DIALOG(R)File      1:ERIC
(c) format only 1998 The Dialog Corporation. All rts. reserv.

EJ536974          TM519883
  The University Entrance Examinations in Turkey.
  Berberoglu, Giray
  Studies in Educational Evaluation; v22 n4 p363-73 1996
  ISSN: 0191-491X
  Language: English
  Document Type: PROJECT DESCRIPTION (141); JOURNAL ARTICLE (080)
  Journal Announcement: CIJMAY97
  Issues related to the two-stage college entrance examinations used in
Turkey are explored. Focus is on the first stage, the selection phase of
the examination, rather than on the second stage, the placement phase.
Further study is needed of the dimensionality of the test and sources of
item bias. (SLD)
  Descriptors: *College Entrance Examinations; Foreign Countries; *Higher
Education; *Item Bias; *Selection; Student Placement; *Test Use; Test
Validity
  Identifiers: Dimensionality (Tests); *Turkey


 7/5/2
DIALOG(R)File      1:ERIC
(c) format only 1998 The Dialog Corporation. All rts. reserv.

EJ528234          PS525393
  Anxiety and the Processing of Emotionally Threatening Stimuli:
Distinctive Patterns of Selective Attention among High- and
Low-Test-Anxious Children.
  Vasey, Michael W.; And Others
  Child Development; v67 n3 p1173-85 Jun 1996
  ISSN: 0009-3920
  Available from: UMI
  Language: English
  Document Type: RESEARCH REPORT (143); JOURNAL ARTICLE (080)
  Journal Announcement: CIJDEC96
```

Tested for bias toward shifting attention toward threatening stimuli among high-anxious children and away from such stimuli among low-anxious children, ages 11-14. Results supported the predicted attentional bias toward threat cues among high-test-anxious children. Unexpectedly, the predicted attentional bias away from threat cues among low-anxious children was found only for boys. (HTH)
  Descriptors: *Anxiety; Attention; *Early Adolescents; *Emotional Response; Personality Traits; Sex Differences; Test Anxiety

  7/5/3
DIALOG(R)File   1:ERIC
(c) format only 1998 The Dialog Corporation. All rts. reserv.

EJ521000   TM519386
  A Blended Qualitative-Quantitative Assessment Model for Identifying and Rank-Ordering Service Needs of Indigenous Peoples.
  Loos, Gregory P.
  Evaluation and Program Planning; v18 n3 p237-44 Jul-Sep 1995
  Research supported by a consortium of human care agencies and funded by the Bishop Estate, a private trust in Hawaii.
  ISSN: 0149-7189
  Available from: UMI
  Language: English
  Document Type: EVALUATIVE REPORT (142); JOURNAL ARTICLE (080)
  Journal Announcement: CIJJUL96
  This article describes a series of qualitative and quantitative methods used to test a community-based needs assessment model that is bias free and socioculturally relevant for indigenous populations. Results of a field test involving 100 Hawaiian children are presented, and implications for policy formation are discussed. (SLD)
  Descriptors: Children; *Community Programs; Cultural Awareness; Field Tests; *Indigenous Populations; Models; *Needs Assessment; *Policy Formation; *Qualitative Research; Statistical Analysis; *Statistical Bias
  Identifiers: Hawaii

Again, the above citations are marginal at best—documents that have the two words within 10 words of each other but not within three. Narrowing still further, we get the following:

?s test(n)bias

```
        71282    TEST
        14735    BIAS (AN INCLINATION, OR A LACK OF BALANCE (NOTE: ...)
   S8    2009    TEST(N)BIAS
?s s6 not s8

        2068     S6
        2009     S8
   S9      59    S6 NOT S8
?t 9/5/1-3
```

  9/5/1
DIALOG(R)File   1:ERIC
(c) format only 1998 The Dialog Corporation. All rts. reserv.

EJ519378   CG548093
  Perceiver Bias in Expectancies for Sexually Abused Children.
  Briggs, Kathleen; And Others

Family Relations; v44 n3 p291-98 Jul 1995
ISSN: 0197-6664
Available from: UMI
Language: English
Document Type: RESEARCH REPORT (143); JOURNAL ARTICLE (080)
Journal Announcement: CIJJUL96
Presents a study in which 134 college students judged children in vignettes varying on child gender and family history to test perceiver bias. Perceiver bias was confirmed. Perceptions of female sexual abuse victims were more biased than perceptions of male victims. (Author/SR)
  Descriptors: Behavior Problems; Child Abuse; Child Behavior; Children; *Questionnaires; *Sex Bias; Sex Differences; Sex Stereotypes; *Sexual Abuse; Surveys
  Identifiers: Child History Expectation Questionnaire

  9/5/2
DIALOG(R)File   1:ERIC
(c) format only 1998 The Dialog Corporation. All rts. reserv.

EJ503271   HE533895
  Effect of Anonymous Test Grading on Passing Rates as Related to Gender and Race.
  Dorsey, J. Kevin; Colliver, Jerry A.
  Academic Medicine; v70 n4 p321-23 Apr 1995
  ISSN: 1040-2446
  Available from: UMI
  Language: English
  Document Type: RESEARCH REPORT (143); JOURNAL ARTICLE (080)
  Journal Announcement: CIJSEP95
Because of concern about potential gender and racial bias in medical test grading, score patterns were examined for male and female and for white and African American medical freshmen (n=476) before and after implementation of an anonymous test grading policy. Results indicate no widespread grading bias before the policy change. (Author/MSE)
  Descriptors: Black Students; Females; *Grading; Higher Education; Males; *Medical Education; Professional Education; *Racial Bias; *Sex Bias; *Testing Problems; White Students
  Identifiers: African Americans

  9/5/3
DIALOG(R)File   1:ERIC
(c) format only 1998 The Dialog Corporation. All rts. reserv.

EJ497098   TM518438
  Comparison of Empirical and Judgmental Procedures for Detecting Differential Item Functioning.
  Hambleton, Ronald K.; Jones, Russell W.
  Educational Research Quarterly; v18 n1 p21-36 Sep 1994
  ISSN: 0196-5042
  Available from: UMI
  Language: English
  Document Type: EVALUATIVE REPORT (142); JOURNAL ARTICLE (080)
  Journal Announcement: CIJMAY95
A judgmental method for determining item bias was applied to test data from 2,000 Native American and 2,000 Anglo-American students for a statewide proficiency test. Results indicated some shortcomings of the

```
judgmental method but supported the use of cross-validation in empirically
identifying potential bias. (SLD)
   Descriptors: American Indians; Anglo Americans; Comparative Analysis;
*Decision Making; *Evaluation Methods; *Identification; *Item Bias; *Test
Items
   Identifiers: Cross Validation; *Empirical Research
```

The above documents are getting closer. The words are now within three words of each other but not directly adjacent. There are probably some good retrievals in there. But we can go still further with the following:

```
?s test(w)bias

         71282      TEST
         14735      BIAS (AN INCLINATION, OR A LACK OF BALANCE (NOTE: ...)
   S10    2002      TEST(W)BIAS
?s s8 not s10

          2009      S8
          2002      S10
   S11       7      S8 NOT S10
?t 11/5/1


   11/5/1
DIALOG(R)File     1:ERIC
(c) format only 1998 The Dialog Corporation. All rts. reserv.

EJ213055          RC503536
   In North Carolina: Overlooked Causes and Implications of School Finance
Disparities.
   Nord, Stephen; Ledford, Manfred H.
   Growth and Change; v10 n4 p16-19 Oct 1979
   Available from: Reprint: UMI
   Language: ENGLISH
   Document Type: JOURNAL ARTICLE (080); RESEARCH REPORT (143)
   Journal Announcement: CIJAPR80
   Describes model, data, results, and implications of a study attempting to
clarify two issues previously overlooked in studies of financing public
education with local property taxes: (1) that regionally aggregated data
may bias test results, and (2) that local fiscal response to grant programs
may vary with the wealth of school districts. (SB)
   Descriptors: Assessed Valuation; *Educational Finance; *Equalization Aid;
Federal Aid; *Financial Policy; *Government School Relationship; Grants;
Models; Policy Formation; *Property Taxes; Public Education; *School Taxes;
State Aid; State School District Relationship; Tax Allocation
   Identifiers: *North Carolina
```

Asking for the two words directly adjacent but in either order pulls up false drops like this. This is to be expected in this case because "bias test" is not the same as "test bias." However, a strategy such as BIAS(2N)TEST, which would look for "bias of a test," would also pull up documents such as the one above. Note that there are very few documents in this set.

As an aside, let us see what happens when we qualify one of these sets down to the title field alone:

```
?s test(w)bias/ti

        10163    TEST/TI
         1407    BIAS/TI (AN INCLINATION, OR A LACK OF BALANCE (NOTE: ...)
S12        76    TEST(W)BIAS/TI
```

The unqualified set, S10, had more than 1,700 documents; this one has 76. Obviously, the vast majority of occurrences of "test bias" as a phrase are in the abstract, descriptor, or identifier fields. Qualification can be an important tool, but at times it may also be too specific.

We can narrow still further with the following:

```
?s test bias

S13      1951    TEST BIAS (UNFAIRNESS IN THE CONSTRUCTION, CONTENT, ADM...)
?s s10 not s13

         2002    S10
         1951    S13
S14        51    S10 NOT S13
?t 14/5/1-3
```

```
 14/5/1
DIALOG(R)File       1:ERIC
(c) format only 1998 The Dialog Corporation. All rts. reserv.


EJ528731          UD519339
  Black Scholars Hold a Pessimistic Outlook for African American Prospects
in Higher Education.
  Cross, Theodore, Ed.; And Others
  Journal of Blacks in Higher Education; n11 p74-77 Spr 1996
  ISSN: 1077-3711
  Language: English
  Document Type: REVIEW LITERATURE (070); RESEARCH REPORT (143); JOURNAL
ARTICLE (080)
  Journal Announcement: CIJDEC96
  Discusses survey findings that show black academics are highly
pessimistic in their view of the future of blacks in higher education.
Reasons include the following: curtailment of federal support for black
colleges over the next five years; continued built-in test bias against
blacks; no improvement in campus race relations; and persistent racial
barriers against black faculty. (GR)
  Descriptors: Affirmative Action; *Black Colleges; *Black Education; Black
Teachers; Educational Research; Educational Trends; *Financial Support;
Futures (of Society); Higher Education; Postsecondary Education; *Racial
Bias; *Racial Relations; Scores; Surveys; *Teacher Attitudes
  Identifiers: Scholastic Aptitude Test


 14/5/2
DIALOG(R)File 1:ERIC
(c) format only 1998 The Dialog Corporation. All rts. reserv.


EJ296328          UD510634
  Beyond IQ Test Bias: The National Academy Panel"s Analysis of Minority
EMR Overrepresentation.
```

Reschly, Daniel J.
Educational Researcher; v13 n3 p15-19 Mar 1984
Language: English
Document Type: REVIEW LITERATURE (070)
Journal Announcement: CIJJUN84
Questions educational relevance of direct measures of learning such as
the Learning Potential Assessment Device, assessment of biomedical factors,
and adaptative behavior measures. Notes increased discrepancies between EMR
and average students in high school. Suggests a generic classification for
the mildly handicapped and the combining of groups for educational
purposes. (CJM)
   Descriptors: Academic Achievement; *Classification; *Educational
Diagnosis; Elementary Secondary Education; *Learning Disabilities;
Mainstreaming; *Measurement Techniques; *Mild Mental Retardation; Minority
Group Children; Racial Bias; Racial Composition; Research Needs; *Special
Education
   Identifiers: Learning Potential Assessment Device; National Research
Council

   14/5/3
DIALOG(R)File   1:ERIC
(c) format only 1998 The Dialog Corporation. All rts. reserv.

EJ285500   EC152888
   Assessing Adaptive Behavior: Current Practices.
   Cantrell, Joan Kathryn
   Education and Training of the Mentally Retarded; v17 n2 p147-49 Apr 1982
   Available from: Reprint: UMI
   Language: English
   Document Type: JOURNAL ARTICLE (080); RESEARCH REPORT (143)
   Journal Announcement: CIJDEC83
   Twenty-nine elementary school psychologists were interviewed about
assessment of adaptive behavior. Over 95 percent reported they routinely
assess adaptive behavior skills, and 90 percent felt the assessment useful
in planning instruction. They rated methods of assessment (home observation
ranked first), cited safeguards against test bias, discussed school
policies, and recommended changes. (CL)
   Descriptors: *Adaptive Behavior (of Disabled); Attitudes; *Disabilities;
Elementary Education; Evaluation Methods; *School Psychologists; *Student
Evaluation

   Interesting. The second of these documents is about "IQ test bias" among minority
students, and so is marginal at best. The first refers explicitly to "test bias" in the abstract
but has not been indexed with the descriptor TEST BIAS. The indexers must have thought
the concept was marginal in this document. And the third one mentions safeguards *against*
test bias, yet is retrieved along with others that also contain that phrase. We have one further step on the ladder to explore.

?s s13/maj

    S15   1087   S13/MAJ
?s s13 not s15

            1951   S13
            1087   S15
    S16   864   S13 NOT S15
?t 16/5/1-3

16/5/1
DIALOG(R)File   1:ERIC

EJ546747   TM520226
  Flawed Items in Computerized Adaptive Testing.
  Potenza, Maria T.; Stocking, Martha L.
  Journal of Educational Measurement; v34 n1 p79-96 Spr 1997
  ISSN: 0022-0655
  Language: English
  Document Type: JOURNAL ARTICLE (080); EVALUATIVE REPORT (142)
  Journal Announcement: CIJNOV97
  Common strategies for dealing with flawed items in conventional testing,
grounded in principles of fairness to examinees, are re-examined in the
context of adaptive testing. The additional strategy of retesting from a
pool cleansed of flawed items is found, through a Monte Carlo study, to
bring about no practical improvement. (SLD)
  Descriptors: *Adaptive Testing; *Computer Assisted Testing; *Item Banks;
Monte Carlo Methods; Test Bias; *Test Items Identifiers: *Flawed Items

16/5/2
DIALOG(R)File   1:ERIC

EJ543873   CE530793
  Career Assessment with Lesbian, Gay, and Bisexual Individuals.
  Prince, Jeffrey P.
  Journal of Career Assessment; v5 n2 p225-38 Spr 1997
  ISSN: 1069-0727
  Language: English
  Document Type: POSITION PAPER (120); JOURNAL ARTICLE (080)
  Journal Announcement: CIJOCT97
  Sexual identity development and environmental factors are central to the
career assessment of lesbian, homosexual, and bisexual clients. Counselor
biases and biases in career assessment tools must be recognized and dealt
with. (SK)
  Descriptors: *Career Counseling; Environmental Influences; *Homosexuality;
*Lesbianism; Measures (Individuals); *Sexual Identity; Test Bias
Identifiers: *Bisexuality; *Career Assessment

16/5/3
DIALOG(R)File   1:ERIC

EJ541216   HE536582
  Educational Histories and Academic Potential: Can Tests Deliver?
  Yeld, Nan; Haeck, Wim
  Assessment & Evaluation in Higher Education; v22 n1 p5-16 Mar 1997
  ISSN: 0260-2938
  Language: English
  Document Type: EVALUATIVE REPORT (142); JOURNAL ARTICLE (080)
  Journal Announcement: CIJAUG97
  A new South African testing approach designed to assess potential
university students" ability to cope with English-medium academic education
is also designed to take into account the effects of educational
disadvantagement and minimize reliance on students" content-based secondary

school experiences. The approach incorporates principles from constructivist learning theories. Preliminary results of the testing approach are discussed. (Author/MSE)
   Descriptors: *Academic Achievement; Constructivism (Learning); *Educationally Disadvantaged; English; *English for Academic Purposes; Foreign Countries; Higher Education; *Language of Instruction; *Learning Processes; Learning Theories; Program Effectiveness; Secondary Education; Test Bias; *Testing Programs; Test Use
   Identifiers: *South Africa

   The documents above have the descriptor TEST BIAS but not as a major descriptor, and they make up fewer than half of the total number of documents that have been indexed with this term. Clearly, these documents are about test bias, but it appears that this is not a central concept in any of them. If we look at our final /MAJ set, though, we see the following:

?t 15/5/1-3

   15/5/1
DIALOG(R)File   1:ERIC
(c) format only 1998 The Dialog Corporation. All rts. reserv.

EJ546768   UD519986
   Equity and High Stakes Testing: Implications for Computerized Testing.
   Sutton, Rosemary E.
   Equity & Excellence in Education; v30 n1 p5-15 Apr 1997
   ISSN: 1066-5684
   Language: English
   Document Type: JOURNAL ARTICLE (080); POSITION PAPER (120); PROJECT
DESCRIPTION (141)
   Journal Announcement: CIJNOV97
   Considers equity issues of highstakes tests conducted by computer, including whether this new form of assessment actually helps level the playing field for students or represents a new cycle of assessment inequality. Two computer tests are assessed: Praxis I: Academic Skills Assessment; and the computerized version of the Graduate Record Examination. (GR)
   Descriptors: Adaptive Testing; *Computer Assisted Testing; Educational Assessment; Educational Testing; Secondary Education; Student Evaluation; *Test Bias
   Identifiers: Graduate Record Examinations; *High Stakes Tests; Praxis Series

   15/5/2
DIALOG(R)File   1:ERIC
(c) format only 1998 The Dialog Corporation. All rts. reserv.

EJ546752   UD519970
   The Overrepresentation of African American Children in Special Education: The Resegregation of Educational Programming?
   Russo, Charles J.; Talbert-Johnson, Carolyn
   Education and Urban Society; v29 n2 p136-48 Feb 1997
   ISSN: 0013-1245
   Language: English
   Document Type: JOURNAL ARTICLE (080); PROJECT DESCRIPTION (141)
   Journal Announcement: CIJNOV97

Reviews the historical background of special education as a major factor in the placement of many children with disabilities, and examines data that reveal a disproportionately large number of students in these programs are children of color. Suggestions are offered to help lead to a more equitable placement of all children in appropriate educational settings. (GR)
  Descriptors: *Blacks; Educational Change; Instructional Improvement; Minority Groups; School Community Relationship; *Special Education; *Special Needs Students; *Student Placement; Teacher Education; Teacher Recruitment; *Test Bias
  Identifiers: Individuals with Disabilities Education Act

  15/5/3
  DIALOG(R)File   1:ERIC
  (c) format only 1998 The Dialog Corporation. All rts. reserv.

  EJ543826   TM520091
  Test Fairness: Internal and External Investigations of Gender Bias in Mathematics Testing.
  Langenfeld, Thomas E.
  Educational Measurement: Issues and Practice; v16 n1 p20-26 Spr 1997
  ISSN: 0731-1745
  Language: English
  Document Type: EVALUATIVE REPORT (142); JOURNAL ARTICLE (080)
  Journal Announcement: CIJSEP97
  Presents two approaches to evaluating gender measurement bias in mathematics testing, and discusses how to assess these approaches. The two approaches are the study of internal test structure and external test relationships. Ensuring a gender-fair test requires attention to both areas. (SLD)
  Descriptors: *Mathematics Tests; *Measurement Techniques; Psychometrics; *Sex Bias; Sex Differences; *Test Bias
  Identifiers: Internal Structure Analysis

We see immediately that this is a very focused set. For a real search, then, we may decide to begin with a controlled vocabulary term or even limiting that to a major descriptor and then broaden out if necessary. Of course, in practice, one does not have the time or opportunity to know this kind of detail about terms, so make an educated guess about where to begin and then move up or down the ladder as necessary as the search progresses.

> Your initial choice of where on the ladder to start your search depends on your expectations of search outcome. How much material do you expect to find? Postings figures in the thesaurus, when available, can help you make this decision, as can personal experience and perhaps information from the user.
>
> – GW

Search Example

For the search example, we will use (for the last time, I promise) the traumatic brain injury search. Now that we have all of these technical possibilities at our disposal, we can use them to create a high-quality search.

A couple of things should be noted at this point:

This is not a perfect search. There are no perfect searches. It is pretty good and is the result of doing it and refining it many times over many years. Do not despair if such a search seems too involved or complicated right now. (If it seems simple, you've found your career!)

The search uses several different techniques, both controlled vocabulary and free text, and a few other things such as exploding. Not every search uses such a variety of methods; this search is an example of how they can all contribute.

Having said all that, let us proceed.

```
File 11:PsycINFO(R) 1967-1998/Jan
(c) 1998 Amer. Psychological Asso.

    Set    Items    Description
    ---    -----    -----------
?ss brain damage and (injuries/df or trauma)

    S1     4677     BRAIN DAMAGE (1967)
    S2     1521     INJURIES/DF (1973)
    S3     8838     TRAUMA
    S4      219     BRAIN DAMAGE AND (INJURIES/DF OR TRAUMA)
```

This small set is a focused subset of documents with BRAIN DAMAGE as a descriptor; that term is used not only for traumatic brain damage but also (more commonly) for congenital brain damage. The parenthetical component restricts the set only to documents that include the one-word descriptor INJURIES or the word TRAUMA anywhere.

```
?ss head injuries or closed()head()injur?
    S5     2323     HEAD INJURIES (1973)
    S6     5001     CLOSED
    S7    11676     HEAD
    S8    15539     INJUR?
    S9      784     CLOSED(W)HEAD(W)INJUR?
    S10    2437     HEAD INJURIES OR CLOSED()HEAD()INJUR?
?s s4 or s10

            219     S4
           2437     S10
    S11    2589     S4 OR S10
?s children! or adolescents/df

         120906     CHILDREN! (1967)
          32256     ADOLESCENTS/DF (1967)
    S12 141918CHILDREN! OR ADOLESCENTS/DF
```

I chose to explode CHILDREN because it has several narrower terms, including INFANTS, and many of these narrower terms also have narrower terms. It is an economical way to get all those terms. ADOLESCENTS, on the other hand, has only two narrower terms, ADOLESCENT MOTHERS and ADOLESCENT FATHERS, both of which have very few postings. Not worth considering.

```
?s s11 and s12

            2589    S11
          141918    S12
    S13     247     S11 AND S12
?ss psychsocial or behavior/maj or neuropsycholog?

    S14       4     PSYCHSOCIAL
    S15    4565     BEHAVIOR/MAJ (1967)
    S16   14928     NEUROPSYCHOLOG?
    S17   19414     PSYCHSOCIAL OR BEHAVIOR/MAJ OR NEUROPSYCHOLOG?
?s psychosocial or s14

    S18   28364     PSYCHOSOCIAL
              4     s14
    S19   28366     PSYCHOSOCIAL OR S14
?s s19 or s17

          28366     S19
          19414     S17
    S20   47282     S19 OR S17
?s s13 and s20

            247     S13
          47282     S20
    S21      86     S13 AND S20
```

When doing this search for inclusion in this chapter, I made the spelling error you see in S14. I did not catch it until too late and was about to restart the search so it would look perfect for the book when I decided to keep it to demonstrate (a) that we all make mistakes like that, no matter how experienced we get, and (b) how to recover from an error like that. Note that I recreated that concept set by ORing it with the correct spelling. Some indexer made the same mistake I did (hence the 4 hits in S14), and those documents are included in S19.

I took three different approaches with those three terms. PSYCHOSOCIAL, as we have seen, is part of a descriptor, PSYCHOSOCIAL READJUSTMENT, but it also was mentioned by itself by the user in her original request. Because it is a fairly concrete and specific term, even in a psychology database, I chose to search it as is. "Behavior" is a far broader concept, especially in a psychology database, so I searched it very narrowly by restricting it to use in major descriptors. I could have chosen specific descriptors and ORed them together, but again the user gave us just that word, so I let it go to all descriptors, yet limited it as best I could. Finally, I truncated on NEUROPSYCHOLOG?, figuring any word beginning with a stem that specific (and that long, for that matter) would be appropriate.

```
?t 21/8/1-10

 21/8/1
DIALOG(R)File 11:(c) 1998 Amer. Psychological Assn. All rts. reserv.

01523141           1997-38757-001
Head injury in children.

DESCRIPTORS: *Brain Damage; *Head Injuries; *Literature Review; *Traumatic
  Brain Injury; Children
IDENTIFIERS: head injury in children, literature review
SUBJECT CODES & HEADINGS: 3297 (Neurological Disorders & Brain Damage)
```

21/8/2

01512432   1997-36680-006
Frontal lobe dysfunction following closed head injury in children: Findings
   from neuropsychology and brain imaging.

DESCRIPTORS: *Brain Disorders; *Head Injuries; *Literature Review;
   *Neuropsychological Assessment; *Tomography; Children; Neuropsychology;
   Prefrontal Cortex
IDENTIFIERS: neurobehavioral sequelae of & neuroimaging techniques for &
performance on neuropsychological tests & prefrontal brain dysfunctions
following closed head-injuries, children, literature review
SUBJECT CODES & HEADINGS: 3297 (Neurological Disorders & Brain Damage)

21/8/3

01507522   1997-43861-010
Concept formation and problem-solving following closed head injury in
   children.

DESCRIPTORS: *Head Injuries; *Neuropsychological Assessment; *Severity
   (Disorders); Adolescence; Adulthood; Childhood; Longitudinal Studies;
   Preschool Age Children; School Age Children
IDENTIFIERS: Twenty Questions Test & Tower of London & Wisconsin Card
Sorting Test performance, 5-18 yr olds with mild vs severe closed head
injury, 36 mo study
SUBJECT CODES & HEADINGS: 3297 (Neurological Disorders & Brain Damage)

21/8/4

01483092   1997-42970-002
A typology of psychosocial functioning in pediatric closed-head injury.

DESCRIPTORS: *Head Injuries; *Psychodiagnostic Typologies; *Severity
   (Disorders); *Psychosocial Readjustment; Adolescence; Childhood; School
   Age Children
IDENTIFIERS: typology of psychosocial functioning, 6-16 yr olds with mild
vs moderate vs severe closed head injury
SUBJECT CODES & HEADINGS: 3290 (Physical & Somatoform & Psychogenic
   Disorders)

21/8/5

01482579   1997-30097-007
Pediatric neuropsychology.

DESCRIPTORS: *Brain Disorders; *Developmental Stages; *Neuropsychological
   Assessment; *Neural Development; Adolescents; Preschool Age Children;
   School Age Children; Oral Communication; Motor Skills; Head Injuries;
   Cognitive Processes
IDENTIFIERS: development of nervous system & motor & speech & higher
cognitive functions & application to development of neuropsychological
assessment approach, 2-5 & 6-14 yr olds with neuropsychological deficits
SUBJECT CODES & HEADINGS: 3297 (Neurological Disorders & Brain Damage)

21/8/6
DIALOG(R)File 11:(c) 1998 Amer. Psychological Assn. All rts. reserv.

01471818   1997-05606-001
Mild head injury in children and adolescents: A review of studies
   (1970-1995).

DESCRIPTORS: *Head Injuries; *Literature Review; Adolescents; Children
IDENTIFIERS: neuropsychological or academic or psychosocial outcomes,
children & adolescents with mild head injury, literature review, 1970-1995
SUBJECT CODES & HEADINGS: 3297 (Neurological Disorders & Brain Damage)

21/8/7
DIALOG(R)File 11:(c) 1998 Amer. Psychological Assn. All rts. reserv.

01427791   1996-04856-003
Behavioural adjustment and parental stress associated with closed head
   injury in children.

DESCRIPTORS: *Behavior Problems; *Parental Attitudes; *Traumatic Brain
   Injury; *Stress; Adolescents; Children; Mothers; Adulthood
IDENTIFIERS: parental stress levels & perception of children"s behavioral
problems at least 1 yr after injury, 24-50 yr old mothers of children (aged
4.5-15 yrs) who had traumatic brain injury
SUBJECT CODES & HEADINGS: 3297 (Neurological Disorders & Brain Damage)

21/8/8
DIALOG(R)File 11:(c) 1998 Amer. Psychological Assn. All rts. reserv.

01411695   1997-85262-001
Applicazione della Batteria Neuropsicologica Luria Nebraska nell"analisi
   funzionale di soggetti con pregresso trauma cranico e coma.
TRANSLATED TITLE: Application of the Luria-Nebraska Neuropsychological
Battery in the functional analysis of subjects with head injury and
subsequent coma.

DESCRIPTORS: *Coma; *Foreign Language Translation; *Neuropsychological
   Assessment; *Test Reliability; *Head Injuries; Adolescence; Adulthood;
   School Age Children; Childhood
IDENTIFIERS: reliability of Luria-Nebraska Neuropsychological Battery, male
10-22 yr olds with head injury & subsequent coma, Italy
SUBJECT CODES & HEADINGS: 2225 (Neuropsychological Assessment)

21/8/9
DIALOG(R)File 11:(c) 1998 Amer. Psychological Assn. All rts. reserv.

01411183   1997-06130-003
Age at injury as a predictor of outcome following pediatric head injury:
   A longitudinal perspective.

DESCRIPTORS: *Age Differences; *Head Injuries; *Neuropsychological
   Assessment; *Recovery (Disorders); Childhood; Longitudinal Studies;
   School Age Children
IDENTIFIERS: age at injury & recovery from pediatric head injury, children
injured before vs after 7 yrs of age, 4 mo to 2 yr longitudinal study
SUBJECT CODES & HEADINGS: 3297 (Neurological Disorders & Brain Damage);
   2820 (Cognitive & Perceptual Development)

```
21/8/10
DIALOG(R)File 11:(c) 1998 Amer. Psychological Assn. All rts. reserv.

01409782          1996-97000-009
Attention deficits in the long term after childhood head injury.

DESCRIPTORS: *Attention; *Cognitive Ability; *Head Injuries; Adolescence;
  Brain Damage; Neuropsychology; School Age Children; School Learning;
  Preschool Age Children; Memory; Early Experience; Childhood; Adulthood
IDENTIFIERS: long term neuropsychological outcomes of memory & attention in
academic work & daily functions, 5.2-18 yr olds with head injuries
SUBJECT CODES & HEADINGS: 3297 (Neurological Disorders & Brain Damage)
```

These results are quite encouraging. Not perfect by any means, but several look very good, especially the sixth one (a literature review). One is in Italian, so I limited the set down to English:

?s s21/eng

```
    S22      82     S21/ENG
```

and only eliminated 4 documents. Here are the titles of the first 25 documents:

?t 22/6/1-25

```
 22/6/1
01523141          1997-38757-001
Head injury in children.


 22/6/2
01512432          1997-36680-006
Frontal lobe dysfunction following closed head injury in children: Findings
  from neuropsychology and brain imaging.


 22/6/3
01507522          1997-43861-010
Concept formation and problem-solving following closed head injury in
  children.


 22/6/4
01483092          1997-42970-002
A typology of psychosocial functioning in pediatric closed-head injury.


 22/6/5
01482579          1997-30097-007
Pediatric neuropsychology.


 22/6/6
01471818          1997-05606-001
Mild head injury in children and adolescents: A review of studies
  (1970-1995).
```

22/6/7
01427791   1996-04856-003
Behavioural adjustment and parental stress associated with closed head
   injury in children.

22/6/8
01411183   1997-06130-003
Age at injury as a predictor of outcome following pediatric head injury:
   A longitudinal perspective.

22/6/9
01409782   1996-97000-009
Attention deficits in the long term after childhood head injury.

22/6/10
01409781   1996-97000-008
Cognitive, behavioral, and motoric sequelae of mild head injury in a
   national birth cohort.

22/6/11
01409779   1996-97000-006
Discourse as an outcome measure in pediatric head-injured populations.

22/6/12
01409778   1996-97000-005
Neurobehavioral outcome of pediatric closed head injury.

22/6/13
01409774   1996-97000-001
Variability in outcomes after traumatic brain injury in children:
   A developmental perspective.

22/6/14
01409211   1996-93110-001
Differential performances on the WRAML in children and adolescents
   diagnosed with epilepsy, head injury, and substance abuse.

22/6/15
01396784   1996-17735-001
Neuropsychological deficit and academic performance in children and
   adolescents following traumatic brain injury.

22/6/16
01385762   1996-02578-040
Clinical neurological indicators are only moderately correlated with
   quantitative neuropsychological test scores in patients who display
   mild-moderate brain impairment following closed-head injuries.

22/6/17
01381178   1995-98826-019
Neurobehavioral effects of brain injury on children: Hydrocephalus,
   traumatic brain injury, and cerebral palsy.

```
22/6/18
01352975              1996-97159-000
Pediatric traumatic brain injury.
SERIES TITLE: Developmental clinical psychology and psychiatry, Vol. 31.


22/6/19
01338383              1995-25937-001
Clinical neurological trauma parameters as predictors for
  neuropsychological recovery and long-term outcome in paediatric
  closed head injury: A review of the literature.


22/6/20
01330143              1995-14036-001
Cognitive and psychosocial outcome after head injury in children.


22/6/21
01314586              1994-97656-014
The impact of neuropsychiatry upon forensic issues related to children
  and adolescents.


22/6/22
01305613              1994-38159-001
Motor, visual; spatial, and somatosensory skills after closed head injury
  in children and adolescents: A study of change.


22/6/23
01265744              1994-10353-001
Predictors of outcome following severe head trauma: Follow-up data from
  the Traumatic Coma Data Bank.


22/6/24
01253977              1993-97880-009
Traumatic brain injury.


22/6/25
01244067              1993-38257-001
Long-term outcome of head injuries: A 23 year follow up study of children
  with head injuries.
```

Let us look at a summary of the complete search strategy:

?*ds*

```
    Set    Items    Description
    S1      4677    BRAIN DAMAGE (1967)
    S2      1521    INJURIES/DF (1973)
    S3      8838    TRAUMA
    S4       219    BRAIN DAMAGE AND (INJURIES/DF OR TRAUMA)
    S5      2323    HEAD INJURIES (1973)
    S6      5001    CLOSED
    S7     11676    HEAD
    S8     15539    INJUR?
    S9       784    CLOSED(W)HEAD(W)INJUR?
```

(List continues on page 172.)

```
Set     Items       Description
S10      2437       HEAD INJURIES OR CLOSED()HEAD()INJUR?
S11      2589       S4 OR S10
S12    141918       CHILDREN! OR ADOLESCENTS/DF
S13       247       S11 AND S12
S14         4       PSYCHSOCIAL
S15      4565       BEHAVIOR/MAJ (1967)
S16     14928       NEUROPSYCHOLOG?
S17     19414       PSYCHSOCIAL OR BEHAVIOR/MAJ OR NEUROPSYCHOLOG?
S18     28364       PSYCHOSOCIAL
S19     28366       PSYCHOSOCIAL OR S14
S20     47282       S19 OR S17
S21        86       S13 AND S20
S22        82       S21/ENG
```

The Internet

The most important thing to understand about searching using Internet search engines is that the available techniques are far less sophisticated and powerful than that of DIALOG or other commercial search vendors. The databases involved are huge; most search engines have indexed the full text of many tens of millions of Web documents, and as such, the overhead involved in creating the kind of inverted file we have been working with is unrealistic. So while most search engines will allow Boolean searches, there are no proximity operators, for example. AltaVista does, however, have a NEAR operator, which works like a (5N), finding target words within five words of each other.

Two other important factors: First, the underlying documents are encoded in HTML, so there is less information in that structure than in a bibliographic document record—no author, maybe a title, and certainly nothing like subject headings or abstracts, which gives the searcher less to work with and fewer opportunities to use sophisticated search techniques in refining or polishing searches. Those kinds of techniques might become more feasible if and when metadata, information about documents, becomes more widely prevalent in documents. Such metadata is now seen in META tags in HTML documents, listing keywords, authors, publishers, etc. Schemes such as the Dublin Core, which attempt to codify or standardize such metadata, might also assist searchers, but they would require wide compliance, which has not yet occurred.

Second, the type of writing found in Web documents varies greatly. There is a great deal more casual, metaphorical, ironic, and sarcastic usage, not to mention terrible spelling, new words, and new uses of old words (who would have thought "spam," now used to describe unwanted E-mail, would be so common?). This means many more false drops, especially with words or phrases with multiple uses.

On the other hand, if you have a really specific name or word or phrase, it will get better results in this environment than perhaps anywhere else. Take advantage of these circumstances rather than viewing them solely as problems. One of the most common reference questions is "What is the other word in the English language, besides "angry" and "hungry," that ends with -gry?" This is the sort of question that drives reference librarians nuts because there is no really good way to look for the answer, other than in a book of language curiosities, or just knowing it from having dealt with the question several times before.

The Internet is the ideal place to look for this type of query. Do a search on almost any search engine on the words "angry" and "hungry," and besides some junk, what will come up are several, perhaps contradictory, answers to the question. I answered a reference question for someone looking for an old poem. He remembered a fragment of it from childhood (these are horrible questions, too—invariably the lines are half-correct, and these poems are never in books, especially if they are Ann-Landers-type poems), and it had the phrase "piddling pup" in it. I figured there couldn't be *that* many documents on the Net with a phrase like that, so I searched for it, and found exactly one, a page from Australia with the full text of the poem.

Remember that most search engines work this way: if words are entered in the search box and the button is pushed, the words will be searched together; documents will be returned, ranked in order by some proprietary (and therefore unexplained) mechanism; and the first ones on the list are allegedly the best. This is, for all intents and purposes, a big OR, getting all documents that have any of the words asked for, and then ranking them by their frequency of occurrence in the document, perhaps giving higher weight to words in the title, <h1> tag, <meta> tag, or early in the page.

Imagine a search on the Net for recipes that use coconut milk (perhaps someone has a lot of coconut milk about to go bad and needs to use it up). I would probably try a strategy something like

```
+ "coconut milk" recipe
```

which would retrieve documents with the phrase "coconut milk" and prefer documents that also include "recipe." I would really prefer to truncate on "recipe," but not all engines allow you to (most notably HotBot at the moment), while others will implicitly truncate unless specifically told not to.

These search engines continue to evolve, both in operation and interface, so it pays to check the help pages, especially if the front or search pages change, to see if the command language or operation has also changed.

There is a lot of money to be made here. As the Internet becomes more of a presence in lives and commerce, and as more people use it for information, a search engine that consistently outperforms the others will be very popular, generate more business, get more traffic and advertising, and make more money. All of a sudden, information retrieval is big business. Therefore, there is a great incentive to make these engines work as effectively as possible.

In fact, there is a fascinating Web site devoted just to this matter: Search Engine Watch (http://www.searchenginewatch.com). This table, taken from one of their introductory pages, gives an idea of the kinds of information available there. (See Fig. 8.1 on p. 174.)

Fig. 8.1. Search engine watch pages.

Section	Designed For	Description
A Webmaster's Guide To Search Engines	Webmasters	This section explains how search engines find and rank web pages, with an emphasis on what webmasters can do to improve how search engines list their web sites.
Search Engines Facts And Fun	Search Engine Users	This section provides background about search engines, tips on how to use them better, some history, and even a game to test your search engine knowledge
Search Engine Status Reports	Anyone	This section provides some insight on how search engines are performing in different areas. Check out some of the material, and make note of reports you want to keep an eye on.
Search Engine Resources	Anyone	A collection of links to search engine related resources across the web.
Search Engine Report Mailing List	Anyone	It's free, and it will keep you updated on the latest search engine news.

Research in areas such as computational linguistics, natural language processing, improved categorization or classification, intelligent agents, and so on, might well prove to make the difference, but so far, no one engine has emerged as the obvious winner . . . yet. It would be nice to believe that librarians and librarianship will be in on this, helping to design and build technological assistants based on our traditions and expertise in searching and understanding the needs of users.

Notes

1.   At present, DIALOG allows this number to be up to 127 in most files; it is unlimited in files that provide the full text of documents—we'll talk more about this later.

2.   Notice the hyphen in the title: "thirty-item" as it appears in the title. In DIALOG, all internal punctuation (hyphens, apostrophes, slashes, quotation marks, etc.) is removed and replaced by spaces. Thus, when this document was processed, the hyphen was removed, and the words "thirty" and "item" went into the inverted file as separate words.

3. These are based on categories given in an article by Elaine Wagner (September 1986), "False Drops—How They Arise . . . How to Avoid Them." *Online* 10(5): 93–96.

4. Markey et al. (1980), "An Analysis of Controlled Vocabulary and Free Text Search Statements in On-Line Searches." *Online Review* 4(3), 225–36.

Additional Reading

Morton, Douglas (1993), "Refresher Course: Getting Next to Proximity Operators" *Online* 17(6): 55–58.

Rowley, Jennifer (1994), "The Controlled Versus Natural Indexing Languages Debate Revisited: A Perspective on Information Retrieval Practice and Research," *Journal of Information Science* 20(2): 109–19.

ADDITIONAL SEARCH FEATURES

So far, we have discussed some fairly basic search techniques—creating sets, truncation, Boolean and proximity operators, and the like—and these serve as the fundamental tools in the searcher's repertoire. But there are more. Again, we will specifically examine the additional search features provided by the DIALOG service, but recognize as always that other services may have similar ones or quite different features altogether.

Additional search features fall into three major categories: commands that assist in searching (here we will look at prefix searching, limits, KEEP, TARGET, and RANK); those that can affect the display of results (SORT, REPORT, and output formats); and those that deal with how results are distributed or accessed (the PRINT command, the ERA service, and the ability to create permanent or temporary search profiles).

Search Features

Over the years, DIALOG has developed a number of commands to allow searchers to go beyond "standard" searching. These range from the fairly simple, taking further advantage of the structure of records, to the more complex, using the power of the computer to find the most potentially useful descriptors and make use of ranked retrieval to support searches.

Prefix Codes

Most search services allow searchers to view the Basic Index as a means of helping with the selection of subject search terms, and we saw earlier that this is done in DIALOG using the EXPAND command. We also learned that it is possible to reduce postings and increase specificity by limiting a search to one particular subject field through the use of suffix codes. EXPAND can also be used with the other inverted files in order to verify the variant spelling and punctuation conventions for proper names (authors, journals, organizations, etc.) that exist in different files.

When we looked at record structures in chapter 5 we saw that each field can be identified by a two-letter code (AU, TI, JN, etc.). We later saw that searches in the Basic Index can be limited to particular subject fields by using these two-letter codes as suffixes linked to the search terms (/TI or /DE, for example). Similarly, non-subject fields can also be identified by their two-letter codes, but here the codes are used as prefixes rather than suffixes. The use of these codes makes it possible to limit a search to any individual field of the record, and this device is a useful way of reducing postings and increasing specificity. As a reminder, here is a listing of the Additional Index fields for a record in PsycINFO (file 11) taken from the bluesheets for that file.

Fig. 9.1. Additional indexes available on PsycINFO records.

ADDITIONAL INDEXES

SEARCH PREFIX	DISPLAY CODE	FIELD NAME	INDEXING	SELECT EXAMPLES
AA=	AA	PsycINFO Record Identifier	Phrase	S AA=1997-07837-004
AG=	AG	Age Group	Phrase	S AG=ADULTHOOD
AI=	AI	Audience Intended	Phrase	S AI=PSYCHOLOGY?
AU=	AU	Author	Phrase	S AU=MARAS, PAM?
None	AZ	DIALOG Accession Number		
BN=	BN	International Standard Book Number	Phrase	S BN=1-85302-414-7
CL=	CL	Conference Location	Word	S CL=INDIA
CN=	CN	Book Publisher's Country	Phrase	S CN=AUSTRALIA
CS=	CS	Corporate Source or Author Affiliation	Word & Phrase	S CS=(GREENWICH(F)LONDON)
CT=	CT	Conference Title	Word	S CT=(INDIAN(W)SCIENCE(W)CONGRESS)
CY=	CY	Conference Year	Phrase	S CY=1995
DT=	DT	Document Type	Phrase	S DT=JOURNAL ARTICLE
GN=	GN	Geographic Name	Phrase	S GN=USA

JN=	JN	Journal Name	Phrase	S JN=EDUCATIONAL & CHILD PSYCHOLOGY
LA=	LA	Language	Phrase	S LA=ENGLISH
PD=	PD	Publication Date	Phrase	S PD=970400
PG=	PG	Population Group	Phrase	S PG=HUMAN
PU=	PU	Publisher	Word & Phrase	S PU=(CAMBRIDGE(W) UNIVERSITY(W)PRESS) S PU=CAMBRIDGE UNIVERSITY PRESS
PY=	PY	Publication Year	Phrase	S PY=1997
RT=	RT	Record Type	Phrase	S RT=ABSTRACT
SE=	SE	Series Title	Word	S SE=(STRESS(1W) EMOTION?)
SF=	SF	Special Feature	Phrase	S SF=REFERENCES
SH=	SH	Subject Codes and Headings	Phrase	S SH=3250
SN=	SN	International Standard Serial Number (ISSN)	Phrase	S SN=02671611
SO=	SO	Source Information	Word	S SO=(EDUCATIONAL AND 14 AND 1997)
SP=	SP	Sponsor	Word	S SP=(LONDON(W)BUSINESS (W)SCHOOL)
UD=	None	Update	Phrase	S UD=9999

The field to be searched can be specified by linking the appropriate prefix codes (which vary somewhat by database) to the search terms using an equal sign. For example,

    s jn=runner's world

will search only the journal inverted file, while

    s au=cohen, michael

searches only the author file. When a prefix code is used in the SELECT statement, the computer goes directly to the named field.

> *Actually, this isn't strictly true. In fact, there's only one inverted file, which contains the entries we've already discussed, words and phrases from titles, abstracts, descriptors, and so on. However, it also has the entries from these additional indexes, all interfiled in alphabetical order with the others. You can only retrieve those entries by using the appropriate prefix code. Searching on*
>
> ```
> ?s  au=cohen?
> ```
>
> *will not retrieve documents with the word "cohen" in titles or abstracts; you'd need to do*
>
> ```
> ?s  cohen
> ```
>
> *for that. Try EXPANDing on something like*
>
> ```
> ?e  au=zzz
> ```
>
> *and you'll see what I mean. – JWJ*

Because many of these fields contain proper names, the problem when using prefix codes is that the exact form of the name to search may not be certain. Remember that data is entered into the database in the form in which it appears in the original document. Documents come from a variety of sources, and there is no authority control of fields other than the descriptors. There are two fields that are phrase-indexed and particularly difficult to search because there may be variant forms of a single author's name (e.g., forename or initials), in how it is punctuated (comma or space or both) or in the citing of a given journal's name (e.g., abbreviated or in full).

Thus, the same author may have more than one entry in the inverted file, due to inconsistencies in the use of initials, hyphens, Jr., Ed., or other variations in the form of entry. The same type of variation may occur in other fields too. Journals may be entered in full, or abbreviated, or even misspelled! Proper names of organizations, products, or corporate sources may all appear in variant forms.

In addition, the way in which author names are entered varies in different databases. Surname and first name may be separated by a space, a space and a comma, or just a comma. First names may be entered in full or as initials. Initials may be separated by periods or spaces or not separated at all. Given this variety, it is clear that database documentation is vital if online time is not to be wasted and relevant material missed.

The EXPAND command is a useful way to make sure that none of the variations in phrase-indexed fields will be inadvertently overlooked. For example, notice the variations on the name of D. J. Foskett in this example:

```
    Set    Items    Description
    ---    -----    -----------
?e au=foskett, d

    Ref    Items    Index-term
    E1        1      AU=FOSHEIM, ROBIN MELANIE, ED.
    E2        5      AU=FOSKETT, A. C.
    E3        0      *AU=FOSKETT, D
```

```
E4          1      AU=FOSKETT, D.
E5          8      AU=FOSKETT, D. J.
E6          2      AU=FOSKETT, DOUGLAS J.
E7          5      AU=FOSKETT, JOHN M.
E8          1      AU=FOSKETT, WILLIAM
E9          1      AU=FOSLER, R. SCOTT
E10         1      AU=FOSMIRE, F. R.
E11         1      AU=FOSMIRE, MONICA
E12         3      AU=FOSNOT, CATHERINE TWOMEY


                   Enter P or E for more
?s e4:e6
   S1       11      AU="FOSKETT, D.":AU="FOSKETT, DOUGLAS J."
```

The name is not entered in full in the EXPAND command, and it is better not to use truncation when using EXPAND, due to the order in which the computer files the punctuation symbols.

Search terms can be similarly EXPANDed in all the other prefix-coded fields, though the exact fields available will vary by database. The Corporate Source (CS=) field, which gives information on authors' affiliations, is often difficult to search effectively because it is word-indexed in many files, making it necessary to use proximity operators (or even AND) for successful retrieval. Remember to SELECT the appropriate E numbers from the EXPAND list, so they are converted to sets for the search terms that they represent.

In addition to authors and journals, other interesting fields often appear in additional indexes, particularly in numeric or business files. We will discuss these further in the chapter on searching other kinds of databases.

Limiting

As an alternative to SELECTing a term using prefix codes and then ANDing the results with subject terms, some of the prefix codes can also be used as suffixes to limit previously SELECTed sets. It often proves helpful to inspect the initial postings figures before proceeding further with a search. Adding qualifiers to previously SELECTed sets is known as *post-qualification*. For example, these three statements all yield the same results:

```
File 154:MEDLINE 1985-1998/Mar W5

      Set     Items     Description
      ---     -----     -----------
?ss cholesterol and la=english
   S1      51214      CHOLESTEROL
   S2    3889538         LA=ENGLISH
   S3      44878      CHOLESTEROL AND LA=ENGLISH
?s s1/eng
   S4      44878      S1/ENG
?s cholesterol/eng
   S5      44878      CHOLESTEROL/ENG
```

Most databases on DIALOG offer one or more suffix codes that limit retrieval to specific criteria in addition to particular inverted files. Check the database bluesheets under "Limiting" for the codes that are applicable in a particular file. Common options include language, document type, publication year, and major descriptor. Here is a listing of the Limit options taken from the bluesheets for MEDLINE (file 154):

Fig. 9.2. Sample MEDLINE limit parameters.

Sets and terms can be restricted by Basic Index suffixes, i.e., /AB, /DE, /DF, /GS, /ID, /NA and /TI (e.g., S S2/TI), as well as by the following features:

SUFFIX	FIELD NAME	EXAMPLES
/ABS	Records with Abstracts	S S3/ABS
/ENG	English-Language Records	S S5/ENG
/HUMAN	Human Subject	S S7/HUMAN
/MAJ	Major Descriptor	S S8/MAJ
/NOABS	Records without Abstracts	S S4/NOABS
/NONENG	Non-English-language records	S S6/NONENG
/YYYY	Publication Year	S S2/1995:1996

Many of these limits are binary choices—either human or nonhuman, English or non-English. It is allowed to combine more than one qualifier for the same search term or set, separating them by commas. For example,

?ss carcinoma/human,1997

```
S6    130303    CARCINOMA/HUMAN
S7    341783    PY=1997
S8    10796     CARCINOMA/HUMAN,1997
```

limits the search term "carcinoma" to human subjects and the publication year of 1997. These limiting suffix codes can be applied in a number of different ways:

- to single search terms
  e.g., *s video/pat*
- to groups of terms connected by logical or proximity operators
  e.g., *s (immigrant? AND worker?)/eng*
- to set numbers
  e.g. *s s6/maj*
- in combination with other field and/or suffix codes
  e.g. *s diplomacy/de,noneng,1990:92*

Be particularly careful when limiting a set that includes a combination of search terms that have previously been ANDed. The limit may not necessarily have been applied to every term as (probably) intended.

> Look at the difference between these two strategies, for example:
>
> ```
> ?ss monkey and malaria
>
>         S1        789      MONKEY
>         S2       1384      MALARIA
>         S3         92      MONKEY AND MALARIA
>
>   ?ss s3/ti
>
>         S4         18      S3/TI
> ```
>
> Set 4 contains records where at least one of the terms (MONKEY or MALARIA) appears in the title. This is different from the results of the command
>
> ```
>   ?s (monkey and malaria)/ti
>
>         S5          6      (MONKEY AND MALARIA)/TI
> ```
>
> which requires that BOTH terms appear in the title.
>
> Post-qualification using suffixes is most effective when used on sets created using the OR operator or proximity operators. – GW

The LIMIT feature is thus a shortcut to enable certain field restrictions to apply to a search statement or even to a whole search strategy by LIMITing the final set number.

A more effective way to limit an entire search is by using the command LIMITALL (abbreviated to LALL). This is usually entered at the start of a search (but can also be used after reviewing postings) to restrict all subsequent sets to one or more suffix codes. Enter LIMITALL followed by a slash(/) and the suffix codes desired, once again separating multiple codes with commas. Up to 40 characters (including commas and spacing) can be entered following the slash. For example, the use of LIMITALL/eng will cause every subsequent set to include only items written in English, thus being equivalent to combining AND LA=eng with each of the search sets.

```
File 5:BIOSIS PREVIEWS 69-97/JUN BA9401:BARRM4301
    (C. BIOSIS 1992)

    Set    Items    Description
    ---    -----    -----------
?ss forest? or tree? or pine?
Processing
Processing
Processing
    S1    60996    FOREST?
    S2    52809    TREE?
    S3    32421    PINE?
    S4   125102    FOREST? OR TREE? OR PINE?
?limitall/de,ti,eng
>>>LIMITALL started
```

```
?ss s4 and seed()dispersal
    S4    49744
    S5    24249    SEED
    S6     5383    DISPERSAL
    S7      511    SEED(W)DISPERSAL
    S8      119    S4 AND SEED()DISPERSAL
```

Notice in this example how the postings for set 4 are reduced from 125,102 to 49,744 once the selected terms are LIMITed to descriptor or title fields and the English language. The LIMITs have also been automatically applied to sets 5, 6, and 7. This illustrates how the codes following the LIMITALL command are applied to all subsequent SELECT statements, until the LIMITALL is canceled (using LIMITALL CANCEL or LIMITALL-), or until a new LIMITALL command is entered, or the search is ended with LOGOFF.

Notice that when field suffixes (e.g. /TI,DE) are used in a LIMITALL command, all subsequent search terms must be SELECTed from the Basic Index. In this situation, the use of a prefix code, such as AU=, will produce zero results. Because there is no indication in the results that the terms have been SELECTed under the LIMITALL restriction (i.e., suffix codes do not appear with the search terms), it is important to remember that LIMITALL is in operation. LIMITALL may save considerable search time during long searches involving large sets by decreasing retrieval and thus reducing the number of records that must be processed.

KEEP

When preparing lists for electronic ordering, the KEEP command is a useful device. KEEP is used to place selected records into an auxiliary set, numbered set zero (S0), to build up the complete order from a series of searches. One can KEEP chosen records from various sets within a search, creating a single final set of search results, which one may possibly want to SORT.

The format of the command is KEEP (or K) followed by either

- a set number
  e.g., *keep s3*

or

- a set number with selected item numbers
  e.g., *keep s6/3,7,10*

which will put records 3, 7, and 10 from set 6 into set zero,

or

- a DIALOG accession number
  e.g., *keep ej247653*

Set S0 can be TYPEd or PRINTed as well as SORTed, and it can be used in subsequent SELECT commands to combine it with other terms or limit it with suffix codes. When KEEP is used to prepare a DIALORDER request, the system looks for set 0 and automatically places the records it finds there into the DIALORDER request. Once the order has been placed the system will delete set 0, but otherwise it can be manually deleted using the command KEEP CANCEL. The same command followed by a DIALOG accession number will delete a single record from set 0.

The use of the KEEP command to create a really nice set, which DIALOG calls S0, is a great feature to minimize the size of sets that you ask to be TYPEd or PRINTed. I must confess, though, that I don't teach it to my classes until the very end of the course. (The same goes for RANK and TARGET, for similar reasons.) Why? Because they want to create the perfect thirty-item set anyway, and this allows them to do it! It can also be a time-waster, especially if you flip through the articles you've retrieved, one at a time, KEEPing the ones you like, and then dealing with the final S0. KEEP is certainly a valid command, but use it with some discretion. – JWJ

TARGET

The TARGET command is DIALOG's attempt to provide non-Boolean access to its databases. They promote it as being of special use in searching full-text databases, especially those without controlled vocabulary features, and it can be quite helpful there. It would also be useful for novice searchers (perhaps even end users) and for experienced searchers who are in databases out of their normal areas of expertise.

It is, in essence, a ranked-retrieval service and looks a great deal like many Web-based engines with similar commands and features (though it predates the Web engines by many years). There is a command-line version, but the easiest way to use it would be simply to type TARGET at the command prompt and follow the menus:

```
File 11:PsycINFO(R) 1967-1998/Feb
     (c) 1998 Amer. Psychological Assn.

    Set    Items    Description
    ---    -----    -----------
?target
Input search terms separated by spaces (e.g., DOG CAT FOOD). You can
enhance your TARGET search with the following options:
   - PHRASES are enclosed in single quotes
        (e.g., 'DOG FOOD')
   - SYNONYMS are enclosed in parentheses
        (e.g., (DOG CANINE))
   - SPELLING variations are indicated with a question
        (e.g., DOG? to search DOG , DOGS)
   - Terms that MUST be present are flagged with an asterisk
        (e.g., DOG *FOOD)
```

The similarities are evident: Phrases are enclosed in quotations, and required words and phrases take asterisks (similar to the Web engines' +). TARGET also allows grouping of synonyms within parentheses and truncation. One will normally retrieve 50 records of varying relevance. Here's a sample search:

```
?*'head injur?' psychosocial children
```
Your TARGET search request will retrieve up to 50 of the statistically most
relevant records.
Searching 1997-1998 records only
. . . Processing Complete
    Your search retrieved 50 records.
Press ENTER to browse results C = Customize display Q = QUIT H = HELP
?c

BROWSE output includes: TI,JN,PD
Term frequency/relevance: off
Continuous display for COMPLETE TEXT: off
Custom display options:
  1 Change BROWSE output to Title Only (usually free)
  2 Customize BROWSE output with your own choice of display codes
  3 Reset BROWSE output to the default (i.e., title, journal, date)
  4 Change COMPLETE TEXT output to continuous display
  5 Show term frequencies and statistical relevance (%) for each item
Press ENTER for NO CHANGE, or enter option number(s)
(e.g., 1,5) to customize the display. Q = QUIT H = HELP
?5

DIALOG-TARGET RESULTS (arranged by percent RELEVANCE)
------- Item: 1 ------------------------------------
DIALOG(R)File 11:(c) 1998 Amer. Psychological Assn. All rts. reserv.

Mild *head *injury in *children and adolescents: A review of studies
    (1970-1995).
JOURNAL: Psychological Bulletin
19970900
  - Statistical Relevance: 95%
  - Term Frequency: HEAD INJUR? - 8 ; PSYCHOSOCIAL - 2 ; CHILDREN - 4
------- Item: 2 ------------------------------------
DIALOG(R)File 11:(c) 1998 Amer. Psychological Assn. All rts. reserv.

A typology of *psychosocial functioning in pediatric closed-*head *injury.

JOURNAL: Child Neuropsychology
19970800
  - Statistical Relevance: 92%
  - Term Frequency: HEAD INJUR? - 8 ; PSYCHOSOCIAL - 6 ; CHILDREN - 2
------- Item: 3 ------------------------------------
DIALOG(R)File 11:(c) 1998 Amer. Psychological Assn. All rts. reserv.

Effect of mild *head *injury during the preschool years.
JOURNAL: Journal of the International Neuropsychological Society
19971100
  - Statistical Relevance: 71%
  - Term Frequency: HEAD INJUR? - 14 ; PSYCHOSOCIAL - 0 ;
        CHILDREN - 8

Press ENTER to continue browsing or enter item number(s) to see full record
M = Modify search T = New TARGET C = Customize display Q = QUIT H = HELP
?1

DIALOG(R)File 11:PsycINFO(R)
(c) 1998 Amer. Psychological Assn. All rts. reserv.
```
```

01471818   1997-05606-001
Mild *head *injury in *children and adolescents: A review of studies
   (1970-1995).
AUTHOR: Satz, Paul; Zaucha, Kenneth; McCleary, Carol; Light, Roger
AUTHOR AFFILIATION: U California, School of Medicine, Neuropsychiatric
   Inst, Los Angeles, CA, USA
JOURNAL: Psychological Bulletin, Vol 122(2) , 107-131, Sep, 1997
ISSN: 0033-2909

DOCUMENT TYPE: Journal Article; Literature Review/Research Review
SPECIAL FEATURES: References
RECORD TYPE: Abstract
LANGUAGE: English
POPULATION GROUP: Human AGE GROUP: 100 (Childhood (birth-12 yrs)); 200
   (Adolescence (13-17 yrs))

ABSTRACT: (journal abstract) In this article, the authors provide a

Press ENTER for next page. B = Browse M = Modify Q = Quit
?[hit ENTER]

DIALOG(R)File 11:PsycINFO(R)
(c) 1998 Amer. Psychological Assn. All rts. reserv.
   comprehensive review of the research of mild *head *injury in *children
      and adolescents from 1970 to 1995. Because of marked variability in
   methodologies across studies, a preliminary box-score tally was computed,
   without regard to studies' scientific or methodological merit. These
   results revealed 13 adverse, 18 null, and 9 indeterminate findings
   related to neuropsychological, academic, or *psychosocial outcome. When
   studies were classified based on methodological merit, the stronger
   studies were generally associated with null outcomes across domains.
   However, a few of the less stronger neuropsychological studies (5 of 40)
   reported subthreshold and transitory alterations during the early
   postinjury period. At the present time, cautious acceptance of the null
   hypothesis is recommended until more definitive studies are conducted
   that address the problems raised in this review. ((c) 1997 APA
   PsycINFO, all rights reserved)

DESCRIPTORS: *Head *Injuries ; *Literature Review; Adolescents; *Children
IDENTIFIERS: neuropsychological or academic or *psychosocial outcomes,

Press ENTER for next page. B = Browse M = Modify Q = Quit
?m

Press ENTER to continue browsing or enter item number(s) to see full record
M = Modify search T = New TARGET C = Customize display Q = QUIT H = HELP
Your TARGET search includes the following search terms:
   0   DATE(S) TO BE SEARCHED: 1997-1998
   1   'HEAD INJUR?'   <<<MUST be present
   2   PSYCHOSOCIAL
   3   CHILDREN
Enter 0 to change dates, a line number to change a term, the next number to
add a new term, F to flag required terms, or press ENTER to run your TARGET
search. Q = QUIT H = HELP
?0

DATES(S) TO BE SEARCHED: 1997-1998 (equivalent to Current year + 1)
Date options include:
   1   Current year only

```
2  Current year + 1
3  Current year + 2
4  Current year + 3
5  Current year + 4
6  Current year + 5
7  All years of coverage
```
(When CURRENT is not available for a file, it will default to ALL years of coverage.)
Enter a line number to change search dates, or press ENTER to retain present date. Q = QUIT H = HELP
?*3*

Your TARGET search includes the following search terms:
```
0  DATE(S) TO BE SEARCHED: 1996-1998
1  'HEAD INJUR?'                              <<<MUST be present
2  PSYCHOSOCIAL
3  CHILDREN
```
Enter 0 to change dates, a line number to change a term, the next number to add a new term, F to flag required terms, or press ENTER to run your TARGET search. Q = QUIT H = HELP
? *[hit ENTER]*

Your TARGET search request will retrieve up to 50 of the statistically most relevant records.
Searching 1996-1998 records only
...Processing Complete
        Your search retrieved 50 records.
Press ENTER to browse results C = Customize display Q = QUIT H = HELP
? *[hit ENTER]*

DIALOG-TARGET RESULTS (arranged by percent RELEVANCE)
------- Item: 1 ------------------------------------
DIALOG(R)File 11:(c) 1998 Amer. Psychological Assn. All rts. reserv.

Mild *head *injury in *children and adolescents: A review of studies
    (1970-1995).
JOURNAL: Psychological Bulletin
19970900
 - Statistical Relevance: 92%
 - Term Frequency: HEAD INJUR? - 8 ; PSYCHOSOCIAL - 2 ; CHILDREN - 4
------- Item: 2 ------------------------------------
DIALOG(R)File 11:(c) 1998 Amer. Psychological Assn. All rts. reserv.

Cognitive, behavioral, and motoric sequelae of mild *head *injury in a
    national birth cohort. Traumatic *head *injury in *children .
19950000
 - Statistical Relevance: 90%
 - Term Frequency: HEAD INJUR? - 10 ; PSYCHOSOCIAL - 2 ; CHILDREN - 5
------- Item: 3 ------------------------------------
DIALOG(R)File 11:(c) 1998 Amer. Psychological Assn. All rts. reserv.

A typology of *psychosocial functioning in pediatric closed-*head *injury.

JOURNAL: Child Neuropsychology
19970800
 - Statistical Relevance: 90%
 - Term Frequency: HEAD INJUR? - 8 ; PSYCHOSOCIAL - 6 ; CHILDREN - 2

Press ENTER to continue browsing or enter item number(s) to see full record

```
M = Modify search T = New TARGET C = Customize display Q = QUIT H = HELP
? [hit ENTER]

------- Item: 4 -------------------------------------
DIALOG(R)File 11:(c) 1998 Amer. Psychological Assn. All rts. reserv.

The role of self-concept in *children 's *psychosocial adjustment to
   *head-*injury.
JOURNAL: Dissertation Abstracts International: Section B: the Sciences &
Engineering
19960500
  - Statistical Relevance: 90%
  - Term Frequency: HEAD INJUR? - 4 ; PSYCHOSOCIAL - 2 ; CHILDREN - 2
------- Item: 5 -------------------------------------
DIALOG(R)File 11:(c) 1998 Amer. Psychological Assn. All rts. reserv.

Traumatic *head *injury in *children .
19950000
  - Statistical Relevance: 71%
  - Term Frequency: HEAD INJUR? - 28 ; PSYCHOSOCIAL - 0 ;
          CHILDREN - 12
------- Item: 6 -------------------------------------
DIALOG(R)File 11:(c) 1998 Amer. Psychological Assn. All rts. reserv.

Age at injury as a predictor of outcome following pediatric *head *injury:
   A longitudinal perspective.
JOURNAL: Child Neuropsychology
19951200
  - Statistical Relevance: 66%
  - Term Frequency: HEAD INJUR? - 18 ; PSYCHOSOCIAL - 0 ; CHILDREN - 8
-----------------------------------------------------
Press ENTER to continue browsing or enter item number(s) to see full record
M = Modify search T = New TARGET C = Customize display Q = QUIT H = HELP
?q

Ending TARGET search. Enter TARGET to do another search in the present
file(s), or BEGIN new file(s). Enter LOGOFF to disconnect from DIALOG
```

TARGET is an interesting addition to DIALOG, and we have used it successfully, but we would be concerned about relying solely on it and about encouraging end users to use it without professional assistance, primarily because of the connect time costs in exploration. It so resembles free Web searching that the temptation to play might be strong and expensive.

RANK

RANK is another interesting command that does pretty much what one would expect from the name. It will rank the records of a retrieved set based on some field. This either is the answer itself (Which are the most successful car dealerships in Wyoming?) or can be used in refining or improving the search. The form of the command is

rank ≤field codes≥

and is used after a set is created.

As an example, imagine being interested in finding out more about a person's area of research, in this case Karen Drabenstott, a well-known researcher in information and library science who also wrote as Karen Markey. In ERIC, we search first to find articles she wrote:

```
File 1:ERIC 1966-1998/Mar
     (c) format only 1998 The Dialog Corporation

     Set    Items     Description
     ---    -----     -----------
?e au=drabensto

     Ref    Items     Index-term
     E1       1       AU=DRABEK, JOHN
     E2       3       AU=DRABEK, THOMAS E.
     E3       0       *AU=DRABENSTO
     E4       1       AU=DRABENSTOTT, JOHN, ED.
     E5       3       AU=DRABENSTOTT, JON
     E6       6       AU=DRABENSTOTT, JON, ED.
     E7       7       AU=DRABENSTOTT, KAREN M.
     E8       1       AU=DRABENSTOTT, KAREN M., WELLER, MARJORIE S.
     E9       3       AU=DRABENSTOTT, KAREN MARKEY
     E10     12       AU=DRABICK, LAWRENCE W.
     E11      1       AU=DRABIN-PARTENIO, INGRID
     E12      1       AU=DRABKIN, MARJORIE

             Enter P or PAGE for more
?s e7-e9

              7       AU=DRABENSTOTT, KAREN M.
              1       AU=DRABENSTOTT, KAREN M., WELLER, MARJORIE S.
              3       AU=DRABENSTOTT, KAREN MARKEY
     S1      11       E7-E9
?e au=markey

     Ref    Items     Index-term
     E1       1       AU=MARKESSINI, JOAN
     E2       2       AU=MARKEWICH, THEODORE S.
     E3       0       *AU=MARKEY
     E4       1       AU=MARKEY, ELLEN M.
     E5       3       AU=MARKEY, JAMES P.
     E6      25       AU=MARKEY, KAREN
     E7       1       AU=MARKEY, LOWELL
     E8       2       AU=MARKEY, MARTIN J.
     E9       1       AU=MARKEY, PENNY S.
     E10      2       AU=MARKEY, T. L.
     E11      1       AU=MARKEY, WILLIAM L.
     E12      1       AU=MARKEY, WILLIAM L., COMP.

             Enter P or PAGE for more
?s e6

     S2      25       AU="MARKEY, KAREN"

?s s1 or s2

             11       S1
             25       S2
     S3      36       S1 OR S2
```

Note the technique here, using EXPAND to find variant forms of the author's names, as well as pieces she cowrote or edited. We OR the two name-sets together to get the 36 hits in S3. On this set, we use RANK to find the descriptors most frequently found in those documents; this will give us a good indication of her research interests and productivity:

```
?rank s3/de
Started processing RANK
Completed Ranking 36 records
DIALOG RANK Results
----------------------
RANK: S3/1-36 Field: /DE File(s): 1
(Rank fields found in 36 records — 112 unique terms) Page 1 of 14

     RANK
     No.    Items    Term
     ---    -----    -----------
     1       19      SUBJECT INDEX TERMS
     2       18      SEARCH STRATEGIES
     3       16      LIBRARY CATALOGS
     4       16      ONLINE SYSTEMS
     5       14      INFORMATION RETRIEVAL
     6       14      ONLINE CATALOGS
     7       12      ONLINE SEARCHING
     8        9      TABLES (DATA)
P = next page Pn = Jump to page n
P- = previous page M = More Options Exit = Leave RANK

To view records from RANK, enter VIEW followed by RANK number,
format, and item(s) to display, e.g., VIEW 2/9/ALL.
Enter desired option(s) or enter RANK number(s) to save terms.
```

It would appear that Drabenstott focuses on a couple of areas: catalogs and the subject headings found there, and online retrieval systems and how they are searched. We will pursue the subject heading area a bit further, with an eye to seeing who else is working in this field. To do this, we ask for the relevant descriptors to be saved for later use.

```
?1 3 6
RANK numbers saved: 1,3,6
DIALOG RANK Results
------------------------
RANK: S3/1-36 Field: /DE File(s): 1
(Rank fields found in 36 records — 112 unique terms) Page 1 of 14

     RANK
     No.    Items    Term
     ---    -----    -----------
     1       19      SUBJECT INDEX TERMS
     2       18      SEARCH STRATEGIES
     3       16      LIBRARY CATALOGS
     4       16      ONLINE SYSTEMS
     5       14      INFORMATION RETRIEVAL
     6       14      ONLINE CATALOGS
     7       12      ONLINE SEARCHING
     8        9      TABLES (DATA)
P = next page Pn = Jump to page n
P- = previous page M = More Options Exit = Leave RANK
```

To view records from RANK, enter VIEW followed by RANK number,
format, and item(s) to display, e.g., VIEW 2/9/ALL.

Enter desired option(s) or enter RANK number(s) to save terms.
?exit

RANK results will be erased; have you saved all the terms of interest?
(YES/NO)
?y

Creating temporary SearchSave ... TD029

Enter EXS to execute the SearchSave
?exs
Executing TD029
```
    S4      1260    "SUBJECT INDEX TERMS"/DE
    S5      1115    "LIBRARY CATALOGS"/DE (LISTS OF LIBRARY MATERIALS
                    ARRANGED IN SOME ...)
    S6       906    "ONLINE CATALOGS"/DE (MACHINE-READABLE CATALOGS THAT
                    CAN BE ACCESS...)
    S7      2782    S4:S6
```

?s s4 and (s5 or s6)
```
            1260    S4
            1115    S5
             906    S6
    S8       197    S4 AND (S5 OR S6)
```

The EXS command just slaps them all together in a big OR; we rearrange them to focus on subject headings in catalog systems. This produces S8, which we then use RANK on again, this time on the author field:

?rank s8/au
Started processing RANK
...Ranking 100 of 197 records
Completed Ranking 197 records
DIALOG RANK Results

RANK: S8/1-197 Field: AU= File(s): 1
(Rank fields found in 190 records — 180 unique terms) Page 1 of 23

```
    RANK
    No.    Items    Term
    ---    -----    -----------
     1      13      AND OTHERS
     2       9      COCHRANE, PAULINE A.
     3       7      MARKEY, KAREN
     4       5      CHAN, LOIS MAI
     5       5      MANDEL, CAROL A.
     6       4      DRABENSTOTT, KAREN M.
     7       4      LARSON, RAY R.
     8       3      DRABENSTOTT, KAREN MARKEY
P = next page Pn = Jump to page n
P- = previous page M = More Options Exit = Leave RANK
```

To view records from RANK, enter VIEW followed by RANK number, format, and
item(s) to display, e.g., VIEW 2/9/ALL.

```
Enter desired option(s) or enter RANK number(s) to save terms.
?p
DIALOG RANK Results
-----------------------
RANK: S8/1-197 Field: AU= File(s): 1
(Rank fields found in 190 records — 180 unique terms) Page 2 of 23

      RANK
      No.    Items    Term
      ---    -----    -----------
      9       3       FROST, CAROLYN O.
      10      3       HILDRETH, CHARLES R.
      11      3       MICCO, MARY
      12      3       VIZINE-GOETZ, DIANE
      13      3       WELLER, MARJORIE S.
      14      2       BATES, MARCIA J.
      15      2       BERMAN, SANFORD
      16      2       CONNELL, TSCHERA HARKNESS
P = next page Pn = Jump to page n
P- = previous page M = More Options Exit = Leave RANK

To view records from RANK, enter VIEW followed by RANK number, format, and
item(s) to display, e.g., VIEW 2/9/ALL.

Enter desired option(s) or enter RANK number(s) to save terms.
```

RANK can be used on sets as large as 50,000 records, but it will take a while and be expensive. It also will not work with any word-indexed fields but will with most phrase-indexed ones. Check documentation for further details.

Formatting Records and Sets

Once the appropriate set or sets is in the bag, more can be done with them than just typing them all out in format 9 and calling it a day. This section will discuss ways of formatting those sets to make them easier to read or more convenient to use by sorting them, using special formats, or creating reports.

Special Formats

Downloading the search results and entering them into a word-processing program is probably the most obvious way to help provide a more professional-looking output for the user. Records are downloaded as ASCII (American Standard Code for Information Interchange) files so that search results can be uploaded into nearly any standard word processor. This job can be greatly simplified if the citations are first SORTed online, and output in the most appropriate format.

> *A small point—your results are indeed downloaded in ASCII format if you're using a DOS-based machine (an IBM PC or compatible); if you're using a Macintosh, it'll be downloaded in straight text format. The thing to understand is that you'll have no formatting commands or characters in your downloaded output, and you'll have some extraneous-looking spaces and hard carriage returns, which is just how DIALOG produces it. Dump it into your word processor, and reformat it—it'll look fine. – JWJ*

We saw earlier that DIALOG provides a choice of predefined formats that are used to control the fields included in the search output. Standard formats are listed on the database bluesheets, but it is also possible to design one's own preferred format. Four alternative format options are available:

- User-defined (UDF) formats

- Preset customized formats

- Keyword in Context (KWIC) format

- Report format

One way of customizing the content of output records on some databases is through the use of a user-defined format (UDF). UDFs allow the use of two-character field codes to select the fields to include in the records to be output. These formats can be specified in three different ways:

- Using field codes separated by commas. For example: (Yes, this document does have the word MILLENIUM buried deep inside.)

```
File 11:PsycINFO(R) 1967-1998/May
     (c) 1998 Amer. Psychological Assn.

   Set    Items    Description
   ---    -----    -----------
?s millenium

   S1       16     MILLENIUM
?t 1/ti,ab/1


1/TI,AB/1
DIALOG(R)File 11:(c) 1998 Amer. Psychological Assn. All rts. reserv.

Health-promoting and health-compromising behaviors among minority
   adolescents.
SERIES TITLE: Application and practice in health psychology.

ABSTRACT: (jacket) Minority adolescents are at increased risk for
   numerous health problems but are less likely to have a regular
   source of medical care than either adults or children. During this
   critical developmental period, adolescents establish behavior
   patterns that set the stage for adulthood, creating a unique window
   of opportunity for clinicians and health care professionals to
   intervene and promote health. This [book] guides the efforts to
```

```
understand and develop innovative, effective, and culturally
sensitive approaches for minority youth populations.
```

```
"Health-Promoting and Health-Compromising Behaviors Among Minority
Adolescents" [is intended] not only [for] health psychologists but
[for] all clinical and counseling professionals who might treat
minority adolescents. ((c) 1997 APA PsycINFO, all rights reserved)
```

- Combining a pre-defined format number with field codes. For example:

```
?t 1/3,de/1
1/3,DE/1
DIALOG(R)FILE 11:PSYCINFO(R)
(C) 1998 AMER. PSYCHOLOGICAL ASSN. ALL RTS. RESERV.
```

```
01490283               1997-97130-000
HEALTH-PROMOTING AND HEALTH-COMPROMISING BEHAVIORS AMONG MINORITY
   ADOLESCENTS.
SERIES TITLE: APPLICATION AND PRACTICE IN HEALTH PSYCHOLOGY.
AUTHOR: WILSON, DAWN K., ED); RODRIGUE, JAMES R., ED); TAYLOR,
   WENDELL C., ED)
AUTHOR AFFILIATION: VIRGINIA COMMONWEALTH U, MEDICAL COLL OF VIRGINIA,
   DIV OF CLINICAL PHARMACOLOGY & HYPERTENSION, RICHMOND, VA, USA,
   XXII, P388, 1997
BOOK PUBLISHER: AMERICAN PSYCHOLOGICAL ASSOCIATION, WASHINGTON, DC,
   USA
```

```
DESCRIPTORS: *At Risk Populations; *Cross Cultural Treatment; *Health
   Promotion; *Health Behavior; *Minority Groups; Adolescents;
   Disorders;  Health Care Policy; Early Intervention
```

- Using the SET command to store a UDF for the length of a search. For example:

```
?set u1 ti,ab,de
User Defined Format 1 is set to TI AB DE.
   Type/Display Estimated Cost: $ 0.30 - (File 11).
```

When the output is TYPEd later, U1 can be used in place of a regular format number. Nine different formats can be defined in this way by using the SET command followed by the desired display codes.

The formats set remain available for use in any database having those fields during the current search session. All UDFs are erased when the search session is terminated with a LOGOFF command. It is possible to save a UDF long-term by SETting it as a parameter of one's user profile, though this may be counterproductive unless the range of files normally searched all use compatible field codes.

Other uses of the SET command are mentioned in association with the commands with which they are most commonly used. One of these is its use with the KWIC (Keyword in Context) option, which is available on a number of DIALOG databases. KWIC is a format option that displays only those portions of a record that contain the SELECTed search terms. It shows them in the context in which they occur, which is useful in helping to determine the relevance of search results. KWIC displays are generally taken from textual fields such as title, descriptors, or text, and the command is particularly useful with full-text records, where matching terms may be far apart and not related to one another at all.

To view only the KWIC portions of search results, enter either KWIC or K in place of the numbered format in the TYPE command. The amount of text shown when KWIC is used consists of the search term within a 30-word "window," with approximately 15 words on either side of the search term. Using the SET command, it is possible to change the size of the KWIC window to anything between 2 and 50 words. For example, one can enter the command

```
set kwic 50
```

at the beginning of the search, and the KWIC window will display 25 words before and after the search terms. The new size will remain in operation until LOGOFF, unless it is changed with another SET KWIC command. In the following example, notice how groups of three periods appear between windows to indicate that text has been omitted.

```
        Set    Items     Description
        ---    -----     -----------
?s self()esteem
               36191     SELF
                1299     ESTEEM
        S1      1251     SELF()ESTEEM
?t 1/kwic/1

1/KWIC/1
... being 11.5 years. All subjects were given the Children's Depression
Inventory, the Coopersmith Self Esteem Inventory and the Children's
Attributional Style Questionnaire. Teachers completed the Child Behaviour
Checklist and... Scale. The results indicated that in the older subjects,
the medicated group had lower social self - esteem than the nonmedicated
group and in younger subjects the medicated group had higher academic
self - esteem than the nonmedicated group. There were no significant
differences among the groups with respect to...
```

Because the KWIC format used alone displays only the portions of the text that contain the "hit" terms, it is usual to combine it with one of the predefined formats in order to retrieve the citation itself. For example,

```
?t 1/3,k/2

 1/3,K/2
08121915            92259915
  Sharing the memories. The value of reminiscence as a research tool.
  Newbern VB
  J Gerontol Nurs (UNITED STATES) May 1992, 18 (5) p13-8, ISSN 0098-9134
Journal Code: IAX
  Languages: ENGLISH
  Document type: JOURNAL ARTICLE
  ... is a tool for life review, storytelling, creation of a meaningful
myth, and maintenance of self - esteem that gerontological nurses cannot
continue to neglect.
```

will display the citation (format 3) and KWIC window of the second record in set 1.

Another SET command that is particularly useful in association with KWIC is the HILIGHT (HI) command. This system feature highlights the occurrence of the search terms in the KWIC window so that they are easier to spot. The command to implement the HILIGHT feature is

```
set hi on
```

entered at the beginning of the search. Depending on the terminal type, highlighted terms may display more brightly (as in the above examples), in reverse video, or with a surplus character on either side (e.g., *self-esteem*) as a marker. The default HILIGHT is the asterisk (*), but it is possible to SET it to any preferred 1-3 characters by using the command

```
set hi #
```

where # is the character selected to HILIGHT the hit terms. This command is helpful in drawing attention to the search terms that have caused the document to be retrieved, and the KWIC format provides a context that helps to assess the relevance of the document. HILIGHT is canceled at LOGOFF or by entering SET HI OFF. Have a look at this example:

```
?set hi #
HILIGHT set on as '#'
?ss inferen?(2n)statistic?
    S2     6071     INFEREN?
    S3    43207     STATISTIC?
    S4      288     INFEREN?(2N)STATISTIC?

?t 4/5/2

 4/5/2
DIALOG(R)File 11:PsycINFO(R)
(c) 1998 Amer. Psychological Assn. All rts. reserv.

01532760          1998-07264-009
Aligning everyday and mathematical reasoning: The case of sampling
  assumptions.
SERIES TITLE: Studies in mathematical thinking and learning.
AUTHOR: Schwartz, Daniel L.; Goldman, Susan R.; Vye, Nancy J.; Barron,
  Brigid J.
AUTHOR AFFILIATION: Vanderbilt U, Learning Technology Ctr, Nashville, TN,
  USA

CORPORATE SOURCE: Cognition & Technology Group at Vanderbilt, USA
BOOK SOURCE: Lajoie, Susanne P. (Ed); et al. Reflections on statistics:
Learning, teaching, and assessment in Grades K-12 ., 233-273, xxip, 336,
1998
BOOK PUBLISHER: Lawrence Erlbaum Associates, Inc., Publishers, Mahwah, NJ,
  USA
ISBN: 0-8058-1971-1 (hardcover); 0-8058-1972-X (paperback)

DOCUMENT TYPE: Chapter; Empirical Study
SPECIAL FEATURES: References
RECORD TYPE: Abstract
AUDIENCE: Psychology: Professional & Research
LANGUAGE: English
POPULATION GROUP: Human AGE GROUP: 100 (Childhood (birth-12 yrs)); 180
  (School Age (6-12 yrs))
```

ABSTRACT: (chapter) We present results from 3 studies that examined and supported 5th- and 6th-grade children's evolving notions of sampling and #statistical# #inference#. Our primary finding has been that the context of a statistical problem exerts a profound influence on children's assumptions about the purpose and validity of a sample. In our design of instructional and assessment materials, we try to acknowledge and take advantage of the role that context plays in statistical understanding.

In the 1st section of the chapter, we present evidence on the piecemeal and context-sensitive nature of statistical understanding. We use this as a basis for proposing that statistical instruction should often be situated in everyday contexts. In the 2nd section, we examine the commonsense basis of early statistical understanding. We present evidence that children understand statistical contexts by drawing on schemas for more familiar situations, such as advertising, that have family resemblances to various aspects of a #statistical# #inference#. In the 3rd section, we describe the results of our efforts to build on children's piecemeal, context-sensitive common sense. ((c) 1998 APA PsycINFO, all rights reserved)

DESCRIPTORS: *Mathematical Ability; *Mathematics Education; *School Learning; *Statistics; Childhood; Cognitive Development; Elementary School Students; Mathematics (Concepts)
IDENTIFIERS: development of understanding sampling & #statistical# #inference# for everyday contexts, 5th & 6th graders
SUBJECT CODES & HEADINGS: 3550 (Academic Learning & Achievement)

RELEASE DATE: 19980501

SORT

Records are normally output in descending order of their DIALOG accession numbers, which in most databases reflects reverse input or chronological order. That is, the record most recently input has the highest accession number, and is retrieved first.

In many databases (but not all), the SORT command can be used to alter the order in which records are output. The final search results can be rearranged by SORTing either alphabetically or numerically on a selected field. The SORT command creates a new set, which could then be used for output with a TYPE or PRINT command. The fields available for SORTing vary by database, so once again the DIALOG bluesheets will need to be checked thoroughly. Here is an example from the bluesheets for the Sociological Abstracts database.

Fig. 9.3. Sort Fields available on Sociological Abstracts.

SORTABLE FIELDS	EXAMPLES
Online (SORT) and offline (PRINT)	SORT S13/ALL/AU/TI
AU, CS, CT, JN, PY, TI	PRINT S5/5/1-24/AU

The format for the SORT command is

$$sort \leq n/all/ff,o\geq$$

where n is the number of the SORTed set, *all* specifies to sort the entire set, *ff* is the field to be used for SORTing, and o is the desired order of the SORT. Output can be SORTed by fields such as author name, journal name, zip code, or sales figures, which are all identified by their two-character field codes (e.g., AU, JN, ZP, SA). SORT orders are either ascending/alphabetical (a) or descending (d), with alphabetical being the system default.

The SORT option enables the production of bibliographies in alphabetic order by author using

> *sort s5/all/au*

or financial reports in descending order of total sales figures using

> *sort s5/all/sa,d*

It is also possible to specify more than one field code in a SORT command, though this is not a frequently used option. When this multiple SORT option is used, codes are listed separated by either commas or slashes, and sorting precedence operates from left to right. For example, the command

> *sort s5/all/au,ti*

sorts all items in set 5 first by author (AU), and within author by title (TI). A SORTed set cannot be used again with SELECT or SORT commands, but can only be used to TYPE or PRINT results. If a different sequence is desired, the original set that was SORTed must be SORTed again by a different field.

In order to get accurate results, though, the whole set must be SORTed. Even when only a subset of the data is needed (e.g., the top 50 companies), the entire retrieved set has to be SORTed.

A SORTed set is normally TYPEd or PRINTed straight away. However, when it is not necessary to inspect the set online, it is more efficient to combine the SORT parameters into the PRINT command. This is done by using a normal PRINT statement and adding at the end the two-letter codes of the fields to be used for SORTing following a slash (with a *d* if descending order is required). For example,

> *print s5/2/1-50/au*
> *or*
> *print s8/3/all/zp,d*

SORTing is a good first step towards providing a "value-added" output for the user. It makes it possible to provide a customized bibliography, arranged alphabetically by author, or a business report arranged in order by a chosen criteria. It can also be used quite effectively with the REPORT command.

REPORT

Another output option available on a number of DIALOG databases, particularly files containing statistical, financial, or demographic data, is the REPORT command. It arranges selected data from a retrieved set of records into useful tables, displaying the information in columns. The extraction of selected fields of data from lengthy records in this way can save not only online time but also time for the user. This is definitely a value-added feature for busy managerial staff. Imagine having to read right through the long record at the end of the last chapter in order to gather one or two specific pieces of information!

Reports are only available online, and the results are most effective when used in combination with the SORT command, so that the data is presented in a logical order. In order to use this command the fields that are available for use with REPORT must first be checked in the bluesheets of the database being used. (An example showing the fields available for use with REPORT on one of the Dun and Bradstreet databases [file 520] is presented in Figure 9.4.) Then calculate the total lengths of the fields to be included. This is necessary because the number of fields that can be displayed readably is limited by the length of the print line. The display line is set to 75 characters, which matches the line length of most printers, but the maximum line length available on the system is 132 characters. Building a line of more than 75 characters, however, will cause the data to wrap around and spoil the appearance of the report. (It is worth pointing out that data that have been formatted using the REPORT command can be difficult to handle in a word processor and may need some rearranging).

Fig. 9.4. Fields for use with REPORT on Canadian Dun's Market Identifiers (File 520).

REPORT S2/CO,SL,EM/ALL

DISPLAY CODE	REPORT FIELD LENGTH	FIELD NAME
AN	11	DIALOG Accession Number
A1	32	Street Address
A2	32	Mailing Address
CE	21	Top Executive Name
CN	9	Country Name
CO	32	Company Name
CX	21	County Name
CY	32	City
DC	13	D-U-N-S Corporate Number
DH	13	D-U-N-S Headquarters Number

Fig. 9.4. Fields for use with REPORT on Canadian Dun's Market Identifiers (continued).

DN	13	D-U-N-S Number
DP	13	D-U-N-S Parent Number
EG	10	Employee Growth
EH	12	Employees Here
EM	12	Employees Total
HC	15	Headquarters City
HS	10	Headquarters State/Province
IP	32	Parent Company Name
IS	10	Parent State/Province
IY	15	Parent City
MC	7	SMSA Code
MN	22	SMSA Name
NW	13	Net Worth
OS	14	Organizational Status
PC	9	Primary SIC Code
PL	9	Primary SIC Code - Local (Canada)
PO	15	Top Executive Position
RD	12	Record Update Date
SA	14	Sales (U.S. $)
SG	8	Sales Growth
SL	14	Sales - Local Currency (Canadian $)
ST	10	State/Province
TE	14	Telephone Number
YR	8	Latest Year Organized
ZP	9	Postal Code

The REPORT command has a format similar to the other output formats:

report ≤n/ff,ff,ff/b-e≥

where *n* is the set number, *ff* are the field codes separated by commas, and *b-e* are the beginning and ending record numbers. There can be as many field codes in this expression as needed, so long as the resulting report can fit across the page. For example,

    report s5/co,sa,ta,nt/1-10

presents a table of the first 10 records from set 5. The table will include company name, total sales figures, total assets, and net assets, with the sequence of columns in the order in which the field codes were entered in the REPORT command. Remember to SORT before using the REPORT command, so that the records in the REPORT are presented in a logical order. Here is an example:

```
File 100:Disclosure(R) Database 1998/Feb 11
(c) 1998 Disclosure Inc.

    Set   Items    Description
    ---   -----    -----------
?s pc=2731
    S1       13    PC=2731
?sort s1/all/sa,d
    S2       13    Sort S1/ALL/SA,D
?report s2/co,sa,ni/1-10

Align paper; press ENTER
?
                      DIALOG(R)File 100:Disclosure(R) Database
                      (c) 1998 Disclosure Inc. All rts. reserv.
                                     Net         Net
Company                             Sales      Income
Name                                (000s)      (000s)
------------------------------    --------    --------
SCHOLASTIC CORP                    966,300         400
HOUGHTON MIFFLIN CO                717,863      43,622
JOHN WILEY & SONS INC              431,974      20,340
GOLDEN BOOKS FAMILY ENTERTAINM     255,005    -197,503
THOMAS NELSON INC                  243,436      26,077
WAVERLY INC                        170,961       6,347
STECK VAUGHN PUBLISHING CORP        85,505       3,170
PAGES INC DE                        29,887       1,529
WILLIAM H SADLIER INC               23,686         707
GOODHEART WILLCOX CO INC            16,631       2,775
```

A useful feature is the ability to eliminate records that do not contain data in essential fields before entering the REPORT command. This can be done by using Boolean NOT to link the field code (sa) equals not available (na) to the final subject set

    s s8 not sa=na

This removes all records that have no data in the total sales (sa) field. (It is a feature that is also useful with the SORT command in a lot of other situations). If no range of records is given, the system defaults to PRINTing all the records in the set, so be careful!

Getting Search Results

There are now many alternatives to viewing search results online. Over the last several years, DIALOG has developed a number of mechanisms to make distribution of results easier and more efficient. Two fairly basic, yet valuable, options are to have results faxed or E-mailed. Both require searchers to create address records within the DIALOG system, specifying fax numbers or E-mail addresses. Once these are available, a version of the PRINT command (previously used just to have an offline print copy of the search results made and mailed back) is used. Both have clear advantages: a fax copy saves the connect time and trouble of downloading a digital version from the direct search and then printing; an E-mail copy is in digital form (but still without spending the connect time) for post-processing before printing.

Perhaps more interesting, though, is the ERA service (Electronic Redistribution and Archiving), which enables companies or organizations to distribute multiple copies of DIALOG output without fear of violating copyright law or policies. More than 250 files within DIALOG can take advantage of ERA; the producers of these databases have reached an agreement with DIALOG to permit this redistribution and gain royalties from it.

Redistribution can be via print or digital copies of DIALOG output. The COPIES command (again used with PRINT) will produce up to 100 paper copies, which DIALOG will print and mail:

```
?print s2/9/1 copies 100
```

will send 100 copies of the first document in set S2 in format 9. Price depends on the file and number of copies requested.

Digital copies are requested with the REDIST command, used either with PRINT or TYPE:

```
?type s6/3/1-15 redist 75
```

will display as would be expected, but then grants the right to make up to 75 copies of this digital version for other people in the user's organization.

A third command, ARCHIVE, permits remote storage on a local area network for later consultation (as compared to actively making copies as with REDIST):

```
?type s15/3/all archive 15
```

will show all records in the set in format 3, and allow up to 15 people to access a remote copy of that set on the LAN.

Making or permitting such multiple copies is, of course, more expensive than making a single copy and sharing it. But it does have the advantage of being legal and allowing companies that are justifiably concerned about handling intellectual property properly in an increasingly digital and litigious world to know they are safely within the constraints of the law.

This chapter has covered a whole range of new commands, many of which can be used together in varying combinations—SORT with PRINT, SET with UDF, SORT with ORDER, and so on. Most of them are intended to improve the appearance of the search output. The intention is to help provide a professional-looking, customized end product for the user. This factor is likely to become increasingly important as users become more aware of online information resources and as they learn to perform simple searches for themselves.

> I believe that as people learn to do simple searches themselves, the role of the professional searcher will depend increasingly on the provision of a value-added end-product. – GW

10 BEYOND THE BASIC SEARCH

We have seen that databases come from many different sources, and are intended for many different audiences. They vary not only by their subject content but by the way the data are presented, the level of detail provided, and the currency of the information. Four basic types of data are in databases found on the DIALOG system:

- Bibliographic
- Numeric
- Directory/dictionary
- Full text

Bibliographic databases are the most common type of file on the older online systems, and their records, as we saw earlier, take the form of bibliographic citations (title, author, source, etc.), sometimes accompanied by an abstract. Numeric databases contain records that are mainly tables of statistical data but often include some textual comment. Directory/dictionary files give factual information about companies, organizations, products, and the like, often in tabular form. Full-text databases contain records that may be several pages long and contain the complete text of magazine articles, newswire stories, encyclopedia entries, and so forth.

> More and more full-text material is becoming available, especially on the Internet. Many of the major vendors are also offering the option of full-text, either directly or as a link from the citation. It seems likely that this is the wave of the future. – GW

Bibliographic databases direct users to a source of information that must be accessed elsewhere, while numeric, directory, and full-text databases provide the information itself.

With hundreds of databases to choose from, selection of the most appropriate files is not always easy. This chapter explains where to find help in making this choice and some of the techniques necessary when searching multiple databases.

Choosing Which System to Search

When a searcher has access to a range of different search systems, the decision about which to use in any given situation will normally depend on what is available on each system. If the same file is available from more than one vendor, the deciding factor is likely to be cost. The price per hour of connect time and the cost per record are what contribute to total search costs, and both may vary, even for the same file, on different systems. In certain cases it is thus possible to save money by preferring one system to another, and Internet of course is "free."

Many search topics require the use of multiple files to obtain comprehensive results, and it is common for searches nowadays to be performed on at least two or three databases. When more than one file needs to be searched, the availability of the full range of files on one system will possibly influence the choice of search system because it will often save time and money to be able to complete the search on a single system.

In some small proportion of searches, the availability of a particular search feature may also be a deciding factor in the choice of system because the same file may be mounted differently, and thus offers different search features on different systems. It pays to check all the available documentation with great care.

A number of sources provide information on the range of databases available across all the search services. For example, the *Gale Directory of Databases* provides excellent overviews of current services and a wealth of information on databases of all types.[1]

Choosing Databases

Many of the criteria used in selecting printed reference resources are also relevant when choosing online files. The following are some points to note when considering the choice of files for searching:

- Subject scope (and how subjects are covered in the file)
- Access points (searchable fields)
- Type of material (popular, research, etc.)
- Type of data (bibliographic, numeric, etc.)
- Time period covered
- File currency (how up-to-date it is)

In addition to these general reference considerations, each of the online retrieval systems offers an extensive range of helpful directories, guides, and newsletters to help choose among their own databases. For example, the DIALOG Database Catalog provides:

- a description of each database (in alphabetical order) detailing subject content, dates of coverage, publisher, etc.;
- charts indicating the type of data, special features, services, and the update frequency of each database;
- a list of database suppliers and the databases they produce; and
- a listing of DIALINDEX/OneSearch Subject Categories which group files by subject.

Database bluesheets summarize the content and list the specific search features that are available on each individual file; they are now available on the Internet from DIALOG's website (www.dialog.com). Each bluesheet includes a sample record (to show what a typical record in the database looks like) and lists the record formats in which output can be displayed. More detailed information for each individual file covering each field of the record, including details of how to search it, is available online.

Despite this variety of search aids intended to assist with the choice of appropriate databases, personal experience suggests that choosing the "best" file to use is not an easy task for the beginning searcher. It may be important to consider factors such as intended audience, type of indexing used, or fields available for searching on particular files. The type of source document required (e.g., patents or research reports) may help narrow the choice of database. There is sometimes considerable overlap between databases, though the amount tends to vary by subject and by file. If a comprehensive search is required, it may be necessary to ignore the likelihood of overlap and accept that some records will necessarily be duplicated. They can be easily eliminated from the final output by using the REMOVE DUPLICATES or RD command.

As has been mentioned, the vendors sometimes group files by their type and coverage in some of their system documentation, and this is another useful resource to assist in database selection. But be aware that the suggested groupings should not necessarily be accepted without question because they often include files that will prove inappropriate.

DIALINDEX

In order to help searchers with the task of choosing appropriate databases, each of the major vendors provides an index file, a kind of "database of databases," which is accessible online. It is a composite of all the inverted files, both Basic Indexes and Additional Indexes, of the whole range of databases available on the system. On the DIALOG system this file is called DIALINDEX (File 411), and it allows the searcher to browse selected search terms in files that look potentially useful so as to compare postings figures. In this way DIALINDEX helps users check which databases have higher postings on a specific topic before the actual search is conducted in more expensive databases. It is particularly useful when there are a whole group of possible files for a given query, and there is uncertainty as to which of them will prove the most useful. DIALINDEX allows the searcher to select anywhere from two to the total of potential files to browse, though of course a small selection would normally be appropriate for consideration in a given search.

It is important to remember that this is an index file. It contains no records and no sets are formed when it is searched, so certain commands (e.g., TYPE, DISPLAY, PRINT, or EXPAND) cannot be used. In order to use this browse facility, we need a new command (usable only in DIALINDEX) to enable us to select the group of files we think may be useful for our search. After we have selected the DIALINDEX database the first command is always going to be SET FILES or SELECT FILES (abbreviated SF) followed by a listing of files, in order to limit the search to that particular group. Be careful not to omit this SET FILES command, or an error message will appear!

The SET FILES command can be used with:

- *file numbers*
    e.g., `select files 38,56,191`

- *acronyms for database categories* to select subject groups (see the Database Catalog for details of the available categories)
    e.g., `sf compsci, software`

- *a combination of numbers and acronyms* to add files to a subject category
  e.g., `sf humanit,47,111`

- *the Boolean NOT operator* to exclude file numbers from a subject category.
  e.g., `sf chemlit not 34,87,94`

A space must be entered after the SF command, and file numbers and acronyms must be separated with commas. Hyphens can be used to indicate a range of file numbers. Following the selection of files, the system confirms the databases chosen, and a list of their file banners can be obtained by using the command SHOW FILES.

When the system issues the next prompt, a single SELECT statement, containing up to 240 characters, is entered in the usual DIALOG format. It is probably most useful to limit this SELECT to the most important concepts of the search linked by appropriate logic. Terms can be linked using Boolean or proximity operators and can be nested using parentheses. Prefix and suffix codes are also acceptable on DIALINDEX, but it is important to check their availability on all of the files selected. (Certain prefix codes may need to be ORed together in order to make sure that a particular feature is covered in all the selected files.) The system responds to the SELECT command by displaying the number of items retrieved from each database for the final logical statement.

DIALINDEX is begun as would be any other file; its file number is 411:

```
?b 411

File 411:DIALINDEX(tm)

DIALINDEX(tm)
(Copr. DIALOG Info.Ser.Inc.)

*** DIALINDEX search results display in an abbreviated ***
*** format unless you enter the SET DETAIL ON command. ***
?select files 10,51,79,155
  You have 4 files in your file list.
  (To see banners, use SHOW FILES command)
?show files

          File    Name
          ----    -----------
           10:    AGRICOLA_70-1998/Jan
           51:    Food Sci.&Tech.Abs_1969-1998/Feb
           79:    Foods Adlibra(TM)_1974-1998/Nov
          155:    MEDLINE(R)_1966-1998/Mar W4

?s low()cholesterol()diet?

Your SELECT statement is:
  s low()cholesterol()diet?

          Items   File
          -----   -----------
            283    10: AGRICOLA_70-1998/Jan
             13    51: Food Sci.&Tech.Abs_1969-1998/Feb
             26    79: Foods Adlibra(TM)_1974-1998/Nov
            269   155: MEDLINE(R)_1966-1998/Mar W4

All files have one or more items; file list includes 4 files.
```

What we are interested in here are the postings figures for each file, in order to determine which databases we will use for our actual search. We can see in this case MEDLINE and AGRICOLA are going to be far and away the most useful files to use for information on low-cholesterol diets. The actual search in those files may be elaborated, but at least we know the most useful files to search.

Here is an example of the use of DIALINDEX with one of the Subject Category acronyms.

```
?set files people
You have 17 files in your file list.
  (To see banners, use SHOW FILES command)
?s bella()abzug

Your SELECT statement is:
s bella()abzug

          Items     File
          -----     -----
            187       47: Magazine Database(TM)_1959-1998/Feb 09
            137       88: IAC BUSINESS A.R.T.S._1976-1998/Feb 10
             36      111: Natl.Newspaper Index(SM)_1979-1998/Feb 10
             70      141: Readers Guide_1983-1997/Dec
             74      148: IAC Trade & Industry Database_1976-1998/Feb 10
              4      211: IAC Newsearch(TM)_1997-1998/Feb 10
             14      234: Marquis Who's Who(R)_ 1997/July.
              1      236: Bowker(r) Biographical Directory_1997/Oct
              1      466: Info Latino America_1988-1995/Dec W1
            130      484: Periodical Abstracts Plustext_1986-1998/Jan W3
             18      603: Newspaper Abstracts_1984-1988
              2      648: TV AND RADIO TRANSCRIPTS_1997-1998/Feb W2
             51      799: Textline Curr.Glob.News_1995-1997/Oct 12
   13 files have one or more items; file list includes 17 files.
```

The most helpful files for this search appear to be Magazine Database, IAC BUSINESS A.R.T.S., and Periodical Abstracts.

The next example illustrates the use of the Boolean NOT to eliminate unsuitable files. The best files for this search on the use of intervention techniques with potential teenage suicides are clearly file 1 (ERIC) and 88 (IAC). This example also shows how the command RANK FILES can be used to arrange files in order of postings figures, which is particularly useful when checking a large group of files.

```
?select files psych not 7
You have 12 files in your file list.
  (To see banners, use SHOW FILES command)
?s teenage()suicide and intervention

Your SELECT statement is:
  s teenage()suicide and intervention

          Items     File
          -----     -----
             16        1: ERIC_1966-1997/Dec
              4       11: PsycINFO(R)_1967-1998/Jan
              2       37: Sociological Abstr._1963-1997/Dec
              2       46: A-V Online_1997/Dec. Q4
              4       86: Mental Health Abstracts_1969-1998/Feb
             26       88: IAC BUSINESS A.R.T.S._1976-1998/Feb 10
              1      121: Brit.Education Index_1976-1997/Q4
   7 files have one or more items; file list includes 12 files.
```

```
?rank files
Your last SELECT statement was:
  S TEENAGE()SUICIDE AND INTERVENTION

      Ref    Items    File
      ---    -----    -----
      N1      26       88: IAC BUSINESS A.R.T.S._1976-1998/Feb 10
      N2      16        1: ERIC_1966-1997/Dec
      N3       4       11: PsycINFO(R)_1967-1998/Jan
      N4       4       86: Mental Health Abstracts_1969-1998/Feb
      N5       2       37: Sociological Abstr._1963-1997/Dec
      N6       2       46: A-V Online_1997/Dec. Q4
      N7       1      121: Brit.Education Index_1976-1997/Q4
      N8       0       35: Dissertation Abstracts Online_1861-1998/Mar
      N9       0      111: Natl.Newspaper Index(SM)_1979-1998/Feb 10
      N10      0      142: Social Sciences Abstracts_1983-1997/Dec
      7 files have one or more items; file list includes 12 files.
```

Keep in mind there are no records available in DIALINDEX. All we have learned so far is which are the "best" files to search. We now need to change to the appropriate database in order to find the relevant documents.

Journal Name Finder

Another useful feature provided by DIALOG to aid in database selection is the Journal Name Finder (file 414). Like DIALINDEX, the Journal Name Finder contains information from all other files in the system. In this case, that information consists of which files contain citations to articles from individual journals. This is particularly useful if the user knows of a good journal or two in the field, or if the subject area is interdisciplinary—some fields of study cross several database boundaries, and material in good journals may escape notice because it is not in an obvious file.

Here is an example. There is no one good file available on DIALOG that covers the area of anthropology, and you encounter a user who is interested in urban anthropology. There is a good journal, *Urban Anthropology*, so the librarian searches the Journal Name Finder and see what files incorporate it. We begin the search with an EXPAND command, as there may be variant forms of the journal's name in different databases.

```
?b 414
File 414:DIALOG Journal Name Finder(TM) 1997/Oct
     (c) 1998 Dialog Corporation

      Set    Items    Description
      ---    -----    -----------
?e urban anthropol

      Ref    Items    Index-term
      E1       1       URBAN AND SOCIAL CHANGE REVIEW V 15 N 1 SPE
      E2       2       URBAN ANTHROP
      E3       1      *URBAN ANTHROPOL
      E4       1       URBAN ANTHROPOL STUD CULT SYST
      E5       9       URBAN ANTHROPOLOGY
      E6       3       URBAN ANTHROPOLOGY AND STUDIES OF CULTURAL SYS
      E7       1       URBAN ANTHROPOLOGY STUDIES OF CULTURAL SYSTE
      E8       1       URBAN APPALACHIAN ADVOCATE
      E9       1       URBAN CLIMATES SYMPOSIUM ON URBAN CLIMATES AN
```

```
     E10        2        URBAN COASTAL AREA MANAGEMENT THE EXPERIENCE
     E11        1        URBAN CONGESTION MANAGEMENT
     E12        1        URBAN DATA SERVICE REPORT V 8 N 12 DECEMBER

                  Enter P or PAGE for more
?s e2,e3,e5
                2        URBAN ANTHROP
                1        URBAN ANTHROPOL
                9        URBAN ANTHROPOLOGY
     S1        12        E2,E3,E5
?t 1/5/1-3


 1/5/1
DIALOG(R)File 414:DIALOG Journal Name Finder(TM)
(c) 1998 Dialog Corporation. All rts. reserv.

 02100013
URBAN ANTHROPOLOGY      (JN=)
     DIALOG FILE     7: SOCIAL SCISEARCH(R) 1972-1997/NOV W1
                        (C) 1997 INST FOR SCI INFO
     This file contains BIBLIOGRAPHIC records.
     Number of Records for this Journal, 31 OCTOBER 1997: 589


 1/5/2
DIALOG(R)File 414:DIALOG Journal Name Finder(TM)
(c) 1998 Dialog Corporation. All rts. reserv.

 01962304
URBAN ANTHROPOLOGY      (JN=)
     DIALOG FILE     37: SOCIOLOGICAL ABSTR. 1963-1997/OCT
                         (C) 1997 SOCIOLOGICAL ABSTRACTS IN
     This file contains BIBLIOGRAPHIC records.
     Number of Records for this Journal, 31 OCTOBER 1997: 285


 1/5/3
DIALOG(R)File 414:DIALOG Journal Name Finder(TM)
(c) 1998 Dialog Corporation. All rts. reserv.

 01846758
URBAN ANTHROPOLOGY      (JN=)
     DIALOG FILE     48: SPORTDISCUS 1962-1997/OCT
                         (C) 1997 SPORT INFORMATION RESOURCE CENTR
     This file contains BIBLIOGRAPHIC records.
     Number of Records for this Journal, 31 OCTOBER 1997: 2
?sort 1/all/rc,d
     S2        12        Sort 1/ALL/RC,D
?report 2/jn,fn,rc/all

Align paper; press ENTER
?
```

```
DIALOG(R)File 414:DIALOG Journal Name Finder(TM)
     (c) 1998 Dialog Corporation All rts. reserv.
```

JOURNAL NAME	FILE NUMBER	RECORD COUNT
URBAN ANTHROPOLOGY	7	589
URBAN ANTHROPOLOGY	37	285
URBAN ANTHROPOLOGY	292	196
URBAN ANTHROPOLOGY	1	99
URBAN ANTHROPOLOGY	88	96
URBAN ANTHROPOLOGY	142	78
URBAN ANTHROPOL	142	78
URBAN ANTHROPOLOGY	50	27
URBAN ANTHROPOLOGY	162	7
URBAN ANTHROP	38	3
URBAN ANTHROPOLOGY	48	2
URBAN ANTHROP	39	1

This method of TYPEing provides a nice display, organized by file number, and helps to identify easily the most useful files—7, 37, and 292.

Saving Searches (SAVE)

The availability of access to so many different databases and the ability to use the same search strategy on several files is an important feature of the major online systems. However, such cross-file searching is not as simple as it might seem because files vary in content, record format, and searchable fields. It is important to realize that the search system may be inconsistent in the way in which it treats features such as prefix or suffix codes, parse rules, and limit qualifiers in different files. Extra effort is needed in the planning of a search that is to be run on multiple databases, and careful scrutiny of the documentation for each of the files is crucial.

The SAVE command enables the searcher to store a search strategy in the mainframe computer to use on another database or for use again at a later date. A stored strategy on DIALOG is known as a SearchSave, and there are three possible types of SearchSave:

- A *temporary* SearchSave, using the SAVE TEMP command, assigns a name to the search strategy and stores it for one week on the system mainframe machine. There are no storage charges for this type of SAVE, and the search will be erased automatically after seven days. This can be used to hold a search for a brief time while the searcher consults with documentation or the user. If the searcher will be offline for only a very short time, the LOGOFF HOLD command should also be considered. This will log the user off from DIALOG but will preserve the sets. The searcher can log back on within a half hour (on the same password), do a DS, and see that the sets are still there.

- A *standard* SearchSave, using the SAVE command, stores a search permanently at a nominal cost. This type of search is saved until released by the user. It is often used to store searches that may be accessed later as part of a library's current awareness service, or for hedges that can be used in the future as part of another search. *Hedges* are complicated blocks that include a great number of synonymous terms used to represent a single concept such as "secondary education," which the searcher may well want to use again in the future. It can save a great deal of the effort involved in search preparation to be able to store such blocks for repeat use, when they can be combined with different concept blocks.

> *Saved searches are charged for storage on DIALOG's mainframe machine at a cost of 40 cents per month plus 15 cents per command line. – GW*

Here's an example of the use of such a hedge:

```
?b 1

File   1:ERIC   66-97/MAY.

    Set    Items    Description
    ---    -----    -----------

?exs sasec
    S1     57845    SECONDARY EDUCATION (EDUCATION PROVIDED IN GRADE
                    7, 8, OR 9 THRO
    S2      8208    JUNIOR HIGH SCHOOLS (PROVIDING FORMAL EDUCATION
                    IN GRADES 7, 8, A...)
    S3     14893    HIGH SCHOOLS (PROVIDING FORMAL EDUCATION IN GRADES
                    9 OR 10...)
    S4      1864    GRADE 9
    S5      1290    GRADE 10
    S6      1232    GRADE 11
    S7      1403    GRADE 12
    S8      3014    SECONDARY SCHOOLS
    S9       728    HIGH SCHOOL EQUIVALENCY PROGRAMS (ADULT EDUCATIONAL
                    ACTIVITIES CONC
    S10    83402    SECONDARY EDUCATION OR JUNIOR HIGH SCHOOLS OR HIGH
                    SCHOOLS OR GRADE 9 OR GRADE 10 OR GRADE 11 OR GRADE
                    12 OR SECONDARY SCHOOLS OR HIGH SCHOOL EQUIVALENCY
                    PROGRAMS
?s science fiction
    S11      360    SCIENCE FICTION
?s s10 and s11
           83402    S10
             360    S11
    S12      114    S10 AND S11
?s s12/1989:1992
             114    S12
           78173    PY=1989 : PY=1992
    S13       11    S12/1989:1992
?t 13/8/1-4

 13/8/1
EJ421924          SE547242
  Science Fiction Stories with Reasonable Astronomy.
  Descriptors: *Astronomy; *Bibliographies; *College Science; Earth
Science ; Educational Resources; Higher Education; Physical Sciences;
Physics; Science Education; *Science Fiction; *Science Materials;
Secondary Education; *Secondary School Science; Space Exploration;
Space Sciences
  Identifiers: Planets; *Solar System
```

```
     13/8/2
EJ421125            CS741037
  Dragons, Dystopias, and Time Travel: Fantasy and Science Fiction
for Everyone (Books for the Teenage Reader).
  Descriptors: *Adolescent Literature; Adolescents; Annotated
Bibliographies; Book Reviews; *Fantasy; Reading Interests; Reading
Materials; *Science Fiction; Secondary Education


     13/8/3
EJ412339            SE546462
  Science Fiction Aids Science Teaching.
  Descriptors: *College Science; *Films; Higher Education; *Inservice
Teacher Education; *Physics; Postsecondary Education; Science
Education; *Science Fiction; *Scientific Concepts; Secondary
Education; Secondary School Science


     13/8/4
EJ406735            CS739668
  Using Film in the Humanities Classroom: The Case of "Metropolis."
  Descriptors: Class Activities; *Film Criticism; *Films; Popular
Culture; *Science Fiction; Secondary Education; Teaching Methods
  Identifiers: *Metropolis (Film); Weimar Republic
```

- A *current awareness* or *SDI* (Selective Dissemination of Information) SearchSave, using the SAVE ALERT command, is saved and automatically called up and executed on every new collection of update records as they are added to the selected database. It is stored permanently until released by the user, and the results will be sent to the searcher, either through the postal service or via DIALMAIL. Charges for this service vary by database, but the costs cover any number of search terms and a maximum of 25 records printed in full format. This command cannot be used on all files, so once again it is important to check the documentation carefully.

The use of this SDI service means that new information is received by the user automatically as soon as it is available, without the need for the searcher to log on repeatedly to check for new information. This type of current awareness service can be used to:

- Keep up-to-date with the latest research

- Monitor the activities of competitors

- Track product announcements

- Watch for new patents

- Stay abreast of the market

It is often useful to store a title or some comments using the comment feature * (an asterisk) as part of the SearchSave because this simplifies the identification of the offline prints when they arrive in the mail.

Combining SAVE with the DIALINDEX feature, we can see that by using the SAVE TEMP command it is possible to enter a search once in DIALINDEX in order to discover which files will provide the highest retrieval, and then move to each file in turn in order to retrieve actual records.

SearchSave strategies are prepared in the same way as regular searches, but only set-generating commands can be saved. Run a search online and then enter the command SAVE after TYPEing the results. All SELECT, SELECT STEPS, SORT, and PRINT commands that have been entered since the last BEGIN will be saved. Notice that SAVE does not store other commands (e.g., EXPAND, DISPLAY SETS, TYPE) that may have been entered during the same search because these commands relate to file-specific data.

The response from the system will confirm that the strategy has been stored and will assign it an identifying number consisting of three digits preceded by two letters. An attractive option allows the user to assign a three- to five-character name to a SAVEd search, making it easier to identify it in the future. Note that two letters will be automatically added to the front of the name chosen in order for the system to identify it. Make a note of this number for future reference. Here is an example:

```
File 191:Art Lit. Intl.(RILA) 1975-1989
        (c) 1989 The Paul Getty Trust-RILA


    Set    Items    Description
    ---    -----    -----------
?ss (church or churches or cathedral? ?) and byzantine and (style or
architecture)
    S1     5877     CHURCH
    S2     4602     CHURCHES
    S3     3481     CATHEDRAL? ?
    S4     2070     BYZANTINE
    S5     4677     STYLE
    S6    31854     ARCHITECTURE
    S7      416     (CHURCH OR CHURCHES OR CATHEDRAL? ?) AND BYZANTINE AND
                    (STYLE OR ARCHITECTURE)
?save temp arch
Temp SearchSave "TDARCH" stored
```

Note the name to remember is TDARCH.

In order to use a previously SAVEd search strategy, connect to the database in which the search will be run using a normal BEGIN command. Then enter the command EXECUTE (EX) or EXECUTE STEPS (EXS), followed by the serial number of the search. The search will be run as though each line of the search strategy were entered separately, with the set numbers being adjusted automatically. The command EXECUTE can be used, but it only returns a single set number (S1) for the complete search strategy. This makes it impossible to modify the search, a move that may well be necessary when searching a different file. The use of EXECUTE STEPS is thus preferable because it returns a set number for each command line of the stored search, enabling it to be easily modified by the use of additional SELECT commands. Note the difference in set numbers between these two examples, where we EXECUTE our SAVEd result on two different databases.

```
?b 179

File 179:Architecture DB 1987-1998/Jan
        (c) 1998 Royal Inst. of Brit. Architects


    Set    Items    Description
    ---    -----    -----------
?ex tdarch
           2685     CHURCH
           2960     CHURCHES
```

```
            1086      CATHEDRAL? ?
              62      BYZANTINE
            1310      STYLE
           26422      ARCHITECTURE
              16      (CHURCH OR CHURCHES OR CATHEDRAL? ?) AND BYZANTINE AND
                      (STYLE OR ARCHITECTURE)
     S1       16      Serial: TDARCH
?b 56


File 56:ARTbibliographies Modern 1974-1997/Jun
      (c) 1997 ABC-CLIO

     Set   Items    Description
     ---   -----    -----------
?exs tdarch
     S1     1428    CHURCH
     S2      654    CHURCHES
     S3      496    CATHEDRAL? ?
     S4      184    BYZANTINE
     S5    14044    STYLE
     S6    12418    ARCHITECTURE
     S7        9    (CHURCH OR CHURCHES OR CATHEDRAL? ?) AND BYZANTINE AND
                    (STYLE OR ARCHITECTURE)
```

Because a SearchSave is stored as a series of command lines, it is possible to review it without actually running the search through the use of the RECALL command with the search name (RECALL TDARCH in this example). It is also useful to be able to review all saved searches using the RECALL SAVE option. This will list all the serial numbers and names of searches that are stored under the password currently in use.

```
?recall temp
Name      Date       Time        Size
-------   --------   --------    ----
TDARCH    10feb98    14:49:42      1
```

When a SAVEd search is no longer needed it should be deleted from memory using the RELEASE command because all SAVEd searches incur ongoing storage charges. As a safety measure, searches can only be EXECUTEd or RELEASEd using the same password with which they were created. Here we are releasing the search we had previously SAVEd and EXECUTEd.

```
?release tdarch
TDARCH released
```

The sequence of commands when saving and using a search is thus:

```
begin ≤file number≥

select ≤search terms and logical combinations≥

save ≤name≥ (3 to 5 characters)

begin ≤another file number≥

execute steps ≤search name≥

release ≤search name≥
```

The sequence can, of course, be repeated in as many files as necessary, without the need to SAVE the search between each file. Remember, it is being SAVEd automatically until it is RELEASEd.

OneSearch™

The use of the SAVE TEMP command to move from file to file, repeating the same search, has been superseded on the DIALOG system by the development of an improved search feature known as OneSearch. This enables a group of databases to be accessed with a single BEGIN command, using both file numbers and DIALINDEX Subject Categories. The system responds with a list of the file banners for the selected databases and then the usual prompt for the search statement.

When using the OneSearch option, the search looks exactly like a search run on a single file, though the postings figures will be those for the whole group of files together. If separate postings figures for the individual files are required, enter the SET DETAIL ON command before entering the search strategy.

OneSearch tends to provide a confusing amount of detail when used with the SELECT STEPS or EXPAND commands across a range of databases, so be careful!

This is what our brain injury search looks like when using OneSearch:

```
?b 11,155, 151

SYSTEM:OS - DIALOG OneSearch
  File 11:PsycINFO(R) 1967-1998/May
        (c) 1998 Amer. Psychological Assn.
  File 155:MEDLINE(R) 1966-1998/Jul W3
        (c) format only 1998 Dialog Corporation
  File 151:HealthSTAR 1975-1998/Jun
        (c) format only 1998 The Dialog Corporation

   Set   Items   Description
   ---   -----   -----------

?s (head or brain)()injur? and (psychosocial or neuropsycholog?)
        146487   HEAD
        559642   BRAIN
        437818   INJUR?
         48618   (HEAD OR BRAIN)(W)INJUR?
         56944   PSYCHOSOCIAL
         41121   NEUROPSYCHOLOG?
   S1     3773   (HEAD OR BRAIN)()INJUR? AND (PSYCHOSOCIAL OR
                 NEUROPSYCHOLOG?)

?s s1 and adolescent? ?
         3773   S1
        144595   ADOLESCENT? ?
   S2     152   S1 AND ADOLESCENT? ?

?set detail on
DETAIL set on
?ds
```

```
Set    File   Items   Description
        11     1547
        155    1312
        151     914
S1             3773    (HEAD OR BRAIN)()INJUR? AND (PSYCHOSOCIAL OR
                       NEUROPSYCHOLOG?)
        11       82
        155      40
        151      30
S2              152    S1 AND ADOLESCENT? ?
```

Notice the difference once we SET DETAIL ON. We get the same results (152 postings), but we can see the breakdown of terms between the three files.

Records retrieved using OneSearch may be TYPEd, DISPLAYed, or PRINTed in the usual manner, save that all the records from the first file are displayed first, followed by all the records from the second file, and so on. A sampling of records from the full range of files can be viewed by using the FROM EACH option with the TYPE command.

For example, the command:

t s5/6/1-5 from each

will view the first five titles from each of the files searched, and is useful to provide a "flavoring" of the material retrieved.

?t 2/3/1-2 from each

```
 2/3/1                (Item 1 from file: 11)
DIALOG(R)File 11:PsycINFO(R)
(c) 1998 Amer. Psychological Assn. All rts. reserv.

01522928            1997-38595-016
Predictors of family functioning after traumatic brain injury in children
   and adolescents.
AUTHOR: Max, Jeffrey E.; Castillo, Carlos S.; Robin, Donald A.; Lindgren,
   Scott D.; Smith, Wilbur L.Jr.; Sato, Yutaka; Mattheis, Philip J.;
   Stierwalt, Julie A. G.
AUTHOR AFFILIATION: U Iowa, Hosps & Clinics, Dept of Psychiatry, Iowa City,
   IA, USA
JOURNAL: Journal of the American Academy of Child & Adolescent Psychiatry,
Vol 37(1) , 83-90, Jan, 1998



 2/3/2                (Item 2 from file: 11)
DIALOG(R)File 11:PsycINFO(R)
(c) 1998 Amer. Psychological Assn. All rts. reserv.

01510431            1997-04974-001
Neuropsychological sequelae of head injury in a New Zealand adolescent
   sample.
AUTHOR: Leathem, Janet M.; Body, Catherine M.
AUTHOR AFFILIATION: Massey U, Dept of Psychology, Psychology Clinic,
   Palmerston North, New Zealand
JOURNAL: Brain Injury, Vol 11(8) , 565-575, Aug, 1997
```

```
 2/3/83              (Item 1 from file: 155)
DIALOG(R)File 155:MEDLINE(R)
(c) format only 1998 Dialog Corporation. All rts. reserv.


09492469           98152734
  Assessment of syntax after adolescent brain injury: effects of memory on
test performance.
  Turkstra LS; Holland AL
  National Center for Neurogenic Communication Disorders, University of
Arizona, Tucson, USA.
  J Speech Lang Hear Res (UNITED STATES) Feb 1998, 41 (1) p137-49,
ISSN 1092-4388 Journal Code: CT1
  Contract/Grant No.: DC-01409, DC, NIDCD
  Languages: ENGLISH
  Document type: JOURNAL ARTICLE


 2/3/84              (Item 2 from file: 155)
DIALOG(R)File 155:MEDLINE(R)
(c) format only 1998 Dialog Corporation. All rts. reserv.


09484148           98153980
  Social and behavioural effects of traumatic brain injury in children.
  Andrews TK; Rose FD; Johnson DA
  Department of Psychology, University of East London, UK.
  Brain Inj (ENGLAND) Feb 1998, 12 (2) p133-8, ISSN 0269-9052
Journal Code: BRA
  Languages: ENGLISH
  Document type: CLINICAL TRIAL; JOURNAL ARTICLE


 2/3/123             (Item 1 from file: 151)
DIALOG(R)File 151:HealthSTAR
(c) format only 1998 The Dialog Corporation. All rts. reserv.


03255019           98144329
  Child and adolescent traumatic brain injury: correlates of injury
severity.
  Max JE; Lindgren SD; Knutson C; Pearson CS; Ihrig D; Welborn A
  Department of Psychiatry, University of Iowa, Iowa City, USA.
  Brain Inj (ENGLAND) Jan 1998, 12 (1) p31-40,
  ISSN: 0269-9052 JOURNAL CODE: BRA
  Contract/Grant No.: MH 31593 MH NIMH; MH 40856 MH NIMH; MHCRC 43271
  Languages: ENGLISH
  Document Type: JOURNAL ARTICLE


 2/3/124             (Item 2 from file: 151)
DIALOG(R)File 151:HealthSTAR
(c) format only 1998 The Dialog Corporation. All rts. reserv.


03204777           98015798
  Child and adolescent traumatic brain injury: psychiatric findings from a
paediatric outpatient specialty clinic.
  Max JE; Lindgren SD; Knutson C; Pearson CS; Ihrig D; Welborn A
  Department of Psychiatry, University of Iowa, Iowa City, USA.
  Brain Inj (ENGLAND) Oct 1997, 11 (10) p699-711,
  ISSN: 0269-9052 JOURNAL CODE: BRA
  Languages: ENGLISH
  Document Type: JOURNAL ARTICLE
```

Note how the record numbers move from 1 and 2 in file 11, to 83 and 84 in file 155, to 123 and 124 in file 151. It is particularly useful to use the REMOVE DUPLICATES (RD) command we mentioned earlier before TYPEing or PRINTing results when using OneSearch because of possible overlaps in file coverage. Using it on our previous example removes documents.

```
?rd s2
...examined 50 records (50)
...examined 50 records (100)
...examined 50 records (150)
...completed examining records
   S3      110    RD S2 (unique items)
```

Using the OneSearch option incurs no additional costs and in fact is probably cheaper than searching on a file-by-file basis. DIALOG tracks the time spent in each file during a OneSearch session, and charges accordingly. The search output is charged at the appropriate rate for each of the files used.

Problems of Multifile Searching

With the vast increase in the number of databases being produced today and the proliferation of full-text and nonbibliographic files, there has been an increase in the likelihood that coverage for almost any given topic will be found in a range of different files. Many, perhaps most, search topics now require the use of multiple files to obtain comprehensive results, even in areas as "isolated" as many fields in the humanities. It has become clear that one database alone will not provide comprehensive coverage of the literature of any field.[2]

Multifile searching is something of an art in itself. It certainly necessitates additional search preparation in the choice of search terms and the accurate use of prefix and suffix codes. It must be remembered that controlled vocabularies will vary between files, as will the availability of different Additional Indexes. This suggests that it will be preferable to use natural language with proximity operators. Lists of do's and don'ts that have appeared in the literature provide some useful suggestions regarding the problems that need to be addressed when searching multiple files[3]:

- Database documentation and thesauri are important as sources of terminology, but don't rely on a single controlled vocabulary.

- Prefer natural language terms linked by proximity operators because controlled vocabularies will vary.

- Use truncation to cover variant word forms and English/American spellings.

- Be particularly careful with classification numbers and prefix codes, as different fields may need to be ORed together to make sure that the concept is covered in all files.

- Note the variations in the punctuation of author's names in different files—use truncation if appropriate.

A couple more caveats: remember that if in more than one database, the sets are probably going to be much bigger than in a single file, so do not be thrown by big sets. Use the FROM command to see what is in each file; if only one or two files contribute usable material, search in them only (again using FROM):

```
s madonna(1n)enthrone? from 56, 191
```

Also watch truncation; as we say in the free-text chapter, a little goes a long way, and that is especially true in a multifile search. Be especially careful truncating on author's names; there are many ways in which databases represent authors' names, and all the variant forms should be obtained, but be careful not to truncate too far:

```
s au=smith?
```

in five files is probably not a good idea!

Good preparation is always the key to successful searching. It is even more important when using multiple databases. Allow plenty of time for search preparation, and make full use of the available documentation.

Search Example

Here is an example of a full-blown search that makes use of many of the techniques discussed in this chapter.

```
?b 411

File 411:DIALINDEX(R)

DIALINDEX(R)
   (c) 1998 Knight-Ridder Info

*** DIALINDEX search results display in an abbreviated ***
*** format unless you enter the SET DETAIL ON command. ***
?sf psych,educat not 88
You have 13 files in your file list.
   (To see banners, use SHOW FILES command)
?s (premarital(n)(pregnan? or birth) or birth?(2n)(out(1w)wedlock)) and
((marital or marriage??)(2n)(satisfact? or stable or stability or
instability or well?))

Your SELECT statement is:
   s (premarital(n)(pregnan? or birth) or birth?(2n)(out(1w)wedlock)) and
((marital or marriage??)(2n)(satisfact? or stable or stability or
instability or well?))

        Items    File
        -----    -----
            5       1: ERIC_1966-1998/Mar
            1       7: Social SciSearch(R)_1972-1998/May W4
            6      11: PsycINFO(R)_1967-1998/May
            7      35: Dissertation Abstracts Online_1861-1998/May
            5      37: Sociological Abstr._1963-1998/Apr
            5      86: Mental Health Abstracts_1969-1998/May
            1     211: IAC Newsearch(TM)_1997-1998/May 26

  7 files have one or more items; file list includes 13 files.
```

?save temp preg

Temp SearchSave "TDPREG" stored
?rank files

Your last SELECT statement was:
    S (PREMARITAL(N)(PREGNAN? OR BIRTH) OR BIRTH?(2N)(OUT(1W)WEDLOCK)) AND
((MARITAL OR MARRIAGE??)(2N)(SATISFACT? OR STABLE OR STABILITY OR
INSTABILITY OR WELL?))

```
    Ref    Items    File
    ---    -----    -----
    N1        7      35: Dissertation Abstracts Online_1861-1998/May
    N2        6      11: PsycINFO(R)_1967-1998/May
    N3        5       1: ERIC_1966-1998/Mar
    N4        5      37: Sociological Abstr._1963-1998/Apr
    N5        5      86: Mental Health Abstracts_1969-1998/May
    N6        1       7: Social SciSearch(R)_1972-1998/May W4
    N7        1     211: IAC Newsearch(TM)_1997-1998/May 26
    N8        0      46: A-V Online_1998/Mar. Q1
    N9        0     111: Natl.Newspaper Index(SM)_1979-1998/May 22
    N10       0     121: Brit.Education Index_1976-1998/Q1
```

    7 files have one or more items; file list includes 13 files.

        - Enter P or PAGE for more -

We can now select our files using these N numbers.

?b n1:n5

```
SYSTEM:OS - DIALOG ONESEARCH
   FILE 35:DISSERTATION ABSTRACTS ONLINE 1861-1998/MAY
         (C) 1998 UMI
   FILE 11:PSYCINFO(R) 1967-1998/MAY
         (C) 1998 AMER. PSYCHOLOGICAL ASSN.
   FILE 1:ERIC 1966-1998/MAR
         (C) FORMAT ONLY 1998 THE DIALOG CORPORATION
   FILE 37:SOCIOLOGICAL ABSTR. 1963-1998/APR
         (C) 1998 SOCIOLOGICAL ABSTRACTS INC
   FILE 86:MENTAL HEALTH ABSTRACTS 1969-1998/MAY
         (C) 1998 IFI/PLENUM DATA CORP.

   SET    ITEMS    DESCRIPTION
   ---    -----    -----------
```

?exs

```
EXECUTING TDPREG
         3341    PREMARITAL
        28701    PREGNAN?
        48160    BIRTH
          262    PREMARITAL(N)(PREGNAN? OR BIRTH)
        53337    BIRTH?
       215068    OUT
          539    WEDLOCK
          168    BIRTH?(2N)OUT(1W)WEDLOCK
        51258    MARITAL
        56456    MARRIAGE??
```

```
           100290    SATISFACT?
            49646    STABLE
            53202    STABILITY
            13576    INSTABILITY
           385814    WELL?
             8763    (MARITAL OR MARRIAGE??)(2N)((((SATISFACT? OR STABLE) OR
                     STABILITY) OR INSTABILITY) OR WELL?)
   S1         28     (PREMARITAL(N)(PREGNAN? OR BIRTH) OR
                     BIRTH?(2N)(OUT(1W)WEDLOCK)) AND ((MARITAL OR
                     MARRIAGE??)(2N)(SATISFACT? OR STABLE OR STABILITY OR
                     INSTABILITY OR WELL?))
```

?*rd s1*

...completed examining records
```
   S2       21     RD S1 (UNIQUE ITEMS)
```
?*t 2/8/1-2 from each*

 2/8/1 (Item 1 from file: 35)
DIALOG(R)FILE 35:(C) 1998 UMI. ALL RTS. RESERV.

01621170   ORDER NO: AAD98-17965
MARRIAGE AS AN INSTITUTION: THEORY AND EVIDENCE (COMMITMENT, CHILD WELFARE,
COUPLES)
   DESCRIPTORS: ECONOMICS, LABOR ; SOCIOLOGY, INDIVIDUAL AND FAMILY STUDIES
   DESCRIPTOR CODES: 0510; 0628

 2/8/2 (ITEM 2 FROM FILE: 35)
DIALOG(R)FILE 35:(C) 1998 UMI. ALL RTS. RESERV.

01326135   ORDER NO: AAD94-01193
TRANSITIONS TO ADULTHOOD AMONG YOUNG WOMEN: THE SEQUENCING OF NEST-LEAVING,
MARRIAGE, AND FIRST BIRTH (WOMEN)
   DESCRIPTORS: SOCIOLOGY, DEMOGRAPHY; SOCIOLOGY, INDIVIDUAL AND FAMILY
               STUDIES; WOMEN'S STUDIES
   DESCRIPTOR CODES: 0938; 0628; 0453

 2/8/8 (Item 1 from file: 11)
DIALOG(R)FILE 11:(C) 1998 AMER. PSYCHOLOGICAL ASSN. ALL RTS. RESERV.

01132991   1991-32992-001
MARITAL STABILITY AND CHANGES IN MARITAL QUALITY IN NEWLY WED COUPLES: A
   TEST OF THE CONTEXTUAL MODEL.

DESCRIPTORS: *DEMOGRAPHIC CHARACTERISTICS; *MARITAL RELATIONS; *REMARRIAGE;
   *STEPCHILDREN; *PERSONALITY TRAITS; ADULTHOOD; SPOUSES; MARITAL STATUS;
   MARITAL SATISFACTION; LONGITUDINAL STUDIES
IDENTIFIERS: DEMOGRAPHIC & PERSONALITY CHARACTERISTICS & MARITAL HISTORY &
PRESENCE OF STEPCHILDREN, MARITAL QUALITY & STABILITY, NEWLYWEDS, 1 YR
STUDY
SUBJECT CODES & HEADINGS: 2953 (DIVORCE & REMARRIAGE)
```
```

```
 2/8/9 (ITEM 2 FROM FILE: 11)
DIALOG(R)FILE 11:(C) 1998 AMER. PSYCHOLOGICAL ASSN. ALL RTS. RESERV.


01035301          1990-04358-001
DEMOGRAPHIC DETERMINANTS OF DELAYED DIVORCE.

DESCRIPTORS: *DEMOGRAPHIC CHARACTERISTICS; *DIVORCE; *MARITAL RELATIONS;
  *PREDICTION; ADOLESCENCE; ADULTHOOD
IDENTIFIERS: PREDICTORS OF DELAYED DIVORCE & MARITAL STABILITY, 15-44 YR
OLD FEMALES
SUBJECT CODES & HEADINGS: 2953 (DIVORCE & REMARRIAGE)


 2/8/12 (ITEM 1 FROM FILE: 1)
DIALOG(R)FILE 1:(C) FORMAT ONLY 1998 THE DIALOG CORPORATION. ALL RTS.
RESERV.

EJ355111          UD512881
  SHOULD WE DISCOURAGE TEENAGE MARRIAGE?
  DESCRIPTORS: *ADOLESCENTS; ATTITUDE CHANGE; *EARLY PARENTHOOD; FAMILY
CHARACTERISTICS; FATHERS; *ILLEGITIMATE BIRTHS; *MARITAL INSTABILITY;
*MARRIAGE; MARRIED STUDENTS; *UNWED MOTHERS


 2/8/13          (ITEM 2 FROM FILE: 1)
DIALOG(R)FILE 1:(C) FORMAT ONLY 1998 THE DIALOG CORPORATION. ALL RTS.
RESERV.

EJ280692          CG524249
  EARLY MARRIAGE, PREMARITAL FERTILITY, AND MARITAL DISSOLUTION: RESULTS
FOR BLACKS AND WHITES.
  DESCRIPTORS: *CHRONOLOGICAL AGE; COHORT ANALYSIS; FAMILY PROBLEMS;
FEMALES; *ILLEGITIMATE BIRTHS; *MARITAL INSTABILITY; *PREGNANCY; *RACIAL
DIFFERENCES; *SPOUSES


 2/8/16 (ITEM 1 FROM FILE: 37)
DIALOG(R)FILE 37:(C) 1998 SOCIOLOGICAL ABSTRACTS INC. ALL RTS. RESERV.

290771          89W10729
A STUDY ON THE STABILITY OF FIRST MARRIAGE FOR MARRIED WOMEN OF
  CHILDBEARING AGE IN TAIWAN-AN EXPLORATION OF THE RELATIONSHIP OF AGE AT
  FIRST MARRIAGE, DIMENSIONS OF PREMARRIED PREGNANCY, AND MARITAL
  DECISION-MAKING
TITLE IN CHINESE
DESCRIPTORS: TAIWAN (D851100); FERTILITY (D298200); FECUNDITY (D294300);
  MARITAL RELATIONS (D490800); STABILITY (D828700)
IDENTIFIERS: FIRST MARRIAGE STABILITY, WOMEN OF CHILDBEARING AGE, TAIWAN;
  SURVEY DATA;
SECTION HEADINGS: SOCIAL WELFARE- MARITAL & FAMILY PROBLEMS (6144)


 2/8/17 (ITEM 2 FROM FILE: 37)
DIALOG(R)FILE 37:(C) 1998 SOCIOLOGICAL ABSTRACTS INC. ALL RTS. RESERV.

074245          76H7893
THE INSTABILITY OF TEENAGE MARRIAGE IN THE UNITED STATES; AN EVALUATION OF
  THE SOCIO-ECONOMIC STATUS HYPOTHESIS
```

```
DESCRIPTORS: MARRIAGE, MARRIAGES, MARITAL (259000); TEENAGE, TEENAGERS
   (456900); INSTABILITY (234976); SOCIOECONOMIC ; (SEE ALSO SOCIOECONOMIC
   STATUS) (434455)
IDENTIFIERS: SOCIOECONOMIC FACTORS OF INSTABILITY IN TEENAGE MARRIAGES
SECTION HEADINGS: THE FAMILY AND SOCIALIZATION- ADOLESCENCE & YOUTH (1939)


 2/8/18 (Item 1 from file: 86)
DIALOG(R)FILE 86:(C) 1998 IFI/PLENUM DATA CORP. ALL RTS. RESERV.

   0423895
   HER1982-19261
   DIVORCE RESEARCH: WHAT WE KNOW; WHAT WE NEED TO KNOW.
   DESCRIPTORS: FAMILY
   IDENTIFIERS: JOURNAL; HUMAN; OVERVIEW; NIMH; MH-22575


 2/8/19 (Item 2 from file: 86)
DIALOG(R)FILE 86:(C) 1998 IFI/PLENUM DATA CORP. ALL RTS. RESERV.

   0337194
   HER1979-29203
   DIVORCE AND SEPARATION: CONTEXT, CAUSES, AND CONSEQUENCES.
   DESCRIPTORS: FAMILY; CHILD-CHILD AND FAMILY STUDIES
   IDENTIFIERS: BOOK; HUMAN; OVERVIEW; HISTORY
?DS
```

This set looks good and offers a good example of the use of REMOVE DUPLICATES. We are searching in five files here, and there are 21 unique documents in that original set of 28. Viewing the same document over and over again is a waste of money, and so for reasonable-sized sets (say, under 100), RD is a nice technique. It would appear that we got some good results here. If we wanted to, we could pearl grow using some of the terms from the best documents here: MARITAL RELATIONS, PARENTHOOD STATUS, MARITAL INSTABILITY, PREGNANCY, DIVORCE, and the like.

Notes

1. K. L. Nolan, ed. (1998), *Gale Directory of Databases* (Detroit: Gale).

2. Geraldene Walker (October 1990), "Searching the Humanities: Subject Overlap and Search Vocabulary" *Database* 13(5): 37–46.

3. Donald T. Hawkins (April 1978), "Multiple Database Searching" *Online* 2(2): 9–15.

Additional Reading

Bjorner, Susan N. (November 1990), "One-Minute Management on DIALOG: Is One-Search an Answer?" *Online* 14: 52–59.

Ojala, M. (1991), "Locating Companies with DIALOG's Company Name Finder," *Database* 15(2): 87–91.

Pagell, Ruth A. (1988), "OneSearch: How and When to Use It," *Database* 11(4): 39–46.

Snow, Bonnie (January 1991), "When One Database Isn't Enough: Creating Composite Bibliographies on DIALOG or BRS," *Online* 15: 82–86.

11 SEARCHING OTHER KINDS OF DATABASES

Up to this point, we have concentrated on bibliographic databases, which provide us with citations to articles and other items that appear in the published literature. The techniques we have discussed so far (controlled vocabulary searching, free text searching, other special features) have all been aimed at this type of retrieval.

Some of these techniques can also be of use in searching other kinds of databases: files that are online versions of print reference or directory sources, files that provide information on citation patterns in the scientific literature, and files that give not only pointers to the literature, but that also contain the full text of the original documents. These files are all available via the major online vendors as well as on the Internet, and each has special techniques and tricks that are necessary in order to search them effectively. In this chapter, we will look at these different files, discuss their use and usefulness, and explore some of these "tricks."

Reference and Directory Files

Many reference sources and directories that are in common use, particularly in libraries, are also available in online formats. As with so many of the bibliographic databases, many of these sources were produced using computer-assisted techniques, so the raw data was available in electronic form. It was thus a relatively easy matter to mount those files and provide online access to them.

The first question to ask when considering using an online system to search a reference database is: Is it worth it? If the user's question is straightforward and the library has the printed tool, it is probably a better idea to use that. Many of the ready-reference files are among the more expensive files available on online systems because of their wide availability and ease of use in print form, and because searching in these files tends to be rather quick.

However, there are situations in which online searching of these sources may well be more efficient and more cost-effective. The library may not have the print version, or it may be out of date.[1] The particular query being searched may require more in-depth work than the usual source can readily support. Also keep in mind the time and effort of the library professional. If a query will necessitate 30 minutes of time manually as opposed to five minutes online, it may be cheaper, in the long run, to use online.

Once the decision is made to go online, the appropriate source must be chosen. In many cases this will be much easier than choosing files for a bibliographic search. The print versions of these sources may already be familiar, or there may be only one potential source.

In some cases, though, it may not be so clear. In that case, examine documentation or consult other staff for advice. Many of the techniques we discussed in the previous chapter for database selection (DIALINDEX, Journal Name Finder, OneSearch) probably will not work here because they are primarily designed for use with bibliographic databases.

Searching in reference databases is often quite different from searching bibliographic databases. We are not interested as much in creating sets of potentially good documents as we are in zeroing in on the one (or more) right answer. More "special" features of the databases will be used and far less (if any) controlled vocabulary/free text searching. In DIALOG terms, this translates into much more extensive use of prefix and suffix searching: additional indexes, limits, qualifiers, and the like.

In reference searching, the database documentation is particularly crucial. DIALOG bluesheets provide detailed information on database coverage, construction, record structure, search technique, output formats, and more. This is even more important here than in the bibliographic files, due to the highly structured nature of the data in these files.

> *Remember, the bluesheets are available for free on DIALOG's website. – GW*

We will look at a few specific examples. First, here is a search in a source that is probably familiar in the print domain: *Books in Print®* (File 470 in DIALOG). In early 1998, a patron wonders if Danielle Steel has got any new books coming out in the next few months. Because the online version of *Books in Print®* also incorporates *Forthcoming Books*™, we can find this out. We begin by EXPANDing on her name because we want to be sure of the spelling.

```
File 470:Books in Print(R) 1997/Dec
        (C) 1998 R.R. BOWKER, REED ELSEVIER INC

    Set    Items    Description
    ---    -----    -----------
?e au=steel, da

    Ref    Items    Index-term
    E1        3      AU=STEEL, D.
    E2        1      AU=STEEL, D. R.
    E3        0      *AU=STEEL, DA
    E4        1      AU=STEEL, DANIEL I.
    E5      103      AU=STEEL, DANIELLE
    E6        6      AU=STEEL, DAVID
    E7        2      AU=STEEL, DAWN
    E8        1      AU=STEEL, DON
    E9        2      AU=STEEL, DONALD
    E10       2      AU=STEEL, DUNCAN
    E11       1      AU=STEEL, DYNE
    E12       1      AU=STEEL, E. W.
        Enter P or PAGE for more
?s e5
    S1      103      AU="STEEL, DANIELLE"
?s s1 and pd>9802
            103      S1
          20684      PD>9802
    S2        5      S1 AND PD>9802
?t 2/5/all
```

2/5/1
DIALOG(R)File 470:Books in Print(R)

08557640   09202679
  TITLE: The Long Road Home
  AUTHOR: Steel, Danielle
  ISBN: 0-385-32410-3 (1997/10)
    STATUS: Active Record
    EDITION: Autographed; Limited ed.
    PUBLISHER: Delacorte
    PUBLICATION DATE: 041998 (199804)
    BINDING: Trade Cloth - $200.00 (Retail Price)
  DATE IN FILE: 1997/10

2/5/2
DIALOG(R)File 470:Books in Print(R)

08446566   09184095
  TITLE: The Long Road Home
  AUTHOR: Steel, Danielle
  ISBN: 0-385-33285-8 (1997/09)
    STATUS: Active Record
    PUBLISHER: Delacorte
    PUBLICATION DATE: 051998 (199805)
    BINDING: Trade Cloth - (Write/Call Publisher for information)
  DATE IN FILE: 1997/09
  DEWEY DECIMAL NUMBER: 813/.54

2/5/3
DIALOG(R)File 470:Books in Print(R)

08446564   09184092
  TITLE: The Long Road Home
  AUTHOR: Steel, Danielle
  ISBN: 0-385-31992-4 (1997/09)
    STATUS: Active Record
    EDITION: Large Type ed.
    PUBLISHER: Delacorte
    PUBLICATION DATE: 041998 (199804)
    BINDING: Trade Cloth - $29.95 (Ingram Price), $29.95 (Retail Price)
  DATE IN FILE: 1997/09
  DEWEY DECIMAL NUMBER: 813/.54
  SUBFILE: LT (Large Type Books in Print)
  LIBRARY OF CONGRESS SUBJECT HEADINGS: LARGE TYPE BOOKS (0066067X)

2/5/4
DIALOG(R)File 470:Books in Print(R)

08446563   09184090
  TITLE: The Long Road Home
  AUTHOR: Steel, Danielle
  ISBN: 0-385-31956-8 (1997/09)

```
   STATUS: Active Record
   PUBLISHER: Delacorte
   PUBLICATION DATE: 051998 (199805)
   NO. OF PAGES: 408p.
    BINDING: Trade Cloth - $25.95 (Ingram Price), $25.95 (Retail Price)
 DATE IN FILE: 1997/09
 TITLE NOTES: P
 DEWEY DECIMAL NUMBER: 813/.54


 2/5/5
DIALOG(R)File 470:Books in Print(r)
(c) 1998 R.R. Bowker, Reed Elsevier Inc. All rts. reserv.

08348426           09031255
  TITLE: Special Delivery
  AUTHOR: Steel, Danielle
  ISBN: 0-385-31691-7 (1997/02)
    STATUS: Active Record
    PUBLISHER: Delacorte
    PUBLICATION DATE: 061997 (199706)
    BINDING: Trade Cloth - $16.95 (Ingram Price), $16.95 (Retail Price)
  ISBN: 0-440-22481-0 (1997/12)
    STATUS: Active Record
    PUBLISHER: Bantam
    PUBLICATION DATE: 071998 (199807)
    BINDING: Trade Paper - (Write/Call Publisher for information)
    SUBFILE: PB (Paperbound BIP)
  DATE IN FILE: 1997/02
```

An interesting file available since 1990 is EventLine (File 165), which is a database of events: trade shows, conferences, exhibitions, sporting events, and so forth. Suppose a patron came in and explained that she was traveling to Ann Arbor in June of 1998 and wanted to know if there would be any interesting events going on there then. A search like this will inform her quickly:

```
File 165:EventLine(TM) 1990-1998/Dec
        (c) 1998 Elsevier Science B.V.

     Set    Items    Description
     ---    -----    -----------
?e cy=ann arbor

     Ref    Items    Index-term
     E1        1     CY=ANKARAN
     E2        3     CY=ANKENY
     E3      125     *CY=ANN ARBOR
     E4       63     CY=ANNAPOLIS
     E5       28     CY=ANNECY
     E6        1     CY=ANNISTON
     E7        2     CY=ANNONAY
     E8        1     CY=ANS
     E9       33     CY=ANTALYA
     E10       3     CY=ANTANANARIVO
     E11      31     CY=ANTIBES
     E12       2     CY=ANTIGONISH
             Enter P or PAGE for more
```

```
?s e3
    S1        125      CY=ANN ARBOR

?s es=9806?
    S2      1807       ES=9806?
?s s1 and s2
            125        S1
           1807        S2
    S3        1        S1 AND S2
?t 3/5/1


3/5/1
DIALOG(R)File 165:EventLine(TM)
(c) 1998 Elsevier Science B.V. All rts. reserv.

   00226078
EVENT TITLE:         Ann Arbor Summer Festival (provisional dates)
  TYPE OF EVENT:     Cultural / ArtLine
  EVENT DATE(S):     June 1-July 31, 1998
  HOST SITE:         Ann Arbor Summer Festival
  EVENT CITY:        Ann Arbor
  EVENT COUNTRY:     USA
  REGION:            North America
  EXHIBITION:        No
  ORGANIZER:         Ann Arbor Summer Festival
                     P.O. Box 4070
                     Ann Arbor USA
  TELEPHONE:         1-313-747-2278
  FAX:               1-313-936-3393
  TRANSLATION:       No
  RECORD INPUT DATE: 941118
```

Here's another example, closer to home. The *American Library Directory* is available online (File 460 in DIALOG), and we want a sorted list of public libraries in central New York State of medium size, say between 40,000 and 60,000 volumes. We go to the documentation and find that the library type field is an additional index, so we will use LT=PUBLIC. Central New York is a bit tougher—the ST= field will get all of New York State, but how do we get any more specific? Well, it is not perfect, but the TE= field will search by area code, and the 315 area code covers roughly the territory we are interested in. Regarding the size of collection, there are two potential fields we could use: BK= and VO= . One says it describes number of book titles, the other the number of book volumes. Which do we want? VO= does refer to *volumes*, so we will use that. We are searching for a numeric range here, so we use a colon to specify it:

```
?S VO=40000:60000
```

Notice there are no commas in the numbers.[2]

That should just about do it. Let us execute the search and see what happens.

```
File 460:American Library Directory 1997
        (c) 1997 Reed Elsevier, Inc.

      Set    Items      Description
      ---    -----      -----------
?s te=315
      S1      285       TE=315
?s lt=public
      S2    10605       LT=PUBLIC
?s s1 and s2
              285       S1
            10605       S2
      S3      159       S1 AND S2
?s vo=40000:60000
      S4     2333       VO=40000:60000
?s s3 and s4
              159       S3
             2333       S4
      S5       10       S3 AND S4
?sort s5/all/vo,d
      S6       10       Sort S5/ALL/VO,D
?report s6/on,cy,vo/all

Align paper; press ENTER
?
        DIALOG(R)File 460:American Library Directory
        (c) 1997 Reed Elsevier, Inc. All rts. reserv.


                                     Library      Book
      Name                           City         Volumes
      --------------------------     ----------   -------
      CANASTOTA PUBLIC LIBRARY       Canastota    56,711
      OSWEGO CITY LIBRARY            Oswego       55,879
      NEWARK PUBLIC LIBRARY          Newark       53,000
      ONEIDA LIBRARY                 Oneida       52,189
      DUNHAM PUBLIC LIBRARY          Whitesboro   51,151
      OGDENSBURG PUBLIC LIBRARY      Ogdensburg   49,190
      DE WITT COMMUNITY LIBRARY      De Witt      47,285
      CANTON FREE LIBRARY            Canton       41,900
      FULTON PUBLIC LIBRARY          Fulton       40,080
      ILION FREE PUBLIC LIBRARY      Ilion        40,000
```

    Here is another example. A patron wants a list of large minority-owned businesses in the United States, those with annual sales of more than $2 billion. Where would we search for this? There are a number of potential databases we could try: D&B - Dun's Electronic Business Directory; Standard & Poor's Register – Corporate; or American Business Directory. We notice, though, that one file, D&B-Duns Market Identifiers (File 516), has an additional index, SF= , for special features, and one of these features is MINORITY OWNED. We therefore choose this file and will search on SF=MINORITY OWNED. The SA= field gives annual sales, and we can search on SA>2B to get all companies with sales greater than $2 billion. The result set is sorted and displayed for the patron.

```
File 516:D & B - Duns Market Identifiers 1997/Dec
        (Copr. 1997 D&B)


    Set   Items    Description
    ---   -----    -----------
?s sf=minority owned
    S1   446154    SF=MINORITY OWNED
?s s1 and sa>2b
         446154    S1
           1178    SA>2B
    S2       36    S1 AND SA>2B
?sort s2/all/sa,d
    S3       36    Sort S2/ALL/SA,D
?t 3/5/1
```

3/5/1
DIALOG(R)File 516:D & B - Duns Market Identifiers
(Copr. 1997 D&B). All rts. reserv.

00294132
Toyota Motor Sales USA Inc
Toyota Accessory
19001 S Western Ave
Torrance, CA 90501-1106

MAILING ADDRESS:
  P O Box 2991
  Torrance, CA 90509

TELEPHONE: 310-618-4000
COUNTY: LOS ANGELES   MSA: 4480 (Los Angeles-Long Beach, CA)
REGION: Pacific

BUSINESS: Whol Autos

PRIMARY SIC:
  5012   Automobiles and other motor vehicles, nsk
    50120200   Motor vehicles, commercial

SECONDARY SIC(S):
  6159   Miscellaneous business credit institutions, nsk
    61590201   Automobile finance leasing

LATEST YEAR ORGANIZED: 1957
STATE OF INCORPORATION: CA DATE OF INCORPORATION: 10/31/1957
ANNUAL SALES REVISION DATE: 01/31/1997

	LATEST YEAR		TREND YEAR (1995)		BASE YEAR (1993)
SALES	$ 27,500,000,000	$	NA	$	NA
EMPLOYEES TOTAL:	5,100		NA		NA
EMPLOYEES HERE:	1,800				

  SALES GROWTH: NA % NET WORTH: $ NA
  EMPLOYMENT GROWTH: NA %

SQUARE FOOTAGE: 387,000 Owned

```
NUMBER OF ACCOUNTS: 9
BANK: Nationsbank NA                BANK DUNS: 08-786-4583
THIS IS:

     A SUBSIDIARY HEADQUARTERS LOCATION
     A CORPORATION
     A MINORITY OWNED BUSINESS

DUNS NUMBER:              00-959-5505
PARENT DUNS:             96-355-0769   Toyota Motor North America
CORPORATE FAMILY DUNS:   96-355-0769   Toyota Motor North America
PRESIDENT:               Ishizaka, Yoshio /President-Chief Executive Offi
                         Maling, Robert /President/Airflite
VICE PRESIDENT:          Turmell, John R /Group Vp-Customer Srvs Div
                         Gallio, Richard /Group Vp-Gnrl Mngr-Tie/Marine
                         McGovern, John E /Group Vp-Dealer Relations
                         Press, James /Senior Vice President-Gen Mana
                         Buckman, Anthony /Vp
                         Chitty, Richard /Vp, New Era Business Strategy
                         Broman, Philip /Vp/Programs
                         Cooper, Barbara /Vp-Information Systems
                         Daly, Robert /Vp/Toyota Logistics Svcs
                         Danzer, David /Vp/Corp Strategy & Planning
                         Johnson, Marshall /Vp/Gm-New York Region
                         Breene, Patrick /Vp/Corporate Controller/Toyota
                         W
EXECUTIVE VICE PRESIDENT:Gieszl, Yale /Executive Vice President
SENIOR VICE PRESIDENT:   Illingworth, Davis /Sr Vp-Gen Mgr/Toyota Div
                         West, Douglas M /Sr Vp-Fin-Information & Human

LATEST UPDATE TO RECORD:  03/06/97
?report 3/co,st,sa,em/all

Align paper; press ENTER
?
           DIALOG(R)File 516:D & B - Duns Market Identifiers
               (Copr. 1997 D&B) All rts. reserv.
```

Company Name	State	Sales Dollars	Total Employees
Toyota Motor Sales USA Inc	CA	27,500,000,000	5,100
Nissho Iwai American Corporati	NY	11,910,913,000	430
Marubeni America Corporation	NY	11,700,000,000	4,545
Mitsui & Co USA Inc	NY	11,564,167,000	1,800
Honda of America Manufacturing	OH	10,000,000,000	12,000
Toys R Us, Inc (delaware)	NJ	9,932,400,000	60,000
Mitsubishi International Corpo	NY	9,753,586,000	710
U S West Communications Group,	CO	9,484,000,000	50,000
Sumitomo Corporation of Americ	NY	7,536,553,000	1,344
Canon U.S.A., Inc	NY	7,500,000,000	7,000
Guardian Life Insurance Compan	NY	6,904,050,000	5,155
Toshiba America, Inc	NY	6,300,000,000	7,500
Office Depot, Inc.	FL	6,068,598,000	31,000
Vons Companies, The Inc	CA	5,407,400,000	29,600
Toyota Motor Manufacturing Ken	KY	5,000,000,000	6,900
Lucky Stores, Inc	CA	4,882,400,000	45,000
Dominion Resources Inc	VA	4,842,300,000	10,943
Mazda Motor of America, Inc	CA	4,500,000,000	785

Mitsubishi Motor Sales of Amer	CA	4,100,000,000	1,900
American Honda Motor Co Inc	CA	4,068,000,000	13,774
Computer Associates Internatio	NY	4,040,000,000	9,850
Mitsubishi Electric America (i	CA	4,000,000,000	3,900
McCann-Erickson Worldwide Inc	NY	3,518,500,000	8,500
Willamette Industries, Inc	OR	3,425,173,000	13,700
Pdv America, Inc (de Corp)	NY	3,022,200,000	5,000
Bosch, Robert Corporation	IL	3,010,688,000	10,665
Toyota Motor Credit Corporatio	CA	2,978,000,000	1,950
Samsung Semiconductor Inc	CA	2,713,580,158	465
Toshiba America Information Sy	CA	2,675,290,000	3,600
Dominick's Finer Foods, Inc	IL	2,511,962,000	17,700
Sony Electronics Inc	NJ	2,495,700,000	22,000
Inter-American Development Ban	DC	2,444,924,000	1,604
Denso International America In	MI	2,300,000,000	3,600
Tomen America Inc	NY	2,296,237,000	827
Polaroid Corporation	MA	2,275,200,000	10,046
Goodrich B F Company, The Inc	OH	2,238,800,000	12,654

A final example of a search that could probably only be conducted online: A patron asks about the name of the Chancellor of Syracuse University in 1991. How to find it quickly? It is tempting to simply call the University and ask, but because this is an online searching textbook, we will pretend you do not think of that and choose to go online instead. Marquis Who's Who is file 234 in DIALOG. This is not a typical way of searching a biographical source; usually we have a person's name and are trying to get information about them. Here, we have an official position and are trying to find the name of the person to whom it applies. This gives you some idea of the power of online versions of "traditional" reference sources—the ability to search them in much more flexible and effective ways.

Anyway, in examining the documentation, we see fields like PO= and ON= for position held and occupation name, CO= for company name, YE= for year of employment, CY= for address city, and /DE for descriptor, which incorporates several other fields.

Putting in a variety of these, we get

```
File 234:MARQUIS WHO'S WHO
        (COPR. MARQUIS WHO'S WHO, INC)

    Set    Items    Description
    ---    -----    -----------
?s po=chancellor? or on=chancellor?
           1017     PO=CHANCELLOR?
            125     ON=CHANCELLOR?
    S1     1029     PO=CHANCELLOR? OR ON=CHANCELLOR?
?s co=syracuse?
    S2      363     CO=SYRACUSE?
?s ye=1991
    S3    64313     YE=1991
?s s1 and s2 and s3
           1029     S1
            363     S2
          64313     S3
    S4       12     S1 AND S2 AND S3
?s s4 and cy=syracuse
             12     S4
            189     CY=SYRACUSE
    S5        5     S4 AND CY=SYRACUSE
?t 5/na,ca/all
```

```
5/NA,CA/1
 Eggers, Melvin Arnold
 CAREER:
  also pres., Syracuse U.
  chancellor, Syracuse U., 1971-
  vice chancellor for acad. affairs, also provost, Syracuse U., 1970-71
  chmn. dept., Syracuse U., 1960-70
  prof. econs., Syracuse U., 1963-70
  mem. faculty, Syracuse U., 1950-70
  instr. econs., Yale, 1947-50
  Clk., Peoples Trust & Savs. Co., Ft. Wayne, 1934-38

5/NA,CA/2
 Prucha, John James
 CAREER:
  bd. dirs., Syracuse U. Press, 1985-90
  pres., Syracuse U. Press, 1973-85
  vice chancellor acad. affairs, Syracuse U., 1972-85
  dean Coll. Arts and Scis., Syracuse U., 1970-72
  chmn. dept., Syracuse U., 1963-70, 88-89
  prof. emeritus, Syracuse U., 1990-
  prof. geology, Syracuse U., 1963-90
  rsch. geologist, Shell Devel. Co., 1956-63
  sr. geologist, N.Y. State Geol. Survey, 1951-56
  Asst. prof. geology, Rutgers U., 1948-51

5/NA,CA/3
 Shaw, Kenneth Alan
 CAREER:
  chancellor, Syracuse U., 1991-
  pres., U. Wis. System, Madison, 1986-91
  chancellor, so. Ill. U. System, Edwardsville, 1979-86
  pres., So. Ill. U., Edwardsville, 1977-79
  v.p. acad. affair, dean, Towson State U., Balt., 1969-76
  asst. to pres., lectr. sociology, Ill. State U., 1966-69
  counselor, Office Dean of Men, Purdue U. (Office Student Loans), 1965-66
  counselor, Office Dean of Men, Purdue U., 1964-65
  residence hall dir., instr. edn., Ill. State U., 1963-64
  Tchr. history, counselor, Rich Twp. High Sch., Park Forest, Ill., 1961-63

5/NA,CA/4
 Tolley, William Pearson
 CAREER:
  chmn., pres., Mohawk Airlines Inc., 1971-72
  chmn. bd., Mohawk Airlines Inc., 1970-71
  chancellor emeritus, Syracuse (N.Y.) U., 1969-
  chancellor, Syracuse (N.Y.) U., 1942-69
  pres., Allegheny Coll., 1931-42
  prof. philosophy, Drew Theol. Sem. (Brothers Coll.), 1930-31
  dean, Drew Theol. Sem. (Brothers Coll.), 1929-31
  acting dean Brothers Coll., instr. in philosophy, Drew Theol. Sem.,
   1928-29
  asst. to pres., Drew Theol. Sem., 1927-28
  instr. systematic theology, Drew Theol. Sem., 1926-28
  alumni sec., Drew Theol. Sem., 1925-27
  Ordained to ministry, Meth. Episcopal Ch., 1923
```

```
5/NA,CA/5
Vincow, Gershon
CAREER:
 vice chancellor for acad. affairs, Syracuse (N.Y.) U., 1985-
 dean Coll. Arts and Scis., Syracuse (N.Y.) U., 1978-85
 v.p. research and grad. affairs, Syracuse (N.Y.) U., 1977-78
 prof. chemistry, Syracuse (N.Y.) U., 1971-
 prof. chemistry, U. Wash., Seattle, 1961-71
```

and we find not only the correct entry (for Kenneth Shaw) but also several false drops. It is easy to see how the false drops were retrieved—position titles that include the word "chancellor," as in vice chancellor, and even a chancellor emeritus. Some of these files are organized more effectively and consistently than others.

Quality control and update frequency are particularly important. An error in a bibliographic record (e.g., spelling error, bad index term) may eliminate one hit from a good retrieval set, but a similar error in a reference record means that it is not retrieved at all and the search comes up empty. Further, if the file is updated infrequently (or never), it may be of limited use in a ready-reference environment for current information.

What lessons have we learned from these examples? Pay attention to documentation, take advantage of special features of files and systems, and expect the unexpected.

Full-Text Databases

Full-text databases resemble bibliographic databases in a number of ways. They have a similar structure; many have abstracts; and some have indexing. Indeed, many bibliographic databases now include both citations and full texts. The key difference, of course, is the full text. Many people believe that the availability of full text will solve the problems of information retrieval, but so far this has not proven to be the case. Indeed, the presence of full text often serves as a distraction rather than an assistance, and we often search more effectively in full-text files when we do not search the full text.

There are definite advantages to full-text files, of course, chief among them the availability of the text itself. Users are often more pleased when they leave an online search session with the actual texts that satisfy their requests, rather than merely bibliographic citations to articles that they must then hunt down. Full text can also provide improved access to the literature—many of the comments we made when discussing free text searching apply here. The use of a term or phrase or figure of speech in the body of a document (but not in a title or abstract) certainly will assist in retrieving it, but it may not prove relevant to the request.

However, there are also disadvantages. With current technology, what we retrieve is not a facsimile of the original document but rather a copy of its text. In general, we are not able to retrieve graphics, photographs, or other images except from the Internet. However, systems, often using CD-ROM technology, allow retrieval of bitmapped images of documents that have been scanned in. Some of these systems provide traditional title/abstract/ indexing access; some permit full-text searching as well. The quality of the output (sometimes including advertising) is not yet as high as in a magazine or newspaper, but it is more than adequate for almost any need.

The primary disadvantage to full-text searching is *false drops*. As we saw when discussing free-text searching, when we search on fields, particularly large fields, that include natural language, the problems of ambiguity and conflation arise. There are ways around this, but using full-text files one can now retrieve a document based on a single, perhaps offhand use of a word buried deep in a 3,000-word text. In files with rudimentary or no indexing (like many newspaper databases), this presents a potentially difficult situation.

A word about newspaper databases: These are becoming ever more popular, and more of them are becoming available in full text all the time. Most of them provide a convenient method of searching that takes advantage of the structure of a typical newspaper article. Most news articles (excluding features and other "auxiliary" stories) have the most important information up front, in the first paragraph or two—what journalists call "the lead."

This can be very useful in searching, as the lead often serves as a kind of abstract of the story. Many news databases permit searching in just the first one or two paragraphs—some call it /LP (lead paragraph) or even /AB or /TI.[3]

Also keep in mind the audience for newspaper stories. They are written for a general readership and are much more likely to use euphemisms and catchy terminology, and less likely to use technical terms (unless they are the focus of the story). These characteristics are important to bear in mind while searching newspaper files.

> In addition to their availability through DIALOG and other commercial systems, more and more newspapers are making themselves available on the Web. Some are providing only fragments of their content, others only a few days' worth of full text (with archives searchable for a fee), and still others are mounting complete archives for free. The newspaper industry is figuring out this new technological opportunity, as is everybody else, and so this too may change quickly. While you lose search facility, and the ability to search multiple papers simultaneously, going directly to www.nytimes.com or the like may well be a reasonable approach to articles in particular newspapers. – JWJ

The subject inverted file (Basic Index) for a full-text database usually includes every term from the text, plus a few other fields (titles, if any, perhaps descriptors), so a simple search command will retrieve based on full text by default. If a search should be restricted further, then the appropriate prefixes or suffixes must be used.

There are several kinds of full-text files available. We have discussed newspapers, but there are also journal articles, newsletters, dictionaries (Dictionary of Substances and their Effects), directories (Encyclopedia of Associations), other sources (Magill's Survey of Cinema), and my all-time favorite DIALOG file, the Bible (King James Version). The strategies and techniques we discuss here should help with most of these files.

We have said that searching full-text databases resembles searching using free text, that often no controlled vocabulary is available, and that false drops are a significant problem. This means we need to recall the ladder of specificity from Chapter 8. The situation we have described seems to imply that we want to be as high on that ladder as possible. AND is often just too broad to be helpful here; a strategy like AIDS AND DRUG? (in a search on drug therapies for AIDS) in the *Chicago Tribune* is hopeless, as illustrated below.

```
File 632:CHICAGO TRIBUNE 1985 - 16 Jun 1992
        (c) 1992 Chicago Tribune

      Set   Items      Description
      ---   -----      -----------
?s aids and drug?
            10218      AIDS
            39459      DRUG?
      S1    3146       AIDS AND DRUG?
?t 1/5/1

 1/5/1
01979609
EVENING. People - K mart, Walgreens refuse to sell Magic's AIDS book
Chicago Tribune (CT) - FRIDAY June 12, 1992
By: Compiled from Chicago Tribune wires
Edition: EVENING UPDATE Section: NEWS Page: 2 Zone: C
Word Count: 119

LEAD PARAGRAPHS:
  Some store chains are refusing to sell Magic Johnson's book on
preventing AIDS because of its blunt language about how to avoid the
sexually transmitted disease, the book's publisher in Troy, Mich. said
Friday.

  Times Books Publisher Peter Osnos said K mart Corp. and the Walgreens
drug store chain were among retailers objecting to the book. The book,
"What You Can Do To Avoid AIDS," was written by Johnson, who retired from
professional basketball because he has the AIDS virus.

  "We're not a bookstore," said a K mart spokesman. "The book is very
informative, but it's also very graphic. It should be available to
teen-agers, . . . (but not) a 3-year-old while their mother is buying a
lawnmower."
DESCRIPTORS: BUSINESS; DECISION; SALE; BOOK; SEX; DISEASE; CELEBRITY

             Copyright (c) 1992, Chicago Tribune
```

Because controlled vocabulary is probably not an option to begin with, we must try using proximity operators: (5N), (2W), and the like. For a specific phrase, use (W):

```
?s dead(w)sea(w)scroll?
            30360      DEAD
            13171      SEA
              570      SCROLL?
      S2      72       DEAD(W)SEA(W)SCROLL?
```

To be more specific, use qualifiers:

```
?s democratic(w)national(w)committee
            28630      DEMOCRATIC
           131158      NATIONAL
            48845      COMMITTEE
      S3     662       DEMOCRATIC(W)NATIONAL(W)COMMITTEE
?s s3/lp                                (limiting to lead paragraph)
      S4     171       S3/LP
```

Another interesting technique for a possibly ambiguous or conflated term is to look for it twice in the same document. A search on CRACK(20W)CRACK will retrieve documents with the word "crack" twice within 20 words. Such a document is perhaps more likely to have something to do with the drug "crack" because it is less likely to be an offhand use of the word (e.g., "the crack of dawn," "crack of the bat").

An interesting example is searching for documents about AIDS. Clearly, there are a large number of articles being published on this topic, and many of them appear in newspapers and other full-text sources. Yet the four-character sequence AIDS is also a word ("this drug aids patients' mobility"). So how do we get at documents about AIDS? This is a good strategy:

```
?s aids(20w)aids or acquired()immun? or hiv
         10218    AIDS
         10218    AIDS
          2764    AIDS(20W)AIDS
         15204    ACQUIRED
          6432    IMMUN?
          1300    ACQUIRED(W)IMMUN?
          1088    HIV
  S5      3833    AIDS(20W)AIDS OR ACQUIRED()IMMUN? OR HIV
```

The first of these three expressions searches for multiple adjacent occurrences of "AIDS"; the second searches for "acquired immune deficiency syndrome" or "acquired immunodeficiency syndrome"; the final searches for "HIV," the abbreviation for human immunodeficiency virus. (Do not truncate on HIV, or the search will retrieve HIVE, HIVES, etc.)

Another proximity operator is often useful in full-text searching: (S), which specifies that two words occur in the same subfield. In full-text databases, this corresponds to paragraphs or sentences (check the documentation to determine which). This operator takes advantage of the natural structure in the document. Rather than guessing with (W)'s, the searcher can ask for AIDS(S)AIDS or NBA(S)PLAYOFF? and get documents where the author uses these words in a natural language unit.

Also take advantage of /LP or /TI or /AB fields. If the topic being searched for is relatively broad, or one that might retrieve a large number of documents, it might be better to search in these more restrictive fields:

```
?s (higher()education or college? ? or universit?)/lp
          7841    HIGHER/LP
         10234    EDUCATION/LP
           565    HIGHER/LP(W)EDUCATION/LP
         16775    COLLEGE? ?/LP
         26058    UNIVERSIT?/LP
  S6     38852    (HIGHER()EDUCATION OR COLLEGE? ? OR UNIVERSIT?)/LP
?s president?(1n)election
        160931    PRESIDENT?
         31527    ELECTION
  S7      2267    PRESIDENT?(1N)ELECTION
?s s7/ti
  S8        18    S7/TI
?s s7/lp
  S9       768    S7/LP
```

On the other hand, it might be better to search narrower or less popular topics in full text (i.e., unqualified):

```
?s minh()city
           317     MINH
        132571     CITY
   S10     147     MINH()CITY
?s science()fiction
         16580     SCIENCE
          5187     FICTION
   S11    1193     SCIENCE()FICTION
```

The first of these searches deserves a comment. If searching for documents about Ho Chi Minh City, Vietnam, it would be tempting to search HO(W)CHI(W)MINH(W)CITY, but what documents would satisfy MINH(W)CITY but not the longer expression? None. So save a bit of searching time and use the shorter strategy.

```
?s ho()chi()minh()city
          1938     HO
          1402     CHI
           317     MINH
        132571     CITY
   S12     147     HO()CHI()MINH()CITY
```

This is also an illustration of a good technique to use in searching full text: Get a "hook"—a very definite piece of strategy that will effectively reduce the size of the database to be searched in. It could be a personal name, geographic location, company name, data, organization—anything—but if one can get a subset of only several thousand or hundred (or even dozen!) records to search through, and it is reasonably certain that the ones needed are in there, it makes the job considerably easier.

In many cases, the database will be of help—there may be additional indexes for some of these proper names, the data field is almost always there, and use of these special features will make searching easier. Here is an example. A patron is interested in articles in trade magazines about marketing strategies by Celestial Seasonings, the herbal tea company. It seems proper to search in *IAC Trade and Industry* (File 148), which covers a number of business-oriented magazines. It has a CO= field for company names, so "Celestial" is EXPANDed on to get:

```
File 148:IAC Trade & Industry Database 1976-1998/Feb 17
         (c) 1998 Info Access Co

    Set   Items   Description
    ---   -----   -----------
?e co=celestial

    Ref   Items   Index-term
    E1      1     CO=CELESTE STEIN DESIGN
    E2      1     CO=CELESTE UPHOLSTERING INC.
    E3      0     *CO=CELESTIAL
    E4      1     CO=CELESTIAL ARTS
    E5      1     CO=CELESTIAL FARMS INC.
    E6      1     CO=CELESTIAL HOMES
    E7      1     CO=CELESTIAL REALTY GROUP INC.
    E8      1     CO=CELESTIAL SEASONING INC.
    E9    183     CO=CELESTIAL SEASONINGS INC.
```

```
        E10         1     CO=CELESTIAL SYSTEMS INC.
        E11         2     CO=CELESTIAL VENTURES CORP.
        E12         1     CO=CELESTICA

                Enter P or PAGE for more
?s e8,e9
                    1     CO=CELESTIAL SEASONING INC.
                  183     CO=CELESTIAL SEASONINGS INC.
        S1        184     E8,E9
?s s1 and marketing/de
                  184     S1
               323594     MARKETING/DE
        S2         13     S1 AND MARKETING/DE
?s s2/1995-1998
                   13     S2
              1823937     PY=1995 : PY=1998
        S3          4     S2/1995-1998
?t 3/3/all



  3/3/1
DIALOG(R)File 148:IAC Trade & Industry Database
(c) 1998 Info Access Co. All rts. reserv.

09575103          SUPPLIER NUMBER: 19542544
Halls brand will move into natural remedies.(introduction of Halls Zinc
   Defense lozenges and other products)
Wilke, Michael
Advertising Age, v68, n25, p1(2)
June 23, 1997
ISSN: 0001-8899    LANGUAGE: English    RECORD TYPE: Abstract



  3/3/2
DIALOG(R)File 148:IAC Trade & Industry Database
(c) 1998 Info Access Co. All rts. reserv.

08875127          SUPPLIER NUMBER: 18581699
Celestial Seasonings - a taste of success many find attractive.
International Journal of Retail & Distribution Management, v24, n5, pIV(2)
Summer, 1996
ISSN: 0959-0552    LANGUAGE: English    RECORD TYPE: Abstract



  3/3/3
DIALOG(R)File 148:IAC Trade & Industry Database
(c) 1998 Info Access Co. All rts. reserv.

08312859          SUPPLIER NUMBER: 17422459 (USE FORMAT 7 OR 9 FOR FULL TEXT)
Celestial Seasonings takes aim at RTD tea - again.(ready-to-drink tea)
Miller, Hilary S.
Beverage Industry, v86, n7, p22(1) July, 1995
ISSN: 0148-6187    LANGUAGE: English    RECORD TYPE: Fulltext; Abstract
WORD COUNT: 467    LINE COUNT: 00039
```

```
  3/3/4
DIALOG(R)File 148:IAC Trade & Industry Database
(c) 1998 Info Access Co. All rts. reserv.

08287262          SUPPLIER NUMBER: 17729884 (USE FORMAT 7 OR 9 FOR FULL TEXT)
HERBAL COMFORT(TM) INTRODUCES TEAS THAT PROMOTE GOOD HEALTH WITH GOOD TASTE
PR Newswire, p1122LAW009
Nov 22, 1995
LANGUAGE: English    RECORD TYPE: Fulltext
WORD COUNT: 312      LINE COUNT: 00039
```

It is also possible to pearl grow in full-text files, or at least in those that have indexing. In many files, this indexing is rudimentary at best, but in full text one needs all the advantages one can get. An example from IAC Health & Wellness (File 149) illustrates this. We are searching for information about difficulties in ensuring that AIDS patients stick to their pharmaceutical regimens of "cocktails" of protease inhibitors.

```
File 149:IAC(SM)Health&Wellness DB(SM) 1976-1998/Feb W3
       (c) 1998 Info Access Co

     Set    Items    Description
     ---    -----    -----------
?s aids(20w)aids or acquired()immun? or hiv
            47863    AIDS
            47863    AIDS
            13416    AIDS(20W)AIDS
            15393    ACQUIRED
            57859    IMMUN?
             6510    ACQUIRED(W)IMMUN?
            32903    HIV
     S1     38709    AIDS(20W)AIDS OR ACQUIRED()IMMUN? OR HIV
?s s1/ab
     S2      6430    S1/AB
?s s2(4n)(cocktail? ? or protease)
             6430    S2
             1371    COCKTAIL? ?
             2249    PROTEASE
     S3        42    S2(4N)(COCKTAIL? ? OR PROTEASE)
?t 3/8/1-5


  3/8/1
DIALOG(R)File 149:(c) 1998 Info Access Co. All rts. reserv.

01735172          SUPPLIER NUMBER: 20080207 (USE FORMAT 7 OR 9 FOR FULL TEXT)
Adherence to prescribed HIV-1 protease inhibitors in the home
  setting.(Adherence Issues in HIV Therapeutics)
WORD COUNT: 6606    LINE COUNT: 00568

DESCRIPTORS: AIDS (Disease)--Care and treatment; Protease inhibitors--Usage;
  Home care--Psychological aspects; Patient compliance--Health aspects
```

```
3/8/2
DIALOG(R)File 149:(c) 1998 Info Access Co. All rts. reserv.

01735168          SUPPLIER NUMBER: 20080203 (USE FORMAT 7 OR 9 FOR FULL TEXT)
Adherence as a particular issue with protease inhibitors.(Adherence Issues
   in HIV Therapeutics)
WORD COUNT: 4525    LINE COUNT: 00391
SPECIAL FEATURES: graph; illustration
DESCRIPTORS: Patient compliance--Health aspects; AIDS (Disease)--
   Psychological aspects; Retroviruses--Care and treatment; Protease
   inhibitors--Usage; Patient education—Health aspects


3/8/3
DIALOG(R)File 149:(c) 1998 Info Access Co. All rts. reserv.

01735167          SUPPLIER NUMBER: 20080202 (USE FORMAT 7 OR 9 FOR FULL TEXT)
Adherence issues in HIV therapeutics, introduction: the
   situation.(Adherence Issues in HIV Therapeutics)
WORD COUNT: 1473    LINE COUNT: 00121

DESCRIPTORS: Protease inhibitors--Health aspects; Patients--Psychological
   aspects; AIDS (Disease)--Care and treatment; Patient compliance--
   Psychological aspects


3/8/4
DIALOG(R)File 149:(c) 1998 Info Access Co. All rts. reserv.

01713995          SUPPLIER NUMBER: 19732668
A natural polymorphism in beta-lactamase is a global suppressor.

SPECIAL FEATURES: photograph; table; graph; illustration
DESCRIPTORS: Genetic polymorphisms--Research; Beta lactamases--Research;
   Suppressor cells--Research; Drug resistance--Research
FILE SEGMENT: AI File 88


3/8/5
DIALOG(R)File 149:(c) 1998 Info Access Co. All rts. reserv.

01710879          SUPPLIER NUMBER: 19638096
Crystalluria and urinary tract abnormalities associated with indinavir.

SPECIAL FEATURES: photograph; table; diagnostic image; illustration
DESCRIPTORS: Kidney stones—Causes of; Proteolytic enzyme inhibitors--
   Adverse and side effects
PRODUCT/BRAND NAMES: Indinavir (Medication)-Adverse and side effects
FILE SEGMENT: HI File 149


?s (aids or hiv)(f)(patient()(compliance or education))/de
           23790    AIDS/DE
           17882    HIV/DE
            6159    PATIENT/DE
             603    COMPLIANCE/DE
            9716    EDUCATION/DE
    S4       53     (AIDS OR HIV)(F)(PATIENT()(COMPLIANCE OR EDUCATION))/DE
```

?s s4 and protease
```
              53    S4
            2249    PROTEASE
    S5         9    S4 AND PROTEASE
```
?t 5/3/all

5/3/1
DIALOG(R)File 149:IAC(SM)Health&Wellness DB(SM)
(c) 1998 Info Access Co. All rts. reserv.

01735173   SUPPLIER NUMBER: 20080208 (USE FORMAT 7 OR 9 FOR FULL TEXT)
HIV therapeutics: confronting adherence.(Adherence Issues in HIV
  Therapeutics)
Katzenstein, David A.; Lyons, Catherine; Molaghan, J.P.; Ungvarski, Peter;
Wolfe, Gary S.; Willians, Ann
Journal of the Association of Nurses in AIDS Care, v8, nSUPP, p46(11)
Annual, 1997
PUBLICATION FORMAT: Magazine/Journal; Refereed ISSN: 1055-3290
LANGUAGE: English RECORD TYPE: Fulltext; Abstract TARGET AUDIENCE:
  Professional
WORD COUNT: 7454   LINE COUNT: 00652

5/3/2
DIALOG(R)File 149:IAC(SM)Health&Wellness DB(SM)
(c) 1998 Info Access Co. All rts. reserv.

01735172   SUPPLIER NUMBER: 20080207 (USE FORMAT 7 OR 9 FOR FULL TEXT)
Adherence to prescribed HIV-1 protease inhibitors in the home
  setting.(Adherence Issues in HIV Therapeutics)
Ungvarski, Peter
Journal of the Association of Nurses in AIDS Care, v8, nSUPP, p37(9)
Annual, 1997
PUBLICATION FORMAT: Magazine/Journal; Refereed ISSN: 1055-3290
LANGUAGE: English RECORD TYPE: Fulltext; Abstract TARGET AUDIENCE:
  Professional
WORD COUNT: 6606   LINE COUNT: 00568

5/3/3
DIALOG(R)File 149:IAC(SM)Health&Wellness DB(SM)
(c) 1998 Info Access Co. All rts. reserv.

01735169   SUPPLIER NUMBER: 20080204 (USE FORMAT 7 OR 9 FOR FULL TEXT)
Antiretroviral therapy: factors associated with adherence.(Adherence Issues
  in HIV Therapeutics)
Williams, Ann
Journal of the Association of Nurses in AIDS Care, v8, nSUPP, p18(6)
Annual, 1997
PUBLICATION FORMAT: Magazine/Journal; Refereed ISSN: 1055-3290
LANGUAGE: English RECORD TYPE: Fulltext; Abstract TARGET AUDIENCE:
  Professional
WORD COUNT: 3524   LINE COUNT: 00304

```
5/3/4
```
DIALOG(R)File 149:IAC(SM)Health&Wellness DB(SM)
(c) 1998 Info Access Co. All rts. reserv.

01735168   SUPPLIER NUMBER: 20080203 (USE FORMAT 7 OR 9 FOR FULL TEXT)
Adherence as a particular issue with protease inhibitors.(Adherence Issues
   in HIV Therapeutics)
Katzenstein, David A.
Journal of the Association of Nurses in AIDS Care, v8, nSUPP, p10(8)
Annual, 1997
PUBLICATION FORMAT: Magazine/Journal; Refereed ISSN: 1055-3290
LANGUAGE: English RECORD TYPE: Fulltext; Abstract TARGET AUDIENCE:
   Professional
WORD COUNT: 4525   LINE COUNT: 00391

```
5/3/5
```
DIALOG(R)File 149:IAC(SM)Health&Wellness DB(SM)
(c) 1998 Info Access Co. All rts. reserv.

01735167   SUPPLIER NUMBER: 20080202 (USE FORMAT 7 OR 9 FOR FULL TEXT)
Adherence issues in HIV therapeutics, introduction: the situation.
   Adherence Issues in HIV Therapeutics)
Molaghan, J.B.
Journal of the Association of Nurses in AIDS Care, v8, nSUPP, p7(3)
Annual, 1997
PUBLICATION FORMAT: Magazine/Journal; Refereed ISSN: 1055-3290
LANGUAGE: English RECORD TYPE: Fulltext; Abstract TARGET AUDIENCE:
   Professional
WORD COUNT: 1473   LINE COUNT: 00121

```
5/3/6
```
DIALOG(R)File 149:IAC(SM)Health&Wellness DB(SM)
(c) 1998 Info Access Co. All rts. reserv.

01720209   SUPPLIER NUMBER: 19799923 (USE FORMAT 7 OR 9 FOR FULL TEXT)
Compliance/adherence and care management in HIV disease.
Crespo-Fierro, Michele
Journal of the Association of Nurses in AIDS Care, v8, n4, p43(12)
July-August, 1997
PUBLICATION FORMAT: Magazine/Journal; Refereed ISSN: 1055-3290
LANGUAGE: English RECORD TYPE: Fulltext; Abstract TARGET AUDIENCE:
   Professional
WORD COUNT: 8938   LINE COUNT: 00774

```
5/3/7
```
DIALOG(R)File 149:IAC(SM)Health&Wellness DB(SM)
(c) 1998 Info Access Co. All rts. reserv.

01680413   SUPPLIER NUMBER: 19240782 (USE FORMAT 7 OR 9 FOR FULL TEXT)
Follow PI doses or don't prescribe them at all, researchers say. (states
   setting compliance criteria for protease inhibitors)(includes related
   information)
AIDS Alert, v12, n4, p37(4)
April, 1997
PUBLICATION FORMAT: Newsletter ISSN: 0887-0292 LANGUAGE: English
RECORD TYPE: Fulltext TARGET AUDIENCE: Professional
WORD COUNT: 1960   LINE COUNT: 00163

```
5/3/8
DIALOG(R)File 149:IAC(SM)Health&Wellness DB(SM)
(c) 1998 Info Access Co. All rts. reserv.

01674538              SUPPLIER NUMBER: 19104974 (USE FORMAT 7 OR 9 FOR FULL TEXT)
Clinicians explore ways to ensure compliance: more counseling needed.
AIDS Alert, v12, n2, p17(2)
Feb, 1997
PUBLICATION FORMAT: Newsletter ISSN: 0887-0292 LANGUAGE: English
RECORD TYPE: Fulltext TARGET AUDIENCE: Professional
WORD COUNT: 1326    LINE COUNT: 00115


5/3/9
DIALOG(R)File 149:IAC(SM)Health&Wellness DB(SM)
(c) 1998 Info Access Co. All rts. reserv.

01663921              SUPPLIER NUMBER: 18995735 (USE FORMAT 7 OR 9 FOR FULL TEXT)
Patient compliance and drug failure in protease inhibitor
  monotherapy.(Letter to the Editor)
Vanhove, Geertrui f.; Schapiro, Jonathan M.; Winters, Mark A.; Merigan,
Thomas C.; Blaschke, Terrence F.
JAMA, The Journal of the American Medical Association, v276, n24, p1955(2)
Dec 25, 1996
DOCUMENT TYPE: Letter to the Editor PUBLICATION FORMAT: Magazine/Journal
  ISSN: 0098-7484 LANGUAGE: English RECORD TYPE: Fulltext
TARGET AUDIENCE: Professional
WORD COUNT: 665    LINE COUNT: 00056
```

A final, obvious, but nonetheless worthwhile point: do not TYPE or PRINT these documents in full format without first checking their relevance. First of all, displaying records in format 9 (full text) will incur higher charges, but remember while TYPEing that some of these records are documents of considerable length. Get an indication (format 3 or 8, usually) of how long the document is in words or lines. Often, these fields are also searchable (in practice, one could ask for documents of less than 1,500 words), but typically a bigger concern is how large the documents are that have already been retrieved for display purposes.

Full-text databases are an exciting development that offer great potential, but they must be searched with additional care and preparation.

> *Joe is right about being particularly careful when TYPEing these full-text documents. It is sometimes sufficient to type only the KWIC sections where the "hits" actually occur. Particularly if you are dealing with a ready-reference question, the client may not need the entire article – GW*

Citation Databases

This category of databases is quite different from the others we have discussed so far. In fact, in a way, searching citation databases is almost backwards from searching "normal" bibliographic files. Citation databases were developed in the 1970s to provide access to documents in a new and different way—not by subject, words in titles or abstracts, or index terms, but by how the documents had been cited as references by other authors in the scientific literature. This could easily be confusing; we have been using the word "citation" throughout this book to refer to the bibliographic representations of documents found in databases. Here we are going to use "citation" in a quite different way.

As an example, consider a journal article, "A Re-Examination of Relevance: Toward a Dynamic, Situational Definition," which appeared in *Information Processing & Management* in 1990 (vol. 26, p. 755-776). This review article (written by three good friends of ours, Linda Schamber, Michael Eisenberg, and Mike Nilan) summarized the research literature on relevance up to that date and presented a new framework for thinking about such research. As it was a review article, it contained a large number of citations or references to the already-existing literature. This reference list, or bibliography, appeared at the end of the article.

One of the articles in this reference list is by Michael Eisenberg and is titled "Measuring Relevance Judgments." It appeared in *IP&M* in 1988. This is a report of his doctoral dissertation and is really a seminal work on the measurement of relevance judgments. As researchers in the area of relevance and user evaluation, we would like to know who else has cited this paper specifically, and the rest of Mike's work as well. Anyone else who has read this material and found it worthy of citation is probably working in a similar area, and we would like to know who they are and what they are doing.

> *Just a word about citations—don't always assume that because an author is citing another author's work, he or she believes that work to be any good. One does run across negative citations: "As Smith (1978) quite incorrectly stated…" But at least they're in the same subject area. – JWJ*

This kind of searching is possible using citation databases. The Institute for Scientific Information (ISI) has been compiling these databases since 1972, scanning the scientific, social science, and (later) arts and humanities literature, and collating the citations to other works. These databases are available in manual format (a true pain to search) as well as online and on CD-ROM.

What we seek in citation databases, then, is who has cited whom. The original article (in this case Eisenberg 1988) is the *cited work,* the article that refers to it (Schamber et al. 1990) is the citing work, and the link between them is the citation.

Fig. 11.1. A citation.

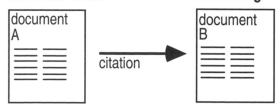

Schamber et al. have cited quite a number of works, and there are many works that cite Eisenberg 1988, so we really have a complex web of citations at work here.

Fig. 11.2. A simple citation web.

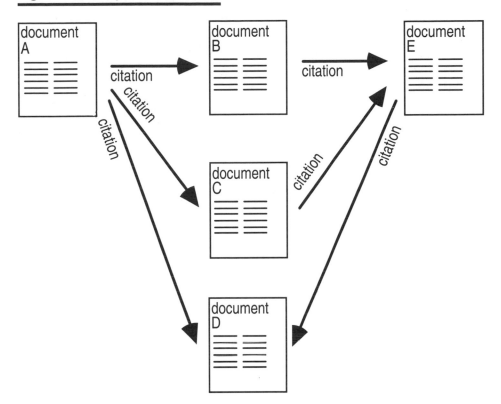

In fact, there is an entire body of research on citation patterns themselves falling under the general heading of *bibliometrics* and including work on scientific communication, citation patterns, co-citation patterns, self-citation, and the like.

This kind of searching presupposes that one has a good "seed" article to begin with. This is often the case with researchers or faculty who have a reasonably good idea of the field and want to see material that has recently appeared. This can prove to be a more efficient method of searching the literature than straightforward topic searches in standard databases.

Citation databases can also be a good way to search topics that cross disciplinary boundaries. More and more interdisciplinary and multidisciplinary research is being conducted, and finding literature that reports on it can be difficult at times. Because there are only three citation databases covering very broad subject areas (science, social science, and arts and humanities), they can be a good source for broad or crossdisciplinary work. Until recently, those searches could be only rudimentary, as the only subject access was via titles of citing works, but ISI has now started adding indexing terms and even some abstracts, so more recent articles will be easier to retrieve in the future.

However, we still primarily search these databases using specialized techniques. The citation databases have highly structured records, and there is very little to go on for searching. The database is composed of more recent records that are the citing works, not necessarily cited works (although many of them will also appear as *cited works* eventually). It can be very convoluted: finding everyone who has cited an article by Armstrong but not searching for Armstrong. We will look at our sample record as it appears in *Social SciSearch* (File 7)[4]:

```
1/5/5
0218096              6Genuine Article#: EK779 Number of References: 64
Title: A REEXAMINATION OF RELEVANCE - TOWARD A DYNAMIC, SITUATIONAL
    DEFINITION
Author(s): SCHAMBER L; EISENBERG MB; NILAN MS
Corporate Source: SYRACUSE UNIV,SCH INFORMAT STUDIES/SYRACUSE//NY/13244
Journal: INFORMATION PROCESSING & MANAGEMENT, 1990, V26, N6, P755-776
Language: ENGLISH Document Type: ARTICLE
Subfile: SocSearch; SciSearch; Scisearch; CC ENGI—Current Contents,
    Engineering, Technology & Applied Sciences; CC SOCS—Current Contents,
    Social & Behavioral Sciences
Journal Subject Category: INFORMATION SCIENCE & LIBRARY SCIENCE
Cited References:
    ALLEN TJ, 1969, V4, P3, ANN REV INFORMATION
    BARHILLEL Y, 1960, P42, AD236772
    BARHILLEL Y, 1960, PB161547
    BEGHTOL C, 1986, V42, P84, J DOC
    BELKIN NJ, 1982, V38, P61, J DOC
    BELKIN NJ, 1982, V38, P145, J DOC
    BELKIN NJ, 1980, P187, THEORY APPLICATION I
    BOOKSTEIN A, 1979, V30, P269, J AM SOC INFORM SCI
    BOYCE BR, 1985, V20, P153, ANNU REV INFORM SCI
    BRITTAIN JM, 1982, V2, P139, SOC SCI INFORM
    COOPER WS, 1971, V7, P19, INFORMATION STORAGE
    COOPER WS, 1973, V24, P87, J AM SOC INFORM SCI
    COOPER WS, 1978, V25, P67, J ASSOC COMPUT MACH
    CUADRA CA, 1967, V23, P291, J DOC
    CUADRA CA, 1967, NSF TM352000100 SYST
    DERR RL, 1985, V21, P489, INFORM PROCESS MANAG
    DERVIN B, 1986, V21, P3, ANNU REV INFORM SCI
    DERVIN B, 1983, INT COMMUNICATION AS
    DERVIN B, 1983, P153, KNOWLEDGE STRUCTURE
    EISENBERG M, 1986, V23, P80, P AM SOC INFORM SCI
    EISENBERG MB, 1988, V24, P373, INFORM PROCESS MANAG
    ELLIS D, 1984, V8, P25, J INFORM SCI
    FAIRTHORNE RA, 1963, P109, INFORMATION RETRIEVA
    FOSKETT DJ, 1972, V8, P77, INFORMATION STORAGE
    GARDNER H, 1987, MINDS NEW SCI
    HALPERN D, 1988, V25, P169, P ASIS ANNU MEET
    INGWERSEN P, 1984, V4, P83, SOC SCI INFORM STUD
    KATZER J, 1987, V12, P15, CANADIAN J INFORMATI
    KEMP DA, 1974, V10, P37, INFORMATION STORAGE
    KOCHEN M, 1974, PRINCIPLES INFORMATI
    LANCASTER FW, 1979, INFORMATION RETRIEVA
    MACCAFFERTY M, 1977, V1, P121, J INFORMATICS
    MACMULLIN SE, 1984, V3, P91, INFORMATION SOC
    MARON ME, 1977, V28, P38, J AM SOC INFORM SCI
    NILAN MS, 1987, V24, P186, P ASIS ANNU MEET
    NILAN MS, 1988, V25, P152, P ASIS ANNU MEET
    NILAN MS, 1989, V26, P104, P ASIS ANNU MEET
    OCONNOR J, 1968, V19, P200, AM DOC
    PAISLEY WJ, 1968, V3, P1, ANN REV INFORMATION
    REES AM, 1966, V18, P316, ASLIB P
    REES AM, 1967, V1, FIELD EXPT APPROACH
    REGAZZI JJ, 1988, V39, P235, J AM SOC INFORM SCI
    ROBERTSON SE, 1979, P202, ANAL MEANING
    ROBERTSON SE, 1979, 3RD INT RES FOR INF
    RORVIG ME, IN PRESS J AM SOC IN
    ROUSE WB, 1984, V20, P129, INFORM PROCESS MANAG
```

```
SALTON G, 1983, INTRO MODERN INFORMA
SARACEVIC T, 1970, P111, INTRO INFORMATION SC
SARACEVIC T, 1975, V26, P321, J AM SOC INFORM SCI
SARACEVIC T, 1988, V39, P197, J AM SOC INFORM SCI
SIMON HA, 1981, V32, P364, J AM SOC INFORM SCI
SWANSON DR, 1977, V47, P128, LIBRARY Q
TAYLOR RS, 1986, VALUE ADDED PROCESSE
TESSIER J, 1977, V68, P383, SPEC LIBR
TESSIER JA, 1981, THESIS SYRACUSE U
TIAMIYU MA, 1988, V24, P391, INFORM PROCESS MANAG
VICKERY BC, 1959, V2, P1275, 1958 P INT C SCI INF
VICKERY BC, 1959, V2, P855, 1958 P INT C SCI INF
WALKER DE, 1981, V32, P347, J AM SOC INFORM SCI
WERSIG G, 1985, V5, P11, SOC SCI INFORM STUD
WILSON P, 1973, V9, P457, INFORMATION STORAGE
WILSON P, 1968, P45, 2 KINDS POWER
WILSON TD, 1984, V4, P197, SOC SCI INFORM STUD
WINOGRAD T, 1986, UNDERSTANDING COMPUT
```

There is little information about the subject content of this document: title, authors, authors' affiliations, bibliographic citation, some rudimentary subject information, and a list of cryptic references. These references are the heart of the citation databases and are the major access point when searching them. Here we see the 64 articles that the authors cite in the body of this particular paper. The one we are interested in is:

Fig. 11.3. Sample cited reference.

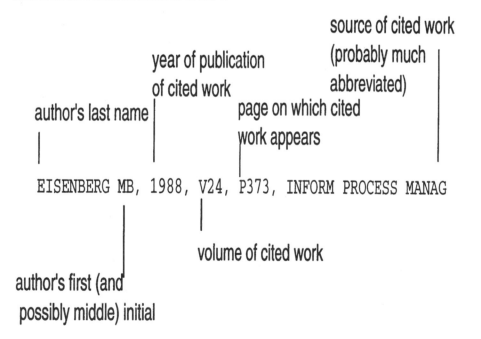

This figure shows the structure of reference fields in citation databases. We strongly advise reading the bluesheets carefully before attempting a citation search, as this is only one example of how such a field is structured; it is immediately evident that there are many more kinds of structures corresponding to books, conference papers, reports, doctoral dissertations, and the like than we have been searching previously.

These references are contained in an additional index, CR= , and are phrase-indexed, so one cannot search by individual words or parts of the field. That is not entirely true—in addition to having the whole thing available as a cited reference, three parts of the field are also separately available: CA= (the cited author's name), CY= (the year of the cited work), and CW= (the name of the cited work), but it is probably a better idea to stick with CR= for citations to a specific work.

We will look at a couple of sample citation searches, starting with the search for articles that cite Eisenberg's 1988 paper. We begin the search by EXPANDing on the CR= field, looking for citations to articles by Mike Eisenberg. We use his middle initial, B., because we know it; if we did not, or if he did not use it, we would have to try CR=EISENBERG M instead. *BE SURE NOT TO TRUNCATE ON THIS EXPAND REQUEST!*

```
File    7:Social SciSearch(R) 1972-1998/Feb W3
        (c) 1998 Inst for Sci Info

        Set   Items   Description
        ---   -----   -----------
?e cr=eisenberg mb

        Ref   Items   Index-term
        E1      1     CR=EISENBERG MA, 1995, V47, P225, STANFORD LAW RE
        E2      2     CR=EISENBERG MA, 1995, V47, P240, STANFORD LAW RE
        E3      0     *CR=EISENBERG MB
        E4      1     CR=EISENBERG MB, IN PRESS J AM SOC IN
        E5      1     CR=EISENBERG MB, 1979, P32, MEDIA METHODS MAR
        E6      1     CR=EISENBERG MB, 1986, MAGNITUDE ESTIMATION
        E7      1     CR=EISENBERG MB, 1986, THESIS SURACUSE U SY
        E8      3     CR=EISENBERG MB, 1986, THESIS SYRACUSE U
        E9      1     CR=EISENBERG MB, 1986, THESIS SYRACUSE U SY
        E10     1     CR=EISENBERG MB, 1986, 49TH P AM SOC INF SC
        E11     1     CR=EISENBERG MB, 1987, P66, 50TH P AM SOC INF SC
        E12     1     CR=EISENBERG MB, 1987, THESIS SYRACUSE U SY

            Enter P or PAGE for more

?p

        Ref   Items   Index-term
        E13     1     CR=EISENBERG MB, 1987, V24, P66, 50TH P AM SOC IN
        E14     1     CR=EISENBERG MB, 1987, 50TH P AM SOC INF SC
        E15     1     CR=EISENBERG MB, 1988, CURRICULUM INITIATIV
        E16     3     CR=EISENBERG MB, 1988, V24, P373, INFORM PROCESS
        E17     27    CR=EISENBERG MB, 1988, V24, P373, INFORMATION PRO
        E18     1     CR=EISENBERG MB, 1988, V39, P293, J AM SOC INFORM
        E19     5     CR=EISENBERG MB, 1990, INFORMATION PROBLEM
        E20     1     CR=EISENBERG MB, 1990, TRENDS ISSUES LIBRAR
        E21     1     CR=EISENBERG MB, 1990, V18, P139, SCH LIBRARY MED
        E22     1     CR=EISENBERG MB, 1990, V18, SCH LIBRARY MEDIA Q
        E23     1     CR=EISENBERG MB, 1991, V26, P243, ANNU REV INFORM
        E24     2     CR=EISENBERG MB, 1993, V2, P2, ERIC REV

            Enter P or PAGE for more
```

We see two items that look like the 1988 *IP&M* article: E16 and E17. Notice the two variant forms of the journal name for *Information Processing & Management*; we must select both of these to get all the citations to this work.

```
?s e16-e17
                 3      CR=EISENBERG MB, 1988, V24, P373, INFORM PROCESS
                27      CR=EISENBERG MB, 1988, V24, P373, INFORMATION PRO
      S1        30      E16-E17
?t 1/3/1-5
```

```
1/3/1
DIALOG(R)File 7:Social SciSearch(R)
(c) 1998 Inst for Sci Info. All rts. reserv.

03131927          GENUINE ARTICLE#: YN805 NO. REFERENCES: 28
TITLE: Partial relevance judgments during interactive information
  retrieval: An exploratory study
AUTHOR(S): Spink A; Greisdorf H
CORPORATE SOURCE: UNIV N TEXAS,/DENTON//TX/76203 (REPRINT)
JOURNAL: PROCEEDINGS OF THE ASIS ANNUAL MEETING, 1997, V34, P111-122
PUBLISHER: INFORMATION TODAY INC, 143 OLD MARLTON PIKE, MEDFORD, NJ
  08055-8750
ISSN: 0044-7870
LANGUAGE: English DOCUMENT TYPE: Article (ABSTRACT AVAILABLE)
```

```
1/3/2
DIALOG(R)File 7:Social SciSearch(R)
(c) 1998 Inst for Sci Info. All rts. reserv.

03108503          GENUINE ARTICLE#: YD202 NO. REFERENCES: 16
TITLE: Measurement in information science - Boyce,BR, Meadow,CT, Kraft,DH
AUTHOR(S): Dubin D
CORPORATE SOURCE: UNIV ILLINOIS,GRAD SCH LIB & INFORMAT SCI, 501 E DANIEL
  ST/CHAMPAIGN//IL/61820 (REPRINT)
JOURNAL: JOURNAL OF CLASSIFICATION, 1997, V14, N2, P327-330
PUBLISHER: SPRINGER VERLAG, 175 FIFTH AVE, NEW YORK, NY 10010
ISSN: 0176-4268
LANGUAGE: English DOCUMENT TYPE: Book Review
```

```
1/3/3
DIALOG(R)File 7:Social SciSearch(R)
(c) 1998 Inst for Sci Info. All rts. reserv.

03104105          GENUINE ARTICLE#: YB504 NO. REFERENCES: 24
TITLE: Users' partial relevance judgements during online searching
AUTHOR(S): Spink A; Greisdorf H
CORPORATE SOURCE: UNIV N TEXAS,SCH LIB & INFORMAT SCI, POB
  13796/DENTON//TX/76203 (REPRINT)
JOURNAL: ONLINE & CDROM REVIEW, 1997, V21, N5 (OCT), P271-280
PUBLISHER: LEARNED INFORMATION LTD, WOODSIDE, HINKSEY HILL, OXFORD, ENGLAND
  OX1 5AU
ISSN: 1353-2642
LANGUAGE: English DOCUMENT TYPE: Article (ABSTRACT AVAILABLE)
```

```
1/3/4
DIALOG(R)File 7:Social SciSearch(R)
(c) 1998 Inst for Sci Info. All rts. reserv.

03090300          GENUINE ARTICLE#: XV698 NO. REFERENCES: 57
TITLE: A framework for retrieval in case-based reasoning systems
AUTHOR(S): Montazemi AR; Gupta KM
CORPORATE SOURCE: MCMASTER UNIV,SCH BUSINESS/HAMILTON/ON L8S 4M4/CANADA/
JOURNAL: ANNALS OF OPERATIONS RESEARCH, 1997, V72, P51-73
PUBLISHER: BALTZER SCI PUBL BV, ASTERWEG 1A, 1031 HL AMSTERDAM, NETHERLANDS
ISSN: 0254-5330
LANGUAGE: English DOCUMENT TYPE: Article (ABSTRACT AVAILABLE)


1/3/5
DIALOG(R)File 7:Social SciSearch(R)
(c) 1998 Inst for Sci Info. All rts. reserv.

03082458          GENUINE ARTICLE#: XR166 NO. REFERENCES: 51
TITLE: Empirical evaluation of retrieval in case-based reasoning systems
  using modified cosine matching function
AUTHOR(S): Gupta KM; Montazemi AR
CORPORATE SOURCE: ATLANTIS AEROSP CORP,/BRAMPTON/ON L6T 5E6/CANADA/
  (REPRINT); MCMASTER UNIV,MICHAEL G DEGROOTE SCH BUSINESS/HAMILTON/ON
  L8S 4M4/CANADA/
JOURNAL: IEEE TRANSACTIONS ON SYSTEMS MAN AND CYBERNETICS PART A-SYSTEMS
  AND HUMANS, 1997, V27, N5 (SEP), P601-612
PUBLISHER: IEEE-INST ELECTRICAL ELECTRONICS ENGINEERS INC, 345 E 47TH ST,
  NEW YORK, NY 10017-2394
ISSN: 1083-4427
LANGUAGE: English DOCUMENT TYPE: Article (ABSTRACT AVAILABLE)
```

There are a number of other variations in this display. E7-E9 and E12 are all citations to Eisenberg's dissertation but with subtle differences; E11, E13, and E14 are all variations on a conference paper he presented at the 1987 ASIS conference; some of these cites have page numbers, some do not. Further, not every citation uses his middle initial—so we also need to EXPAND on his name without the B:

```
?e cr=eisenberg m, 1986

    Ref    Items      Index-term
    E1       1        CR=EISENBERG M, 1985, UNPUB THEORY ADJUDIC
    E2       1        CR=EISENBERG M, 1985, V33, P1, AM ARCH REHABILITA
    E3       0        *CR=EISENBERG M, 1986
    E4       1        CR=EISENBERG M, 1986, P80, P AM SOC INFORM SCI
    E5       2        CR=EISENBERG M, 1986, THESIS SYRACUSE U SY
    E6       1        CR=EISENBERG M, 1986, V114, P31, MED TIMES
    E7       1        CR=EISENBERG M, 1986, V23, P80, ASIS 86
    E8       5        CR=EISENBERG M, 1986, V23, P80, P AM SOC INFORM S
    E9       1        CR=EISENBERG M, 1987, EMPIRICAL STUDIES PR
    E10      1        CR=EISENBERG M, 1987, P14, EMPIRICAL STUDIES PR
    E11      1        CR=EISENBERG M, 1987, P66, P AM SOC INFORM SCI
    E12      2        CR=EISENBERG M, 1987, P66, 50TH P AM SOC INF SC

            Enter P or PAGE for more
?p
```

```
Ref      Items      Index-term
E13        1        CR=EISENBERG M, 1987, UNPUB FINANCIAL SERV
E14        1        CR=EISENBERG M, 1987, UNPUB ISP DRUG TESTI
E15        4        CR=EISENBERG M, 1987, V24, P66, P ASIS ANNU MEET
E16        1        CR=EISENBERG M, 1987, V5, P370, ANN EMERG MED
E17        4        CR=EISENBERG M, 1987, V51, P28, FED PROBAT
E18        2        CR=EISENBERG M, 1987, 50TH P AM SOC INF SC
E19        1        CR=EISENBERG M, 1988, CURRICULUM INITATIVE
E20       17        CR=EISENBERG M, 1988, NATURE COMMON LAW
E21        1        CR=EISENBERG M, 1988, PROGRAMMING SCHEME
E22        3        CR=EISENBERG M, 1988, P1, NATURE COMMON LAW
E23        1        CR=EISENBERG M, 1988, P104, NATURE COMMON LAW
E24        1        CR=EISENBERG M, 1988, P135, NATURE COMMON LAW

          Enter P or PAGE for more
?p

Ref      Items      Index-term
E25        4        CR=EISENBERG M, 1988, P14, NATURE COMMON LAW
E26        1        CR=EISENBERG M, 1988, P15, NATURE COMMON LAW
E27        1        CR=EISENBERG M, 1988, P156, NATURE COMMON LAW
E28        1        CR=EISENBERG M, 1988, P164, ASIS MIDYEAR P
E29        1        CR=EISENBERG M, 1988, P164, ASIS P
E30        1        CR=EISENBERG M, 1988, P164, ASIS P ATLANTA
E31        1        CR=EISENBERG M, 1988, P164, 51ST P ASIS ANN M
E32        1        CR=EISENBERG M, 1988, P2, NATURE COMMON LAW
E33        1        CR=EISENBERG M, 1988, P209, CORPORATIONS
E34        1        CR=EISENBERG M, 1988, P50, NATURE COMMON LAW
E35        1        CR=EISENBERG M, 1988, P58, NATURE COMMONLAW
E36        1        CR=EISENBERG M, 1988, P83, NATURE COMMON LAW

          Enter P or PAGE for more
?p

Ref      Items      Index-term
E37        1        CR=EISENBERG M, 1988, R7, NATURE COMMON LAW
E38        1        CR=EISENBERG M, 1988, THESIS U PENNSYLVANI
E39        6        CR=EISENBERG M, 1988, V25, P164, P ASIS ANNU MEET
E40        1        CR=EISENBERG M, 1988, V39, P292, J AM SOC INFORM
E41       17        CR=EISENBERG M, 1988, V39, P293, J AM SOC INFORM
E42        1        CR=EISENBERG M, 1989, V89, P1462, COLUMBIA LAW RE
E43        1        CR=EISENBERG M, 1990, CORPORATIONS BUSINES
E44        1        CR=EISENBERG M, 1990, INFORMATION PROBLEM
E45        1        CR=EISENBERG M, 1990, PROBLEM SOLVING BIG
E46        1        CR=EISENBERG M, 1990, PROGRAMMING MACSCHEM
E47        2        CR=EISENBERG M, 1990, V113, P408, ANN INTERN MED
E48        1        CR=EISENBERG M, 1990, V51, P971, U PITT L REV

          Enter P or PAGE for more
```

Several of these are citations to Mike Eisenberg's work: E4, E7-E8, E11-E12, E28-E31. How can we tell? We have to figure it out from abbreviated titles and a general knowledge of the field and his work. In practice, it may be difficult to disambiguate these, and we see also that another M. Eisenberg is prolific in legal research. Separating their citations could be tricky because we have no further information, such as where they are located, to help us.

Citation searching can be tricky, but it can also be rewarding if the right strategies are found. Notice that although citations are entered as they appear in the citing article (including any errors), there is a strict format to entries. The order of elements and the punctuation and spacing have to be entered exactly:

```
?s cr=eisenbman gr, 1957, v126, p831
```

> Unless you are pretty familiar with an author's work, this selection of appropriate records can be difficult and time-consuming. You may need to check many pages of EXPANDs, selecting appropriate entries as you go along. With common surnames, it can be a nightmare! – GW

Here is a more straightforward example: searching for citations to the work of Elfreda Chatman, who has done some superb research on the information needs of groups of people who have not been much studied (older women, janitors, etc.). We begin by expanding on her name in the CA= (cited author) field:

```
?e ca=chatman e

    Ref    Items    Index-term
    E1        1     CA=CHATMAN D
    E2       10     CA=CHATMAN DL
    E3        3     *CA=CHATMAN E
    E4       30     CA=CHATMAN EA
    E5       11     CA=CHATMAN J
    E6      191     CA=CHATMAN JA
    E7        1     CA=CHATMAN JE
    E8        2     CA=CHATMAN LM
    E9      144     CA=CHATMAN S
    E10       2     CA=CHATMAN SB
    E11      17     CA=CHATMAN SP
    E12       5     CA=CHATMAN T

          Enter P or PAGE for more
?s e3-e4
              3     CA=CHATMAN E
             30     CA=CHATMAN EA
    S2       32     E3-E4
?t 2/6/1-5
```

```
  2/6/1
  03131941        GENUINE ARTICLE#: YN805 NUMBER OF REFERENCES: 11
  TITLE: Information seeking and information needs of low income African
     American households: Wynnewood Healthy Neighborhood Project (ABSTRACT
     AVAILABLE)


  2/6/2
  03115515        GENUINE ARTICLE#: YG454 NUMBER OF REFERENCES: 22
  TITLE: Discovering information behavior in sense making .3. The person
     (ABSTRACT AVAILABLE)
```

```
2/6/3
03115513          GENUINE ARTICLE#: YG454 NUMBER OF REFERENCES: 30
TITLE: Discovering information behavior in sense making .1. Time and timing
  (ABSTRACT AVAILABLE)


2/6/4
03083799          GENUINE ARTICLE#: XR820 NUMBER OF REFERENCES: 24
TITLE: Nurses' perceptions of their needs for community information -
  Results of an exploratory study in southwestern Ontario (ABSTRACT
  AVAILABLE)


2/6/5
03009441          GENUINE ARTICLE#: WJ555 NUMBER OF REFERENCES: 66
TITLE: A discipline independent definition of information (ABSTRACT
  AVAILABLE)
```

These all look correct; there is only one E. Chatman, and because all these citing works seem to be in the general area, it appears that we have the right one.

Another interesting (and useful) feature of the citation databases is that all[5] of the works by a particular author can be found. We expand on the AU= field to find Elfreda Chatman's work:

?e au=chatman e

```
    Ref     Items      Index-term
    E1         1       AU=CHATMAN AB
    E2         1       AU=CHATMAN DL
    E3         1      *AU=CHATMAN E
    E4        13       AU=CHATMAN EA
    E5         4       AU=CHATMAN J
    E6         8       AU=CHATMAN JA
    E7         1       AU=CHATMAN JE
    E8         1       AU=CHATMAN L
    E9         5       AU=CHATMAN S
    E10       10       AU=CHATMAN SP
    E11        1       AU=CHATO F
    E12        1       AU=CHATO P

          Enter P or PAGE for more
?s e3-e4
               1       AU=CHATMAN E
              13       AU=CHATMAN EA
    S3        14       E3-E4
?t 3/6/1-8


3/6/1
02864209          GENUINE ARTICLE#: TX290 NUMBER OF REFERENCES: 64
TITLE: THE IMPOVERISHED LIFE-WORLD OF OUTSIDERS (Abstract Available)


3/6/2
02759909          GENUINE ARTICLE#: RB250 NUMBER OF REFERENCES: 1
TITLE: BARRIERS TO INFORMATION - HOW FORMAL HELP SYSTEMS FAIL BATTERED
  WOMEN - HARRIES,RM, DEWDNEY,P
```

```
3/6/3
02677273 GENUINE ARTICLE#: PP078 NUMBER OF REFERENCES: 1
TITLE: INVESTIGATING SUBJECTIVITY - RESEARCH ON LIVED EXPERIENCE - ELLIS,C,
  FLAHERTY,MG


3/6/4
02566481          GENUINE ARTICLE#: MN245 NUMBER OF REFERENCES: 1
TITLE: PUBLIC-LIBRARIES AS AGENTS OF COMMUNICATION - A SEMIOTIC ANALYSIS -
  WAGNER,GS


3/6/5
02415720          GENUINE ARTICLE#: JV325 NUMBER OF REFERENCES: 0
TITLE: DAILY INFORMATION NEEDS - IMPLICATIONS FOR POLICY


3/6/6
02350780          GENUINE ARTICLE#: HP254 NUMBER OF REFERENCES: 51
TITLE: THE ROLE OF MENTORSHIP IN SHAPING PUBLIC-LIBRARY LEADERS (Abstract
  Available)


3/6/7
02327031          GENUINE ARTICLE#: HD038 NUMBER OF REFERENCES: 52
TITLE: CHANNELS TO A LARGER SOCIAL WORLD - OLDER WOMEN STAYING IN CONTACT
  WITH THE GREAT SOCIETY (Abstract Available)


3/6/8
02253985 GENUINE ARTICLE#: FU468 NUMBER OF REFERENCES: 96
TITLE: LIFE IN A SMALL WORLD - APPLICABILITY OF GRATIFICATION THEORY TO
  INFORMATION-SEEKING BEHAVIOR
```

If we were to look at a full record for any of these, we would see what works Chatman has cited. This example allows one to envision the network of citations encompassed by this file. It is a fascinating but potentially perilous area, not the least because these files are very expensive to search, so speed and careful preparation are most important.

Finally, it is also possible to conduct a rudimentary topic search in these files. A search for review articles on information needs in the information/library science area can be quickly done (SC= is the additional index for subject codes, one of which is "Information Science and Library Science"; it is word-indexed, so we search just on SC=INFORMATION):

```
?s information(1n)need? ?/ti
        40745     INFORMATION/TI
        14680     NEED? ?/TI
    S4     413     INFORMATION(1N)NEED? ?/TI
?s s4 and sc=information
         413     S4
      125771     SC=INFORMATION
    S5     240     S4 AND SC=INFORMATION
?t 5/8/1-5

  5/8/1
DIALOG(R)File 7:(c) 1998 Inst for Sci Info. All rts. reserv.

03138219          GENUINE ARTICLE#: YR755 NUMBER OF REFERENCES: 1
TITLE: Assessing information needs: Tools and techniques - Nicholas,D
JOURNAL SUBJECT CATEGORY: INFORMATION SCIENCE & LIBRARY SCIENCE
```

5/8/2

03131941   GENUINE ARTICLE#: YN805 NUMBER OF REFERENCES: 11
TITLE: Information seeking and information needs of low income African
  American households: Wynnewood Healthy Neighborhood Project (ABSTRACT
  AVAILABLE)
JOURNAL SUBJECT CATEGORY: INFORMATION SCIENCE & LIBRARY SCIENCE
IDENTIFIERS--KeyWord Plus(R): PATTERNS

5/8/3

03127650   GENUINE ARTICLE#: YM280 NUMBER OF REFERENCES: 24
TITLE: Information needs of rural health professionals: a retrospective use
  study (ABSTRACT AVAILABLE)
JOURNAL SUBJECT CATEGORY: INFORMATION SCIENCE & LIBRARY SCIENCE
IDENTIFIERS--KeyWord Plus(R): SMALL MEDICAL-LIBRARY; PHYSICIANS; JOURNALS;
  BOOKS; LIST

5/8/4

03120392   GENUINE ARTICLE#: YJ027 NUMBER OF REFERENCES: 19
TITLE: University professional and managerial staff: Information needs and
  seeking (ABSTRACT AVAILABLE)
JOURNAL SUBJECT CATEGORY: INFORMATION SCIENCE & LIBRARY SCIENCE
IDENTIFIERS--KeyWord Plus(R): ADMINISTRATORS; HUMANITIES; PATTERNS

5/8/5

03033549   GENUINE ARTICLE#: WU813 NUMBER OF REFERENCES: 8
TITLE: Assessing information needs: A case study of journalists (ABSTRACT
  AVAILABLE)
JOURNAL SUBJECT CATEGORY: INFORMATION SCIENCE & LIBRARY SCIENCE
?s s5/review
    S6   6   S5/REVIEW
?t 6/8/all

6/8/1
01645355   Genuine Article#: E2565 Number of References: 136
Title: INFORMATION NEEDS AND USES
Journal Subject Category: INFORMATION SCIENCE & LIBRARY SCIENCE

6/8/2
01398228   Genuine Article#: TN709 Number of References: 24
Title: THE INFORMATION NEEDS AND USES OF SCHOLARS IN THE HUMANITIES - A
  REVIEWING OF STUDIES IN THE HUMANITIES
Journal Subject Category: INFORMATION SCIENCE & LIBRARY SCIENCE

6/8/3
0117268   3Genuine Article#: PW511 Number of References: 86
Title: HUMANITIES SCHOLARS - INFORMATION NEEDS AND USES
Journal Subject Category: INFORMATION SCIENCE & LIBRARY SCIENCE

```
6/8/4
00658757          Genuine Article#: FT055 Number of References: 107
Title: INFORMATION NEEDS AND USES
Journal Subject Category: INFORMATION SCIENCE & LIBRARY SCIENCE


6/8/5
00401662          Genuine Article#: CG627 Number of References: 1
Title: INFORMATION NEEDS OF SOCIAL-SCIENTISTS - REVIEW ARTICLE
Journal Subject Category: INFORMATION SCIENCE & LIBRARY SCIENCE


6/8/6
00222374          Genuine Article#: V6856 Number of References: 35
Title: INFORMATION NEEDS AND USES
Journal Subject Category: INFORMATION SCIENCE & LIBRARY SCIENCE
```

As is evident, we searched this file primarily using the EXPAND command, then SE-LECTing from the E-display. This does not have to be done; AU=CHATMAN E? or CR=EISENBERG MB? will work (note the truncation operators, though—remember, these are phrase-indexed fields), but this example should give one a sense of the inconsistencies in this file. Citations are entered into the database exactly as they appear in the citing work, abbreviations, spacing, errors, and all. Because there is little authority control, working with an E-display makes it possible to identify variant forms and lends more confidence to the search. As with full-text searching, citation databases are powerful but require thorough preparation and some advanced skills.

> These are particularly difficult files to search because of all the inconsistencies. Nevertheless, they are worth the effort required to learn to search them efficiently—largely because the manual files are so awful. Not only is the typeface practically illegible without a magnifying glass, but it is also very easy to miss relevant material. – GW

Notes

1.   Don't be fooled, though, into believing that all online files are more up-to-date than print versions. Some of these reference databases are updated infrequently, intermittently, or not at all. Always check the documentation before you log on and the database banner as you BEGIN to search the file to see when the last update was.

2.   Searching on numeric ranges is not difficult, as you can see, but there are several shortcuts and special features you should know about. Check for numeric fields in system documentation to get complete details.

3.   Why /TI? Headlines, which you might think of as titles, are often little use to us in searching, since their stilted style and cryptic wording make them unreliable subject indicators.

4.   The other two citation databases are *SciSearch* (File 34) and *Arts & Humanities Search* (File 439).

5.   or virtually all; not everything goes into the citation databases, but most of the good journals and conferences are indexed, along with a selection of monographs, technical reports, and other sources.

Additional Reading

Aluri, R. et al. (1991), "Keyword Subject Access and Citation Indexing." In *Subject Analysis in Online Catalogs* (Englewood, CO: Libraries Unlimited): 98–112.

Basch, Reva (April 1990), "The Seven Deadly Sins of Full-Text Searching," *Database* 12(4): 15–23.

Chandler, Helen E., and Vincent de P. Roper (October 1991), "Citation Indexing: Uses and Limitations," *The Indexer* 17: 243–49.

12 EVALUATING YOUR RESULTS

When discussing evaluation in the context of online searching and information retrieval, we need to talk about it from two different perspectives: the practical and the theoretical. The practical kinds of evaluation are those used in day-to-day, real-life searching settings. The theoretical kinds are used in research into online and information retrieval issues and in design of online systems.

These two perspectives are related, but there are important differences as well. Ideally, they should support each other—practical work providing grist for the mill of theory and research, and research better informing the practice of searching. This is not always the case, unfortunately, but in this chapter we will examine evaluation from both points of view and perhaps see how they can better relate in the future.

The Basic Measures: Precision and Recall

Before we can go far in discussing evaluation and the issues that surround it, we must begin with the basics. There are two evaluative measures that have been used for decades in this area. They are used both in practical settings and in virtually all information retrieval research and design. As will be seen, they are quite simple to compute and understand, but there are some problems with their use and interpretation. Both are expressed as ratios (or sometimes percentages) and attempt to tell us how effective or efficient a particular search or system is.

The first is *precision*, and this is defined as the proportion of documents retrieved in a given search that are relevant.[1] In formula form, it is expressed as

$$\text{precision} = \frac{\# \text{ of relevant documents retrieved}}{\# \text{ of documents retrieved}}$$

So if a given search retrieves 50 documents, 17 of which are relevant, that search gets a precision rating of 17/50, which is 0.34, or 34%. A search that retrieves nothing but relevant documents would have a precision rating of 1.00, the maximum; a search retrieving no relevant documents gets a precision rating of 0.00, the minimum.

The other measure used is *recall*, and this is defined as the proportion of relevant documents in the database that are retrieved by a particular search. Its formula is

$$recall = \frac{\text{\# of relevant documents retrieved}}{\text{\# of relevant documents in database}}$$

Our search above netted 17 documents; if there were in fact 72 relevant documents in the database, we have a recall rating of 17/72, which is 0.236 or 23.6%. If a search retrieves all relevant documents available, it gets a recall rating of 1.00; if it retrieves no relevant documents, it gets a recall rating of 0.00.

A couple of things may be immediately striking. First of all, how can we know, in practice, how many relevant documents there are in the database? If we knew that, could we not retrieve them all? That is a good observation, and in fact recall is impossible to calculate in real life. An attempt to calculate something like it has been developed, called *normalized recall*. Here, several searchers perform searches on a particular topic, see how many relevant documents are in the big merged set, and calculate recall figures for each individual search. This is better than no total recall figure at all, but not much.

In research settings, testing different search modules or improvements, one may actually know all the relevant documents in a test collection so one can actually calculate real recall. However, this type of research typically is done with very small document collections (several hundred to a few thousand), and systems that perform well on small collections do not necessarily do so well on big ones (millions of documents), so such conclusions may not be all that helpful either. The bottom line is that recall is, at best, a metaphysical measure, and it is not really used much or taken very seriously.

This notion of using numbers of documents (relevant and otherwise) to measure effectiveness is easy and straightforward, but perhaps also simpleminded. A number of researchers (most notably Bertram Brookes[2]) have contended that it is not possible to add up "relevance" like one would add up bricks. If one has a pile of 25 bricks and adds one more, the result is 26 bricks, and this will be the same operation no matter how many bricks one starts with—add one, and there is one more. With information, it is not so easy. Does a user have the same amount of "extra" information with the retrieval of the 54th relevant document as she did with the fourth, for example? And does it not also depend on the quantity and quality of the information in those documents? Some of them may be "relevant" (more problems with the definition of this word) but not contain much that is new, while others may answer all of a user's questions and satisfy their information needs.

These issues are not as simple as they seem at first. Recall and precision are gross measures that we can use to get a rough idea of the performance of systems and searchers, but they cannot give us detailed information. True, they are easy to calculate, but they mask some serious and deep theoretical questions that are as yet unresolved. Nonetheless, they are used constantly, both in research and in everyday settings.

The Recall-Precision Tradeoff

If recall and precision are not of much use as fine measurement tools, they can be helpful in establishing a mindset for a particular search. If we take them literally, then the "ideal" search would be one where recall and precision were both equal to 1.00—a search that retrieves all the relevant documents in the database and no others. In practical terms, this is virtually impossible (except when searching for a single known item or doing a search to demonstrate that there are no relevant documents), but it is often perceived as the goal for which we shoot in searching.

These mindsets are often discussed in the online searching literature and recommended in practice for planning a "high-recall search" or a "high-precision search." These phrases come from experiences and conversations with users, but also from the perception that there is a tradeoff between the two—that it is very difficult to do a search that is both high-recall and high-precision, so we must choose between them.

That may be true in the current situation, but we can always hope that better-designed systems and a better understanding of some of the fundamental concepts underlying information retrieval can improve our searches. But that is another story. The recall-precision tradeoff is widely discussed and believed, both for particular searches and for system design. In many cases it can be useful in planning searches.

High-Precision Searches. Conventional wisdom tells us that high-precision searches are best for users who are looking for a few good documents in a small set without a lot of garbage to wade through. The stereotypical user here is a senior researcher, faculty member, businessperson, or other individual who is familiar with the field in question and only wants to pick up a few good citations. Other high-precision users might include people who cannot afford extensive, comprehensive searches; people who do not have the time or energy to wade through a long list of potentially good documents; and people for whom only a few good documents will be necessary (e.g., high school students with term paper assignments).

To conduct a high-precision search, we often use much more specific strategies that seek to produce small, high-quality sets. This is a perfect opportunity to use controlled vocabulary or narrow free-text techniques, limiting to major descriptors, articles from only the last few years, in English, and so forth. Perhaps the user knows authors or journals that could be used in focusing the search—ANDing them in with bigger result sets.

High-Recall Searches. The quintessential high-recall user is the doctoral student doing a literature review. She is going to want everything ever written that even remotely relates to the topic, so a big, high-recall set is going to make her happy. She is not going to mind getting junk (but there are limits to how much you should retrieve), so long as she gets a pretty good sense that most of the good documents have been retrieved. Getting everything is unrealistic, but the net should be cast pretty wide.

High-recall searches often use lots of terms ORed together, may use free-text as well as controlled vocabulary techniques (and broader free-text strategies at that), and probably do not use year limits extensively. Knowledge of authors or journals are especially useful in broadening the search through pearl growing techniques.

Beware, though, of the notions that these are the only two kinds of searches we do and that they are mutually exclusive. A user who requests a high-precision search may really want more than just a few good things, and the doctoral student may quickly decide she needs a more focused set. Be flexible and open; listen to the user.

We have discussed the necessity of broadening and narrowing search strategies already; here is a collection of techniques we have found to be useful:

Fig. 12.1. Refining a search.

To *Narrow* a Search Strategy:	To *Broaden* a Search Strategy:
AND in a new concept set.	Stop using a concept set, especially the one *least* crucial to the query.
Use *fewer* terms in concept sets.	OR in *more* terms in concept sets.
Move *up* the ladder of specificity: Use narrower proximity operators, go from free-text to controlled vocabulary, limit to major descriptors.	Move *down* the ladder of specificity: Stop using major descriptors, go to free text, use broader proximity operators.
Truncate further to the *right.*	Truncate further to the *left.*
Use *narrower* controlled vocabulary terms.	Use *broader* controlled vocabulary terms.
Qualify search strategies to titles, descriptors, abstracts.	Remove qualifiers; search full-text if available.
Limit by language, publication year, publication type, age group, etc.	Remove limitations.

Other Measures of Performance

Recall and precision are fine as far as they go, but in the big bad world, other factors often intrude. For instance, a library may have policies in place that restrict searches to a particular length of time, number of citations retrieved, or total cost. In these circumstances, searching will be constrained. High-quality searching can still be done in an environment such as this, but there are added considerations.

There may not be much opportunity for pearl growing, so the initial strategy for a high-recall search may have to be broader than normal. Such a search may even not be possible, if the library's limit is 10 or 15 citations. In a high-precision search, the focus may not be quite as effective, but these constraints are usually less of a problem here because this kind of search lends itself more to such a setting.

Searching may also be evaluated using cost or time measures. Because the system provides detailed information at the end of each search and on monthly invoices, it becomes an easy matter for management to see just how long searches are taking and how much they cost. This could be good or bad. Using this information alone may give a misleading impression of search performance, but taking users' evaluations of retrievals into account as well can form a more realistic picture of what is going on.

This also leads to another interesting question: When should a search be stopped? Beginning searchers often ask this, and there is really no good answer.

There are a few rules of thumb here. The first is the easiest: If the user is happy, then stop. If, upon later reflection, they think there might be more to be had, the search can always be resumed. In situations where the user is not present during the search, the searcher must rely on their own impressions of how the search is going, depending on whether the user wanted a high-precision or high-recall search (or some other kind), and the searcher's perception, or the user's, of how many documents constitute an ideal set. If limits have been set by policies on length or cost, they will certainly help decide when a search stops. Also, after searching for a while, it may become evident that there is just nothing more (or nothing at all) to be found. Or the search simply does not go well. In such a circumstance, it may be best to save the search, get off, regroup, and try again rather than staying online and flailing around for no good reason.

Self-Evaluation

So far, we have talked about ways and measures used to evaluate searches from a neutral perspective. Recall, precision, time, cost—these are all objective measures used to evaluate searches and systems and searchers. However, there are other evaluation possibilities.

Beginning searchers may feel unsure as they search. They are still learning the commands and techniques of searching, and they are probably not all that comfortable with the process yet. As they gain practice and experience, though, they will start to feel more comfortable and more confident, and this will lead them to be better searchers. Some simple self-evaluation tactics will make the process happen more quickly and more easily.

Here are some ideas for questions you can ask yourself as you review searches that you've conducted:

- *What were my best sets?* Look for sets you are particularly pleased with. Be honest—even if your search did not go particularly well, there has to be a least one set you think was pretty good. How did you get it? What techniques or strategies did you use? Is there any way you could improve on it?

> *A major temptation is to "fall in love" with your results, so be strict with yourself. I find students selecting citations as "relevant" when they really have minimal usefulness. OK, I know you feel good when you complete your first few searches, but let's get real with the results. – GW*

- *What sets caused me trouble?* It is easy to create a set that does not work and not see it as you are doing it. Often, beginning searchers make spelling or typing errors and get sets with no items or the wrong items. When combining sets, neglecting an S in a set number can result in searching on a number rather than a set. Notice the difference between sets S4 and S5 in this example:

```
File 1:ERIC 66-98/JUN.

        Set    Items    Description
        ---    -----    -----------
?ss stress variables or stress management
        S1     5232     STRESS VARIABLES (CAUSES AND CONSEQUENCES OF
                        PSYCHOLOGICAL AND...)
        S2     1685     STRESS MANAGEMENT (TECHNIQUES TO HANDLE PSYCHOLOGICAL
                        AND/OR PH...)
        S3     6280     STRESS VARIABLES OR STRESS MANAGEMENT
?s 3 and beginning teacher induction
            156021     3
               646     BEGINNING TEACHER INDUCTION (STRUCTURED PROCESSES OR
                        PROGRAMS DESIGNED TO...)
        S4      194     3 AND BEGINNING TEACHER INDUCTION
?s s3 and beginning teacher induction
              6280     S3
               646     BEGINNING TEACHER INDUCTION (STRUCTURED PROCESSES OR
                        PROGRAMS DESIGNED TO...)
        S5        1     S3 AND BEGINNING TEACHER INDUCTION
```

See the error?

The second search statement searched on the digit 3, finding all documents that have the number 3 in Basic Index fields, rather than set S3. S4 will have very little of use, while S5 is a very focused result set. An error like this can be very hard to notice online.

These technique difficulties are easier to see once the search is over and you have a chance to review the printout at leisure. Do not fret about them—just make notes to yourself and try not to repeat the things that did not work. Also look for terms that are too broad or narrow, and sets that are too big or too small (too many or too few terms, or search expressions at the wrong level on the ladder of specificity).

- *What did you learn through this search?* Did you use any new techniques or system features? How did they work? Would you use them again, and in what situations?

- *How will you improve as a result of this search?* It sounds like a cliché, but you should aim to be a better searcher after each search you do. Explicitly thinking about what you learned and how you'll improve can help you to see that process, and thus feel better about your searching in general.

The Other Side: Research and Theoretical Notions of Evaluation

Recall and precision are common practical methods of evaluation, but they also are used in a wide variety of research into system design, search and searcher performance, and other topics in information retrieval and online searching. Underlying these methods, though, are the central questions of evaluation: What are people looking for, and how can we measure this? This part of the chapter will give an idea of how these questions have been attacked over the last few decades.

When we talked about recall and precision earlier, in both cases we defined them in terms of the number of "relevant" documents retrieved. What exactly do we mean by "relevant"? This is not a flip question, although most people probably have a pretty good idea of what they think "relevant" means. That is the problem—everybody thinks they know what is "relevant." The definition of "relevance" has occupied many researchers in the area of evaluation. Many possible alternate terms, expressions, and ideas have been offered over the years: "topicality" (documents that are on the same topic as the search request), "satisfaction" (documents that the user or someone else says satisfy the request), "utility" (documents that are useful to the user), "pertinence" (related to topicality and "aboutness") and on and on. One of the best definitions comes from Saracevic, who in 1975 called relevance "a primitive 'y'know' concept."[3]

Each of these definitions seems to have some applicability and some relationship to the others. Most "relevant" documents are on the topic of the request and satisfy and are useful to the user. Yet we have all probably had the experience of running across a "rogue" document that is way off the topic, yet brings a new insight or point of view, so we pursue it, use it, and eventually are satisfied with it. Conversely, we may retrieve a beautiful document, spot on the topic—yet we have already seen it, perhaps even violently disagree with it, so it will never be used. Is this document "relevant" to the question at hand?

The initial response to that question may well be that it depends—on the information about the document that we have, the query, the situation, the time and place in which that judgment is made, the user's state of mind, other documents that have been seen, and, probably most important, who is doing the judging.

All of these (and more) have been identified as variables that affect or influence the processes of relevance judgment. Some experimental research has been conducted to examine these issues, but there is a great deal more to be learned. We do know, for example, that relevance can be measured in much the same ways as other physical or psychological stimuli,[4] that the order in which documents are presented affects the judgments people make,[5] that judgments change in many different ways as people get more information about documents,[6] that there are many different criteria people use to make these judgments,[7] and that librarians and students make rather different judgments from users—typically overestimating relevance, but with some other interesting patterns.[8]

Schamber et al., in an excellent article reviewing more than three decades of work on relevance and related issues,[9] end with the following conclusions about the nature of relevance and its role in information behavior:

1. Relevance is a multidimensional cognitive concept whose meaning is largely dependent on users' perceptions of information and their own information need situations.

2. Relevance is a dynamic concept that depends on users' judgments of the quality of the relationship between information and information needs at a certain point in time.

3. Relevance is a complex but systematic and measurable concept if approached conceptually and operationally from the user's perspective.

Note these words: "multidimensional," "dynamic," "complex," "systematic," "measurable." Note also the heavy emphasis on the user.

What does all this mean to the searcher? Outside of the intellectual interest of trying to find out how and why people make judgments about documents, evaluation research can offer useful information and assistance for searching:

- *Have the user with you during searching.* The practical online searching literature has been suggesting this for years, but research tells us that the judgments we as professionals make are sometimes quite different from those of users. Having the user there relieves you of this burden and will probably lead to better searches, especially as the search progresses, using information about good documents to retrieve even more good ones (known as "feedback").

- *If you can't have the user with you, be liberal in judgment.* This is probably not a problem—many of us seem to do this naturally, and we are trained to do it as well, but research shows us that some information professionals and students are conservative in judgment, which may exclude potentially good documents or lead the search down a less productive path.

- *You'll get better at judgment.* Your ability to approximate users' judgments will probably improve as you gain experience in the profession—although it will probably plateau within a few years.

- *Give the user as much information as you can about documents*, but ask them or find out what kinds of information they will find most helpful. Titles, certainly—abstracts also help, as does information about authors and sources, especially if the user is experienced in the area. Experienced users tend to make less use of index terms in decision-making; less-experienced users may find them more helpful. We as professionals also seem to use subject information.

- *Don't ask yes/no questions about relevance*—ask how good the citations are and why; find out what features are important and whether the "good" documents are *really* good or just okay. It is more than a black-or-white decision (or should be).

- *Be sensitive to the dynamism of the process.* Users may actually change what they are looking for as the search progresses but might not actually say so or even realize it themselves. Also, be aware that seemingly marginal (or worse) documents may pique a user's interest for reasons we can only guess at.

As is evident, there is considerable overlap between these two perspectives on evaluation. A recent renaissance in interest and research into these issues is encouraging because if we better understand how users make judgments about information items, we may gain insight into their information needs and assistance with designing systems, interfaces, and document representations to assist in answering those needs.

Notes

1. This is, in my mind at least, the crux of the whole evaluation issue: What is "relevant" anyway, and is that the best measure to use to evaluate searching? We'll discuss this in more detail later in this chapter; in the meantime, rely on your intuitive notion of "relevance" for the rest of this discussion.

2. See, for example, Brookes, B. C. (1980), "Measurement in Information Science: Objective and Subjective Metrical Space," *Journal of the American Society for Information Science* 31: 248–55.

3. Tefko Saracevic (1975), "Relevance: A Review of and a Framework for the Thinking on the Notion in Information Science," *Journal of the American Society for Information Science* 26(6): 321–43.

4. Michael B. Eisenberg, (1988), "Measuring Relevance Judgments," *Information Processing & Management* 24(4): 373–89.

5. Michael B. Eisenberg and Carol Barry (1986), "Order Effects: A Preliminary Study of the Possible Influence of Presentation Order on User Judgments of Document Relevance," *Proceedings of the 49th Annual Meeting of the American Society for Information Science*: 80–86.

6. Joseph W. Janes (1991), "Relevance Judgments and the Incremental Presentation of Document Representations," *Information Processing & Management* 27(6): 629–46.

7. Carol Barry (1994), "User-Defined Relevance Criteria: An Exploratory Study," *Journal of the American Society for Information Science* 45: 149–59.

8. Joseph W. Janes and Reneé McKinney (1992), "Relevance Judgments of Actual Users and Secondary Judges: A Comparative Study," *Library Quarterly* 62(2): 150–68.

9. Linda Schamber, Michael B. Eisenberg, and Michael S. Nilan (1990), "A Reexamination of Relevance: Toward a Dynamic, Situational Definition," *Information Processing & Management* 26: 755–76.

Additional Reading

Bruce, Harry (1994), "A Cognitive View of the Situational Dynamism of User-Centered Relevance Estimation," *Journal of the American Society for Information Science* 45: 142–48.

Harter, S. (1996), "Variations in Relevance Assessments and the Measurement of Retrieval Effectiveness," *Journal of the American Society for Information Science* 47: 37–49.

Mizzaro, Stefano (1997), "Relevance: The Whole History," *Journal of the American Society for Information Science* 48: 810–32.

Park, Taemin (1994), "Toward a Theory of User-Based Relevance: A Call for a New Paradigm of Inquiry," *Journal of the American Society for Information Science* 45: 135–41.

Schamber, Linda (1994), "Relevance and Information Behavior," *Annual Review of Information Science and Technology* 29: 3–48.

13 RUNNING A LIBRARY SEARCH SERVICE

We have seen that the earliest users of online information retrieval services were professional librarians in specialized information agencies. But over the years the use of online systems has become increasingly common in libraries of all types, and the advent of new electronic services has made access possible from almost anywhere. Electronic information is available in such a variety of forms, from CD-ROM, from mainframe computers, and from the Internet, that the task of providing maximum access in the most efficient manner has become increasingly complicated. This chapter looks at some of the issues involved in setting up and managing access to electronic information resources in libraries.

Decisions regarding the allocation of available library resources in times of financial constraint and the rising prices of print materials have tended to favor a move to increasing reliance on electronic resources and interlibrary lending. The issues involved include not only the choice between different formats in which the same information may be available, but also the often-conflicting claims of promoting direct user access versus the provision of a service using trained searchers. Funding is likely to be the crucial factor in such decision-making because the objective is to maximize efficient access to all types of information in the most cost-effective manner.

The following discussion is concerned with four aspects of operating such electronic search services in libraries:

- The allocation of resources between formats,
- Policies and administration,
- Professional searching, and
- Training users.

The Allocation of Resources

The last five or six years have seen a massive shift towards CD-ROM as the format of preference in most major libraries, particularly academic libraries. It seems clear that users much prefer this format, at least when compared with the parallel printed indexes. So does this mean that libraries should buy all their indexes in this format? Indeed, is everything required available in CD-ROM format? The enormous growth we have seen in interlibrary lending in recent years suggests that there is increasing use of indexes in electronic form as pointers to information materials of all types. The availability of electronic full text for much material is also a positive incentive for many users, and the access to unique documents and visual materials available via the WWW make for a growing body of library users. There can be no doubt about the demand for these materials, but the question for most libraries is how to provide access and how to afford it.

CD-ROMs are available from a range of producers, each with their own customized search software. This means that the knowledge gained from searching a database produced by one vendor will not necessarily transfer to products produced by another vendor. This is particularly confusing to users because CD-ROMs appear to be physically identical. In the library situation, where products from a range of vendors are (of necessity) available, this indicates a need for ongoing user training. (More on this later in this chapter.) Many libraries have attempted to minimize the problem by favoring the products of one major vendor when there is a choice of different vendors for the same file. Even so, some files are only available from other smaller vendors, so there is bound to be a variety of search software in use in any library with a large number of databases on CD-ROM.

Libraries with heavy CD-ROM use and dispersed sites have tended to network the most heavily used of their databases, allowing multiple users to access a single file at the same time. These libraries also make it possible to permit remote access from homes or dorms so that use can be dispersed to hours when the library is not open. The pattern appears to be to network the most popular files and allow stand-alone access to less-used databases. Stand-alone access requires that the discs be stored offline and only mounted as needed, while networked access has all the networked files always available from a group of machines.

In parallel with in-house CD-ROMs, many major libraries are providing remote access to other electronic resources via systems such as DIALOG, databases such as OCLC's FirstSearch, databases mounted in-house and accessed via the library's OPAC, and (of course) the vast resources available on Internet. This smorgasbord of information in electronic format makes one wonder why (or even how) we are still buying printed books and journals! The choices of how to divide the materials budget have become increasingly complicated, and libraries are having to base decisions on perceptions of user needs within their individual institutions. Selection criteria and evaluation of both use and content have become more important than ever before.

Policies and Administration

All decisions regarding how the different search services will operate need to be implemented through the design of appropriate policies. Decisions will need to be made regarding the following matters:

- When will an online (DIALOG) search be offered? Presumably, if the appropriate database is available on CD-ROM, then that would be searched first. If the most recent information is needed in addition, then an online search incorporating a time concept (either PY= or UD=) will complement the CD-ROM search of the same database. Because this is largely a question of economics, presumably any eligible user who is prepared to pay the full cost of a search would be accommodated regardless of CD-ROM availability. If no appropriate CD-ROM file is available, online may be the only alternative.

- Who are eligible users of the search services? Are these services intended to serve only internal users, or will outsiders be able to use the electronic resources as well as print materials? How will these policies relate to online commercial services for which the library is billed direct costs? Most libraries that receive public funding are normally available for in-house use by the public at large, and this access would apparently apply also to electronic resources that are paid for up front (CD-ROMs and in-house files). In fact, some CD-ROM publishers limit access to in-house users as part of their contract with the library. This restriction can be enforced by requiring a password for access (usually the user number); and commercial services available through the WWW often restrict access to individual machines with an appropriate IP address (e.g., albany.edu or mich.edu).

Regarding online searches performed using commercial services, many libraries will operate a differential policy regarding access, with different user categories being treated differently in terms of both access and costs. For example, searches may be available to only faculty and graduate students at some academic libraries, or they may be free to all registered users, though they are not normally provided free to library users from outside the parent organization.

- How will searches be paid for? Many librarians see this "fee versus free" debate as an important ethical issue involving the concept of equal access for all. Traditionally, most libraries funded by public money have supported this professional ideal espoused in the American Library Association's (ALA's) Code of Ethics.[1] The rationale is that information obtained from a computer is no different from information obtained from any other reference source because all information has to be paid for in some way. It is also assumed that charging for information will inhibit its use, at least for certain groups of users. It was demonstrated early on that search requests were less common in libraries that charged the user than in those offering a free service.[2] Nevertheless, there now appear to be emerging groups of professional users who seem willing to pay for speedy and efficient access to information, and this may well be a growing trend. Some public libraries, for example, will charge business users, while offering free searching to individual patrons.

On the other hand, many libraries would be unable to offer online search services at all without being able to charge for them. Opinions on how to do this vary considerably, and any library contemplating fees will need to study the question carefully. The more complicated the pricing structure, the more paperwork is involved, so that charging fees may in fact be counterproductive. Most search vendors charge for their services by a combination of connect time per hour plus charges for each individual record retrieved. Typical connect charges range from $15 to $120 per hour, with certain chemical and business files going as high as $350 per connect hour. Charges for bibliographic records range from 10¢ to $10 per record, though records from some of the highly valued business files and those in full text may cost as much as $120 each. Many libraries are forced by financial realities to recoup at least a part of these expenses, though few charge users the total cost of their searches including overheads.

> I am becoming increasingly fed up with the fee versus free argument. No information is free (even the stuff on the Net—it takes time and attention to search for and identify what you want), but to hear some people go on about it, the mere thought of charging for information is a betrayal of a sacred trust and means that we might as well all give up and go to work for Barnes & Noble. That's an exaggeration, but not by much.
>
> In continually reinforcing the notion (everywhere but in special libraries, which often make internal charges) that everything is "free," we do our users and ourselves a disservice. It denies the reality of increasingly expensive information and, more important, binds us to an eternal poverty, without options for alternative sources of revenue. It renders us feckless and naive. – JWJ

- What do we do if a paid-for search is not successful? The cause of a failed search is often difficult to determine, and sometimes searches are unproductive through no fault of the professional searcher. Many users find it difficult to express their information needs exactly. Users have a well-documented tendency to ask for a topic broader than the one they actually require, though this kind of misunderstanding should, of course, be remedied during the reference interview. (More on this later.) On occasion the searcher may be at fault through failure to clarify the search topic, inexperience on a particular database, or lack of subject knowledge. Regardless of the cause of a search failure, it is probably politic to have an official policy of offering a free search if a user is seriously dissatisfied.

> Just to be difficult—some patrons want a zero hit search. I call these "disconfirmatory" searches; others have called them "negative" searches. The most common type are patent searches, where users really want to find nothing, meaning that they have a better chance of patenting their new, improved onion peelers. Other researchers though, especially doctoral students, may want to be reassured that no one has done or reported a particular study, so the way is clear for them to do so. Zero hit searches are not always failures and should be paid for somehow. – JWJ

- Administrative details. A clear set of policy statements, such as those discussed here, provides a sound framework for the administration of electronic services. In addition, a whole range of paperwork will be needed to cover record-keeping and user instruction. One of the major tasks for the online service will be keeping a search log to track all the searches performed. Such a log should include details of the searcher, search service and databases used, date and time of the search, and costs incurred. These elements are important for checking the accuracy of the monthly bills, and it is most convenient to update the search log at the time the search is performed. Each organization will have its own record-keeping requirements, but a chart something like figure 13.1 will probably suit most situations.

Fig.13.1. Search service log.

Date	Time	System	Database(s)	Cost	Searcher

It is important for all searchers to be conscientious about keeping this log because discrepancies will have to be resolved before bills can be passed to the accounts department for payment. Most host systems have mechanisms for automatically chasing unpaid accounts and may resort to threats to terminate the service when payments are unduly delayed.

> *Some specialized searching software (I'm thinking here about examples like DIALOGLINK or ProSearch) will create automatic search logs that have billing and invoice modules, so if you elect to use software like this, some of this record-keeping may be done for you. It could be a big time-saver and also increase your confidence in the accuracy of your logs. – JWJ*

Some procedures will also need to be devised to match users with machines, or with professional searchers for the online searches. Bookings can either be incorporated into the regular reference desk duties, or sign-up sheets can be made available for self-booking in busy libraries. This can get quite complicated when there are whole banks of machines, many of then accessing different databases and some of them providing access only to the Internet or the library catalog. A booking form will be necessary for each individual terminal, clearly stating which databases are available from it. This author's own library has all the machines numbered, and both they and their database handouts are color-coded. This also simplifies the choice of appropriate search handouts, which are summary sheets of search software. A great deal of the administration of the different services will revolve around forms of one sort or another, so it is worth investing some time and thought in their design. These investments will pay in terms of staff time by making them as self-explanatory as possible, though it is not possible to make electronic searching entirely self-service.

For the online search service, a search request form is an important starting point. It has been found that a search request expressed in narrative form and natural language is likely to produce better results than a list of potential search terms. A known citation that can be used for pearl growing is also a useful starting point, and it is helpful to know if there are any limitations of time period or language to be imposed on the search. Is the aim of the search to be high recall or high precision? In addition to information about the search topic itself, most libraries also collect demographic data about the user for internal use. Figure 13.2 on page 278 is an example of such a form.

Fig. 13.2. Sample request form from University at Albany Libraries.

CONTROL/REQUEST NO.

```
                          SUNY ALBANY LIBRARIES
                        COMPUTER SEARCH SERVICE
                             REQUEST FORM

LAST NAME_____FIRST_____PHONE: DAY_____
                                                      EVE._____

ADDRESS_____
        _____    A.   Have you done a CSS search here
        _____          before?
                                        PLEASE CIRCLE ONE (YES/NO)
B.  Please circle categories which apply and check (C) the appropriate
box/boxes.  Users must sign and date agreement.


ACTIVE SUNYA                                NON-SUNYA (Y)
SUNYA DEPT. OR MAJOR     SUNYA STATUS       (includes SUNYA Alumni
                                            and other SUNY units)

Business. . . . . . . .B  Faculty. . . . . . . .F  For-Profit Business. . B
Criminal Justice. . . .C  Graduate Student. . . G  Non-Profit Organiz. . .P
Education. . . . . . . E  Undergraduate. . . . .U  Other SUNY Unit. . . . N
Humanities. . . . . . .H  Staff. . . . . . . . .S  Academic (non-SUNY). . A
Library & Info Sci. . .L  Other. . . . . . . . .O  Empire State Coll. . . E
Natural Science/Math. .N                           Other. . . . . . . . . O
Public Affairs. . . . .P
Soc/Behavioral Sci. . .S  C. ┌─┐ I agree to pay 50% (SUNYA), or 100% plus $6
SUNYA Resrch Ctr/Inst. R     └─┘ for (non-SUNYA), of cost of the online time
Univ. Admin. . . . . . A         required for this search and 100% of the
Univ. Libraries. . . . V         cost of such printing as I designate at the
Univ. Lib.-Lib. Wk. . J         time of the search.
College of Gen Study. .G
Social Welfare. . . . .W     Signature_____Date_____
Undeclared Major. . . .M                     OR
Other. . . . . . . . .O  ┌─┐ I have arranged for this search to be
                         └─┘ charged to a valid account.
                             Account #_____

                             Signature_____Date_____
```

D. PURPOSE OF SEARCH	LANGUAGE SPECIFICATIONS	SEARCH RESTRICTION
_____Term Paper	_____English Only	Please indicate search
_____Thesis or Diss	_____Other (Specify)	limitations such as:
_____Research		human; animal; plant;
_____Other (Specify)		age; female; male; grade
		level; time period;
		racial or ethnic group;
		geographic area.

E. Please give a narrative description* of the information you seek and
titles of relevant citations, if you have them.

---

* Search topics are confidential and, except for necessary library faculty consultation, will not be shared with others without patron consent. If confidentiality is
of concern, please write the description of the information you seek on a separate
sheet and request to retain the sheet and your search strategy.

In the early days, online search services invested considerable effort in the production of amusing and eye-catching publicity materials, though it seems that the new electronic services now require little in the way of introductory advertising. It is more a case of trying to keep up with the demand! When new services are initiated, a flyer is obviously required, and ongoing training sessions for all files and all systems provide advertising of a sort. In an academic setting in particular, the user population is always changing, so there is a continuing need for promotional materials and training. Most use of electronic resources has traditionally come from repeat users and personal recommendations, but we are now seeing the emergence of a more technically oriented user population who are familiar with computers and happy to try their hands on new systems. They have yet to learn that computer know-how does not necessarily translate to an ability to search!

Professional Searching

Over the years, much has been written about the importance of the *reference interview* in the traditional library setting. It is generally agreed that the reference process involves an "interaction between the librarian, the library patron, and the library's resources in order to satisfy the patron's information needs."[3] In general, the term "reference interview" refers to the conversation that takes place between a reference librarian and a library patron for the purpose of clarifying the patron's information needs. The librarian's goals are to determine exactly what information the patron needs, how much information is needed, and the form in which the information is required. This interaction differs from an ordinary conversation in that it is generally more formal and more structured, especially in the online situation. It is clear that many of the strategies recommended for the manual interview will also apply to the interactions between reference librarians and users who are searching online or using CD-ROM databases.

The traditional approach to the reference interview has been to try to match users to resources, based on a series of "closed" questions that elicit responses from a specified range of choices. Recently, interest has moved from listing the steps to be followed to focusing on the relationships among the four interacting elements of the reference process. In consequence, a number of models of reference interaction have been developed.

Models of the Reference Process

The development of such behavioral models of the reference process rely on theories taken from a number of other fields, including social work, psychology, journalism, and communication theory. The interaction between the requester and the librarian searcher has been described as "one of the most complex acts of human communication . . . where one person tries to describe to another person not something he knows, but rather something he does not know."[4] The inquiry is viewed as "a description of an area of doubt in which the question is open ended, negotiable, and dynamic."[5] The emphasis is on the requester's difficulty in articulating an information need. It has also been suggested that the belief that the analyst may not understand or the system may not suit the request may lead a user to distort how the information need is expressed.[6]

Taylor has suggested a model that divides the information-seeking cycle into four successive levels: the visceral (unexpressed) need, the conscious (recognized) need, the formalized (expressed) need, and the compromised need. The compromised version is how the query is finally presented to the information system. The experienced information specialist has to work back through these levels in order to determine what is really required.

> *Remember how we started the eight-step procedure in chapter 6?*
>
> 1. *Read the query.*
> 1a. *Listen to the query.*
> 1b. *Understand the query.*
>
> *This may require quite a bit of negotiation, a lot of patience, and the use of all your communication skills. – GW*

It has been suggested that the use of "open" rather than "closed" questions improves the pace of the interchange between question and response and elicits more helpful responses from the requester.[7] Open questions begin with query words (what, when, why, etc.) and allow the respondent to answer at length, as opposed to the searcher using closed questions to control the discussion.

Dervin has suggested the idea of a "sense making" model, focusing on "movement through time space," which she believes underlies all information-seeking situations.[8] Information is depicted as a construct of the user rather than having an independent existence in isolation. Information is required by individuals to fill a gap in a given real-life situation. Dervin argues for the uniqueness of each information need and suggests that the same question may not require the same answer for different people or at different times.

Based on this idea and developing the open or closed question debate is her introduction of the idea of "neutral" questions. These are questions intend to help the librarian learn the nature of the underlying situation, the gaps faced by the user, and the expected uses of the answers provided. This approach is user-oriented in that it allows users to retain control over describing their needs and to identify the most important aspects for themselves. Here are some examples of neutral questions, taken from Dervin:[9]

To assess the situation:

Tell me how this problem arose.

What are you trying to do in this situation?

What happened that got you stopped?

To assess the gaps:

What would you like to know about X?

What seems to be missing in your understanding of X?

What are you trying to understand?

To assess the uses:

How are you planning to use this information?

If you could have exactly the help you wanted, what would it be?

How will this help you? What will it help you do?

Despite extensive research, little of this theoretical base has so far been incorporated into professional training courses. Nevertheless, communication skills are obviously important for any public service professional, and all models stress that they are particularly important in the online negotiation interview, where misunderstandings are apt to be expensive. "What transpires during this exchange affects the formulation, the search itself, and even the user's opinion of the results. The interview, then, becomes the crucial step in the overall computer search process."[10]

Explaining Online Systems

Many clients still have minimal ideas about what a computer search can provide and what it cannot.

> *Reminds me of the undergraduate who arrived at 6:15 P.M. asking for an online search because he had to make a class presentation at 7 P.M.! He was sadly disillusioned to discover that there are no instant answers. I notice the same lack of understanding in relation to CD-ROM databases. Students are determined to use them, regardless of whether the most appropriate file for their particular query is available only in print format. – GW*

Library users need to be educated to the fact that they are not going to receive instantaneous information unless it is available in full text. In that case it may be expensive to acquire online and will still require synthesis and interpretation. They need to be told that in many situations the result of their search will be a list of citations that they will have to follow up in the library or elsewhere. Making this clear from the outset will prevent disappointment.

The searcher also needs to explain what types of searches can be best performed on a computer system. In general, the more complicated the question, the better it is suited to online searching, largely because it is more difficult to perform manually. The advantages of multiple access points, the ability to combine terms using logical operators, and the interactive nature of the search process all need to be explained. The limitations of online searching also need to be admitted, such as the limited time coverage of some databases and the impossibility of defining other than logical relationships (e.g., dog bites man versus man bites dog). It is important to confirm that an online search is appropriate for a specific query because otherwise the request should be referred back to regular reference services.

Cost structures of the online system obviously need to be discussed, particularly when the client is expected to pay any part of the cost. The client must understand that costs are assessed on a per-record basis and that different formats are available. The option of printing citations with or without abstracts, online or offline, needs to be offered, together with an explanation of the likely time delays and cost differences. It is important to determine a rough estimate of the number of citations required and give an estimate of the likely cost of the search. The client may wish to review the choices made on the search request form in light of these explanations (see figure 13.2 on page 278).

The Interview

Having established that an online search is indeed the correct way to go for a specific query, and that the patron understands the limitations and costs involved, we are ready to start discussing the search topic. The starting place is normally the written information request provided on the standardized request form. In some library situations this will be the only communication between the searcher and the requester; therefore, the design of the form is crucially important. It should help the client define exactly what information is needed, how much output is required, and any limitations of time or language that exist. It should also help the searcher understand those needs.

Needless to say, most online searchers prefer to have a face-to-face interview with the requester, and most writers stress the importance of this style of negotiation. Many searchers also like to have the client present while the search is being conducted. This opportunity for the user to refine the search while it is being conducted is one of the major advantages of online systems. Cleverden has also stressed the importance of feedback in improving search results: "Frequently the search results will change as the user, having found some related documents, develops a clearer idea of exactly what he needs. . . . Alternatively, it may be that . . . he will be guided to more effective search terms."[11]

This positive feedback between patron and system minimizes the disadvantages of the delegated search process. Used in conjunction with the written request and presearch interview, these personal interactions save time and money, help to ensure that the results of the search are satisfactory, and in the long term may prevent the need for a follow-up search.

It is helpful for the searcher to know something about the subject field of the search topic and the relevant jargon and terminology, which may entail some background reading. It has been observed that the role of the librarian is to know how information is organized and where to find the answers, rather than to know the answers directly, but it certainly seems that we need to know at least a little about almost everything. Knowing a little about a search topic is important not only in helping with the selection of search terminology but also in communicating with the client and maintaining professional credibility. The librarian is not expected to be an expert in everything (indeed, many clients will be delighted to take that role) but does need to be able to interact intelligently with them.

The major portion of the reference interview in the online setting is conducted prior to the search itself to minimize search costs. This means that it is important to establish effective communication strategies because the role of the intermediary is "to clarify, expand, delimit, or otherwise modify the user's request so that it can be developed into an effective search strategy."[12]

There are many reasons why patrons' initial questions do not provide the librarian with accurate guidance to their real information needs. The librarian must be careful to avoid assumptions based on initial statements, past experience, or the user's appearance. The exact questions to ask cannot be specified because every situation will be different, but neutral questions will prevent premature diagnosis. This clarification of the exact information need is particularly important in the online situation, where results cost money.

Negotiating Search Terms

We have talked about controlled vocabulary and free-text searching but have not really addressed the question of how to choose search terms. It has been found that allowing the user to suggest terms is not necessarily a productive strategy, and most search request forms specify a narrative statement of the information need. This may seem a strange approach, for who can know better what the user really needs than the user himself? Unfortunately, it appears that the user's ability to express what is wanted is inhibited by perceptions of the system and its abilities. Talking through the whole information problem will help to expand or redefine the initial search statement. The librarian must make sure that the question is understood. The good searcher does not hesitate to consult a dictionary or ask questions, and the understanding of new ideas or concepts is often based on analogies to things that are familiar.[13]

We know that the initial search statement is a source of natural-language terms, which can also provide lead-ins to the controlled vocabulary. Aside from the obvious terms, ask the user about key terminology and key sources. Oftentimes, a crucial search term will not appear in the search statement or the thesaurus. It may be a new term, a colloquialism, a proper name, or an acronym.

> A good example of this was a search request I received asking for information on the effect of teacher expectations on student academic performance and classroom behavior. I decided that ERIC was the appropriate database to search, and there were some useful thesaurus terms available, such as teacher attitudes, student behavior, and academic achievement. I also decided to incorporate the term "teacher expectations" from the language of the query. This initial search turned out to be way too broad, even after it was limited by /MAJ or /DE, and the term "teacher attitudes" was dropped. Furthermore, the records did not look very useful. A pause for further discussion produced the term "Pygmalion effect," which had never been mentioned in the presearch interview and was unfamiliar to me. But it turned out to be exactly what was needed. – GW

Search terms come from many different places, and do not forget that new descriptors are being added to thesauri all the time. Word frequency lists, when available, and online EXPANDs can aid in the selection of free-text terms. Some search services and Internet search engines have introduced their own equivalency links. These terms can include obvious linguistic matches, such as singular or plural and alternative spellings, or obvious conceptual links, such as alternative names for the same thing (e.g., USSR = Russia = Soviet Union).[14]

The meaning of free-text searching may need to be explained so that the requester understands the difference between natural-language and controlled vocabulary terms and the value and limitations of each. Discuss the possibility of using truncation, and select potential terms to be covered by truncating. When discussing phrases, point out that it is probably best to rely on the most essential words and allow for variant forms rather than to be exactly specific. Learn whether the aim is for a comprehensive search or just a few good references, as this affects the number of synonymous terms to be included.

> When looking for search terms and preparing a search strategy, I find it helpful to play a kind of game. I try to dream up titles that would make good answers to the query. (This requires a bit of imagination, but it is rather fun!) I then test my prepared strategy to check whether it would retrieve my imagined titles. If it would not, I have to do some adapting. – GW

Understand the search topic thoroughly, especially the desired relationships among concepts. Ask intelligent questions about the information situation in general and how the information is to be used. Above all, act interested. Try to act as if it is a team project. Talk about what WE will do. In general, "the librarian should assume a strong role in developing the search strategy."[15] This is the librarian's area of expertise, but remember that every search is a partnership affair.

Finally, anticipate problems that may crop up. At the very least have two alternative strategies prepared in advance. One will be used if too few references are retrieved—a broadening strategy. The other is for use if too many postings appear—a limiting strategy. Despite one's best efforts, one may still have to improvise while online, and indeed one of the major advantages of an online search is its interactive nature. If necessary, slow down and view some titles in order to let the user provide feedback by identifying the records that satisfy the search needs completely. Look for possible new terms in them that might be incorporated into the search (pearl growing). These new terms may also suggest possible alternative databases to search. Stop searching when enough material has been found or the cost cap has been hit. And most important, check with the user that the search results are satisfactory.

Presenting Search Results

Traditionally, the post-search role of the librarian has been to review the printout with the user, explain the search strategy, and make sure that the requester can decipher the printout and knows how to find the material. In the case of an absentee requester, the role of the searcher may be even simpler: stuff and address an envelope or phone for a pickup.

The fact that most searchers nowadays use a microcomputer as their search terminal has provided new opportunities for enhancing the presentation of search results. Searches can be easily downloaded, reformatted on a word processor, and delivered to the client as a value-added professional end product, customized to the client's requirements.

The searcher can edit out confusing fields (e.g., code numbers or accession numbers) and possibly add information on local holdings and interlibrary loan options. The search results can be presented either as print via mail or fax, or as machine-readable data, either on disk or transmitted by E-mail. Policy decisions are needed regarding the amount of searcher time to be committed to editing and refining search results, and how that time will be budgeted. There is an interesting potential for improving the image of the search service overall through upgrading the presentation of the finished product. The presentation of numeric information in report or spreadsheet format, and the increased use of alternative telecommunications channels to transmit results, will provide dramatic evidence of the library's use of advanced technology to enhance its user services. Such enhancements are particularly important in a situation where most searching is done by information seekers themselves using CD-ROM. It becomes vital that the professional search output should stand out as different and look like a professional product.

CD-ROM User Training

The interview associated with CD-ROM database searching tends to be more relaxed than that for online, largely because charges will not be incurred directly during the search. Because CD-ROM searching is usually conducted by the user, most of this interaction is likely to occur during the search rather than before and to center on the use of the equipment and how to structure a search strategy. Less effort will normally be invested by the professional searcher in the analysis of the query and the choice of appropriate search terms, because the librarian's role has changed from online searcher/partner to CD-ROM search assistant/trainer.

The elimination of the full reference interview in this situation has its unfortunate side. Examples abound of end users scanning hundreds of citations looking for that elusive "needle in the haystack" because they do not know how to reduce postings. It seems that libraries are currently committing more and more reference staff time to CD-ROM instruction and help, often employing student assistants to deal with the more mechanical tasks.

It is good practice for reference staff to check on first-time users while they are searching because this is when explanations are apt to make the most sense. This will also encourage new client searchers to use CD-ROM systems again, and they will probably feel more comfortable asking for assistance when they need it in the future. The variations in command languages and system features among competing vendors make multiple CD-ROMs a particular problem for novice searchers. (And some professionals are not too happy either. Imagine having to remember five different truncation symbols on seemingly identical systems, as our reference staff have to!) Although most CD-ROM products provide online or printed documentation or both, they are not always as helpful as they might be, and it is a fact of life that when faced with any type of technology, users will turn to the documentation only as a last resort.

> *It is well known that many people will not use documentation at all; they prefer either to try to find online help systems, which are common but not inevitable and often not particularly helpful; to flail about and hope they get the idea; or even to just abandon ship. – JWJ*

Many libraries are devoting increased amounts of time to bibliographic instruction—not the old-fashioned "tour of the library" type, but focused sessions on the idiosyncrasies of particular databases or Web search engines, or the finer aspects of search term selection and search strategy development. The librarian's role is moving more and more away from the things that we traditionally regard as "librarianly," and more and more towards teaching and instruction in the use of the automated IR systems.

Notes

1. American Library Association (1995), *Code of Ethics*. Chicago: ALA.

2. I. R. M. Mowat and S. E. Cannell (July 1986), "Charges for Online Searches in University Libraries: Follow-up to 1981 Survey," *Journal of Librarianship* 18(3): 193–211.

3. Gerald Jahoda and Judith S. Braunagel (1980), *The Librarian and Reference Queries* (New York: Academic Press).

4. Robert S. Taylor (May 1968), "Question Negotiation and Information Seeking in Libraries," *College & Research Libraries* 29(3): 178–94.

5. Ibid.

6.   Sara D. Knapp (Spring 1978), "The Reference Interview in the Computer-Based Setting," *RQ* 17(3): 320–24.

7.   Taylor, op.cit.

8.   Brenda Dervin and Patricia Dewdey (Summer 1986), "Neutral Questioning: A New Approach to the Reference Interview," *RQ* 25: 506–13.

9.   Ibid.: 509.

10.   Stuart J. Kolner (January 1981), "Improving the MEDLARS Search Interview: A Checklist Approach," *Bulletin of the Medical Library Association* 69(1): 26–33.

11.   Cyril Cleverden (September 1972), "On the Inverse Relation of Recall and Precision," *Journal of Documentation* 28(3): 199.

12.   Carolyn K. Warden (Winter 1977), "Online Searching and Bibliographic Databases—The Role of the Intermediary," *Bookmark* 36: 35–41.

13.   Knapp, op.cit.: 323.

14.   Barbara Quint (July 1991), "Inside the Searcher's Mind: The Seven Stages of an Online Search—Part 2," *Online* 15(4): 28–35.

15.   Arleen N. Somerville (February 1982), "The Pre-Search Reference Interview—A Step by Step Guide," *Database* 5(1): 32–38.

Additional Reading

Budd, John (September 1994), "It's Not the Principle, It's the Money of the Thing," *Journal of Academic Librarianship* 15(4): 218–22.

Halliday, Jane (October 1991), "Fee or Free: A New Perspective on the Economics of Information," *Canadian Library Journal* 48(5): 327–32.

Jacso, Peter (May/June 1996), "Watching Your Online Bottom Dollar," *Online* 20(3): 51–53.

Katz, William A. (1997), *Introduction to Reference Work. Vol. 2: Reference Services and Reference Processes*, 7th ed. (New York: McGraw-Hill).

O'Leary, Mick (January 1993), "Flat-Rate Online: A New Online Era Begins," *Online* 17(1): 34–5238.

14 RUNNING YOUR OWN SEARCH SERVICE

The need to manage printed information has long demanded specialists to select, organize, store, and help with retrieval. We call these specialists *librarians*. The current glut of information, the variety of new formats (CD–ROM, Internet, etc.), and the new technologies that allow direct access to the layperson have, in fact, increased rather than lessened the need for this specialized professional expertise. Information retrieval is becoming a more precise science, and the importance of timely and accurate information especially in today's fast-moving business environment gives the information professional a crucial role in any decision-making process. Information may be more easily accessible than ever, but it is the experience and expertise of the professional searcher, not the information per se, that is the product when we talk about marketing information.

This chapter explains the role of the independent *information broker*, who offers knowledge of and access to available information resources, both manual and electronic, as products for sale. It is becoming increasingly impossible for any layperson to keep up with the information being published in even a relatively small subject field when things are changing so rapidly. A commercial information service can help a client not only to identify what information is required but also to find it, interpret it, and decide how to use it. Unfortunately, many people are as yet unaware of the need for professional help, so that it will often be necessary to "sell" the value of such assistance, at least initially.

Information brokering is a job that requires many of the traditional skills of the librarian plus an entrepreneurial turn of mind and business acumen. A good starting point is to join the Association of Independent Information Professionals, as they can offer experience and advice to the novice entrepreneur. Certain innate characteristics will also prove to be particularly useful, such as a logical and analytic mind, good communication skills, enthusiasm, and the ability to make decisions. In addition, learned assets that are useful are (obviously) information search skills, especially knowledge of online information sources and how to use them effectively, and an area of subject expertise that will provide a focus for a proposed business.

Making a Business Plan

The first step for anyone intending to enter the information-providing marketplace as an entrepreneur is the preparation of a business plan. Information is finally being recognized as a major product in today's marketplace, and the number of independent information providers is growing rapidly. Burwell reported that there were 1,776 such businesses worldwide in 1996, representing 51 countries and 49 of the 50 American states.[1] However, most such operations are small in scale, often employing only one person. It is obvious that there will only be a viable market in major population centers, and even there it is probably not possible for a business to survive on the provision of information alone. Most independent information professionals have a variety of skills for sale—document provision, training workshops, desktop publishing, and the like. This means that versatility and flexibility are prime requirements for anyone planning on setting up their own business.

There are more than half a million new incorporations in the United States every year, and a large percentage of them fail, largely as a result of poor planning. A helpful starting place is a general book on starting any small business.[2] Probably the most important step for any aspiring new business is the development of a business plan. It should serve three main functions:

- A communications tool

- A basis for management

- A yardstick to measure progress and evaluate changes

This plan reflects the person who prepares it and that person's ability to organize, to think, to manage, and to communicate. It also demonstrates that person's ability to compete in the business arena, and it is the face presented to potential funders, as well as a way to keep track of progress. Here we suggest the essential elements of any properly prepared business plan.

1. *The Business Concept.* This presents a summary of the idea for the business and is based on research into local business information needs, particularly information needs within a specialized subject field. It needs to demonstrate how an information service could fit into the local marketplace and that it has potential for future development.

2. *The Service Provided.* This should give a complete description of the different types of service to be provided. It will need to explain the benefits and advantages of such an information-providing service because many people are unaware that a viable market for information even exists. This section is aimed at "selling" the concept of an information service to a complete stranger with no knowledge of the field.

3. *The Market.* The big picture needs to be explained first—the growing importance of information in the global marketplace and the growth in information-providing agencies of all kinds. Discuss local competition in the field, evaluate the performance of the competition, and show how a new business could fill a niche created by their deficiencies. Show that there is a potential customer base for information services in the selected field.

4. *Marketing Strategy.* Describe how the services will be sold, including pricing strategies, estimated business, and market share for the first three years. Add plans for advertising and public relations, and include service and warranty policies.

5. *Operation Plans.* Explain the resources available for information provision (local libraries, interlibrary loan, online vendors, the Web, etc.). Outline the office space, equipment, and professional and online memberships that will be required.

6. *Personnel.* Most information brokers are a one-person operation, at least at first. Make a list of the qualifications, skills, and talents needed to achieve success, and explain convincingly why you believe that you have them.

7. *Financial Plans.* A personal financial statement is the bare minimum required here for someone with no past business history. Demonstrate a plan to cover startup expenses and estimate the likely level of business for the first year. How will this increase over the following years? What will be the likely levels of repeat business, and what strategies can be used to maximize repeat business?

The business plan must be well organized, easy to read, sound, logical and factual. It must demonstrate a direct relationship between future growth and past knowledge and experience. But it is not cast in stone and will probably need considerable fine tuning at first. Adequate planning involves setting a series of objectives, with the specific time and resources need to fulfill those objectives. Each action needs to be prioritized into a logical order and given a time frame for execution. Every detail needs to be covered, and a reason has to be available for every step to be taken along the way. It may be necessary to explain or defend any action in the plan!

Making a Budget

In order to decide whether a business is likely to be successful, it is necessary to try to determine how much money it will cost to organize and plan the operation (seed money) and to get started (startup financing), and what level of business will be necessary to recoup that investment and sustain operations (growth financing). A first budget will be at best a guess, but it must be a realistic and educated guess. Subsequent budgets will generally be better informed, but it is essential to make the initial guesses. The budget will consist of three sections:

- Fixed expenses
- Variable expenses
- Profits

Fixed expenses are those incurred regardless of the level of business—rent, utilities, publicity, equipment, memberships, and so forth. *Variable expenses* vary according to the level of business—online access charges, printing, photocopying, and the like—and will depend entirely on the needs of individual clients. *Profit* needs to include not only the provider's own remuneration but also items that are normally provided by an employer, such as health insurance. There should also be enough profit to plow back into the business to finance future growth and cover lean times, and to show some return on the initial investment. In basic terms, the level of sales is adjusted until enough is being sold to cover the fixed and variable expenses and to return the necessary profit. Before the doors of the business open, there should be enough money not only to get started but also to operate for at least six months without income. It is essential to be prepared for business to be slow at first. When planning the first budget, it is better to err on the side of estimating expenses high and income low.

It will often be the case that additional funding besides one's own resources will be necessary. There are several ways to look for money, but if it has to be borrowed and secured with personal assets, be aware that these assets may be entirely lost in the event of failure. Anyone prepared to lend money (usually at a considerable rate of interest) will require detailed information about the would-be entrepreneur, their personal financial situation, and the business plans. This is where the business plan comes in: to give the investor confidence in the potential of the business and demonstrate that it is properly planned. Looking for possible sources of capital requires a *loan proposal* tailored to the individual investor. Commercial banks are the largest single source of loans to both small and large businesses. They are in the money business and make money by lending money. If the borrower is a member of a credit union, it is a good idea to investigate their loan rates, which may be lower than the regular banks or insurance companies. There are also various grant funding agencies, both professional organizations and government-sponsored. Small Business Investment Companies (SBIC) are privately owned companies licensed by the Small Business Administration (SBA) to provide capital to small firms. Community Development Companies have also been established by many local communities with the aim of attracting business into their community. Local Chambers of Commerce are good places to start looking for possible resources and advice. There are also special grants available to encourage the growth of women and minority-owned small businesses, and sometimes local funding for specific projects. They are all worth investigating.

Marketing

Despite the widespread belief that "information is power," it is surprisingly hard to sell information as a commercial product or service, so the effective promotion of any potential service is crucial. A regular user base is necessary for success because casual users will not provide a reliable long-term income. Traditionally, the information business has been geared to respond to requests rather than to a sales initiative. That is, it has responded to the needs articulated by clients in most cases. Most information professionals are unused to the idea of promoting a service, and most potential users are unaware of the value of such a service to their operation. This means that more is required than merely advertising and sending out flyers. A personal relationship, *referrals*, word of mouth, and industry reputation all take time to build.

An effective marketing strategy includes:

- Defining the service

- Identifying a client base

- Pricing the service competitively

- Advertising and selling the service

A crucial factor in defining the scope of an information service is a geographical one. What are the major commercial activities of the area and what are the projections for future development? Clearly, a major center of population and white-collar businesses is necessary to support a viable level of information service. Business people often have little understanding of the role, sources, and value of information, but they all have problems related to *information needs*. In order to sell this service it is necessary to relate information provision to the solving of these problems, and the presentation of these solutions in a manner useful to the client is the value-added product that an information service can provide. Rather than presenting merely a bibliography of useful sources, the real professional will provide the actual information. Rather than providing pages of detailed statistics. the professional will provide analyzed summaries.

National commercial services and products aimed at the end-user market can help to identify potential client bases for a local information service. Possible *target populations* might include business, medical, or legal professionals; all have enormous information needs and some understanding of the cost and value of information. A point to consider when looking for a client base is "What are their current information sources?" It will be necessary to provide something they are not currently receiving, or to provide it more conveniently or more cheaply. Many of the larger organizations will have in-house information services with which they are familiar and reasonably satisfied, so it would seem that smaller groups might be a better target for independent services. On the other hand, major corporations with in-house information systems do sometimes make use of outside searchers to "pick up the slack."

As online services continue their push for the end-user market, and alternative sources (e.g., CD-ROMs, the Internet) become more widely available, some potential clients will favor the "do it yourself" approach. Part of the appeal of end-user searching is the belief that the ability to use computer systems will translate into the ability to do online research. Personal experience suggests that even when clients have access to appropriate resources, they are not necessarily adept at using them. The expertise brought to the task by the information professional is information expertise, not computer expertise—knowing how to frame the query, the resources that are available to answer it, where to find them, and how to present them in the most useful fashion.

If there are other independent information providers in the area, any new service must fill a separate niche and be priced in relation to them. It is doubtful if any of these others will be offering exactly the same services to the same market, but it would be helpful to offer additional services (e.g., document delivery, online delivery) to identify the new service as being different. *Pricing policies* are somewhat subjective, but points to consider are: costs, profit margins, competitor pricing, and the importance of the information to the client.

Information services tend to use the usual range of *advertising* techniques: sales calls, brochures, word of mouth, professional meetings and journals, and advertisements in local papers and yellow pages. Obviously, where and how to advertise depends on the chosen market. Most early business will come as a result of direct contacts, either individual calls, introductions at professional meetings, or from colleagues. Because information is an unfamiliar product to many potential customers, it is important to couch the service in very practical terms. A published article in a professional journal or an oral presentation at a professional meeting are useful publicity. Business cards and brochures (with logos) are important, but even the most casual encounter can be turned into a marketing opportunity.

Keeping old clients is as important as gaining new ones. One technique for encouraging repeat business is using *deposit accounts*, which will also help stabilize the cash flow problem. Follow-up calls are important, and the offer of a current awareness service is often appropriate. Offers of in-house training sessions or presentations can be additional sources of income, and consulting can be particularly lucrative. It is important to diversify the services offered, not only because variety makes life more interesting but also to attract additional business.

Fees and Charges

The United States traditionally thinks of information as being free and believes that it should be universally available. Most people would probably agree with this idea, but in fact information is never free. Even information available from the public library is not free. It is paid for by public taxes. The cost of online time varies considerably for different databases and different database vendors, so it pays to have access to a range of services. One way of determining the value of information is to look at the cost of not having it. Its value lies in its usefulness, so that the relationship between cost and value is complicated and will vary widely in different situations and for different clients.

The general opinion within the profession regarding charges for information services is that most entrepreneurs do not value their services enough. It is not sufficient just to charge what the opposition is charging, or even to select a desirable hourly rate. The hourly rate charged needs to cover fixed expenses (rent, telephone, supplies, etc.), as well as the time actually spent. These fixed charges will be divided among the client base so that the more clients there are, the less of this amount each will have to pay. The catch here is estimating the number of clients necessary to achieve solvency while still keeping charges at a level acceptable to clients. Variable costs (e.g., database charges) are usually billed separately, so that clients using more online time pay more than those using less. Choosing to set fees too low in order to attract initial business is not good judgment because they will need to be raised over time.

Start-up and initial operating costs can be kept low by working alone from a home office and drawing minimum expenses for the first few months. Not many people can afford to work for free for an extended period, but it will take time to build a client base and also to start money coming in. There is also likely to be a time lag between money being earned and money being received. Most businesses operate on a *monthly billing* arrangement, but many independent information services operate on a *retainer* basis, with full or partial payment in advance based on an estimate of the final bill. An acceptable alternative is the method of regular period *deposit accounts*, against which client services are billed as expenses occur. Accepting credit cards requires recognition by a bank of merchant status and the payment of charges set by the bank, so it is best to insist on cash or checks. It is prudent to hire the assistance of an accountant (and a lawyer; see below) from the very beginning.

There will always be the odd overdue client account. In general, the older the bill, the more difficult it is to collect, so it is advisable to send out both bills and past-due notices promptly. This is where the policy of advance payments has definite advantages. Discussion of payment terms should be dealt with up front and stated as being regarded as part of business ethics. (More on this later.) It is a given that it is really hard to pin a specific value on information because it will vary by time, by individual, and by form of presentation.

Legal Issues

Going into business today is a complex legal process. Here we will look at some of the areas of particular concern for the independent information professional.

Copyright

As soon as people consider the information business, the question of copyright emerges. Two important concepts to consider are the form of the information and an awareness of what exactly is being sold. As to this latter question, we have already stressed that what we are selling is expertise, professional time, and the ability to use information resources effectively. The search intermediary is acting on behalf of the ultimate client in terms of research. Copyright Law recognizes that the way in which an idea is expressed is what is copyrightable, not the information itself. This means that facts cannot be copyrighted. DIALOG has a policy of granting information brokers permission to use search output so long as no systematic photocopying and redistribution (i.e., to more than one client) take place. Most communications packages have the ability to store captured data in ASCII (plain-text) format, which is compatible with most word processors. It is thus possible to rearrange, reformat, merge, and repackage online output to suit individual clients and remain within the guidelines of copyright law.

If material is used exactly as retrieved, it may be necessary to pay a *copyright fee* to the producer of the information. There are different copyright concerns in the area of document delivery. The law requires the payment of a royalty fee for the photocopying of source documents for sale to clients. Fortunately, it is not necessary to continually pay small sums to individual publishers because the Copyright Clearance Center (CCC) takes care of this. Nevertheless, individual agreements need to be negotiated with publishers who are not members of CCC.

Liability

Another major area of concern for information brokers is liability. Most experts agree that the searcher is not liable for the accuracy of the information discovered and supplied to the client, nor for any consequences the client might suffer because of that information. There have been a number of cases involving damage caused by computer software (and many that have been settled out of court), but there appears to be no consensus in determining responsibility. On the other hand, the courts have been reluctant to impose liability on authors, publishers, and booksellers for defective information in books because of concern for the effect that such liability would have on the *free exchange of ideas* and information.[3] Whether the "no liability" rule applicable to print information providers will be extended to electronic information providers remains to be seen. There are some differences between the print world and the electronic world that may put electronic information providers at a greater risk of liability than print information providers.[4]

How does this affect the information broker, the middleman in the information chain? It would appear that if the information provided is honestly and fairly delivered, then *contractual liability* has been satisfied. Because this might not seem a very professional approach, a written agreement that specifies sources of the search, means to be used, and estimated costs will provide protection to both sides. The basis is mutuality of obligation, the information professional to deliver and the client to pay. Nevertheless, the exact nature and limitations of liability are not clearly defined by the courts, and merely claiming that one is not liable for damages does not necessarily make one immune from prosecution. There is after all, a difference between implied warranty of accuracy and negligence. Many independent information professionals are looking at the possibilities of some kind of error and omission (E & O) insurance coverage. The wide variety of disclaimers in use by information providers suggests that it will be wise to seek competent legal advice on this point.

Ethics and Confidentiality

Much has been written about the invasions of privacy and the loss of confidentiality resulting from the input of large amounts of personal data to machine-readable format and the development of worldwide telecommunications networks for the transfer of all types of data. The American Library Association (ALA) has long been zealous in defending the rights of library users to confidentiality. In the face of several attempts by U.S. government officials from the 1970s onwards to obtain information about reading habits from library circulation records, the ALA Intellectual Freedom Committee revised and expanded its policy to protect from scrutiny all library records that identify users, and urged that libraries refrain from making these records available save by a court order.[5] Most libraries have now endorsed and applied statement III of the ALA's Code of Ethics adopted by the membership at its 1981 conference, which reads:

> "III. Librarians must protect each user's right to privacy with respect to information sought or received, and materials consulted, borrowed or acquired." [6]

Although these guidelines were originally developed to ensure the confidentiality of library circulation records, they apply equally to confidential data about the nature of patron requests and searches. They provide a useful basis for the development of policy guidelines to be used by independent information professionals. The confidentiality of this kind of data may well be particularly important in the cases of business, legal, and financial data. For example, the same information broker has been known to find herself providing information to two clients representing opposite sides of a lawsuit. Results of client searches must be confidential, and even when requests for the same or similar information are received from different clients, it would be a breach of professional ethics (not to mention copyright) to use the results of the first search to answer the second one. Information professionals have a powerful role as gatekeepers to the information sources and must be careful to maintain the highest ethical standards.

Conclusion

As the need for information grows and as the systems for finding it proliferate, the role of the information professional, both within and outside libraries, is a crucial and expanding one. But the key element for success as an independent information broker appears to be marketing. Clients are not going to come knocking on the door, especially in the early months. In order to survive, it is important to offer a whole range of information-related services, ranging from acquisition services (for hard-to-find and out-of-print material) to document delivery, from print and database searching to training seminars, from electronic delivery to current awareness services. A very wide range of skills is required, and it may prove wise to find a partner whose talents complement one's own. For those who have the basic skills and favor an independent approach to life, information brokering may be just the right career.

Notes

1. Helen P. Burwell, ed. (1996), *Burwell World Directory of Information Brokers 1995/6* (Houston, TX: Burwell).

2. Max Faller (1993), *How to Set Up Your Own Small Business* (Minneapolis, MN: American Institute of Small Business).

3. Roy Arnold (Spring 1992), "The Persistence of Caveat Emptor: Publisher Immunity from Liability for Inaccurate Factual Information," *Univ. of Pittsburgh Law Review* 53: 777–811.

4. Pamela Samuelson (Jan 1993), "Liability for Defective Electronic Information," *Communications of the ACM* 36(1): 21–26.

5. American Library Association (Sept 1975), "IFC Report to Council," *Newsletter on Intellectual Freedom* 24: 135–55.

6. Lilian N. Gerhardt and Bertha M. Cheatham (Aug 1981), "ALA's Happy 100th Conference," *School Library Journal* 27: 20–29.

Additional Reading

Ardito, S. C. (Feb/Mar.1995), "The Information Broker and Intellectual Property Rights," *Bulletin of the American Society for Information Science* 21(3): 19–20.

Buschman, John (1990), "A Critique of the Information Broker: Context of Reference Services," *Reference Librarian* 31: 131–51.

Dragich, Martha J. (Sept 1989), "Information Malpractice: Some Thoughts on the Potential Liability of Information Professionals," *Information & Technology Libraries* 8(3): 265–72.

Everett, John H., and Elizabeth P. Crowe (1994), *Information for Sale*, 2d ed. (New York: Windcrest/McGraw-Hill).

Gray, John A. (1988), "Personal Malpractice Liability of Reference Librarians and Information Brokers," *Journal of Library Administration* 9(2): 71–83.

Isbell, M. K., and M. K. Cook (Summer 1986), "Confidentiality of Online Bibliographic Searches: Attitudes and Practices," *Reference Quarterly* 25(4): 483–87.

Mason, R. O. (Fall 1990), "What is an Information Professional?" *Journal of Education for Library & Information Science* 31(2): 122–38.

Mintz, Anne P. (Sept 15, 1985), "Information Practice and Malpractice," *Library Journal* 110(15): 38–43.

Nasri, William Z. (Winter 1986), "Professional Liability," *Journal of Library Administration* 7(4): 141–45.

Pritchard, Teresa, and Michelle Quigley (May 1989), "The Information Specialist : A Malpractice Risk Analysis," *Online* 13(3): 57–62.

Rugge, Sue, and Alfred Glossbrenner (1997), *The Information Broker's Handbook* (New York: McGraw-Hill).

Sabine, Denis, and Yves Poullet (1990), "Questions of Liability in the Provision of Information Services," *Online Review* 14(1): 21–32.

Shaver, D. B. et al. (Fall 1985), "Ethics for Online Intermediaries," *Special Libraries* 76(4): 238–45.

Warner, Alice Sizer (1989), *Making Money: Fees for Library Services* (New York: Neal-Schuman).

—— (1987), *Mind Your Own Business: A Guide for the Information Entrepreneur* (New York: Neal-Schuman).

GLOSSARY
OF ONLINE TERMS

ACCESS: To identify, locate, and use information. We talk about access points to records, meaning the fields on which they can be searched. See also FIELD.

ACCESSION NUMBER: The unique number assigned to each record in a database as it is entered into the system. Similar to library accession numbers.

ADDITIONAL INDEXES: The nonsubject inverted files that enable the searching of fields such as author or publication year. These fields are identified by two-letter codes such as AU or PY. See also FIELD.

ADJACENCY SEARCHING: See PROXIMITY SEARCHING.

ANALOG: Data encoded in signals that are continuous over some range of values. Analog must be converted to digital data before being processed by computers. (cf. DIGITAL.)

ASCII: American Standard Code for Information Interchange.

ASK: Anomalous State of Knowledge. A model for information retrieval based on the assumption that the foundation of a question by a user signifies the recognition by the user that information is needed.

AUTHORITY CONTROL: The means used to ensure consistency in entering variant names, titles, spellings, and so forth into a database.

BASIC INDEX: The subject-inverted file that combines all subject-related terms (usually from the title, the abstract, and the descriptor fields) into a single alphabetic sequence. Attached to each term is information regarding the field it came from, its position in that field, and its record address (accession number). See also ACCESSION NUMBER; FIELD.

BAUD RATE: A measure of the speed of data transmission controlled by the modem. Baud rate divided by 10 is the number of characters per second.

BIBLIOGRAPHIC RECORD: A description of an item of recorded information, which includes all the data necessary to uniquely identify it.

BIBLIOGRAPHIC UTILITY: A commercial service that maintains an online bibliographic database to support library functions such as cataloging and interlibrary loan (e.g., OCLC and RLIN). Such services are easier to search than other online databases in that one is normally looking for a known item.

BIT: Binary digit, a 0 or a 1.

BOOLEAN OPERATORS: Set logic used to indicate relationships between search terms; named after mathematician George Boole. The Boolean operator AND requires both the linked terms to be present simultaneously. OR requires at least one term in a concept block to be present, while NOT excludes any reference to a term. See also LOGICAL OPERATORS.

BUILDING BLOCKS: An approach to search strategy by building blocks of synonymous terms to be ORed together.

BYTE: Any meaningful collection of bits that specifically defines a character or function. Eight-bit bytes are the most common.

CD-ROM (Compact Disc Read-Only Memory): A dense storage medium used to hold databases, which can then be accessed and read, but the data cannot be altered.

CHARACTER: Any letter, number, or other symbol in the computer. A space is also considered a character.

COMMAND LANGUAGE: A subset of language used to tell the computer to carry out a particular operation. Commands are normally followed by some data element on which they act. Examples of commands in DIALOG are B (BEGIN) or SS (SELECT STEPS).

CONCEPT: The idea of a thing, regardless of the name used to define it in a given instance. Such terms are combined into concept blocks using Boolean OR. For example: automobile OR car OR motor car.

CONNECT TIME: The length of time a user is connected to a particular system and database. This will determine the cost of a search, together with print and telecommunications charges.

CONTROLLED VOCABULARY: A list of subject terms, such as the ERIC Thesaurus, used to assign index terms to records in a uniform manner in a given database. Not all databases use a controlled vocabulary; these can only be searched free-text. See also DESCRIPTOR; THESAURUS.

DATABASE: A collection of related records in machine-readable form. Databases may be of various types—bibliographic, numeric, directory, or full-text. It is the computer version of a file.

DATABASE PRODUCER: An organization that compiles a file of machine-readable records; it decides what information will be included and how it will be indexed.

DEFAULT: An operation that the computer is programmed to perform when it receives no instruction with regard to the file, field, or set on which to perform an operation.

DESCRIPTOR: A subject heading or index term chosen by an indexer from a controlled vocabulary and assigned to a particular record. A "bound" descriptor is a multiword phrase indexed as a complete phrase in the Basic index. Such phrases may only be searched in selected fields that are datebase specific.

DOCUMENT DELIVERY: Provision of actual copies of articles and other documents whose references were found by database searches. Some vendors provide for online document ordering and delivery.

DOWNLOAD: The transfer of data from one electronic storage medium (the host system) to another (the user machine), usually the results of a search, for offline printing, or for word processing.

DUPLEX: The mode of transmission between two computers. In half duplex, messages can be either sent or received, but only one way at a time. Full duplex allows sending and receiving to be simultaneous over the same connection.

END USER: A person who actually performs their own search, most frequently on CD-ROM databases or the Internet.

ETHERNET: A local data network system popular on terminal and PC networks. It is a broadband system that uses coaxial cable.

FALSE DROP: A citation produced from a logically correct search statement that is not relevant to the user's needs. This is usually the result of an incorrect relationship between search terms.

FIBER OPTICS: Plastic or glass fibers or fiber bundles used to carry information.

FIELD: The area of a record set aside for a specific type of information. For example, there are usually author fields, title fields, descriptor fields, and so on. Fields need to be identified in order for them to be searchable. A fixed-length field will contain a predetermined number of characters, while a variable-length field may contain any number of characters.

FILE: A collection of related records from a single source. Although the term "file" is often used as synonymous with "database," some of the larger databases may be divided into more than one file, usually by date.

FIXED FIELD: A field in a record that has a predetermined length. (cf. VARIABLE FIELD.)

FORMAT: In online search terms, this refers to the form of output, which determines how much of the selected record(s) will be printed (e.g., full record, title only). Each database offers a selection of predetermined formats, or the searcher may define an original format.

FREE-TEXT SEARCHING: Searching for words or phrases in fields other than the descriptor field, usually by title, abstract, or full text. Proximity operators are used to specify word positions and to search for phrases in these uncontrolled fields. It is generally better to choose highly specific search terms when searching free-text.

GATEWAY: Equipment or system designed to connect two or more dissimilar networks. Usually involves protocol conversion and large buffers.

GIGO: Garbage in, garbage out.

HITS: See POSTINGS.

HOST SYSTEM: See VENDOR.

HTML: Hypertext Markup Language; used to "construct" Web pages.

HTTP: Hypertext Transport Protocol; allows servers and browsers to communicate on the Web.

HYPERTEXT: A system of writing and displaying text that enables the text to be linked in multiple ways, to be available at several levels of detail, and to contain links to related documents. The World Wide Web is a multimedia hypertext environment.

IDENTIFIER: An index term assigned to a record by an indexer other than from the controlled vocabulary. These are usually proper nouns, which make useful search terms but are too numerous to be included in the thesaurus (e.g., geographical places, personal names, acronyms).

INFORMATION: Often used very broadly to encompass all ideas, facts, and imaginative works. Not easy to define satisfactorily.

INFORMATION BROKER: Individual or organization providing information services to clients for a fee.

INTERMEDIARY: A searcher who formulates a search strategy and performs a search for someone else (the "user"). In libraries the intermediary is normally a specially trained reference librarian.

INTERNET: An international network of many computer networks linked via common communications protocols.

INVERTED FILE: An alphanumeric index of the searchable terms found in all the records of a given database, with an annotation of the exact location of the term within a particular record. The Basic Index is an inverted file, as are the other searchable sequences (author, date of publication, etc.). Inverted files are intended to speed searching in the same way that a back-of-the-book index speeds access to particular topics.

ISDN: Integrated Services Digital Network.

KEYWORD: Individual word searchable in any field of a record.

KWIC (Keyword in Context): A format for search output that shows only those portions of a record where the search terms occur. Particularly useful for searching full-text.

LC: The Library of Congress, the unofficial national library of the United States, which serves the information needs of Congress and provides services to all types of libraries.

LCSH: Library of Congress Subject Headings. The controlled vocabulary used for indexing records by many libraries and bibliographic utilities.

LIFO (Last-in-first-out): An acronym that represents the order in which records are retrieved from a database, with the most recently added item being output first.

LIMITING: Searching for terms when they are combined with some other characteristic, such as language or date of publication (e.g., /eng or /1997). See also QUALIFICATION.

LINEAR FILE: The file in which the complete records are stored, normally in accession number order. This is a large file that uses inverted files (indexes) to access selected records. That is, the linear file is not searched directly and is only accessed to TYPE or PRINT a record.

LISTSERV: Software that allows the creation of electronic discussion lists for a particular group or purpose.

LOCAL AREA NETWORK (LAN): A connection between multiple computers intended to allow the individual stations to share resources and exchange files (e.g., ETHERNET).

LOGICAL OPERATORS: The Boolean operators AND, OR, and NOT, which are used to arrange search terms into logical groups to form a search strategy. The order in which the computer executes these operators is NOT, AND, OR, with parentheses used to override this order when necessary. See also BOOLEAN OPERATORS.

LOGON/LOGOFF: The process of connecting or disconnecting from a local machine to the remote host computer of the search service. This access includes a dial-up procedure to connect to the telecommunications network, a procedure to sign on to the system using a private password, and a signoff procedure.

MARC (Machine-Readable Catalog): A database of Library of Congress holdings used by librarians as an authority for cataloging data.

MODEM (Modulator/Demodulator): A device used to connect a computer terminal to a telephone communication system. The modem translates the digital signals of the computer into sounds to be transferred over the telephone lines and determines the speed at which they will be transferred.

MOUNTING: The process used by the system vendor to transform a linear file of records into inverted files suitable for searching.

NESTED LOGIC: The use of logical operators to form compound search statements and determine the order in which they will be executed. For example, (pets NOT (cats OR dogs)) AND (fleas OR lice). See also LOGICAL OPERATORS.

NETWORK: An interconnection of systems that includes computers, terminals, and communications facilities.

NODE: A connection or switching point in a network. It may be a workstation, a dedicated server, or a connection point for routing messages.

OCLC (Online Computer Library Center): A bibliographic utility used by libraries to trace, acquire, and catalog library materials or to arrange interlibrary loans.

OFFLINE: Any activity that takes place while the searcher is not connected to the mainframe machine. Many communications software packages allow for the uploading of search strategies entered offline and for the processing or printing of search results after the searcher has disconnected. See also DOWNLOAD.

OFFLINE SEARCHING: Noninteractive searching, where the search is processed without the searcher being connected to the mainframe. This normally involves a delay in the receipt of results, which may well be unacceptable, though SDI searches are processed offline. See also SDI.

ONESEARCH: A search mode on DIALOG that allows the simultaneous searching of multiple databases.

ONLINE CATALOG: A catalog based on MARC records accessible in an interactive mode. See also MARC.

ONLINE SEARCHING: An interactive means of searching a database, where the searcher is directly connected to the search system and can modify a search as it is being conducted. (cf. OFFLINE SEARCHING.)

ONLINE THESAURUS: Some databases that use a controlled vocabulary make this vocabulary available online using the EXPAND command. This enables the searcher to find descriptor terms without having the printed version of the thesaurus available. See also THESAURUS.

OPAC: Online Public Access Catalog.

OPERATORS: See BOOLEAN OPERATORS; LOGICAL OPERATORS; PROXIMITY OPERATORS.

PACKET: A group of binary digits that is transferred as a composite whole. Most packet transmission is bit-oriented.

PACKET SWITCHING: A communication process in which information is transferred through a network in the form of discrete units called "packets."

PARSE: To separate and sort the words and phrases in a field so that each word and phrase can be accessed separately. The parsing operation is part of the mounting of a database in order to make it searchable.

PASSWORD: An identification assigned by the search service to a customer to provide access to the service.

PEARL GROWING: The idea of using terms from a relevant retrieved record in order to find more material on the same topic.

POST-COORDINATION: The combination of individual concepts describing a query into compound or complex subjects at the time of retrieval. (cf. PRE-COORDINATION.)

POSTINGS: The number of documents retrieved for any term used in a search.

POST-QUALIFICATION: Limiting a previous set to terms to a particular field Basic Index in order to reduce postings and increase specificity (e.g., SS S4/TI).

PRECISION: The percentage of records in a retrieved set that are relevant to the search topic. This figure is arrived at by dividing the number of relevant records retrieved by the total number of records retrieved and multiplying that number by 100. Precision measures the ability to retrieve only relevant records. (cf. RECALL.)

PRE-COORDINATION: The combination of individual concepts describing a document into compound index strings at the time of input to the system. (cf. POST-COORDINATION.)

PRINTOUT: Printed output from an online search. Also known as "hard copy."

PROMPT: A system indication (on DIALOG, a question mark) that lets the user know that the system is ready to receive a command.

PROTOCOL: A set of rules for how information is exchanged over a network.

PROXIMITY OPERATOR: Symbol used for searching phrases in fields other than the Descriptor field. They include (W), meaning adjacent in the given order; (N), meaning adjacent in either order; (F), meaning in the same field; (S), meaning in the same subfield; and (L), meaning linked terms in the Descriptor field.

PROXIMITY SEARCHING: A method of searching for phrases in fields other than the Descriptor field, where the order of terms and the distance between them can be specified. Care has to be taken to allow for the presence of stopwords, which are not searchable in themselves. Proximity searching is more precise than searching with logical operators. See also PROXIMITY OPERATOR.

QUALIFICATION: Limiting a search to terms in a particular field by specifying title (/TI) or Descriptor (/DE). See also LIMITING.

REAL TIME: A mode of operation in which user transactions are handled immediately and answers are returned as interactive responses.

RECALL: The percentage of relevant records found by a search. It is measured by dividing the relevant records retrieved by the total relevant records in the database. Recall is a way to measure the ability to retrieve as much as possible of the relevant material. Notice that total relevant records is normally an unknown figure in real-life situations. (cf. PRECISION.)

RECORD: A collection of related items of data treated as a unit and stored in the linear file. A record is the complete description of one document in a database.

RELEVANCE: The degree of match between a search request and the items retrieved as a result of a search for that request. See also PRECISION.

RESPONSE TIME: The elapsed time between the transmission of a command to the computer and the receipt of a response. Response time tends to increase in proportion to the number of searchers on the system at a given time.

RLIN: Research Libraries Information Network, the bibliographic utility that primarily serves very large academic libraries.

SDI (Selective Dissemination of Information): A search option where a user profile is filed with a search service and rerun against new records whenever the file is being updated.

SEARCH SERVICE: See VENDOR.

SEARCH STATEMENT: Instruction to the computer to find records matching the term or combination of terms entered by the searcher.

SEARCH STRATEGY: The plan for how a request will be searched on the computer. It will include a series of search statements combined by Boolean operators, which will normally be planned in advance.

SET: A group of records retrieved by a search statement and assigned a set number by the computer. These set numbers can then be used to refine the search.

SPECIFICITY: The idea of selecting search terms to represent as closely as possible the topic to be searched. The more specific a search statement, the smaller the set retrieved.

STOPLIST: A group of nonsignificant words that are not included in the Basic Index and therefore cannot be searched. The list of stopwords will differ on different systems but will normally include prepositions, articles, and Boolean operators. In DIALOG, there are nine such words: AN, AND, BY, FOR, FROM, OF, THE, TO, and WITH.

SUBFIELD: A subunit within a field (e.g., forename and surname in an author field).

SUBJECT ANALYSIS: The process of identifying the intellectual content of a document.

SUBJECT-RELATED TERMS: See ONLINE THESAURUS.

SURROGATE: Many databases consist of surrogates (or document representations) rather than of the documents themselves. This is the difference between bibliographic files and full-text files—the results of a search of surrogates will be a list of references rather than actual answers to a query.

T1: A wide band carrier designed to operate over twisted pair cables and carry 24 voice channels of 56K bps each.

TELECOMMUNICATIONS NETWORK: Commercial organization that provides connections to the main computer system. Examples are SprintNet and BT TYMNET.

TERMINAL: An input-output device used to send and receive messages with a remote computer system. Nowadays, a terminal is usually a personal computer programmed to act as a "dumb" terminal.

THESAURUS: An alphabetical listing of subject words that comprise the controlled vocabulary for a particular database. Terms from the thesaurus are selected by indexers to describe the document when it is being input, and by searchers to find documents for retrieval. Most thesauri also list the subject-related terms for each entry as an aid to selecting the most specific terms. See also CONTROLLED VOCABULARY.

TIMESHARING: An interactive method of computer use that allows multiple users to perform searches on the same system at the same time, but from different locations. The system actually services each user in sequence by assigning small blocks of time, though the speed of processing gives the impression of receiving individual attention.

TRUNCATION: A search technique that allows for variant spellings and word endings through the use of a special symbol (wildcard). The actual symbol used varies on different systems, and some CD-ROM databases automatically accommodate singular and plural forms of nouns. DIALOG uses the question mark as its truncation symbol.

UDF (User Defined Format): A format for search output where the user can define the fields to be viewed by specifying the desired field codes, as opposed to selecting one of the predetermined formats presented by the system.

UPDATE: The most recent group of records added to a database. On DIALOG the latest update to a file can be accessed online by SELECTing UD=9999.

UPLOAD: The transfer of data from one electronic medium (the user machine) to another (the host system) in order to speed the transfer of data. An efficient means of logging on to the system.

URL: Uniform Resource Locator—a Web address.

VARIABLE FIELD: A field whose length will vary according to the data being entered. (cf. FIXED FIELD.)

VENDOR: A commercial firm, government agency, or database producer in the business of offering access to a database or group of databases. Vendors are responsible for rearranging the information provided by the database producers, loading it onto their computers, and providing software programs to make it searchable.

VENN DIAGRAM: A diagram using closed circles to represent subject sets as an aid in formulating search logic.

VIRTUAL LIBRARY: Access to electronic information in a variety of remote locations through a local online catalog or other gateway, such as the Internet.

WAN (Wide Area Network): A public or private network, usually packet switched, that serves a set of users who are geographically separated. See also PACKET SWITCHING.

WEBSITE: A file of related Web pages of text and graphics linked through hypertext.

WILD CARD: See TRUNCATION.

WWW: The World Wide Web (Web for short), the graphical environment that gives hypertext-linked access to information on the Internet.

Z39.2: The NISO Information Interchange Format, which undergirds library automation by standardizing bibliographic formats, enabling them to be used on a variety of platforms.

Index